RESEARCH METHODOLOGY

Sara Miller McCune founded SAGE Publishing in 1965 to support the dissemination of usable knowledge and educate a global community. SAGE publishes more than 1000 journals and over 800 new books each year, spanning a wide range of subject areas. Our growing selection of library products includes archives, data, case studies and video. SAGE remains majority owned by our founder and after her lifetime will become owned by a charitable trust that secures the company's continued independence.

Los Angeles | London | New Delhi | Singapore | Washington DC | Melbourne

RESEARCH METHODOLOGY

FIFTH EDITION

a step-by-step guide for beginners

RANJIT KUMAR

Los Angeles | London | New Delhi
Singapore | Washington DC | Melbourne

Los Angeles | London | New Delhi
Singapore | Washington DC | Melbourne

SAGE Publications Ltd
1 Oliver's Yard
55 City Road
London EC1Y 1SP

SAGE Publications Inc.
2455 Teller Road
Thousand Oaks, California 91320

SAGE Publications India Pvt Ltd
B 1/I 1 Mohan Cooperative Industrial Area
Mathura Road
New Delhi 110 044

SAGE Publications Asia-Pacific Pte Ltd
3 Church Street
#10-04 Samsung Hub
Singapore 049483

Editor: Aly Owen
Production editor: Ian Antcliff
Marketing manager: Ben Griffin-Sherwood
Cover design: Lisa Harper-Wells
Typeset by: C&M Digitals (P) Ltd, Chennai, India
Printed in the UK

Library of Congress Control Number: 2018952089

British Library Cataloguing in Publication data

A catalogue record for this book is available from the British Library

ISBN 978-1-5264-4989-4
ISBN 978-1-5264-4990-0 (pbk)

At SAGE we take sustainability seriously. Most of our products are printed in the UK using responsibly sourced papers and
boards. When we print overseas we ensure sustainable papers are used as measured by the PREPS grading system.
We undertake an annual audit to monitor our sustainability.

To my daughter, Parul

CONTENTS

List of figures   xii
List of tables   xv
Guided tour   xvi
Acknowledgements   xviii
Preface   xix

1   Research: a way of thinking   1

Research: a way of thinking   4
Research: an integral part of your
    professional practice   4
Research: a way to gather evidence
    for your practice   7
Evidence-based practice   8
Applications of research in practice
    development and policy formulation   8
Research: what does it mean?   9
The research process: its characteristics and requirements   12
Types of research   13
    Application perspective   13
    Objectives perspective   15
    Mode of enquiry perspective   16
Important note to readers   19
The mixed/multiple methods approach   21
    Introduction   21
    Defining the approach   21
    Rationale underpinning the approach   27
    When to use the approach   27
    Ways of mixing methods   29
    Advantages and disadvantages   30
    Considerations to be kept in mind   32

    Situations in which the approach can be used   32
Paradigms of research   33
Summary   34

2   The research process: a quick glance   39

The research process: an eight-step model   42
A: Deciding what to research   46
    Step one: Formulating a research problem   46
B: Planning how to conduct the study   46
    Step two: Conceptualising a research design   46
    Step three: Constructing an instrument for
    data collection   47
    Step four: Selecting a sample   48
    Step five: Writing a research proposal   48
C: Conducting a research study   49
    Step six: Collecting data   49
    Step seven: Processing and displaying data   49
    Step eight: Writing a research report   49
Summary   50

STEP ONE: FORMULATING A RESEARCH PROBLEM   53

3   Reviewing the literature   55

The place of the literature review in research   58
    Bringing clarity and focus to your
    research problem   58
    Improving your research methodology   59
    Broadening your knowledge base in your
    research area   59
    Contextualising your findings   60

Difference between a literature review
   and a summary of the literature   60
How to review the literature   60
   Searching for the existing literature   61
   Reviewing the selected literature   65
   Developing a theoretical framework   66
   Developing a conceptual framework   67
Writing about the literature reviewed   68
Summary   71

4   Formulating a research problem   77

The research problem   80
The importance of formulating a research problem   80
Sources of research problems   81
Considerations in selecting a research problem   83
Steps in formulating a research problem   84
The formulation of research objectives   91
The study population   92
Establishing operational definitions   92
Formulating a research problem in
   qualitative research   94
Summary   95

5   Identifying variables   101

What is a variable?   104
The difference between a concept and a variable   105
Converting concepts into variables   106
Types of variable   107
   From the viewpoint of causal relationship   107
   From the viewpoint of the study design   114
   From the viewpoint of the unit of measurement   115
Types of measurement scale   116
   The nominal or classificatory scale   117
   The ordinal or ranking scale   119
   The interval scale   119
   The ratio scale   120
Summary   120

6   Constructing hypotheses   127

The definition of a hypothesis   130
The functions of a hypothesis   131
The testing of a hypothesis   132
The characteristics of a hypothesis   133
Types of hypothesis   133
Errors in testing a hypothesis   137
Hypotheses in qualitative research   137
Summary   138
Developing a research project: a set of exercises for
   beginners   142
Exercise I: Formulation of a research problem   142

STEP TWO: CONCEPTUALISING A RESEARCH DESIGN   149

7   The research design   151

What is a research design?   154
The functions of a research design   155
The theory of causality and the research design   155
Summary   162

8   Selecting a study design   167

Differences between quantitative and qualitative study
   designs   170
Study designs in quantitative research   171
   Study designs based on the number of contacts   172
   Study designs based on the reference period   177
   Study designs based on the nature of the
      investigation   180
   Other designs commonly used in
      quantitative research   191
Study designs in qualitative research   195
   Case study   196
   Oral history   197
   Focus groups/group interviews   197
   Participant observation   198
   Holistic research   198

	Community discussion forums	199
	Reflective journal log	199
	Other commonly used philosophy-guided designs	199
	Action research	200
	Feminist research	200
	Participatory research and collaborative enquiry	202
	Summary	202
	Exercise II: Conceptualising a study design	206

STEP THREE: CONSTRUCTING AN INSTRUMENT FOR DATA COLLECTION 209

9	Selecting a method of data collection	211
	Differences in the methods of data collection in quantitative, qualitative and mixed methods research	214
	Major approaches to information gathering	215
	Collecting data using primary sources	215
	Observation	217
	The interview	220
	The questionnaire	222
	Constructing a research instrument in quantitative research	234
	Asking personal and sensitive questions	235
	The order of questions	235
	Pre-testing a research instrument	237
	Prerequisites for data collection	237
	Methods of data collection in qualitative research	238
	Unstructured interviews	238
	Observation	241
	Secondary sources	241
	Constructing a research instrument in qualitative research	241
	Collecting data using secondary sources	242
	Problems with data from secondary sources	243
	Summary	244

10	Collecting data using attitudinal scales	249
	Measurement of attitudes in quantitative and qualitative research	252
	Attitudinal scales in quantitative research	252
	Functions of attitudinal scales	253
	Difficulties in developing an attitudinal scale	254
	Types of attitudinal scale	254
	The summated rating or Likert scale	254
	The equal-appearing interval or Thurstone scale	259
	The cumulative or Guttman scale	260
	Attitudinal scales and measurement scales	261
	Attitudes and qualitative research	261
	Summary	261

11	Establishing the validity and reliability of a research instrument	267
	The concept of validity	270
	Types of validity in quantitative research	271
	Face and content validity	272
	Concurrent and predictive validity	272
	Construct validity	272
	The concept of reliability	273
	Factors affecting the reliability of a research instrument	274
	Methods of determining the reliability of an instrument in quantitative research	274
	External consistency procedures	275
	Internal consistency procedures	275
	Validity and reliability in qualitative research	276
	Summary	278
	Exercise III: Developing a research instrument	282

STEP FOUR: SELECTING A SAMPLE 285

12	Selecting a sample	287
	The differences between sampling in quantitative and qualitative research	290
	Sampling in quantitative research	291

The concept of sampling 291
Sampling terminology 292
Principles of sampling 293
Factors affecting the inferences drawn
  from a sample 295
Aims in selecting a sample 296
Types of sampling 296
The calculation of sample size 310
Sampling in qualitative research 311
The concept of saturation point in
  qualitative research 312
Summary 312
Exercising IV: Selecting a sample 317

STEP FIVE: WRITING A RESEARCH PROPOSAL 319

13 Writing a research proposal 321

The research proposal in quantitative and
  qualitative research 324
Contents of a research proposal 325
Preamble/introduction 326
The research problem 329
Objectives of the study 330
Hypotheses to be tested 332
Study design 333
The setting 335
Measurement procedures 336
Ethical issues 336
Sampling 336
Analysis of data 337
Structure of the report 340
Problems and limitations 342
Appendix 342
Work schedule 342
Budget 342
Summary 343
Exercise V: Writing a research proposal 348

STEP SIX: COLLECTING DATA 351

14 Considering ethical issues in data collection 356

Ethics: the concept 356
Stakeholders in research 357
Ethical issues to consider concerning
  research participants 358
Collecting information 358
Seeking informed consent 358
Providing incentives 359
Seeking sensitive information 359
The possibility of causing harm to participants 359
Maintaining confidentiality 360
Ethical issues to consider relating to the researcher 360
Avoiding bias 360
Provision or deprivation of a treatment 360
Using inappropriate research methodology 361
Incorrect reporting 361
Inappropriate use of information 361
Ethical issues regarding the sponsoring organisation 362
Restrictions imposed by the sponsoring organisation 362
The misuse of information 362
Ethical issues in collecting data from
  secondary data 362
Summary 363
Exercise VI: Data collection
  (ethical issues in data collection) 367

STEP SEVEN: PROCESSING AND DISPLAYING DATA 371

15 Processing data 373

Data processing in quantitative studies 376
Editing 376
Coding 378
Developing a frame of analysis 394
Analysing quantitative data manually 400
Data processing in qualitative studies 402

Content analysis in qualitative research – an example   403
Data analysis in mixed methods studies   413
The role of statistics and computers in research   413
Summary   414

16   **Displaying data**   **419**

Methods of communicating and displaying
      analysed data   422
      Text   422
      Tables   423
      Graphs   428
      Statistical measures   442
Summary   442
      Exercise VII: Processing and displaying data   446

STEP EIGHT: WRITING A RESEARCH REPORT   451

17   **Writing a research report**   **453**

Writing a research report   456
Developing a draft outline   457
Writing about variables   461
Referencing   463
Writing a bibliography   463
Summary   463
Exercise VIII: Report writing   467

Glossary   471
Bibliography   490
Index   495

FIGURES

1.1	The applications of research	10
1.2	Types of research	14
1.3	Mixed/multiple methods, quantitative and qualitative approaches in social research	23
1.4	Use of mixed and multiple methods – an example	26
1.5	Mixed/multiple methods study – an example	31
2.1	The research journey	42
2.2	The research process	43
2.3	The chapters in the book in relation to the operational steps	45
3.1a	Developing a theoretical framework – the relationship between mortality and fertility	69
3.1b	Theoretical framework for the 'community responsiveness in health' study	69
3.2a	Sample outline of a literature review	70
3.2b	Main themes from the literature review for the community responsiveness study	71
4.1	Dissecting the subject area of domestic violence into subareas	86
4.2	Steps in formulating a research problem – alcoholism	87
4.3	Formulating a research problem – the relationship between fertility and mortality	88
4.4	Narrowing down a research problem – health	89
4.5	Characteristics of objectives	90
5.1	Types of variable	110
5.2	Types of variable in a causal relationship	111
5.3	Independent, dependent and extraneous variables in a causal relationship	111
5.4	Sets of variables in counselling and marriage problems	112
5.5	Independent, dependent, extraneous and intervening variables	113
5.6	Active and attribute variables	114
6.1	The process of testing a hypothesis	132
6.2	Two-by-two factorial experiment to study the relationship between MCH, NS and infant mortality	135
6.3	Types of hypothesis	136
6.4	Type I and Type II errors in testing a hypothesis	137
7.1	Factors affecting the relationship between a counselling service and the extent of marital problems	157
7.2	The relationship between teaching models and comprehension	159
7.3	The components of total change: independent, extraneous and chance	160
7.4	Building into the design	161

8.1	Types of study design	173
8.2	Before-and-after (pre-test/post-test) study design	174
8.3	The regression effect	176
8.4	The longitudinal study design	177
8.5	Classification of study designs based on the reference period: (a) retrospective; (b) prospective; (c) retrospective-prospective	178
8.6	Experimental and non-experimental studies	180
8.7	Randomisation in experiments	181
8.8	The after-only design	183
8.9	Measurement of change through a before-and-after design	183
8.10	The control experimental design	185
8.11	Double-control designs	188
8.12	Comparative experimental design	189
8.13	The placebo design	190
8.14	The cross-over experimental design	193
8.15	The replicated cross-sectional design	194
8.16	Action research design	201
9.1	Methods of data collection	216
9.2	Observing/recording group interaction on a three-directional rating scale	221
9.3	Types of interview	222
9.4	Where to go? A study of occupational mobility among immigrants	224
9.5	Occupational redeployment: a study among state government employees	225
9.6	Examples of closed questions	230
9.7	Examples of open-ended questions	231
9.8	Types of unstructured interview	239
10.1	An example of a categorical scale	255
10.2	An example of a seven-point numerical scale	256
10.3	An example of a scale with statements reflecting varying degrees of an attitude	256
10.4	The procedure for constructing a Likert scale	257
10.5	Scoring positive and negative statements	258
10.6	Calculating an attitudinal score	259
10.7	The procedure for constructing the Thurstone scale	260
12.1	The concept of sampling	291
12.2	Types of sampling in quantitative research	297
12.3	The procedure for using a table of random numbers	299
12.4	The procedure for selecting a simple random sample	303
12.5	The procedure for selecting a stratified sample	304
12.6	The concept of cluster sampling	305
12.7	Snowball sampling	308

12.8	The procedure for selecting a systematic sample	309
12.9	Systematic sampling	311
15.1	Steps in data processing	377
15.2	Example of questions from a survey	381
15.3	Some selected responses to the open-ended question (no. 11) in Figure 15.2	392
15.4	Some questions from a survey – respondent 3	395
15.5	Some questions from a survey – respondent 59	396
15.6	Some questions from a survey – respondent 81	397
15.7	An example of coded data on a code sheet	398
15.8	Manual analysis using graph paper	401
16.1	The structure of a table	424
16.2a	Two-dimensional histogram	430
16.2b	Three-dimensional histogram	431
16.2c	Two-dimensional histogram with two variables	432
16.3	Different types of bar chart	433
16.4	The stacked bar chart	434
16.5	The 100 per cent bar chart	435
16.6	The frequency polygon	436
16.7	The cumulative frequency polygon	437
16.8	The stem-and-leaf display	437
16.9	Two- and three-dimensional pie charts	438
16.10	The line diagram or trend curve	439
16.11	The area chart	440
16.12	The scattergram	441

TABLES

1.1	Types of research studies from the perspective of objectives	17
1.2	Differences between quantitative, qualitative and mixed methods approaches	20
3.1	Some commonly used electronic databases in public health, sociology, education and business studies	64
4.1	Aspects of a research problem	82
4.2	Operationalisation of concepts and study populations	93
5.1	Examples of concepts and variables	106
5.2	Converting concepts into variables	108
5.3	Categorical/continuous and quantitative/qualitative variables	116
5.4	Characteristics and examples of the four measurement scales	118
9.1	Guidelines for constructing a research instrument	236
10.1	The relationship between attitudinal and measurement scales	255
11.1	Criteria for judging research	277
12.1	The difference between sample statistics and the population mean	294
12.2	The difference between sample statistics and the population mean	295
12.3	Selecting a sample using a table of random numbers	300
12.4	Elements selected using the table of random numbers	302
13.1	Developing a time-frame for your study	343
13.2	Estimated cost of the study	343
15.1	An example of a code book	383
16.1	Respondents by age (frequency table for one population)	425
16.2	Respondents by age (frequency table comparing two populations)	425
16.3	Respondents by attitude towards uranium mining and age (cross-tabulation)	426
16.4	Attitude towards uranium mining by age and gender	427
16.5	Age and income data	441

GUIDED TOUR

DISCOVER YOUR TEXTBOOK AND ITS ONLINE RESOURCES

Get the support you need for your research course or project, when you need it

https://study.sagepub.com/kumar5e

LEARNING ABOUT RESEARCH METHODOLOGY FOR THE FIRST TIME?

BEGINNING YOUR FIRST RESEARCH PROJECT?

HAVE A RESEARCH METHODS ASSIGNMENT?

The fifth edition of *Research Methodology* has everything you need to succeed in your research methods course. Breaking down the process of designing and doing a research project into eight achievable stages, it takes you from research problem to a written research report and helps you find the support you need at every step along the way.

Whether you're confused, up for a challenge, or a combination of both, this book will clarify important concepts, fill you with confidence in your methods knowledge, and inspire you. Each chapter contains checkpoints that flag key concepts and sticking points. Look out for this icon in the margins:

Checkpoints!
Checkpoints!
Checkpoints!

Every checkpoint connects to two online pathways, each of which presents you with videos, weblinks, journal articles, case studies, and other digital resources curated to support your research needs:

PATHWAY 1: Confused about what you just read? These online resources create opportunities to stop and think or look at a concept in a different way.

PATHWAY 2: Are you up for a challenge? These online resources inspire, pique curiosity, and help you delve deeper and impress your lecturer.

At the end of each chapter, you can find a list of that chapter's available resources for each of these two pathways so you can pick and choose which ones would be most useful for you.

No matter what your methods need is, your textbook is ready to meet it. If you want to go beyond the information in the book and the confused and up for a challenge pathways – or just need more general support or want to kickstart your project – you can use the online resources to:

↝ Get up to speed with key terms and increase your confidence around research methods vocabulary with **glossary flashcards**.

↝ Test yourself on important concepts and identify your strengths and weakness for each chapter with **multiple choice questions**.

↝ Build a portfolio of your research ideas and track your project progress with an **exercise workbook**.

↝ Get started on your assessment, keep momentum and get the mark you want with an **assessment toolkit** that provides examples, trouble-shooting tips, supervisor advice and relevant tools and templates for seven common research methodology assignments.

FOR LECTURERS

If you are using this book as a teaching text, the fifth edition of *Research Methodology* is also supported by a wealth of additional resources for instructors only:

↝ A testbank of **multiple choice questions for** each chapter that you can use in class, for exams or as homework.

↝ **PowerPoint slides** for each chapter that you can download and customize for use in your own lecture.

↝ **Instructor guidelines** that provide guidance on different teaching points and possible in-class activities and exercises for each chapter.

These resources are available on the website, formatted to upload to your Learning Management System.

ACKNOWLEDGEMENTS

The author and SAGE would like to thank all of the reviewers and survey responders for their time, help and feedback, which has helped shape the current edition of the book.

We would also like to extend our thanks to Sarah Turpie for her valuable input on the online resources.

Finally, we would also like to give a very special thanks to Stephanie Fleischer, Principle Lecturer at the University of Brighton, for creating the three additional exercises for this edition (steps five through eight), reviewing the assessment toolkit resources, and contributing the student multiple choice questions, instructor guidelines, PowerPoint slides, and testbanks for the supporting online resources. These materials can be viewed on the book's supporting online resources: https://study.sagepub.com/kumar5e.

PREFACE

This book is based upon my experiences in research as a student, practitioner and teacher. The difficulties I faced in understanding research as a student, my discoveries about what was applicable and inapplicable in the field as a research practitioner, my development of the ability to effectively communicate difficult concepts in simple language without sacrificing technicality and accuracy as a teacher, and the feedback of many experts who participated in the evaluations carried out by Pearson Australia on the first edition and Sage UK on the second, third and fourth editions have become the basis of this book. Many aspects of methodology were added on the basis of the feedback of teachers of research methods from a number of countries.

Research methodology is taught as a supporting subject in several ways in many academic disciplines such as health, education, psychology, social work, nursing, public health, library studies and marketing research. The core philosophical base for this book comes from my conviction that, although these disciplines vary in content, their broad approach to a research enquiry is similar. This book, therefore, is addressed to these academic disciplines.

It is true that some disciplines and professionals place greater emphasis on quantitative research, some on qualitative and some on both. My own approach to research is a combination of both. Firstly, it is the objective that should decide whether a study is carried out adopting a qualitative or a quantitative approach. Secondly, in real life most research is a combination of both approaches. Though they differ in the philosophy that underpins their mode of enquiry, to a great extent their broad approach to enquiry is similar. The quantitative research process is reasonably well structured whereas the qualitative one is fairly unstructured, and these are their respective strengths as well as weaknesses. I strongly believe that both are important to portray a complete picture. In addition, there are aspects of quantitative research that are qualitative in nature. It depends upon how a piece of information has been collected and analysed. Therefore I feel very strongly that a good researcher needs to have both types of skill. I follow a qualitative–quantitative–qualitative approach to an enquiry. This book, therefore, has been written to provide information about various methods, procedures and techniques that are used in both the research approaches in a simple step-by-step manner, linked to operational steps. In terms of methods, techniques and procedures, as the mixed/multiple methods approach uses qualitative and/or quantitative approaches, I did not consider it appropriate to describe mixed/multiple methods separately. Thus, although Chapter 1 of this book describes three approaches to a research enquiry in social research, the subsequent chapters describe only the two approaches as the third, mixed methods, is covered under them.

Research as a subject is taught at different levels. The book is designed specifically for students who are newcomers to research and who may have a psychological barrier with regard to the subject. I have, therefore, not assumed any previous knowledge on the part of the reader; I have omitted detailed discussion of aspects that may be inappropriate for beginners; I have used many flow charts and examples to communicate concepts; and areas covered in the book follow a 'simple to complex' approach in terms of their discussion and coverage. I have also made a deliberate attempt not to make this book too theoretical. This primarily is a 'nuts and bolts' book that aims to develop elementary skills rather than a theoretical and philosophical knowledge base.

The structure of this book, which is based on the model developed during my teaching career, is designed to be practical. The theoretical knowledge that constitutes research methodology is therefore organised around the operational steps that form this research process for quantitative, qualitative and mixed methods research. All the information needed to take a particular step, during the actual research journey, is provided in one place. The information is organised in chapters and each chapter is devoted to a particular aspect of that step (see Figure 2.3). For example, 'formulating a research problem' is the first operational step in the research process. To formulate a 'good' research problem, in my opinion, you need to know how to review the literature, formulate a research problem, deal with variables and their measurement, and construct hypotheses. Hence, under this step, there are four chapters. The information they provide will enable you to formulate a problem that is researchable. These chapters are titled: 'Reviewing the literature', 'Formulating a research problem', 'Identifying variables' and 'Constructing hypotheses'. Similarly, for the operational step, Step III, 'Constructing an instrument for data collection', the chapters titled 'Selecting a method of data collection', 'Collecting data using attitudinal scales' and 'Establishing the validity and reliability of a research instrument' will provide sufficient information for you to develop an instrument for data collection for your study. For every aspect at each step, a smorgasbord of methods, models, techniques and procedures is provided for both quantitative and qualitative studies (and thus also, by extension, for mixed/multiple studies) in order for you to build your knowledge base in research methodology and also to help you to select the most appropriate ones when undertaking your own research.

It is my belief that a sound knowledge of research methodology is essential for undertaking a valid study. To answer your research questions, up to Step V, 'Writing a research proposal', knowledge of research methods is crucial as it enables you to develop a conceptual framework that is sound and has merits for undertaking your research endeavour with confidence. Having completed the preparatory work, the steps that follow are more practical in nature, the quality of which entirely depends upon the soundness of the methodology you proposed in your research proposal. Statistics and computers play a significant role in research, but their application is mainly after the data has been collected. To me, statistics are useful in confirming or contradicting conclusions drawn from simply looking at analysed data, in providing an indication of the magnitude of the relationship between two or more variables under study, in helping to establish causality, and in ascertaining the level of confidence that can be placed in your findings. A computer is used primarily in data analysis, the calculation of statistics, word-processing and the graphic presentation of data. It saves time and makes it easier for you to undertake these activities; however, you need to learn this additional skill. This book does not include statistics or information about computers.

I am grateful to a number of people who have helped me in the writing of this book. First of all, to my students, who have taught me how to teach research methods. The basic structure of this book is an outcome of the feedback I have received from them over the years. How, and at what stage of the research process, a concept or a procedure should be taught I have learnt from my students. I thank them all for their contribution to this book.

I am extremely grateful to my friend and colleague Dr Norma Watson, whose efforts in editing the first edition were of immense help. The book would not have reached its present stage without her unconditional help.

I thank Professor Denis Ladbrook, my friend and colleague, for his continuous encouragement, support and critical appreciation of my writing.

I am also grateful to my friend Dr Deenaz Damania, a very well-known expert in qualitative research, for her interest, encouragement and help in the completion of this edition.

I am immensely grateful to the international research experts who participated in the in-depth review of the book, undertaken by Sage Publications, and provided valuable suggestions for its further improvement. A number of changes in the fifth edition are a direct result of their feedback. The many reviews on the Sage website by teachers of research from universities in many countries have been very positive and a source of encouragement, motivation and reinforcement for this edition, and I am immensely grateful to the reviewers.

Ranjit Kumar

xxi

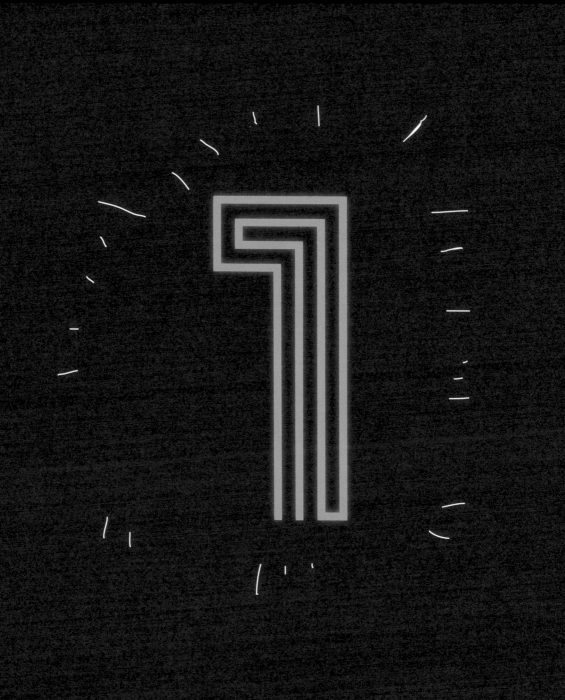

RESEARCH

A WAY OF THINKING

ESSENTIAL TERMS

You should be able to define these by the end of the chapter

- applied research
- descriptive research
- empirical research
- evidence-based practice
- explanatory research

- exploratory research
- paradigm
- qualitative research
- quantitative research
- mixed methods

BONUS TERMS

You will learn more about these by the end of the chapter

- controlled
- correlational
- interpretive paradigm
- positivistic research
- research reliability

- structured enquiries
- unstructured enquiries
- systematic
- validity

LEARNING OBJECTIVES

At the end of this chapter, you will be able to:

- Understand the meaning of research and its benefits and applications for your practice
- Identify situations in which research can be used for practice improvement
- Conceptualise the types of research approaches in the social sciences
- Spot the differences in the applications of quantitative, qualitative and mixed methods approaches
- Name the major paradigms of research in the social sciences

RESEARCH: A WAY OF THINKING

Research: One of the ways of finding answers to your professional and practice questions. It is characterised by the use of tested procedures and methods and an unbiased and objective attitude in the process of exploration.

Research is not only a set of skills, but also a way of thinking. Within this framework of thinking, you usually question what you observe, make an attempt to further explore, understand and explain your observations, and draw conclusions and inferences to enhance your practice skills and their knowledge base. It is looking at your practice or work situation inquisitively, critically and analytically to gain an in-depth knowledge of its rationale, relevance, effectiveness and efficiency. You develop an attitude that encourages you to challenge different aspects of your work situation, to question their purpose, relevance and validity, to find their strengths and weaknesses, and to investigate the possibilities and ways for further improvements and refinements. Research develops this thinking, inquisitive perspective in you. Thinking in this research mode, as a practitioner, you develop the ability to ask yourself questions such as: What am I doing? Why am I doing this? How is it affecting my clients or consumers? How can I improve my work? Such questions naturally come to your mind as a practitioner, and as a researcher you make attempts to find their answers. It is to find answers to such questions that you need to have research skills.

Research develops in you a way of thinking that is logical and rational and that encourages you to critically examine every aspect of your day-to-day situation. It helps you to understand and formulate guiding principles that govern a particular procedure in your practice, and develop and test new ways that contribute to the advancement of your practice and profession. This way of thinking develops in you a very different perspective to your work. Research develops this analytical way of thinking in you, and the knowledge of research methodology provides you with the techniques to find answers to your research questions. This research orientation becomes a cycle of your practice which, in turn, encourages you to further observe, question, explore, test and understand various aspects of your practice.

RESEARCH: AN INTEGRAL PART OF YOUR PROFESSIONAL PRACTICE

Research is an integral part of good professional practice in many professions and has been responsible for greatly influencing the practice procedures and outcomes in these professions. Among many professions such as medicine, public health, psychology and education, research and practice are well integrated, and practice relies very heavily upon what is discovered through research. As a matter of fact, research and practice are two sides of the same coin that should and cannot be separated. It would be appropriate to say that the greater the integration between research and practice in a profession, the greater the advancement in its theoretical and practice knowledge base. As mentioned, research is a habit of questioning what you do, and a systematic way of examining your clinical observations to explain and find answers for what you observe in your practice, with a view to instituting appropriate changes for a more effective professional service. Let us take some disciplines as examples.

Suppose you are working in the field of health. You may be a front-line service provider, supervisor or health administrator/planner. You may be in a hospital or working as an outreach community health worker. You may be a nurse, doctor, occupational therapist, physiotherapist, social worker or other paramedic. In any of these positions, you may ask yourself or be asked some of the following questions:

- How many patients do I see every day?
- What are some of the most common conditions prevalent among my patients?
- What are the causes of these conditions?
- Why do some people have a particular condition whereas others do not?
- What is the average cost of a service to a patient?
- What is the ideal population–worker ratio for this programme?
- What are the health needs of the community?
- What are the benefits of this programme to the community?
- How do I demonstrate the effectiveness of my service?
- Why do some people use the service while others do not?
- What do people think about the service?
- How satisfied are patients with the service?
- How effective is the service?
- How can the service be improved?

You can add many other questions to this list. At times it may be possible to ignore these questions because of the level at which you work; at other times you may make an effort to find answers on your own initiative, or sometimes you may be required to obtain answers for effective administration and planning.

Let us take another discipline: business studies. Assume you work in the area of marketing. Again, you can work at different levels: as a salesperson, sales manager or sales promotion executive. The list of questions that may occur to you is endless. The types of questions and the need to find answers to them will vary with the level at which you work in the organisation. You may just want to find out the monthly fluctuation in the sales of a particular product, or you may be asked to develop a research and development strategic plan to compete for a greater share of the market for your company's products. You may ask yourself or be asked, for example:

- What is the best strategy to promote the sale of a particular product?
- How many salespersons do I need?
- What is the effect of a particular advertising campaign on the sale of this product?
- How satisfied are consumers with this product?
- How much are consumers prepared to spend on this product?
- What do consumers like or dislike about this product?
- What type of packaging do consumers prefer for this product?
- What training do the salespersons need to promote the sale of this product?
- What are the attributes of a good salesperson?

Again, suppose you are a teacher working in a school. In your day-to-day teaching you are likely to encounter many complex questions and issues, the answers to which could directly or indirectly improve your effectiveness as a teacher. Some of these questions could be:

- What do students think about my teaching?
- What do I need to do to become a better teacher?
- Why are some students good at their studies while others are not?
- What effect does the home environment have on the academic achievement of a child?
- What, in students' opinion, are the attributes of a good teacher?
- Do I have the attributes that make a good teacher?
- What is the attitude of students towards homework?
- What determines students' motivation in their studies?
- Is there a relationship between academic achievement and occupational aspirations?

You can go on adding to this list. Answers to these questions will help you to become a better teacher and develop policies and programmes that will improve the system. In an attempt to find valid answers to these questions you need to have research skills.

To take a different example, let us assume that you work as a psychologist, counsellor or social worker. In the course of your work you may ask yourself (or someone else may ask you) the following questions:

- What are my clients' most common presenting problems?
- What are their most common underlying problems?
- What are the reasons for their problems?
- What is the socioeconomic background of my clients?
- Why am I successful in certain cases and not in others?
- What intervention strategies are more effective for the problems of my clients?
- What resources are available in the community to help a client with a particular need?
- What intervention strategies are appropriate for this problem?
- How satisfied are my clients with my services?
- How can I improve the quality of my services?

As a supervisor, administrator or manager of an agency, again different questions relating to the effectiveness and efficiency of a service may come to your mind. For example:

- How many people are coming to my agency?
- What are the socioeconomic-demographic characteristics of my clients?
- How many cases can a worker effectively handle in a day?
- Why do some people use the service while others do not?
- How effective is the service?
- What are the most common needs of clients who come to this agency?
- What are the strengths and weaknesses of the service?
- How satisfied are the clients with the service?
- How can I improve this service for my clients?

Still, at another level of practice, as a professional who feels a responsibility to contribute to the development and enhancement of your profession, you might be interested in finding answers to theoretical questions, such as:

- What is the most effective intervention for a particular problem?
- What causes X, or what are the effects of Y?
- What is the relationship between two phenomena such as unemployment and street crime; stressful living and heart attack; breakdown in marital relationships and personal communication; and immigration and family roles?
- How do I measure the self-esteem of my clients?
- How do I ascertain the validity of my questionnaire?
- What is the pattern of programme adoption in the community?
- What is the best way of finding out community attitudes towards an issue?
- What is the best way to find out the effectiveness of a particular treatment?
- How can I select an unbiased sample?
- What is the best way to find out about the level of marriage satisfaction among my clients?

Let us now consider some questions from the other side of the desk; that is, from the perspectives of consumers of your service. Recent decades have witnessed a tremendous shift in attitudes in the way consumers expect and accept services. It has changed from an obligatory perspective to the right to have a service. The focus is now not only on the service but also on its quality. Therefore in this age of consumerism, you cannot afford to ignore the consumers of a service. Consumers have the right to ask questions about the quality and effectiveness of the service they are receiving and you, as the service provider, have an obligation to answer their questions. Some of the questions that a consumer may ask are:

- How effective is the service that I am receiving?
- Am I getting value for money?
- How well trained are the service providers?

Most professions that are in the human service industry would lend themselves to the questions raised above and you as a service provider should be well prepared to answer them. Irrespective of your field of practice and the level at which you work, in your day-to-day practice, you will encounter many of these questions and to improve your practice you must find their answers. Research is one of the ways to help you do so objectively.

RESEARCH: A WAY TO GATHER EVIDENCE FOR YOUR PRACTICE

In recent decades evidence-based practice (EBP) has gained recognition as a requirement for a good professional practice. In professions such as medicine it has become a service delivery norm, a requirement and an indicator

Evidence-based practice: A service delivery system that is based upon research evidence as to its effectiveness; a service provider's clinical judgement as to its suitability and appropriateness for a client; and a client's preference as to its acceptance.

of practice accountability. Though its origin is credited to medical practice, EBP has become an important part of many other professions such as nursing, allied health services, mental health, community health, social work, psychology and teaching. It is now being promoted as an acceptable and scientific method for policy formulation and practice assessment.

EVIDENCE-BASED PRACTICE

CHECKPOINT
Evidence-based practice

Evidence-based practice is the delivery of services based upon research evidence about their effectiveness; the service provider's clinical judgement as to the suitability and appropriateness of the service for a client; and the client's own preference as to the acceptance of the service. The concept of EBP encourages professionals and other decision-makers to use evidence regarding the effectiveness of an intervention in conjunction with the characteristics and circumstances of a client and their own professional judgement to determine the appropriateness of an intervention when providing a service to a client. In this age of accountability, you as a professional must be accountable to your clients as well as your profession. It is as a part of this accountability that you need to demonstrate the effectiveness of the service(s) you provide.

Research is one of the ways of collecting accurate, sound and reliable information about the effectiveness of your interventions, thereby providing you with evidence of its effectiveness. As service providers and professionals, we use techniques and procedures developed by research methodologists to consolidate, improve, develop, refine and advance clinical aspects of our practice to serve our clients better.

APPLICATIONS OF RESEARCH IN PRACTICE DEVELOPMENT AND POLICY FORMULATION

Very little research in the field is 'pure' in nature; that is, very few people do research in research methodology per se. The use of research skills is mostly 'applied'; that is, they are often used in the development of practice skills and procedures, and the formulation of practice policies. All professions use research methods in varying degrees in many areas. They use the methods and procedures developed by research methodologists in order to increase understanding of different aspects of practice in their own profession and to enhance their professional knowledge base. It is through the application of research methodology that they strengthen and advance their own professional knowledge and skills. Examine your own field. You will find that its professional practice follows procedures and practices tested and developed by others over a long period of time. It is in this testing process that you need research skills, the development of which falls in the category of pure research. As a matter of fact, the validity of your findings entirely depends upon the soundness of the research methods and procedures you adopt.

Within any profession, where you directly or indirectly provide a service, such as health (nursing, occupational therapy, physiotherapy, community health, health promotion and public health), education, psychology or social work, the application of research can be viewed from four different perspectives:

1   the service provider;
2   the service administrator, manager and/or planner;
3   the service consumer; and
4   the professional.

These perspectives are summarised in Figure 1.1. Though it is impossible to list all the issues in every discipline, this framework can be applied to most disciplines and situations in the humanities and the social sciences. You should be able to use this to identify, from the viewpoint of the above perspectives, the possible issues in your own academic field where research techniques can be used to find answers.

RESEARCH: WHAT DOES IT MEAN?

The word 'research' has multiple meanings and its precise definition varies from discipline to discipline and expert to expert. Across disciplines and experts, however, there seems to be agreement with respect to the functions it performs; that is, to find answers to your research questions. You can use any of the research methods/approaches to achieve this objective. These methods range from the fairly informal, based upon clinical impressions, to the strictly scientific, adhering to the conventional expectations of scientific procedures. Research means using one of these methods to find answers to your questions. However, when you say that you are undertaking a research study to find answers to a question, you are implying that the process being applied:

1   is being undertaken within a framework of a set of philosophies;
2   uses procedures, methods and techniques that have been tested for their validity and reliability;
3   is designed to be unbiased and objective.

Your philosophical orientation may stem from one of the several paradigms and approaches in research – positivist, interpretive, phenomenology, action or participatory, feminist, qualitative, quantitative, mixed methods – and the academic discipline in which you have been trained. The concept of 'validity' can be applied to any aspect of the research process. It ensures that in a research study correct procedures have been applied to find answers to a question. 'Reliability' refers to the quality of a measurement procedure that provides repeatability and accuracy. 'Unbiased and objective' means that you have taken each step in an unbiased manner and drawn each conclusion to the best of your ability and without introducing your own vested interest. The author makes a distinction between bias and subjectivity. Subjectivity is an integral part of your way of thinking that is 'conditioned' by your educational background, academic discipline, philosophy, experience and skills. For example, a psychologist may look at a piece of information differently than an anthropologist or a historian. Bias, on the other hand, is a deliberate attempt to either conceal or highlight something because of your vested interest. Adherence to the three criteria mentioned above enables the process to be called 'research'. Therefore, when you say you are undertaking a research study to find the answer to a question, this implies that the method you are adopting fulfils these expectations (discussed later in the chapter).

Bias: A deliberate attempt either to conceal or highlight something that you found in your research or to use deliberately a procedure or method that you know is not appropriate but will provide information that you are looking for because you have a vested interest in it.

Subjectivity: This is an integral part of your way of thinking that is 'conditioned' by your educational background, discipline, philosophy, experience and skills. Bias is a deliberate attempt to change or highlight something which in reality is not there but you do it because of your vested interest. Subjectivity is not deliberate, it is inherent in the way you understand or interpret something.

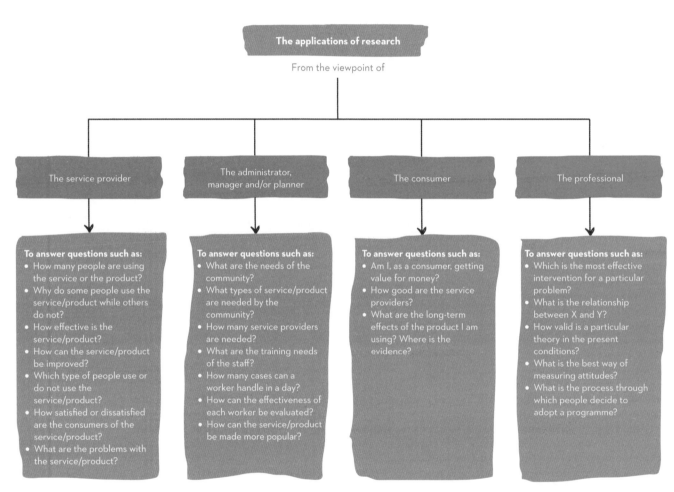

Figure 1.1   The applications of research

However, the degree to which these criteria are expected to be fulfilled varies from discipline to discipline and so the meaning of 'research' differs from one academic discipline to another. For example, the expectations of the research process are markedly different between the physical and the social sciences. In the physical sciences a research endeavour is expected to be strictly controlled at each step, whereas in the social sciences rigid control cannot be enforced as you are studying the human rather than the material world, and sometimes it is not even demanded.

Within the social sciences the level of control required also varies markedly from one discipline to another, as social scientists differ over the need for the research process to meet the above expectations. Despite these differences among disciplines, their broad approach to enquiry is similar. The research model, the basis of this book, is based upon this broad approach.

As a beginner in research you should understand that not all research studies are based upon complex and technical methodologies and have to use statistics and computers. Research can be a very simple activity designed to provide answers to very simple questions relating to day-to-day activities. On the other hand, research procedures can also be employed to formulate intricate theories or laws that govern our lives. The difference between research and non-research activity is, as mentioned, in the way we find answers to our research questions. For a process to be called research, it is important that it meets certain requirements and possesses certain characteristics. To identify these requirements and characteristics let us examine some definitions of research:

> The word *research* is composed of two syllables, *re* and *search*. The dictionary defines the former as a prefix meaning again, anew or over again and the latter as a verb meaning to examine closely and carefully, to test and try, or to probe. Together they form a noun describing a careful, systematic, patient study and investigation in some field of knowledge, undertaken to establish facts or principles. (Grinnell 1993: 4)

Grinnell further adds: 'research is a structured inquiry that utilises acceptable scientific methodology to solve problems and creates new knowledge that is generally applicable' (1993: 4).

Lundberg (1942) draws a parallel between the social research process, which is considered scientific, and the process that we use in our daily lives. According to him:

> Scientific methods consist of systematic observation, classification and interpretation of data. Now, obviously, this process is one in which nearly all people engage in the course of their daily lives. The main difference between our day-to-day generalisations and the conclusions usually recognised as scientific method lies in the degree of formality, rigorousness, verifiability and general validity of the latter. (Lundberg 1942: 5)

Burns (1997: 2) defines research as 'a systematic investigation to find answers to a problem'.

According to Kerlinger (1986: 10), 'scientific research is a systematic, controlled empirical and critical investigation of propositions about the presumed relationships about various phenomena'. Bulmer (1977: 5) states: 'Nevertheless sociological research, as research, is primarily committed to establishing systematic, reliable and valid knowledge about the social world.'

CHECKPOINT
Defining research

11

THE RESEARCH PROCESS: ITS CHARACTERISTICS AND REQUIREMENTS

From these definitions it is clear that research is a process for collecting, analysing and interpreting information to answer research questions. But to qualify to be called 'research', the process must have certain characteristics and fulfil some requirements: it must, as far as possible, be controlled, rigorous, systematic, valid and verifiable, empirical and critical.

Let us briefly examine these characteristics and requirements to understand what they mean:

Controlled: In order to reliably establish a cause-and-effect relationship, it is sometimes important to design a study in such a way that enables you to link cause(s) with the effect(s) and vice versa so that you can study the extent of the impact of the cause on the effect(s).

➤ **Controlled** – In real life there are many forces that affect the outcome(s) of an event. In the social sciences, a particular event seldom occurs for a single reason. It is the multiplicity of factors that determine the outcome of an event. It is true that some relationships are easy to understand while there are others more complex and difficult. In almost every relationship, simple or complex, most outcomes are a result of the interplay of a multiplicity of interacting factors. In order to reliably establish a cause-and-effect relationship, it is therefore important to design a study in such a way that enables you to link cause(s) with the effect(s) and vice versa. It is important for such studies to be able to isolate the effect of all other factors that are of no interest to you as a researcher but have a bearing on the outcomes. The concept of control implies that, in exploring causality in relation to two variables, you set up your study in such a way that it either minimises or quantifies (as it is impossible to eliminate) the effects of factors, other than the cause variable, affecting the relationship. This can be achieved to a large extent in the physical sciences, as most of the research is done in a laboratory. However, in the social sciences it is extremely difficult as research is carried out on issues relating to human beings living in society, where such controls are impossible. Therefore, in the social sciences, as you cannot control external factors, you attempt to quantify their impact.

➤ **Rigorous** – You must be scrupulous in ensuring that the procedures followed to find answers to questions are relevant, appropriate and justified. Again, the degree of rigour varies markedly between the physical and the social sciences and within the social sciences.

➤ **Systematic** – This implies that the procedures adopted to undertake an investigation follow a certain logical sequence. The different steps cannot be taken in a haphazard way. Some procedures must follow others.

➤ **Valid and verifiable** – This concept implies that whatever you conclude on the basis of your findings is correct and can be verified by you and others.

➤ **Empirical** – This means that any conclusions drawn are based upon hard evidence gathered from information collected from real-life experiences or observations.

➤ **Critical** – Critical scrutiny of the procedures used and the methods employed is crucial to a research enquiry. The process of investigation must be foolproof and free from any drawbacks. The process adopted and the procedures used must be able to withstand critical scrutiny.

TYPES OF RESEARCH

As mentioned earlier, to some extent, the definition of research varies from discipline to discipline and expert to expert. This variation in the definition and understanding of research, to a large extent, can be attributed to the different philosophies that underpin research thinking. Your belief in a particular philosophy underpinning the mode of enquiry shapes your opinion about the appropriateness of the methods for finding answers to your research questions. On the basis of the terminology used to describe types of research in the social science research methodology literature, the author has tried to develop a framework for the classification of research from different perspectives (Figure 1.2). The 'mode of enquiry' perspective classifies the research types on the basis of the different philosophies that guide them, while the 'application' and 'objectives' perspectives look at the research classification from the uses and purposes points of view. The three perspectives that form the basis of this classification are:

1 *applications* of the findings of the research study;
2 *objectives* of the study;
3 *mode of enquiry* used in conducting the study.

The classification of the types of research on the basis of these perspectives is not mutually exclusive – that is, a research study classified from the viewpoint of 'application' can also be classified from the perspectives of 'objectives' and 'enquiry mode' employed. For example, a research project may be classified as pure or applied research (from the perspective of application), as descriptive, correlational, explanatory or exploratory (from the perspective of objectives/purposes) and as qualitative, quantitative or mixed methods (from the perspective of the enquiry mode employed).

Application perspective

If you examine a research endeavour from the perspective of its application, there are two broad categories: pure research and applied research. In the social sciences, according to Bailey (1978: 17):

> Pure research involves developing and testing theories and hypotheses that are intellectually challenging to the researcher but may or may not have practical application at the present time or in the future. Thus such work often involves the testing of hypotheses containing very abstract and specialised concepts.

Pure research is also concerned with the development, examination, verification and refinement of research methods, procedures, techniques and tools that form the body of research methodology. Examples of pure research include developing a sampling technique that can be applied to a particular situation; developing a methodology to assess the validity of a procedure; developing an instrument, say, to measure the stress level in people; and finding the best way of measuring people's attitudes. The knowledge produced through pure research is sought in order to add to the existing body of knowledge of research methods.

Pure research is concerned with the development, examination, verification and refinement of research methods, procedures, techniques and tools that form the body of research methodology.

Applied research: Most research in the social sciences is applied in nature. Applied research is one where research techniques, procedures and methods that form the body of research methodology are applied to collect information about various aspects of a situation, issue, problem or phenomenon so that the information gathered can be utilised for other purposes such as policy formulation, programme development, programme modification and evaluation, enhancement of the understanding about a phenomenon, establishing causality and outcomes, identifying needs and developing strategies.

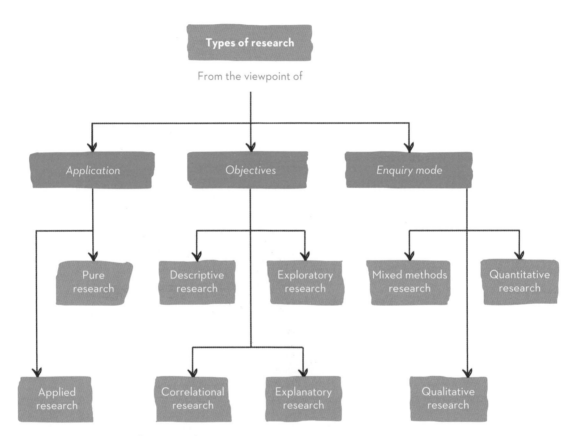

Figure 1.2   Types of research

Most of the research in the social sciences is applied. In other words, the research techniques, procedures and methods that form the body of research methodology are applied to the collection of information about various aspects of a situation, issue, problem or phenomenon so that the information gathered can be used in other ways – such as for policy formulation, administration and the enhancement of understanding of a phenomenon.

Objectives perspective

If you examine a research study from the perspective of its objectives, broadly a research endeavour can be classified as descriptive, correlational, explanatory or exploratory.

A research study classified as a descriptive study attempts to describe systematically a situation, problem, phenomenon, service or programme, or provides information about, say, the living conditions of a community, or describes attitudes towards an issue. For example, it may attempt to describe the types of service provided by an organisation, the administrative structure of an organisation, the living conditions of Aboriginal people in the outback, the needs of a community, what it means to go through a divorce, how a child feels living in a house with domestic violence, or the attitudes of employees towards management. The main purpose of such studies is to describe what is prevalent with respect to the issue or problem under study.

The main emphasis in a correlational study is to discover or establish the existence of a relationship, association or interdependence between two or more aspects of a situation or phenomenon. For example, what is the impact of an advertising campaign on the sale of a product? What is the relationship between stressful living and the incidence of heart attack? What is the relationship between fertility and mortality? What is the relationship between technology and unemployment? What is the effect of a health service on the control of a disease, or the home environment on educational achievement?

Explanatory research attempts to clarify why and how there is a relationship between two aspects of a situation or phenomenon. This type of research attempts to explain, for example, why stressful living results in heart attacks; why a decline in mortality is followed by a fertility decline; or how the home environment affects children's level of academic achievement.

The fourth type of research, from the viewpoint of the objectives of a study, is called exploratory research. This is when a study is undertaken with the objective either of exploring an area where little is known or of investigating the possibilities of undertaking a particular research study. In many situations a study could have multiple objectives; that is, some parts of it could be descriptive, some correlational, and some explanatory. As a matter of fact a good study combines all three of these objectives. When the purpose of a study is to determine its feasibility, it is also called a feasibility study or a pilot study. It is usually carried out when a researcher wants to explore areas about which s/he has little or no knowledge. A small-scale study is undertaken to decide if it is worth carrying out a detailed investigation. On the basis of the assessment made during the exploratory study, a full study may eventuate. Exploratory studies are also conducted to develop, refine and/or test measurement tools and procedures. Table 1.1 shows the types of research study from the viewpoint of objectives.

Although, theoretically, a research study can be classified in one of the above objectives-perspective categories, in practice, most studies are a combination of the first three; that is, they contain elements of descriptive, correlational and explanatory research. In this book the guidelines suggested for writing a research report encourage you to integrate these aspects.

Descriptive study: A study in which the main focus is on description, rather than examining relationships or associations, is classified as a descriptive study. A descriptive study attempts systematically to describe a situation, problem, phenomenon, service or programme, or provides information about, say, the living conditions of a community, or describes attitudes towards an issue.

Correlational study: Study which is primarily designed to investigate whether or not there is a relationship between two or more variables.

Explanatory research: In an explanatory study the main emphasis is to clarify why and how there is a relationship between two aspects of a situation or phenomenon.

Exploratory research: This is when a study is undertaken with the objective either to explore an area where little is known or to investigate the possibilities of undertaking a particular research study. When a study is carried out to determine its feasibility it is also called a feasibility or pilot study.

Feasibility study: When the purpose of a study is to investigate the possibility of undertaking it on a larger scale and to streamlining methods and procedures for the main study, the study is called a feasibility study.

Pilot study: see Feasibility study

Mode of enquiry perspective

Broadly, from the perspective of 'mode of enquiry', there are three approaches that are used in social research to find answers to your research questions. These are:

→ the quantitative or structured approach;
→ the qualitative or unstructured approach; and
→ the mixed methods approach.

The core difference between the three is the extent of flexibility permitted to you as a researcher in the research process. In the quantitative or structured approach of enquiry everything that forms the research process – objectives, design, sample, the questions that you plan to ask of your respondents – is predetermined. The unstructured or qualitative approach, by contrast, allows you as a researcher complete flexibility in all these aspects of the process. The mixed methods approach has attributes from both the other approaches, that is, some aspects of the research process may have flexibility and others may completely lack it, depending upon the paradigm to which they belong.

The **quantitative approach** is rooted in the philosophy of rationalism; follows a rigid, structured and predetermined set of procedures to explore; aims to quantify the extent of variation in a phenomenon; emphasises the measurement of variables and the objectivity of the process; believes in substantiation on the basis of a large sample size; gives importance to the validity and reliability of findings; and communicates findings in an analytical and aggregate manner, drawing conclusions and inferences that can be generalised.

The **qualitative approach,** on the other hand, is embedded in the philosophy of empiricism; follows an open, flexible and unstructured approach to enquiry; aims to explore diversity rather than to quantify; emphasises the description and narration of feelings, perceptions and experiences rather than their measurement; and communicates findings in a descriptive and narrative rather than analytical manner, placing no or less emphasis on generalisations.

The mixed methods approach uses the strengths of both quantitative and qualitative research. It aims to select the best methods, regardless of the qualitative–quantitative divide, to find answers to the research questions. In extremely simple terms, the mixed methods approach to social research combines two or more methods to collect and analyse data pertaining to the research problem. These methods could be either a mix of quantitative and qualitative or belong to only one paradigm. The approach is based upon the rationale that for certain situations qualitative techniques are better and for some others the quantitative. Hence, to get the best outcome for a research study you need to combine both approaches or use more than one method.

The quantitative or structured approach is more appropriate to determine the *extent* of a problem, issue or phenomenon, whereas the qualitative or unstructured approach is predominantly used to explore its *nature*, in other words the variation or diversity per se in a phenomenon, issue, problem or attitude towards an issue. For example, if you want to find out the different perspectives on an issue or the problems experienced by people living in a community, then these are better explored by using unstructured enquiries. On the other hand, to find out how many people have a particular perspective, how many people have a particular problem or how many people hold a particular view, you need to have a structured approach to enquiry. If you need to look into these

Mixed/multiple methods approach: In extremely simple terms, the mixed methods approach to social research is when you combine two or more methods to collect and analyse data pertaining to your research problem. When these methods are from both paradigms, that is, when a study uses both quantitative and qualitative methods, it is classified as mixed methods approach. However, when these are from one paradigm only, it is called multiple methods approach.

The approach is based upon the rationale that for certain situations qualitative techniques are better and for others quantitative ones are better. Hence, to get the best outcome for a research study you need to combine both approaches or use more than one method.

Table 1.1   Types of research studies from the perspective of objectives

Examples	Aim	Main theme	Type of research
• Socioeconomic characteristics of residents of a community • Attitudes of students towards quality of teaching • Types of service provided by an agency • Needs of a community • Sale of a product • Attitudes of nurses towards death and dying • Attitudes of workers towards management • Number of people living in a community • Problems faced by new immigrants • Extent of occupational mobility among immigrants • Consumers' likes and dislikes with regard to a product • Effects of living in a house with domestic violence • Strategies put in place by a company to increase productivity of workers	To describe what is prevalent regarding: • a group of people • a community • a phenomenon • a situation • a programme • an outcome	To describe what is prevalent	Descriptive research
• Impact of a programme • Relationship between stressful living and incidence of heart attacks • Impact of technology on employment • Impact of maternal and child health services on infant mortality • Effectiveness of a marriage counselling service on extent of marital problems • Impact of an advertising campaign on sale of a product • Impact of incentives on productivity of workers • Effectiveness of an immunisation programme in controlling infectious disease	To establish or explore: • a relationship • an association • an interdependence	To ascertain if there is a relationship	Correlational research
• Why does stressful living result in heart attacks? • How does technology create unemployment/ employment? • How do maternal and child health services affect infant mortality? • Why do some people have a positive attitude towards an issue while others do not? • Why does a particular intervention work for some people and not for others? • Why do some people use a product while others do not? • Why do some people migrate to another country while others do not? • Why do some people adopt a programme while others do not?	To explain: • why a relationship, association or interdependence exists • why a particular event occurs	To explain why the relationship is formed	Explanatory research

aspects, you will need to use both approaches; that is, you will need to use the mixed methods approach. Even if your interest is in finding out how many people have a particular problem or hold a particular view, before undertaking a structured enquiry, in the author's opinion, an unstructured enquiry must be undertaken to ascertain the diversity in a phenomenon which can then be quantified through a structured enquiry. Both approaches have their place in research. Both have their strengths as well as weaknesses. Therefore, you should not 'lock' yourself solely into a structured or unstructured approach.

The structured approach to enquiry, as you know, is classified as quantitative research and unstructured as qualitative research, and the mixed methods approach could be either entirely quantitative or qualitative or some sections could be qualitative and some quantitative. The divide between the two is based upon the philosophies of rationalism and empiricism and the difference in attitude towards acquiring knowledge. Rationalism is based upon the belief that 'human beings achieve knowledge because of their capacity to reason' and empiricism upon the belief that 'the only knowledge that human beings acquire is from sensory experiences' (Bernard 1994: 2). Mixed methods, as mentioned earlier, can combine the attributes of both. The distinction between quantitative, qualitative and mixed method research, in addition to the philosophies underpinning them and the structured/ unstructured process of enquiry, is also dependent upon some other considerations which are briefly presented in Table 1.2. The choice between the quantitative, qualitative and mixed methods approaches should depend upon:

→ **the aim of your enquiry** – exploration, confirmation or quantification;
→ **the use of the findings** – policy formulation or process understanding.

A study is classified as qualitative if the purpose of the study is primarily to describe a situation, phenomenon, problem or event; that is, if the information is gathered through the use of variables measured on nominal or ordinal scales (qualitative measurement scales); and if the analysis is done to establish the variation in the situation, phenomenon or problem without quantifying it. The historical enumeration of events, an account of the different opinions people have about an issue, and a description of an observed situation such as the living conditions of a community are examples of qualitative research.

On the other hand, the study is classified as quantitative if you want to quantify the variation in a phenomenon, situation, problem or issue; if information is gathered using predominantly quantitative variables; and if the analysis is geared to ascertaining the magnitude of the variation. Examples of quantitative aspects of a research study are: how many people have a particular problem, and how many people hold a particular attitude.

The use of statistics is *not* an integral part of a quantitative study. The main function of statistics is to act as a test to confirm or contradict the conclusions that you have drawn on the basis of your understanding of analysed data. Statistics, among other things, help you to quantify the magnitude of an association or relationship, provide an indication of the confidence you can place in your findings and help you to isolate the effect of different variables.

It is strongly recommended that you do not lock yourself into becoming either solely a quantitative or solely a qualitative researcher. It is true that there are disciplines that lend themselves predominantly either to qualitative or to quantitative research. For example, such disciplines as anthropology, history and sociology are more inclined towards qualitative research, whereas psychology, epidemiology, education, economics, public health and marketing are more inclined towards quantitative research. However, this does not mean that an economist or a psychologist never uses the qualitative approach, or that an anthropologist never uses quantitative information.

There is increasing recognition by most disciplines in the social sciences that both types of research are important for a good research study. The research problem itself should determine whether the study is carried out using quantitative or qualitative methodologies.

As both qualitative and quantitative approaches have their strengths and weaknesses, advantages and disadvantages, 'neither one is markedly superior to the other in all respects' (Ackroyd & Hughes 1992: 30). The measurement and analysis of the variables about which information is obtained in a research study are dependent upon the purpose of the study. In many studies you need to combine both qualitative and quantitative approaches. For example, suppose you want to find out the types of service available to victims of domestic violence in a city and the extent of their utilisation. Types of service are the qualitative aspect of the study as finding out about them entails description of the services. The extent of utilisation of the services is the quantitative aspect as it involves estimating the number of people who use the services and calculating other indicators that reflect the extent of utilisation. The mixed methods approach combines the strengths of both paradigms to best achieve the objectives of your research. It replaces those weaknesses of a design had we used methods from one paradigm only.

It is important for you to understand that, as compared to mixed methods, both quantitative and qualitative approaches have well-developed methodologies and methods. In most situations the methods and procedures of both quantitative and qualitative approaches are used in the mixed methods approach. Table 1.2 looks at the differences between the three from different perspectives.

IMPORTANT NOTE TO READERS

CHECKPOINT
Qualitative, quantitative and mixed methods research

Both quantitative and qualitative approaches have their own body of theoretical knowledge comprised of their common as well as respective methods, models and procedures. Their respective theoretical knowledge base, in this book, is detailed in relation to the operational steps which provide both the framework and the structure for the book. As the mixed methods approach is of very recent origin, to the best of the author's knowledge and understanding, it does not have an extensive body of methodological literature. It mostly uses methods, models and procedures of the quantitative and/or qualitative approaches. Therefore the book does not detail separately, under each operational step, the theoretical knowledge for the mixed methods approach.

When using mixed methods you first need to decide which methods are most appropriate to best achieve the objectives of your study. Specific methods and procedures that you are likely to use as a part of the mixed methods approach are mostly either quantitative or qualitative, hence are detailed either as quantitative or qualitative methods and procedures in this book. To learn details about these methods you need to consult the pertinent sections describing quantitative or qualitative approaches.

The next section in this chapter provides details about different aspects such as definition, philosophy, advantages and disadvantages, forms of mixing of the mixed methods approach. It details aspects that will help you to develop a greater understanding of the mixed methods approach per se and provides background information about it as appropriate.

The sole aim of the section below is to provide you, as a beginner in research methods, information sufficient to give you some understanding of the mixed methods approach as such. Also, the emphasis is on providing practical

Table 1.2 Differences between qualitative, quantitative and mixed methods approaches

Difference with respect to:	Quantitative approach	Qualitative approach	Mixed methods approach
Underpinning philosophy	Rationalism: 'That human beings achieve knowledge because of their capacity to reason' (Bernard 1994: 2)	Empiricism: 'The only knowledge that human beings acquire is from sensory experiences' (Bernard 1994: 2)	Both are valuable to social research theory and practice. That knowledge can be gained through both the capacity to reason and sensory experiences.
Approach to enquiry	Structured/rigid/predetermined methodology	Unstructured/flexible/open methodology	Can be structured, unstructured or both
Main purpose of investigation	To quantify the extent of variation in a phenomenon, situation, issue, etc.	To describe variation in a phenomenon, situation, issue, etc.	To quantify and/or explore with multiple or mixed methods a phenomenon to enhance accuracy or yield greater depth
Measurement of variables	Emphasis on some form of either measurement or classification of variables	Emphasis on description of variables	Measurement and/or description
Sample size	Emphasis on greater sample size	Fewer cases	Larger sample size for some aspects and smaller for others, depending upon the purpose
Focus of enquiry	Narrows focus in terms of extent of enquiry, but assembles required information from a greater number of respondents/sources	Covers multiple issues but assembles required information from fewer respondents	Narrow or broad, or both, depending upon the methods used
Dominant research topic	Explains prevalence, incidence, extent, nature of issues, opinions and attitude; discovers regularities and formulates theories	Explores experiences, meanings, perceptions and feelings	Both or either, depending upon the methods used
Analysis of data	Subjects variables to frequency distributions, cross-tabulations or other statistical procedures	Subjects responses, narratives or observational data to identification of themes and describes these	Quantitative or qualitative or both, depending upon the objectives
Dominant research value	Reliability and objectivity (value-free)	Authenticity, but does not claim to be value-free	Dominant value of one or both of the paradigms
Communication of findings	Organisation more analytical in nature, drawing inferences and conclusions, and testing magnitude and strength of a relationship	Organisation more descriptive and narrative in nature	Similar to the quantitative and/or qualitative approach

knowledge rather than detailing historical, philosophical and conceptual issues and debates about it. In doing so an attempt is also made not to make things too complicated but simply to make you aware of the mixed methods approach to research enquiry. You can consult books on the mixed methods approach referenced in this book for greater understanding.

THE MIXED/MULTIPLE METHODS APPROACH
Introduction

Though the mixed methods approach in social research has been in use for a 'long time', it has attained its recognition and prominence only during the last two decades. According to Creswell and Clark (2011: xix), 'mixed methods has had its roots over the last 20 years in several disciplines'; however, 'in the past 5 to 10 years we have seen tremendous interest in this approach to research'. According to Teddlie and Tashakkori (2009: 7), 'The [mixed methods] research tradition is less well known than the [quantitative] or [qualitative] traditions because it has emerged as a separate orientation during only the past 20 years'. To the author's mind, it is more than a methodology but a philosophy that has come to be recognised as an approach during the last 20 years or so. It is based upon the assumption that, for certain situations, to enhance the accuracy and meaningfulness of your conclusions, to have a complete picture of a situation and to reconfirm your findings you need to use more than one method belonging to one or both of the paradigms. The core of the mixed/multiple methods approach is the use of multiple methods belonging to both paradigms, or simply of more than one method from one paradigm. Many research experts (Bernard 1994; Brewer & Hunter 1989; Creswell & Clark 2011; Tashakkori & Teddlie 1998; Teddlie & Tashakkori 2009) have advocated the use of mixed methods approach in social research. According to Bernard (1994: 1), 'whatever our theoretical orientation, a sound mix of qualitative and quantitative data is inevitable in any study of human thought and behaviour'. According to Brewer and Hunter (1989: 22), 'Since the fifties, the social sciences have grown tremendously. And with that growth, there is now virtually no major problem-area that is studied exclusively within one method.' According to Tashakkori and Teddlie (1998: 5), 'most major areas of research in social and behavioural sciences now use multiple methods as a matter of course'. Such studies that use more than two or more methods, either from one or both the paradigms, to enhance accuracy of the findings, are said to be using a mixed/multiple methods approach.

Defining the approach

According to Creswell and Clark (2011: 2), 'several definitions for mixed methods have emerged over the years that incorporate various elements of methods, research processes, philosophy, and research design'. In extremely simple terms, mixed methods is an approach, rather a philosophy, to social enquiry that uses two or more methods, processes and (in certain situations) philosophies in undertaking a research study. It is based upon the belief that different paradigms and methods have different strengths and, for certain situations, their combined strength would result in improving the depth and accuracy of the findings. The mixed methods approach aims to best achieve the objectives of a study by combining the strengths of different methods and paradigms. According to Teddlie and Tashakkori (2009: 7), 'Mixed methodologists present an alternative to the QUAN and QUAL traditions by advocating the use of whatever methodological tools are required to answer the research questions under study'. According to them, 'mixed method studies are those that combine the qualitative and quantitative approaches into the research methodology of a single study or multi-phased study' (Tashakkori & Teddlie 1998: 17–18). Writers such as Bryman (2004) and Creswell and Clark (2007) also believe that to be called a mixed methods approach the methods you use must be from both the paradigms. According to Creswell and Clark (2007: 5), 'as a method, it focuses on collecting, analysing, and mixing both quantitative and qualitative data in a single study or series of studies. Its central premise is that the use of quantitative and qualitative approaches, in combination, provides a better understanding of research problems than either approach alone.' Tashakkori and Tedllie (1998: ix) define 'mixed methods as a combining of quantitative and qualitative approaches in the methodology of a study'. They consider the mixed methods design as one where you mix quantitative and qualitative methods. Johnson et al. (2007: 113) define mixed methods research as 'the type of research in which a researcher or team of researchers combine elements of qualitative and quantitative research approaches (e.g., use of qualitative and quantitative viewpoints, data collection, analysis, inference techniques) for the purposes, breadth, depth of understanding, and corroboration'.

However, there are others such as Alexander et al. (in Gilbert 2008: 126) who consider an approach to be a mixed methods approach even if the methods used are from only one paradigm; that is, two or more methods could be from both the paradigms or they can be from one of them. According to them, 'mixed methods research seems, self-evidently, to be the use of two or more methods in a single research project (or research programme)'. Writers such as Cronin et al. (2007) also subscribe to the view of Alexander et al. They 'suggest that those studies that even use two different quantitative or qualitative methods can be said to be using a mixed methods approach'.

It is evident from the above definitions that there are two opinions with respect to the definition of a mixed method study (Figure 1.3). The first advocates that the two methods must be from both the paradigms, that is, one must mix quantitative and qualitative methods (Teddlie & Tashakkori 2009; Tashakkori & Teddlie 1998; Bryman 2004; Cresswell & Clark 2007). The second suggests that even if both the methods are from the same paradigm, a study using two methods is considered as a mixed methods study (Gilbert 2008; Chapter 7, Cronin et al. 2007). The present author also believes that for a study to be classified as a mixed methods study, the two or more methods it uses could come from either or both the paradigms.

Though the term 'multiple methods approach' is not much in use nowadays or is used interchangeably with 'mixed methods approach' by some, the author makes a distinction between 'multiple' and 'mixed' methods approaches. The term 'mixed methods', according to the author, is used for situations where different elements of the research process are combined from both the quantitative and qualitative approaches, and 'multiple methods' when the methods selected are from one paradigm only.

Combining or mixing of different methods in both these viewpoints is done with the aim of taking advantage of the strengths of both paradigms, and, in the case of multiple methods belonging to the same paradigm, of enhancing and enriching the accuracy, validity and reliability of the findings. There is no single approach that, always and in all situations, can accurately find answers to all your research questions. In some situations you need to use different methods for different research questions or objectives that guide your study. Also there are situations 'in which one data source may be insufficient, results need to be explained, exploratory findings need to be generalized, a second method is needed to enhance a primary method, a theoretical stance needs to be employed, and an overall research objective can be best addressed with multiple phases or projects' (Creswell &

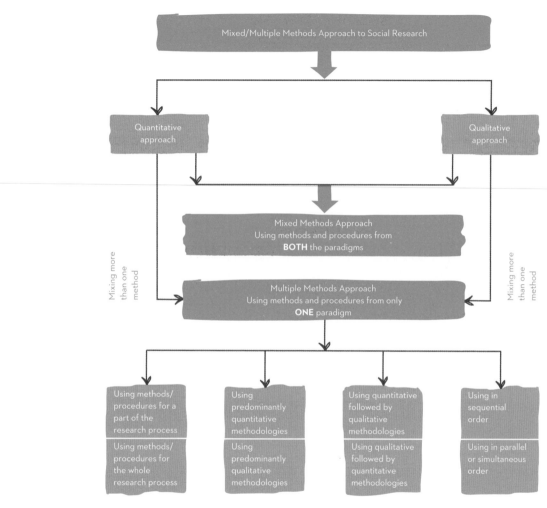

Figure 1.3 **Mixed/multiple methods, quantitative and qualitative approaches in social research**

Clark 2011: 8). The mixed/multiple methods approach lets you choose the methods that are best suited for your study from within or across paradigms.

There is another consideration you need to keep in mind when defining a mixed methods approach. Many researchers often use two different methods, quantitative and/or qualitative, for only one operational step, that of data collection. For example, you may conduct in-depth interviews with some members of the study population to further understand the issues identified by them in the data collected through the use of a questionnaire. A similar situation is when, for example, you want to develop a questionnaire to ascertain the needs of a community and, to do so, you conduct a number of in-depth or focus group interviews with some of the community members or organise a community forum to establish the diversity of needs. This process of identifying the diversity of needs becomes the basis for developing the questionnaire or interview schedule. The issue is: do you classify such studies as mixed or multiple methods studies where you use more than one method only for collecting data? The complete replication of a study, using two approaches, is quite expensive and hence not common. The author considers a study to be using multiple or mixed methods approach even though it uses more than one method for a single operational step. In the author's opinion the use of more than one method in the following situations will qualify a study to be classified as using a mixed/multiple methods approach:

- **Collecting data** using different methods for information gathering; that is, you can collect the same data through a questionnaire or an interview schedule (quantitative methods) as well as through in-depth interviews, focus groups or a community forum (qualitative methods). Using multiple methods for data collection will qualify a study to be classified as mixed/multiple methods (depending upon whether the methods are from both or single paradigm). Of course, you also need to use different methods for data analysis and processing to match with the methods of data collection.

- Collecting the required information from different groups of people, for verification and confirmation of findings, drawn from the same study population (**different samples**). In other words, selecting one sample for administering, say, a questionnaire, selecting another for in-depth interviewing and selecting the third to form a focus group for gathering similar information for validation, verification and greater understanding of the issues.

- Using different ways of **data analysis** and **information dissemination**; that is, analysing data with quantitative as well as qualitative techniques to best achieve the objectives of a study.

Tashakkori and Teddlie (1998) differentiate between the two by using two different names. According to them (p. 1), 'mixed methods combine the qualitative and quantitative approaches to the research methods of a study, while mixed models studies combine these two approaches across all phases of the research process'. In the author's opinion it is the use of two or more methods, either quantitative, qualitative or both, for the whole or a part(s) of the research process, that constitutes the mixed/multiple methods approach.

It is important for you to understand that the way you formulate your research problem or subobjective(s) determines the types of method that are appropriate for finding their answers. Let us take an example (Figure 1.4) to further understand the relationship between the way a subobjective is formulated and the types of method that are appropriate to study it and how the methods used determine the typology of the approach

CHECKPOINT
The mixed methods approach

adopted. Also note that to achieve different objectives you need to use different research approaches. For some it is purely quantitative, for some purely qualitative and for some it is a mixed methods approach.

Suppose you are interested in the area of domestic violence and want to conduct a study with the following subobjectives (you can select just one subobjective to study if you wish):

1   to determine the prevalence of domestic violence in a community;
2   to understand the nature and extent of domestic violence in the community;
3   to find out what it means for a woman and a man to live in a household with domestic violence;
4   to understand why, in spite of domestic violence, some victims, men as well as women, continue to live in the relationship;
5   to describe the types of service available to victims of domestic violence in a community; and
6   to establish the socioeconomic-demographic profile of people who are consumers of these services.

To achieve these objectives, the study needs to be carried out by using different methods. For example:

→ Subobjective 1 can only be studied through methods that fall into the quantitative category (counting the number of households with domestic violence episodes determined by using a predetermined and accepted set of criteria).

→ For subobjective 2, you need to use methods that fall into both paradigms. The 'nature' of domestic violence can best be explored through qualitative methods (such as in-depth interviews, focus groups, narratives, oral histories) and its 'extent' through quantitative methods (such as structured household interview, records of agencies providing services to victims of domestic violence).

→ Subobjective 3 you can best explore using a qualitative methodology (in-depth interviews, group interviews with victims, narratives, oral histories, case studies) as no quantitative method will give you more accurate information on 'what it means' to a victim to live in a house with domestic violence.

→ The reasons for living in the relationship in spite of violence (subobjective 4) can be investigated through a number of methods belonging to both paradigms (you can conduct in-depth interviews, structured interviews, group interviews, focus groups). You can collect information using one method only or a number of them.

→ Similarly 'types of service' (subobjective 5) you can best study through a qualitative approach (in-depth interviews with service providers and consumers of the services).

→ Finally, the 'profile of consumers' (subobjective 6) is best investigated by quantitative methods (questionnaire or interview schedule).

In the above example you will note that we have proposed different methods for different subobjectives of the study. Studies like this that make use of the strengths of different methods, irrespective of the paradigm they

Suppose you are interested in the area of domestic violence and want to conduct a study with the following subobjectives (you can select even one subobjective to study if you so desire):

1 To determine the prevalence of domestic violence in a community;
2 To understand the nature and extent of domestic violence in the community;
3 To find out what it means for a woman and a man to live in a household with domestic violence;
4 To understand why, in spite of domestic violence, some women continue to live in the relationship;
5 To describe the types of service available to victims of domestic violence in a community; and
6 To establish the socioeconomic demographic profile of people who are consumers of these services.

To achieve these objectives, the study needs to be carried out by using different methods. For example:

Subobjective 1 can only be studied through methods that fall into the category of quantitative methods (counting the number of households with domestic violence episodes determined by using a predetermined and accepted set of criteria).

For subobjective 2, you need to use methods that fall into both the paradigms. 'Nature' of domestic violence can best be explored through methods (such as in-depth interviews, focus groups, narratives, oral histories) that fall in the domain of qualitative research and 'extent' through methods (such as structured household interview, records of agencies providing services to victims of domestic violence) that are considered to be belonging to the quantitative paradigm.

Subobjective 3 can best be explored using qualitative methodology (in-depth interviews, group interviews with victims, narratives, oral histories, case studies), as no quantitative method will give you more accurate information on 'what does it mean' to a victim to live in a house with domestic violence.

The reasons for living in the relationship in spite of violence (subobjective 4), can be investigated through a number of methods belonging to both paradigms (you can conduct in-depth interviews, structured interviews, group interviews, focus groups; you can collect information through one method only or through a number of them).

Similarly 'types of service' (subobjective 5) can best be studied through a qualitative approach (in-depth interviews with service providers and consumers of the services).

And

The 'profile of consumers' (subobjective 6), can be better investigated by quantitative methods (questionnaire or interview schedule).

Figure 1.4 Use of mixed and multiple methods – an example

belong to and make use of multiple methods belonging to the same paradigm, are classified as mixed or multiple methods studies. If the methods used are from both paradigms, it is a mixed methods study and if they are from the same paradigm, it is a multiple method study. In brief, any study that uses more than one method belonging to either one and/or the other paradigm for either the total or partial research process, to best achieve the objectives of a study, is classified as mixed/multiple methods study.

Rationale underpinning the approach

The rationale underpinning the mixed/multiple methods approach is primarily based upon two beliefs. The first relates to the ability of the methods of a paradigm to provide accurate answers to all your research questions in all situations. The second relates to the belief that the use of more than one method in most situations will provide a better and more complete picture of a situation or phenomenon than a single method alone. Specifically, these beliefs are:

→ The way you formulate your subobjectives determines whether a study would lend itself to a quantitative or qualitative mode of enquiry. Most of the time a study has several subobjectives (Figure 1.4) not all of which lend themselves to be extensively and accurately explored by the methods of a single paradigm. It often happens that some subobjectives are better explored through quantitative methods and others through qualitative methods. In situations like this if you use methods from only one paradigm, you will compromise the quality of your findings. The mixed methods approach is based upon the belief that, in certain situations, use of methods from both the paradigms will certainly enhance the accuracy and reliability of the findings. Openness to the use of methods from both paradigms in a study to best achieve its objectives is the underpinning philosophy of the mixed methods approach.

→ In certain circumstances a single method may not provide a complete, detailed and accurate picture of the situation. Or, in some instances, to be absolutely certain you may want to double-check your findings by using another method. The use of multiple methods is based upon the belief that in certain situations the accuracy of your findings can be enhanced by using more than one method from a paradigm.

When to use the approach

Several reasons warrant the use of mixed or multiple methods approach. Some of these reasons are as follows:

→ **When you want to explore from both perspectives.** Qualitative and quantitative research will look at a phenomenon from different perspectives. The qualitative perspective looks at the phenomenon in depth but is based upon information collected from a few individuals, hence is limiting in making generalisations and broad conclusions. On the other hand, the quantitative approach gathers information from many individuals so that it has the ability to make generalisations but is limited in terms of in-depth analysis. Taking a purely quantitative or purely qualitative approach would give the study the strengths as well weaknesses of the approach. It is to overcome the weaknesses of the approach and make use of the strengths of the other approach that you combine both. By combining both perspectives you can have a more complete picture and understanding of a phenomenon from both perspectives.

→ **When accurate and complete information from one source is difficult to obtain.** Sometimes there are situations when you are unable to have complete and accurate information about a situation through the use of a single method from either approach. To fill such gaps you need to supplement the information by other methods, thus taking a mixed methods approach. According to Creswell and Clark (2011: 8), 'research problems suited for mixed methods are those in which one data source may be insufficient, results need to be explained, exploratory findings need to be generalized, a second method is needed to enhance a primary method, a theoretical stance needs to be employed, and an overall research objective can be best addressed with multiple phases or projects'. The author was involved in a study to ascertain the number of births and deaths in rural India. To accurately estimate the number of births and deaths two secondary and two primary sources were used. These included: records kept by a government-appointed official responsible for maintaining vital statistics records in rural areas (secondary source); a village midwife who every fortnight was visited by a member of the research team to collect, through informal interviewing, information on births and deaths during the previous fortnight (primary source); ten 'key informants' selected from the residents of the village for the duration of the study and who were contacted every fortnight by a member of the research team (primary source); and the resident midwife nurse, an employee of the research team, who was responsible for sending a monthly report on birth and deaths in her area during the previous month (secondary source). All these reports were compared (triangulated) to ascertain the total number of births and deaths in the area. It is in situations like this, where you want to collect factual information on a longitudinal basis and want to be sure of the accuracy of the information, that you need to use more than one method, the mixed/multiple methods approach.

→ **A must for good quality research.** Almost every good researcher who aims to undertake a study in order to make generalisations first explores different aspects of the study by undertaking an exploratory phase which mostly uses qualitative methodology. Everything needed for a quantitative study is usually developed on the basis of an exploratory study. It is also not uncommon that after completing the study you take your findings back to the respondents for explanations and clarifications. In the author's opinion a good researcher always follows a 'qualitative–quantitative–qualitative' cycle of enquiry. Hence, to enhance the quality of your research, you need to mix both approaches and on occasions use more than one method.

→ **When you need to make generalisations.** When your aim is to make generalisations on the basis of your study as well as share the findings with the study population, it is good practice to develop issues you want to explore and questions you would like to ask your respondents, in consultation with potential respondents. Development and sharing can best be undertaken by qualitative approaches. In such situations you need to combine both qualitative and quantitative methodologies.

→ **When you need to find an explanation for your findings.** There are situations when the findings from a quantitative approach need elaboration as to the exact meaning of the responses given by the respondents. These exact meanings can only be understood when discussed with the respondents. In such situations you need to combine quantitative methods with qualitative ones to further understand the responses. According to Creswell and Clark (2011: 9), 'Sometimes the result of a study may provide an incomplete understanding of a research problem and there is a need for further explanation. In this case, a mixed methods study is used with the second database helping to explain the first database. A typical situation is when quantitative results require an explanation as to what they mean.'

→ **When you want to develop a good data collection instrument and ascertain the validity of the questions.** It is a common practice in quantitative studies to develop data collection instruments in consultation with the potential respondents to ensure their relevance. This consultative process entails the use of qualitative methodologies. In addition, this process will ensure the validity of the questions by exploring whether or not the respondents interpreted and understood them as intended by the researcher.

→ **When you undertake studies with multiple objectives.** Situations when a study has multiple objectives and not all of them lend themselves to a single approach warrant the collection of data through the use of either quantitative and qualitative approaches or having two sets of data collected through two either quantitative or qualitative methods.

Ways of mixing methods

The 'typology' developed here does not strictly reflect the study designs per se but the different ways in which methods and procedures from quantitative and qualitative approaches are mixed with regard to when, what, at what stage, in what order and to what extent. The designs, procedures and methods are primarily those of quantitative and/or qualitative research.

There are several ways in which you can mix methods and procedures belonging to quantitative and/or qualitative paradigms in mixed or multiple methods studies. The types of *mixed methods study design*, as identified by Tashakkori and Teddlie (1998: 18), according to the author, are primarily based upon the way the methods are mixed. The author feels that the classification or 'typology of studies' within mixed and multiple methodologies predominantly depends upon *what* is being mixed (whether mixing is from both paradigms or just one), *when* in the research process the mixing is done (whether mixing is in a sequential or simultaneous order), *at what stage* of the research process mixing is taking place (whether mixing is for a part or whole of the research process), *in what order* mixing occurs (whether it is qualitative followed by quantitative or quantitative followed by qualitative or both together) and *to what extent* (whether predominantly quantitative or qualitative).

In terms of *what*, there are broadly two ways in which you can mix different methods:

→ Mix methods belonging to both paradigms either for the whole or a part of the research process.
→ Mix methods belonging to only one paradigm either for the whole or a part of the process.

In terms of *when*, again there are two ways:

→ Use two or more methods one after the other (sequentially) either for the whole research process or a part of it. Creswell (1995: 177) calls studies using methods one after the other as *sequential studies*.

→ Use two or more methods concurrently either for the whole or a part of the process. Creswell (1995: 177) calls studies using methods concurrently *parallel* or *simultaneous studies*.

In terms of *stage*, there are two ways:

→ Mix them for the whole of the research process.
→ Mix them only for one or some operational steps.

In term of *order*, there are three ways in which you can mix methods:

→ Use qualitative methods followed by quantitative.
→ Use quantitative methods followed by qualitative.
→ Use qualitative methods followed by quantitative followed again by qualitative.

In terms of *extent*, there are two ways of mixing:

→ Use both methodologies equally (equivalent status studies: Creswell 1995: 177).
→ Use one methodology predominantly (dominant/less dominant studies: Creswell 1995: 177). When, in conducting a study, the methods are mixed in such a way that one paradigm dominates, with a small proportion of the methods/procedures drawn from the other.

Equivalent status studies:
A mixed methods study where both methodologies are equally applied is classified as an equivalent status study.

Dominant/less dominant studies:
A mixed methods study where one methodology dominates the study is classified as dominant/less dominant study.

Advantages and disadvantages

The use of mixed methods in a research project has both advantages as well as disadvantages. Some of the main advantages are as follows:

→ **Enhancement of research possibilities.** In situations where you have multiple objectives to achieve in a research study and if not all the objectives lend themselves to be explored with one method, use of multiple methods offers a way to find answers to all your research questions. For instance, in the example in Figure 1.4, subobjective 2 has two dimensions, 'nature' and 'extent'. These two concepts require different methodologies. 'Nature' can be explored more richly through qualitative methods, whereas 'extent' is better explored through quantitative methods as it involves counting the number of households with occurrence of domestic violence. Similarly, suppose you want to ascertain the prevalence of drug use in a community and the process of becoming a drug addict. The first part you can investigate through a number of methods such as structured interviewing or a questionnaire, but the second part is best investigated by unstructured and in-depth interviewing. Thus, the use of mixed/multiple methods approach enhances the research possibilities within the framework of a study.

→ **Better for more complex situations.** Another important advantage of a mixed methods approach is that it provides freedom to use the best methods, irrespective of their paradigm, in more complex situations. We are often confronted with situations with complex structure and dimensions that warrant investigation by multiple methods not only within a paradigm but also across paradigms. A mixed/multiple methods approach provides such freedom and flexibility. According to Creswell and Clark (2011: 21), 'the complexity of our research problems call for answers beyond simple numbers in a quantitative sense or words in a qualitative sense. A combination of both forms of data provides the most complete analysis of problems.'

↱ **Enrichment of data.** There are situations when you collect data with one method but for its supplementation or enrichment you need another set of data. The second set of data primarily looks at the issues from a different perspective. This triangulation enriches the information and enhances the accuracy of the findings and is only possible when a mixed/multiple methods approach is used in undertaking a study. Let us take another example (Figure 1.5), in which the author was involved, that used non-participant observation as a method of data collection but with the recording done, on the spot, in two different formats (descriptive and categorical). Though the data was collected by one method, two different methods of observation recording were employed. Some of the subsequent steps – the analysis and communication of the findings – were treated in two different ways appropriate to the manner in which the data was collected. This enrichment of data was possible only because of the use of mixed methods in recording and subsequent steps that followed.

↱ **Collecting additional research evidence.** For complex and important situations, where you want further evidence to support or contradict your argument, collection of data by two different methods makes good sense. The second set is used for comparison and confirmation or contradiction of the findings of the first method.

Triangulation: Triangulation involves the use of the same set of data from multiple sources to best achieve the objectives of your study. It is based upon the belief that use of the same set of data, collected through different approaches to draw conclusions, and its examination from different perspectives will provide a better understanding of a problem, situation, phenomenon or issue. There are different types of triangulations; data, investigator, theory and methodology.

The author was involved in a study designed to develop a service delivery model for maternal and child health services for rural India. To work out the worker–population ratio, data was collected through a 'two-minute-instantaneous' non-participant observation of the activities being carried out by service delivery workers, on randomly selected days, over four years, taking into consideration the periods of fluctuations in the workload due to seasonality. Different categories of health workers, when delivering services in real-life situations, were observed by an observer every two minutes and their activities were recorded in descriptive as well as predetermined service-activity categories (developed on the basis of pre-test phase) by the observers. Information gathered through descriptive recording was thematically analysed to ascertain the activities carried out by the workers and amount of time spent on each one of them. The data gathered through categorical recording was similarly analysed to establish the time spent on each activity. The two sets of data were compared (triangulated) to ascertain the various activities carried out by the workers and the average time spent on each one of them to form the basis of establishing the optimal worker–population ratio for the service delivery model.

Figure 1.5   Mixed/multiple methods study – an example

Some of the disadvantages are as follows:

→ **More data means more work and resources.** Collecting data through two or more methods means more data to collect and analyse, resulting in more time, financial resources, effort and technical expertise. Instead of one data set you have at least two data sets to handle for data collection, analysis, processing and information dissemination.

→ **Requires additional and diverse skills.** As multi-methods studies use different methods belonging to both quantitative and/or qualitative paradigms, you need to be reasonably well versed in all those methods and procedures that you are likely to use, requiring a wider skill set than for single-method studies. You need to have knowledge and skills in data collection methods that you are proposing to use. Similarly, you need to be competent in data analysis methods suitable for different methods of data collection. Finally, you need to be well versed in data triangulation and information dissemination for different sets of data.

→ **Contacting two study populations.** Using a mixed methods design may involve contacting and establishing rapport with two or more different study populations, with all that that entails.

→ **Resolving disagreements in data.** You may discover a significant disagreement between the data sets. How do you decide as to the reliability of a set of data?

Considerations to be kept in mind

You need to keep in mind a number of things when using a mixed methods approach:

→ Make sure you have sufficient time to complete the additional tasks. Using different methodologies means more work for the whole research project.
→ You also need to be sure that you have the required technical expertise to develop and/or undertake different methods and procedures.
→ You need to decide how to resolve inconsistencies, if encountered, in the findings.
→ How will the findings of different methods be communicated? Will they be triangulated, integrated or communicated in a parallel manner?

Situations in which the approach can be used

A number of reasons justify the use of mixed/multiple methods approaches in social research. To illustrate we will take some examples. The overriding reason for using the mixed/multiple methods approach is the desire to enhance the coverage, depth, reliability and validation of your findings through the use of another method(s). Specifically, multiple methods can be used in the following situations:

1   When, in your opinion, an aspect of your study, either methodologically or within the financial constraints, cannot be reliably investigated through the main research approach you have adopted. To gain a deeper, complete and/or reliable understanding of the subaspects of your study, you may need to use another method. Investigation by another method will hopefully provide you with more accurate information about some aspects of your study. For example, suppose you are conducting a study to ascertain the recreational needs of youth in a community and the community's attitudes towards the **desirability** of those needs. Also suppose you are ascertaining recreational needs by interviewing a random sample of young people. You do not have enough resources to interview a sample of members of the community and, therefore, you decide to set up a community forum for the purpose. In this situation you are using two methods to find out about different aspects of your study that cannot be investigated in the same manner because of lack of resources. Studies like this will be classified as using a mixed methods approach which, in this example, is using both quantitative and qualitative methods.

2   There are situations when you use a particular research approach to find answers to research questions, but, to be doubly sure, you want to compare your findings with the findings determined by another approach. We again take the example of the study designed to determine the needs of youth in a community. To enhance the accuracy and reliability of your findings, you may use a number of methods. For example, you can ascertain the perceived recreational needs of young people by carrying out in-depth interviews of a sample, holding a focus group and holding a community forum. Triangulation of the findings from all three sources will provide you with enriched information. The study will be classified as multiple methods study as it is using three methods, all qualitative, to find answers to your research questions. If, instead of in-depth interviewing, you had used a structured questionnaire or interview schedule (both quantitative techniques), the study, according to the typology suggested by the author, would have been classified as mixed methods study (as you are using quantitative as well as qualitative methods). Such approaches help you to cross-check your findings to ensure their reliability so that you can place greater confidence in your findings, albeit at the risk of creating other problems if there are marked differences between the sources.

PARADIGMS OF RESEARCH

Although there are two main paradigms (quantitative and qualitative) that form the basis of research methodology in the social sciences, the mixed methods paradigm has also emerged during the last two decades as a third approach. Mixed methods, though considered as an approach to social enquiry, has not yet developed its own body of investigative methods and procedures. It mostly uses the methods and procedures of quantitative and qualitative approaches.

The crucial question that divides the two dominant paradigms is whether the methodology of the physical sciences can be applied to the study of social phenomena. The paradigm that is rooted in the physical sciences is called the quantitative, systematic, scientific or positivist approach to social enquiry. The opposite paradigm has come to be known as the qualitative, ethnographic, ecological or naturalistic approach. The advocates of the two opposing sides have developed their own values, terminology, methods and techniques to understand social phenomena. However, since the mid-1960s there has been a growing recognition that both paradigms have their place, and this has led to the mixed methods approach to social enquiry. The author feels very strongly that it is the purpose for which a research activity is undertaken that should determine the mode of enquiry, hence the paradigm. To indiscriminately apply one approach to all research problems can be misleading and inappropriate. Combining quantitative and qualitative methods is a very powerful methodology and should be used where warranted with full realisation that it entails diverse and/or additional knowledge about different approaches to research.

A positivist paradigm lends itself to both quantitative and qualitative data. The author makes a distinction between qualitative data, on the one hand, and qualitative research, on the other, as the former is confined to the measurement of variables, mostly on nominal and ordinary measurement scales, and the latter to the use of a qualitative research methodology.

The author believes that no matter what paradigm the researcher works within, s/he should adhere to certain values regarding the control of bias and the maintenance of objectivity in terms of both the research process itself and the conclusions drawn. It is the application of these values to the process of information gathering, analysis and interpretation that enables it to be called a research process.

CHECKPOINT
*Research
paradigms*

SUMMARY

There are several ways of collecting and understanding information and finding answers to your questions – research is one way. The difference between research and other ways of obtaining answers to your questions is that, in a process that is classified as research, you work within a framework of a set of philosophies, use methods that have been tested for validity and reliability, and attempt to be unbiased and objective.

Research has many applications. You need to have research skills to be an effective service provider, administrator/manager or planner. As a professional who has a responsibility to enhance professional knowledge, research skills are essential.

The typology of research can be looked at from three perspectives: application, objectives and the mode of enquiry. From the point of view of the application of research, there is applied and pure research. Most of the research undertaken in the social sciences is applied, the findings being intended either for use in understanding a phenomenon/issue or to bring change in a programme/situation. Pure research is academic in nature and is undertaken in order to gain knowledge about phenomena that may or may not have applications in the near future, and to develop new techniques and procedures that form the body of research methodology.

A research study can be carried out with four objectives: to describe a situation, phenomenon, problem or issue (descriptive research); to establish or explore a relationship between two or more variables (correlational research); to explain why certain things happen the way they do (explanatory research); and to examine the feasibility of conducting a study or exploring a subject area where nothing or little is known (exploratory research).

From the point of view of the mode of enquiry, there are three types of research: quantitative (structured approach), qualitative (unstructured approach) and mixed or multiple methods (structured and/or unstructured approach). The main objective of a qualitative study is to describe the variation and diversity in a phenomenon, situation or attitude with a very flexible approach so as to identify as much variation and diversity as possible, while

34

quantitative research, in addition, helps you to quantify the variation and diversity. The use of mixed methods aims to draw on the strengths of the other approaches; that is, it uses the best of both the paradigms to enhance the accuracy, depth and reliability of the findings. There are many who strongly advocate a combined approach to social enquiry; that is, use of mixed/multiple methods. The author is strongly in favour of the qualitative-quantitative-qualitative cycle of enquiry. The author feels strongly that it is purpose of research rather than the belief in a paradigm that should determine the mode of enquiry.

Now that you have read the full chapter...

CHECK YOUR UNDERSTANDING

☐ Do you understand the meaning and application of all of the keywords at the start of the chapter? If not, visit the online resources and use the glossary flashcards to get to grips with their definitions.

☐ What is research? What should be the requirements for a process to be called a research process?

☐ How can research provide evidence for your practice?

☐ How would you go about convincing a service provider that evidence-based research might benefit them?

☐ What are the different approaches to research, and what are the differences between them?

☐ Do you consider mixed/multiple methods approach as a third paradigm of research? Give reasons for your answer.

APPLY IT TO YOUR OWN PROJECT

☐ Identify two or three research questions, related to your own academic field or professional area, that could be answered by undertaking each of the following types of research:

  ☐ descriptive research;
  ☐ correlational research;
  ☐ explanatory research;
  ☐ exploratory research.

☐ How could the three approaches to research – quantitative, qualitative and mixed/multiple methods – be applied to improve your practice in your own area of interest?

CONFUSED?

THE ONLINE RESOURCES ARE HERE TO HELP YOU

 https://study.sagepub.com/kumar5e

CHECKPOINT: What is evidence based practice? Visit this website.

CHECKPOINT: What does 'research' mean? Watch this video.

CHECKPOINT: What are the main differences between qualitative, quantitative, and mixed methods studies? Watch this video.

CHECKPOINT: What does it mean to use a mixed methods approach? Review this checklist.

CHECKPOINT: What is a research paradigm? Watch this video.

NEED MORE GENERAL SUPPORT?

Get up to speed on key terms with *glossary flashcards* and test yourself on important concepts with *multiple choice questions*.

UP FOR A CHALLENGE?

THE ONLINE RESOURCES ARE HERE TO INSPIRE YOU

 https://study.sagepub.com/kumar5e

CHECKPOINT: What does an evidence-based practice study look like? Explore this case study.

CHECKPOINT: What are some alternative perspectives on the definition of research? Read this chapter.

CHECKPOINT: When is it better to do a qualitative, quantitative, or mixed methods project? Read this journal article.

CHECKPOINT: What does a mixed methods approach look like? Explore this case study.

CHECKPOINT: What types of research paradigm could you use for your research project? Visit this website.

READY TO WORK ON YOUR OWN PROJECT?

Start building a portfolio of your ideas with the exercise workbook and get support tailored to your specific assignment with the assessment toolkit.

THE RESEARCH PROCESS

A QUICK GLANCE

ESSENTIAL TERMS

You should be able to define these by the end of the chapter

- data collection
- data display
- data processing
- research design
- research instrument

- research objectives
- research proposal
- research report
- sample

BONUS TERMS

You will learn more about these by the end of the chapter

- data
- empiricism
- hypotheses
- interview schedule
- non-probability sample
- primary data
- probability sample
- qualitative research
- questionnaire
- rationalism

- reliability
- research problem
- sample size
- sampling design
- secondary data
- study design
- unstructured interview
- validity
- variables

LEARNING OBJECTIVES

At the end of this chapter, you will be able to:

- Describe the research process and its operational steps
- Explain what it involves to undertake a research study
- Understand the relationship between the research process and the theoretical knowledge needed

THE RESEARCH PROCESS: AN EIGHT-STEP MODEL

Research methodology and methods are taught in several ways in many academic disciplines at various levels by people committed to a variety of research paradigms. Though paradigms vary in their contents and substance, their broad approach to enquiry, in the author's opinion, is similar. Such ideas have also been expressed by Festinger and Katz, who in the foreword to their book *Research Methods in Behavioral Sciences* say: 'Although the basic logic of scientific methodology is the same in all fields, its specific techniques and approaches will vary, depending upon the subject matter' (1966: vi). Therefore, the model developed here is generic in nature and can be applied to a number of disciplines in the social sciences. It is based upon a practical and step-by-step approach to research enquiry that at each step provides a smorgasbord of methods, models and procedures to choose from.

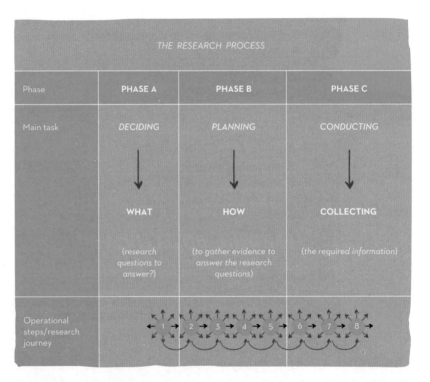

Figure 2.1   The research journey – touch each post and select methods and procedures appropriate for your journey

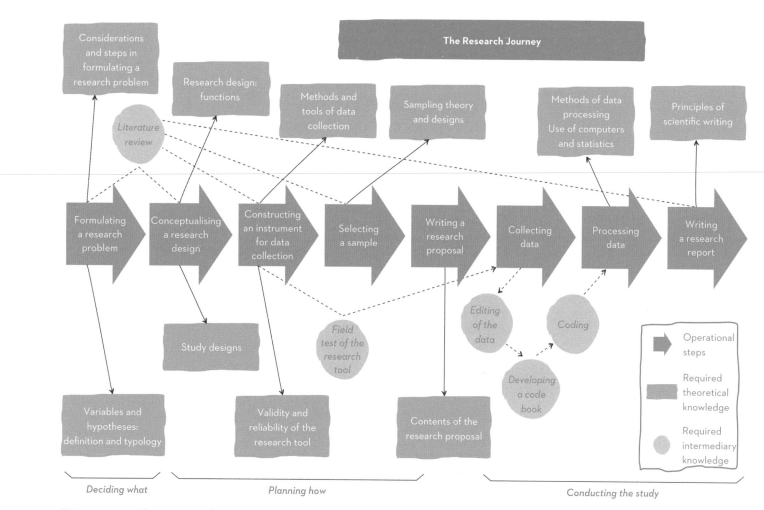

Figure 2.2   The research process

44

CHECKPOINT
*Theoretical
frameworks and
underpinning
philosophy*

Broadly, a research process is very similar to undertaking a journey. Suppose you want to go out for a drive. Before you start, you must decide where you want to go and then which route to take. If you know the route, you do not need to consult a map, but, if you do not know the route, then you need to use one. Your problem is compounded if there is more than one route. You need to decide which one to take. Similarly, for a research journey there are also two important decisions to make. The first is to decide *what you want to find out about* or, in other words, what research questions you want to find answers to. Having decided upon your research questions or research problems, you then need to decide *how to go about finding their answers*. The path to finding answers to your research questions constitutes research methodology. Just as there are signposts along the way as you travel to your destination, so there are practical steps through which you must pass on your research journey in order to find the answers to your research questions (Figure 2.1). The sequence of these steps is not fixed, and with experience you can change it. At each operational step in the research process you are required to choose from a multiplicity of methods, procedures and models of research methodology which will help you best achieve your research objectives. This is where your knowledge base of research methodology plays a crucial role.

The aim of this book is to provide you with knowledge that will enable you to select the most appropriate methods and procedures. The strength of this book lies in anchoring the theoretical knowledge of the steps that you need to go through on your research journey. At each operational step, the book aims to provide, at a beginner's level, knowledge of methods and procedures used by both qualitative and quantitative researchers, though there is an inclination towards the quantitative way of thinking.

Quantitative and qualitative research methodologies differ both in their underpinning philosophy and, to some extent, in the methods, models and procedures used. Though the research process is broadly the same in both, quantitative and qualitative research are differentiated in terms of the methods of data collection, the procedures adopted for data processing and analysis, and the style of communication of the findings. For example, if your research problem lends itself to a qualitative mode of enquiry, you are more likely to use the *unstructured interview* or *observation* as your method of data collection. When analysing data in qualitative research, you go through the process of identifying themes and describing what you have found out during your interviews or observation rather than subjecting your data to statistical procedures. The mixed methods approach to a research enquiry basically uses methods and procedures of quantitative and/or qualitative approaches. Table 1.2 in Chapter 1 compares the qualitative, quantitative and mixed methods approaches to research from different perspectives.

Since, at a number of steps of the research process, the choice of methods and procedures is influenced by the quantitative–qualitative distinction, the methods and procedures discussed in some of the chapters in this book are dealt with separately under qualitative and quantitative sections of the methodology, even though the author does not attach importance to this distinction. The author has tried to minimise this distinction as a number of methods and procedures are applicable to both. Also note that this book is for beginners, it does not cover extensively each method, model and procedure. For a deeper understanding of a method or procedure relating to either, you may wish to consult other books identified in the text or in the Bibliography. You can also visit the companion website for the book on your mobile using the QR code, or by visiting www.uk.sagepub.co.uk/kumar4e where additional information is available.

The proposed research model is shown in Figure 2.2. The tasks identified by *arrows* are the operational steps you need to follow in order to conduct a study, whether quantitative, qualitative or using the mixed methods approach. Topics identified in *rectangles* are the required theoretical knowledge needed to carry out these steps.

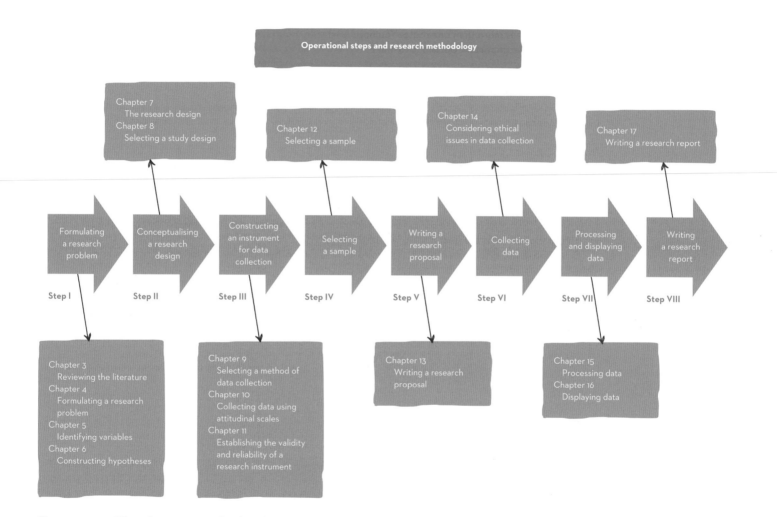

Figure 2.3   The chapters in the book in relation to the operational steps

The tasks identified in *circles* are the intermediary steps that you need to complete to go from one step to another. It is important for a beginner to work through these steps in the proposed sequence, though, as already stated, once you know the route for your research journey you will not need to follow the sequence.

In this book the theoretical knowledge required is written around each operational step and follows the same sequential progression as is needed when actually undertaking a research investigation. For each operational step, the required theoretical knowledge is further organised, in different chapters, around the operational step to which, in the author's opinion, it is most logically related (Figure 2.3). Again, for a beginner, it is important to study this diagram to relate the theoretical knowledge to the operational steps.

The following sections of this chapter provide a quick glance at the whole process to acquaint you with the various tasks you need to undertake to carry out your study, thus giving you some idea of what the research journey involves.

A: DECIDING WHAT TO RESEARCH

Step one: Formulating a research problem

Formulating a research problem is the first and most important step in the research process. A research problem identifies your destination: it should tell you, your research supervisor and your readers *what* you intend to research. The more specific and clearer you are the better, as everything that follows in the research process – study design, measurement procedures, sampling strategy, frame of analysis and the style of writing of your dissertation or report – is greatly influenced by the way in which you formulate your research problem. Hence, you should examine it thoroughly, carefully and critically. The main function of formulating a research problem is to decide what you want to find out about. Chapter 4 deals in detail with various aspects of formulating a research problem.

It is extremely important to evaluate the research problem in the light of the financial resources at your disposal, the time available, and your own and your research supervisor's expertise and knowledge in the field of study. It is equally important to identify any gaps in your knowledge of relevant disciplines, such as statistics required for analysis. Also ask yourself whether you have sufficient knowledge about computers and software if you plan to use them.

B: PLANNING HOW TO CONDUCT THE STUDY

Step two: Conceptualising a research design

An extremely important feature of research is the use of appropriate methods. Research involves systematic, controlled, valid and rigorous exploration and description of what is not known, and establishment of associations and causation that permit the accurate prediction of outcomes under a given set of conditions. It also involves identifying gaps in knowledge, verification of what is already known and identification of past errors and limitations. The strength of *what* you find largely rests on *how* it was found.

The main function of a research design is to decide, describe, justify and explain *how* you will find answers to your research questions. The research design sets out the specific details of your enquiry. A research design should include the following: the study design per se and the logistical arrangements that you propose to undertake, the measurement procedures, the sampling strategy, the frame of analysis and the time-frame. (Do not confuse the study design and research design. The study design is just one part of the research design. The research design also includes other parts which constitute the research process.)

For any investigation, the selection of an appropriate research design is crucial in enabling you to arrive at valid findings, comparisons and conclusions. A faulty design results in misleading findings and is therefore tantamount to wasting human and financial resources. In scientific circles, the strength of an empirical investigation is primarily evaluated in the light of the research design adopted. When selecting a research design it is important to ensure that it is *valid*, *workable* and *manageable*. Chapter 7 provides details about the research design most commonly used in quantitative and qualitative research.

There is an enormous variety of study designs (Chapter 8) and you need to be acquainted with some of the most common ones both in quantitative and qualitative approaches. The chapter does not separately describe study designs for the mixed methods approach as it primarily uses those which are either quantitative or qualitative. Select or develop the design that is most suited to your study. You must have strong reasons for selecting a particular design; you must be able to justify your selection; and you should be aware of its strengths, weaknesses and limitations. In addition, you will need to explain the logistical details needed to implement the suggested design.

Step three: Constructing an instrument for data collection

Anything that becomes a means of collecting information for your study is called a 'research tool' or a 'research instrument', for example interview schedules, questionnaires, notes on field observations, field diaries, information collected from secondary notes, interview guides.

The construction of a research instrument is the first 'practical' step in carrying out a study. You will need to decide how you are going to collect data for the proposed study and then construct a research instrument for data collection. Chapter 9 details the various methods of data collection for qualitative and quantitative studies and the process of developing a research instrument.

If you are planning to collect data specifically for your study (primary data), you need either to construct a research instrument or to select one that has already been constructed. Chapter 10 deals with methods for collecting data using attitudinal scales. The concepts of validity and reliability in relation to a research instrument are discussed in Chapter 11.

If you are using secondary data (information already collected for other purposes), you will need to identify what information is needed and then develop a form to extract the required data. In order to determine what information is required, you need to go through the same process as for primary data.

Field testing (or pre-testing) a research tool is an integral part of instrument construction. As a rule, the pre-test of a research instrument should not be carried out on the sample of your study population but on a similar population which you are not proposing to study. This is covered in greater detail in Chapter 9.

If you are planning to use a computer for data analysis, you may wish to provide space for coding the data on the research instrument. This is explained in Chapter 15.

Research design: A research design is a procedural plan that is adopted by the researcher to answer questions validly, objectively, accurately and economically. A research design therefore addresses questions that determine the path you are proposing to take for your research journey. Through a research design you decide for yourself and communicate to others your decisions regarding what study design you propose to use, how you will collect information from your respondents, how you will select your respondents, how the information you will collect is to be analysed and how you will communicate your findings.

Study design: This term is used to describe the type of design you are going to adopt to undertake your study; that is, if it is going to be experimental, correlational, descriptive, or before and after. Each study design has a specific format and attributes.

Research instrument: Anything that becomes a means of collecting information for your study is called a 'research instrument' or a 'research tool', for example interview schedules, questionnaires, notes on field observations, field diaries, information collected from secondary notes, interview guides.

Primary data: Information collected for the specific purpose of a study either by the researcher or by someone else.

Secondary data: Sometimes the information required is already available in other sources such as journals, previous reports or censuses, and you extract that information for the specific purpose of your study. This type of data is called secondary data.

Step four: Selecting a sample

The accuracy of your findings largely depends upon the way you select your sample. The basic objective of any sampling design is to minimise, within the limitation of cost, the gap between the values obtained from your sample and those prevalent in the study population.

The underlying premise in sampling is that a relatively small number of units, if selected so that they genuinely represent the study population, can provide – with a sufficiently high degree of probability – a fairly true reflection of the sampling population that is being studied.

When selecting a sample you should attempt to achieve two key aims of sampling: (i) the avoidance of bias in the selection of a sample; and (ii) the attainment of maximum precision for a given outlay of resources.

There are three categories of sampling design (Chapter 12): random/probability sampling designs, non-random/non-probability sampling designs, and the 'mixed' sampling design.

There are several sampling strategies within the first two categories. You need to be acquainted with these sampling designs – the strengths and weaknesses of each and the situations in which they can or cannot be applied – in order to select the one most appropriate for your study. The type of sampling strategy you use will influence your ability to make generalisations from the sample findings about the study population, and the type of statistical tests you can apply to the data.

Bias: A deliberate attempt either to conceal or highlight something that you found in your research or to use deliberately a procedure or method that you know is not appropriate but will provide information that you are looking for because you have a vested interest in it.

Step five: Writing a research proposal

Having done all the preparatory work, the next step is to put everything together in a way that provides adequate information about your research study, for your research supervisor and others. This overall plan, called a research proposal, tells the reader about your research problem and how you are planning to investigate it. Broadly, a research proposal's main function is to detail the operational plan for obtaining answers to your research questions. In doing so it ensures – and reassures the reader of – the validity of the methodology to obtain answers accurately and objectively.

Universities and other institutions may have differing requirements regarding the style and content of a research proposal, but the majority of institutions would require most of what is set out here. Requirements may also vary within an institution, from discipline to discipline or from supervisor to supervisor. However, the guidelines set out in Chapter 13 provide a framework which will be acceptable to most.

A research proposal must tell you, your research supervisor and a reviewer the following information about your study:

↪ *what* you are proposing to do;
↪ *how* you plan to proceed;
↪ *why* you selected the proposed strategy.

Therefore it should contain the following information about your study (Chapter 13):

↪ a statement of its *objectives*;
↪ a list of *hypotheses*, if you are testing any;
↪ the *study design* you are proposing to use;

Research proposal: A research proposal details your operational plan as to how you are going to find answers to your research questions. It outlines the various tasks you plan to undertake to fulfil your research objectives or obtain answers to your research questions.

48

- the *setting* for the study;
- the research *instrument(s)* you are planning to use;
- the *sample size* and sampling design;
- the *data processing* procedures;
- an outline of the proposed *chapters* for the report;
- the study's *problems and limitations*; and
- the proposed *time-frame*.

C: CONDUCTING A RESEARCH STUDY

Step six: Collecting data

Having formulated a research problem, developed a study design, constructed a research instrument and selected a sample, you then collect the data from which you will draw inferences and conclusions for your study.

Many methods could be used to gather the required information. As a part of the research design, you decided upon the procedure you wanted to adopt to collect your data. In this phase *you actually collect the data*. For example, depending upon your plans, you might commence interviews, mail out a questionnaire, conduct nominal/focus group discussions or make observations. Collecting data through any one of the methods may involve some ethical issues, which are discussed in Chapter 14.

Step seven: Processing and displaying data

The way you analyse the information you collected largely depends upon two things: the type of information (descriptive, quantitative, qualitative or attitudinal); and the way you want to communicate your findings to your readers. Chapter 15 describes different ways of analysing quantitative and qualitative data and Chapter 16 details various methods of displaying the data that has been analysed.

In addition to the qualitative–quantitative distinction, it is important for data analysis that you consider whether the data is to be analysed manually or by a computer.

If your study is purely descriptive, you can write your dissertation/report on the basis of your field notes, manually analyse the contents of your notes (content analysis), or use a computer program such as NVivo for this purpose.

If you want quantitative analysis, it is also necessary to decide upon the type of analysis required (i.e. frequency distributions, cross-tabulations or other statistical procedures, such as regression analysis, factor analysis and analysis of variance) and how it should be presented. You will also need to identify the variables to be subjected to these statistical procedures.

Step eight: Writing a research report

There are two broad categories of reports: quantitative and qualitative. As mentioned earlier, the distinction is more academic than real as in most studies you need to combine quantitative and qualitative skills. Nevertheless, there are some purely qualitative and some purely quantitative studies.

Writing the report is the last and, for many, the most difficult step of the research process. This report tells the world what you have done, what you have discovered and what conclusions you have drawn from your findings. If you are clear about the whole process, you will also be clear about the way you want to write your report. Your report should be written in an academic style and be divided into different chapters and/or sections based upon the main themes of your study. Chapter 17 suggests some ways of writing a research report.

SUMMARY

This chapter has provided an overview of the research process, which has been broken down into three phases (A, B, C) and eight steps, the details of which are covered in the remainder of this book. At each step the research model provides a variety of methods, models, techniques and procedures so that you can select the one most appropriate for your study. It is like a buffet party with eight tables, each with different dishes made from similar ingredients. You go to all eight tables and select the dish that you like the most from each table. The main difference between the model and this example is that in the model you select what is most appropriate for your study and not what you like the most. For a beginner it is important to go through all the steps, although perhaps not in the same sequence. With experience you can take a number of shortcuts.

The eight steps cover the complete spectrum of a research endeavour, from problem formulation through to writing a research report. The steps are operational in nature, following a logical sequence, and detailing the various methods and procedures in a simple step-by step manner.

CHECKPOINT
Steps of the research process

Now that you have read the full chapter...

CHECK YOUR UNDERSTANDING

☐ Do you understand the meaning and application of all of the keywords at the start of the chapter? If not, visit the online resources and use the glossary flashcards to get to grips with their definitions.

☐ Reflecting on the differences between quantitative and qualitative research (as outlined in Table 1.2), which approach are you more inclined to follow and why? To what extent does this reflect your own underpinning philosophy?

☐ What is the first step in the research process outlined in this chapter? And the last step?

☐ Think about the applicability of the proposed research process for quantitative, qualitative and mixed methods studies. Are there any differences in how you might approach the eight-step model based on your understanding of the different research approaches, objectives and paradigms in Chapter 1?

APPLY IT TO YOUR OWN PROJECT

☐ Critically examine the applicability of this research process to your situation.

CONFUSED?

THE ONLINE RESOURCES ARE HERE TO HELP YOU

 https://study.sagepub.com/kumar5e

CHECKPOINT: What are the main philosophical assumptions underlying qualitative and quantitative research? Visit this website.

CHECKPOINT: What are the eight steps of the research process? Visit this website.

NEED MORE GENERAL SUPPORT?

Get up to speed on key terms with *glossary flashcards* and test yourself on important concepts with *multiple choice questions*.

UP FOR A CHALLENGE?

THE ONLINE RESOURCES ARE HERE TO INSPIRE YOU

 https://study.sagepub.com/kumar5e

CHECKPOINT: How do you discuss your research's theoretical framework? Visit this website.

CHECKPOINT: What are frequently the most time-consuming steps in the research process? Read this project planner.

READY TO WORK ON YOUR OWN PROJECT?

Start building a portfolio of your ideas with the exercise workbook and get support tailored to your specific assignment with the assessment toolkit.

STEP ONE

FORMULATING A RESEARCH PROBLEM

REVIEWING THE LITERATURE

- step one -
FORMULATING A RESEARCH PROBLEM

This operational step includes four chapters:

→ Reviewing the literature   54

Formulating a research problem   76

Identifying variables   100

Constructing hypotheses   126

ESSENTIAL TERMS

You should be able to define these by the end of the chapter

→ literature review
→ summary of literature

→ conceptual framework
→ theoretical framework

BONUS TERMS

You will learn more about these by the end of the chapter

→ catalogue
→ contextualise
→ Internet

→ knowledge base
→ search engines
→ thematic writing

LEARNING OBJECTIVES

At the end of this chapter, you will be able to:

→ Understand the functions of the literature review in research
→ Describe how to carry out a literature search
→ Explain the difference between a literature review and a summary of literature
→ Use the Internet for a literature review
→ Review the selected literature
→ Develop theoretical and conceptual frameworks
→ Write a literature review

THE PLACE OF THE LITERATURE REVIEW IN RESEARCH

Literature review: This is the process of searching the existing literature relating to your research problem to develop theoretical and conceptual frameworks for your study and to integrate your research findings with what the literature says about them. It places your study in perspective to what others have investigated about the issues. In addition, the process helps you to improve your methodology.

One of the essential preliminary tasks when you undertake a research study is to go through the existing literature in order to acquaint yourself with the available body of knowledge in your area of interest. Reviewing the literature can be time-consuming, daunting and frustrating, but it is also rewarding. The literature review is an integral part of the research process and makes a valuable contribution to almost every operational step. It is important even before the first step; that is, when you are merely thinking about a research question that you may want to find answers to through your research journey. In the initial stages of research it helps you to clarify your ideas, establish the theoretical roots of your study and develop your research methodology. Later in the process, the literature review serves to enhance and consolidate your knowledge base in your subject area and helps you to examine your findings in the context of the existing body of knowledge. Since an important responsibility in research is to compare your findings with those of others, it is here that the literature review plays an extremely important role. During the write-up of your report it helps you to integrate your findings with the existing knowledge – that is, to either support or contradict earlier research. The higher the academic level of your research, the more important a thorough integration of your findings with existing literature becomes.

In summary, a literature review has the following functions:

- It provides a theoretical background to your study.
- It helps you establish the links between what you are proposing to examine and what has already been studied.
- It enables you to show how your findings have contributed to the existing body of knowledge in your profession. It helps you to integrate your research findings into the existing body of knowledge.

In relation to your own study, the literature review can help in four ways. It can:

1 bring clarity and focus to your research problem;
2 improve your research methodology;
3 broaden your knowledge base in your research area; and
4 contextualise your findings, that is, integrate your findings with the existing body of knowledge.

Bringing clarity and focus to your research problem

The literature review involves a paradox. On the one hand, you cannot effectively undertake a literature search without some idea of the problem you wish to investigate. On the other hand, the literature review can play an extremely important role in influencing the nature of your research problem thus conditioning your thinking about choosing your research problem. It is therefore important for you to strike a balance between reviewing the literature and its influence on your research problem. The process of reviewing the literature helps you to understand the subject area better and thus helps you to conceptualise your research problem clearly and precisely and makes it more relevant and pertinent to your field of enquiry. When reviewing the literature you learn what aspects of your subject area have been examined by others, what they have found out about these aspects, what gaps they have identified and what suggestions they have made for further research. All these will help you gain a greater insight into your own research questions and provide you with clarity and focus which are central to a relevant and valid study. In addition, they will help you to focus your study on areas where there are gaps in the existing body of knowledge, and where you can to the existing body of knowledge, thereby enhancing your study's relevance and importance.

Improving your research methodology

Going through the literature acquaints you with the methodologies that have been used by others to find answers to research questions similar to the one you are investigating. A literature review tells you if others have used procedures and methods similar to the ones that you are proposing, which procedures and methods have worked well for them and what problems they have faced with them. By becoming aware of any problems and pitfalls, you will be in a better position to select a methodology that is capable of providing valid answers to your research question. This will increase your confidence in the methodology you plan to use and will equip you to defend its use.

Broadening your knowledge base in your research area

The most important function of the literature review is to ensure you read widely around the subject area in which you intend to conduct your research study. It is important that you know what other researchers have found in regard to the same or similar questions, what theories have been put forward and what gaps exist in the relevant body of knowledge. When you undertake a research project for a higher degree (e.g. an MA or a PhD) you are expected to be an expert in your area of research. A thorough literature review helps you to fulfil this expectation. Another important reason for doing a literature review is that it helps you to understand how the findings of your study fit into the existing body of knowledge (Martin 1985: 30).

In summary, in terms of knowledge base, the literature review is extremely useful for it:

- Helps you to identify what has been established, and what are the gaps in the area of your research, thereby ensuring the relevance and usefulness of your research.
- Acquaints you with methods and procedures used in similar studies, helping you to select a robust methodology for your research.
- Helps you to locate your research questions and findings in the existing literature.
- Helps you to justify the selection of your research questions.
- Helps you to develop, expand and demonstrate your knowledge base in the subject area of your study.

CHECKPOINT
Literature reviews

59

Contextualising your findings

Obtaining answers to your research questions is comparatively easy: the difficult part is examining how your findings fit into the existing body of knowledge. How do answers to your research questions compare with what others have found? What contribution have you been able to make to the existing body of knowledge? How are your findings different from those of others? Undertaking a literature review will enable you to compare your findings with those of others and answer these questions. It is important to place your findings in the context of what is already known in your field of enquiry; that is, to integrate what you have found out with the existing literature.

DIFFERENCE BETWEEN A LITERATURE REVIEW AND A SUMMARY OF THE LITERATURE

Some people use the terms 'literature review' and 'summary of the literature' interchangeably. However, there is a difference between the two. A summary of the literature is a description of the significant findings of each relevant piece of work that you have gone through as a part of your literature search. The summary basically entails listing, under each pertinent source, the major findings of relevance to your study. The sources searched can be listed in any order. However, in a literature review the main findings are organised around main themes that emerge from your literature search. Different studies in which the same theme is identified are referenced in one place where the theme is being discussed as a part of the literature review. Under each theme the main findings relating to it from all the sources you have searched are mentioned and compared, pointing to similarities and differences between them. This is usually followed by a statement of conclusions with respect to the theme. The themes are then put together in a logical progression. A summary of the literature is a summary of the main findings from each relevant reference you searched. In a literature review you describe each theme that emerged during the literature search, citing its origin, comparing it with others and integrating it in a logical manner with the rest.

HOW TO REVIEW THE LITERATURE

If you do not have a specific research problem, you should review the literature in your broad area of interest with the aim of gradually narrowing it down to what you want to find out about. It is like funnelling your ideas. To start with, these ideas are very broad and vague but as you get more insight into your research problem you narrow and refine them to select something that you are really interested in. Once you have reasonably narrowed your research problem, the literature review should then be focused around your research problem. There is a danger in reviewing the literature without having a reasonably specific idea of what you want to study. It can condition your thinking about your study and the methodology you might use, resulting in a less innovative choice of research problem and methodology than otherwise would have been the case. Hence, you should try broadly to conceptualise your research problem before undertaking your major literature review. Your literature search should concentrate around the main themes of your research problem and should be undertaken as if you are answering the following questions:

- What is already known in the area?
- What is not known or what are the gaps in the existing body of knowledge?
- What questions have remained unanswered?
- Are there any areas of professional conflict?
- What theories have been put forward relevant to your area of research?
- What suggestions have been made for further research?
- What research strategies have been employed by others undertaking similar research?

There are four steps involved in conducting a literature review:

1   Searching for the existing literature in your area of study.
2   Reviewing the selected literature.
3   Developing a theoretical framework.
4   Developing a conceptual framework.

The skills required for these tasks are different. Developing theoretical and conceptual frameworks is more difficult than the other tasks.

Searching for the existing literature

To search effectively for the literature in your field of enquiry, it is imperative that you have at least some idea of the broad subject area and of the problem you wish to investigate, in order to set parameters for your search. You must also have some idea of the study population. For example, you should decide whether your interest lies in studying immigrants, youth, women, students, or residents of an institution. You also need to have some idea as to what it is about your population that you want to study. For example, in the case of immigrants, you might want to study their settlement process, reasons for immigration or patterns of occupational mobility. Next, compile a bibliography for this broad subject area. There are four sources that you can use to prepare a bibliography:

a   books;
b   journals;
c   conference papers;
d   the Internet.

Books

Though books are a central part of any bibliography, they have their disadvantages as well as advantages. The main advantage is that the material published in books is usually important and of good quality, and the findings are 'integrated with other research to form a coherent body of knowledge' (Martin 1985: 33). The main disadvantage is that the material is not completely up to date, as a year or more may pass between the completion of a work and its publication in the form of a book.

The best way to search for a book is to look at your library catalogues. When librarians catalogue a book they also assign to it subject headings that are usually based on *Library of Congress* **subject headings**. If you are not sure, ask your librarian to help you find the best subject heading for your area. This can save you a lot of time. Publications such as *Book Review Index* can help you to locate books of interest.

Use the *subject catalogue* or *keywords* option to search for books in your area of interest. Narrow the subject area searched by selecting the appropriate keywords. Look carefully through these titles found and identify those books you think are likely to be of interest to you. If you think the titles seem appropriate to your topic, print them out if possible, as this will save you time, or write them down. Be aware that sometimes a title does not provide enough information to help you decide if a book is going to be of use, so you may have to examine its contents too.

When you have selected 10-15 books that you think are appropriate for your topic, examine the bibliography of each one. It will save time if you **photocopy** their bibliographies, provided it is legal. Go through these bibliographies carefully to identify the books common to several of them. If a book has been referenced by a number of authors, you should include it in your reading list. Prepare a final list of books that you consider essential reading.

Having prepared your reading list, locate these books in your library or borrow them from other sources. Examine their contents to double-check that they really are relevant to your topic. If you find that a book is not relevant to your research, delete it from your reading list. If you find that something in a book's contents is relevant to your topic, make an annotated bibliography. An annotated bibliography contains a brief abstract of the aspects covered in a book and your own notes about its relevance. Be careful to keep track of your references. To do this you can prepare your own card index or use a computer program such as Endnotes or Zotero.

Journals

You need to go through the journals relating to your research in a similar manner. Journals provide you with the most up-to-date information, even though there is often a gap of 2-3 years between the completion of a research project and its publication in a journal. You should select as many journals as you possibly can, though the number of journals available depends upon the field of study. There are a number of ways to find the journals you need to examine in order to identify the literature relevant to your study. You can:

- locate hard copies of the journals that are appropriate to your study;
- look at citation or abstract indices to identify and/or read the abstracts of such articles;
- search electronic databases.

If you have been able to identify any useful journals and articles, prepare a list of those you want to examine, by journal. Select one of these journals and, starting with the latest issue, examine its contents page to see if there is an article of relevance to your research topic. If you feel that a particular article is of interest to you, read its abstract. If you think you are likely to use it, depending upon your financial resources, either photocopy it, or prepare a summary and record its reference for later use. When photocopying, make sure to first seek permission of the appropriate authority.

There are several sources designed to make your search for journals easier and save you a great deal of time. They are:

→ indexes of journals (e.g. *Humanities Index*);
→ abstracts of articles (e.g. *ERIC*);
→ citation indices (e.g. *Social Sciences Citation Index*).

Each of these indexing, abstracting and citation services is available in print, or accessible through the Internet.

In most libraries, information on books, journals and abstracts is stored on computers. In each case the information is classified by subject, author and title. You may also have the keywords option (author/keyword; title/keyword; subject/keyword; expert/keyword; or just keywords). What system you use depends upon what is available in your library and what you are familiar with.

CHECKPOINT
More electronic databases

There are specially prepared electronic databases in a number of disciplines. These can also be helpful in preparing a bibliography. For example, most libraries carry the electronic databases shown in Table 3.1.

Select the database most appropriate to your area of study to see if there are any useful references. Of course, any computer database search is restricted to those journals and articles that are already on the database. You should also talk to your research supervisor and other available experts to find out about any additional relevant literature to include in your reading list.

Conference papers

Another important source for the literature review is the papers presented at professional conferences. These can provide you with the most recent research in the area. You should try to get copies of the papers presented at recent conferences in your area of interest.

The Internet

In almost every academic discipline and professional field, the Internet has become an important tool for finding published literature. Through an Internet search you can identify published material in books, journals and other sources with immense ease and speed.

An Internet search is carried out through search engines. There are many search engines (listed on sites such as www.thesearchenginelist.com), and different engines have strengths in searching different areas. Some specialise in business, legal, maps, books, medical or multimedia; others can be considered as all-purpose search engines. However, the most commonly used for your purpose are *Google, scholar.google.com* and *Yahoo!* Another very useful source on the Internet, particularly to describe and explain terms and concepts, is *Wikipedia*. You can use it for definitions, meanings and other details, though do bear in mind that you may not be able to quote from Wikipedia in your academic dissertations as many universities consider it to be unreliable.

Table 3.1   Some commonly used electronic databases in public health, sociology, education and business studies

Electronic database	Description	Printed equivalent
ABI/INFORM	Abstracted Business Information (ABI) contains references to business information worldwide. It covers subjects such as accounting, banking, data processing, economics, finance, health care, insurance, law, management, marketing, personnel, product development, public administration, real estate, taxation and telecommunications	None
ERIC	ERIC is a database of educational material collected by the Education Resources Information Center of the US Department of Education. It covers subjects such as adult career or vocational education, counselling and personnel services, educational management, primary and early childhood education, handicapped and gifted children, higher education, information resources, language and linguistics, reading and communication, rural education, science, mathematics and environment education, social science education, teacher education, secondary education, evaluation and urban education	CIJE: Current Index to Journals in Education
HEALTHROM	HEALTHROM provides references and some full-text publications on the environment, health, HIV/AIDS and communicable diseases, aboriginal health, clinical medicine, nutrition, alcohol and drug addiction	None
MEDLINE	MEDLINE contains references to material in the biomedical sciences, including medicine, pharmacology, nursing, dentistry, allied health professions, public health, behavioural sciences, physiotherapy, occupational therapy, medical technology, hospital administration, and basic sciences such as anatomy and physiology	Index Medicus
CINAHL	Cumulative Indices to Nursing and Allied Health Literature (CINAHL) provides access to virtually all English-language nursing journals and primary journals from 13 allied health disciplines, including health education, medical records, occupational therapy, physical therapy and radiologic technology	CINAHL

Searching the Internet is very similar to the search for books and articles in a library using an electronic catalogue, as it is based on the use of keywords. An Internet search basically identifies all material in the database of a search engine that contains the keywords you specify, either individually or in combination. It is important that you choose words or combinations of words that other people are likely to use.

According to Gilbert (2008: 73), 'Most search facilities use Boolean logic, which allows three types of basic search "AND", "OR" and "NOT"'. With practice you will become more efficient and effective in using keywords in combination with AND, OR and NOT, and so learn to narrow your search to help you identify the most relevant references.

CHECKPOINT
Search engines and strategies

STEP ONE FORMULATING A RESEARCH PROBLEM

Reviewing the selected literature

Now that you have identified several books and articles as useful, the next step is to start reading them critically to pull together themes and issues that are of relevance to your study. Unless you have a theoretical framework of themes in mind to start with, use separate sheets of paper for each theme or issue you identify as you go through selected books and articles. The following examples detail the process.

The author recently examined, as part of an evaluation study, the extent of 'community responsiveness' in the delivery of health services in Western Australia by health service providers. Before evaluating the extent of its use, pertinent literature relating to 'community responsiveness in health' was identified and reviewed. Through this review, many themes emerged, which became the basis for developing the theoretical framework for the study. Out of all of this, the following themes were selected to construct the theoretical framework for the evaluation study:

- Community responsiveness: what does it mean?
- Philosophies underpinning community responsiveness
- Historical development of the concept in Australia
- The extent of use in health planning
- Strategies developed to achieve community responsiveness
- Indicators of success or failure
- Seeking community participation
- Difficulties in implementing community responsiveness
- Attitude of stakeholders towards the concept of community responsiveness.

Let us take another example from education.

Suppose you are studying the determinant of high academic achievement among high school students. As part of building your theoretical framework, you might want to focus your literature search on exploring the relationship between high academic achievement and

- home environment
- peer group pressure
- involvement in sport
- self-esteem
- motivation in studies
- educational background of the parents
- relationship with teacher(s)

Once you develop a rough framework, slot the findings from the material so far reviewed into these themes, using a separate sheet of paper for each theme of the framework so far developed. As you read further, continue slotting the information where it logically belongs under the themes so far developed. Keep in mind that you may need to add more themes as you go along. While going through the literature you should carefully and critically examine it with respect to the following aspects:

CHECKPOINT
*Evaluating
selected
literature*

- Note whether the knowledge relevant to your theoretical framework has been confirmed beyond doubt.
- Note the theories put forward, the criticisms of these and their basis, the methodologies adopted (study design, sample size and its characteristics, measurement procedures, etc.) and the criticisms of them.
- Examine to what extent the findings can be generalised to other situations.
- Notice where there are significant differences of opinion among researchers, and give your opinion about their validity in addition to putting forward your position, with your reasons.
- Ascertain the areas in which little or nothing is known – the gaps that exist in the body of knowledge.

Developing a theoretical framework

Examining the literature can be a never-ending task, but as you have limited time it is important to set parameters by reviewing the literature in relation to some main themes pertinent to your research topic. As you start reading the literature, you will soon discover that the problem you wish to investigate has its roots in a number of theories that have been developed from different perspectives. The information obtained from different books and journals now needs to be sorted under the main themes and theories, highlighting agreements and disagreements among the authors and identifying the unanswered questions or gaps. You will also realise that the literature deals with a number of aspects that have a direct or indirect bearing on your research topic. Use these aspects as a basis for developing your theoretical framework. Your review of the literature should sort the information, as mentioned earlier, within this framework. Unless you review the literature in relation to this framework, you will not be able to develop a focus in your literature search; that is, your theoretical framework provides you with a guide as you read. This brings us to the paradox mentioned previously: until you go through the literature you cannot develop a theoretical framework, and until you have developed a theoretical framework you cannot effectively review the literature. The solution is to read some of the literature and then attempt to develop a framework, even a loose one, within which you can organise the rest of the literature you read. As you read more about the area, you are likely to change the framework. However, without it, you will get bogged down in a great deal of unnecessary reading and note-taking that may not be relevant to your study.

Literature pertinent to your study may deal with two types of information: universal or general; and more specific (local trends or a specific programme). In writing about such information you should start with the general information, gradually narrowing it down to the specific. Look at the example in Figure 3.1.

If you want to study the relationship between mortality and fertility, you should review the literature about:

→ *fertility* – trends, theories, some of the indices and critiques of them, factors affecting fertility, methods of controlling fertility, factors affecting acceptance of contraceptives, and so on;
→ *mortality* – factors affecting mortality, mortality indices and their sensitivity in measuring change in mortality levels of a population, trends in mortality, and so on; and, most importantly,
→ *the relationship between fertility and mortality* – theories that have been put forward to explain the relationship, implications of the relationship.

Out of this literature review you need to develop the theoretical framework for your study. Primarily this should revolve around theories that have been put forward about the relationship between mortality and fertility. You will discover that a number of theories have been proposed to explain this relationship. For example, it has been explained from economic, religious, medical and psychological perspectives. Within each perspective several theories have been put forward: 'insurance theory', 'fear of non-survival', 'replacement theory', 'price theory', 'utility theory', 'extra' or 'hoarding theory' and 'risk theory'.

Your literature review should be written under the following headings, with most of the review involving the examination of the relationships between fertility and mortality:

→ fertility theories;
→ the theory of demographic transition;
→ trends in fertility (global, and then narrow it to national and local levels);
→ methods of contraception (their acceptance and effectiveness);
→ factors affecting mortality;
→ trends in mortality (and their implications);
→ measurement of mortality indices (their sensitivity);
→ *relationships between fertility and mortality* (different theories such as 'insurance', 'fear of non-survival', 'replacement', 'price', 'utility', 'risk' and 'hoarding').

Developing a conceptual framework

The conceptual framework is the basis of your research problem. It stems from the theoretical framework and usually focuses on the section(s) which become the basis of your study. Whereas the theoretical framework consists of the theories or issues in which your study is embedded, the conceptual framework describes the aspects you selected from the theoretical framework to become the basis of your enquiry. For instance, in the example cited in Figure 3.1a, the theoretical framework includes all the theories that have been put forward to explain the relationship between fertility and mortality. However, out of these, you may be planning to test only one, say the fear of non-survival. Similarly, in Figure 3.1b, the conceptual framework is focused only on indicators to measure the success or failure of the strategies to enhance community responsiveness. Hence the conceptual framework grows out of the theoretical framework and relates only and specifically to your research problem. The conceptual framework becomes the foundation of your study.

WRITING ABOUT THE LITERATURE REVIEWED

Now, all that remains to be done is to write about the literature you have reviewed. As mentioned at the beginning of this chapter, two of the broad functions of a literature review are (1) to provide a theoretical background to your study and (2) to enable you to contextualise your findings in relation to the existing body of knowledge, in addition to refining your methodology. The content of your literature review should reflect these two purposes. In order to fulfil the first purpose, you should identify and describe various theories relevant to your field and specify gaps in existing knowledge in the area, recent advances in the area of study, current trends and so on. In order to fulfil the second, you should integrate the results from your study with specific and relevant findings from the existing literature by comparing the two for confirmation or contradiction. Note that at this stage you can only accomplish the first purpose of the literature review, to provide a theoretical background to your study. For the second, the contextualisation of the findings, you have to wait till you are at the research report writing stage.

If you want to study the relationship between mortality and fertility, you should review the literature about:

→ *fertility* – trends, theories, some of the indices and critiques of them, factors affecting fertility,
→ methods of controlling fertility, factors affecting acceptance of contraceptives, and so on;
   mortality – factors affecting mortality, mortality indices and their sensitivity in measuring change in mortality levels of a population, trends in mortality, and so on; and, most importantly,
→ *the relationship between fertility and mortality* – theories that have been put forward to explain the relationship, implications of the relationship.

Out of this literature review you need to develop the theoretical framework for your study. Primarily this should revolve around theories that have been put forward about the relationship between mortality and fertility. You will discover that a number of theories have been proposed to explain this relationship. For example, it has been explained from economic, religious, medical and psychological perspectives. Within each perspective several theories have been put forward: 'insurance theory', 'fear of non-survival', 'replacement theory', 'price theory' 'utility theory, 'extra' or 'hoarding theory' and 'risk theories'.

Your literature review should be written under the following headings, with most of the review involving the examination of the relationships between fertility and mortality:

→ fertility theories;
→ the theory of demographic transition;
→ trends in fertility (global, and then narrow it to national and local levels);

- methods of contraception (their acceptance and effectiveness);
- factors affecting mortality;
- trends in mortality (and their implications);
- measurement of mortality indices (their sensitivity);
- relationships between fertility and mortality (different theories such as 'insurance', 'fear of non-survival', 'replacement', 'price', 'utility', 'risk' and 'hoarding').

Figure 3.1a   Developing a theoretical framework – the relationship between mortality and fertility

Note: *Preliminary discussions with some stakeholders revealed that not much was known to them about community responsiveness and therefore it was proposed that the study be carried out in two phases: preparatory phase and actual evaluation phase. The main aim of the preparatory phase was to ascertain the understanding of the concept, identify the strategies that are being or can be used, and developing a set of indicators for measuring its success or failure. This framework became the basis of the first phase of the study.*

The review of literature for the first phase was written around the following theoretical framework which, of course, emerged from the literature review itself:

Community responsiveness: What do the stakeholders {service providers, service managers and the consumers) understand by community responsiveness, why it is needed and what purpose does it serve?

Historical and philosophical perspectives: Start of the concept, an historical overview of its emergence, philosophical perspective that underpins the concept.

Implementation strategies: What strategies have been used to achieve community responsiveness in the service delivery area?

Attitude of the stakeholders: What are the attitudes of service providers, service managers and consumers of the services towards community responsiveness?

Evaluation of community responsiveness: What indicators can be used to determine the impact of these strategies, what should determine the success or failure of the implementation of the strategies, and by whom and how should it be determined?

Figure 3.1b   Theoretical framework for the 'community responsiveness in health' study

While reading the literature for the theoretical background to your study, you will realise that certain themes have emerged. List the main ones, converting them into subheadings. Some people write up the entire literature review in one section, entitled 'Review of the literature', 'Summary of literature' or 'The literature review', without subheadings, but the author strongly suggests that you write your literature review under subheadings based upon the main themes that you have discovered and which form the basis of your theoretical framework. These subheadings (which will form the basis of your theoretical framework) should be precise, descriptive of the theme in question and follow a logical progression. Now, under each subheading, record the main findings with respect to the theme in question (thematic writing), highlighting the reasons for and against an argument if they exist, and identifying gaps and issues. Figure 3.2a shows the subheadings used to describe the themes in a literature review conducted by the author for a study entitled 'Intercountry adoption in Western Australia'. Figure 3.2b shows themes around which the literature was reviewed for the community responsiveness study.

The second broad function of the literature review – contextualising the findings of your study – requires you to compare very systematically your findings with those made by others. Quote from these studies to show how your findings contradict, confirm or add to them. This places your findings in the context of what others have found. Be sure to provide a complete reference for any quoted material, in an acceptable format. This function is undertaken, as mentioned earlier, when writing about your findings; that is, after analysis of your data.

Thematic writing: A style of writing which is written around main themes.

CHECKPOINT
Writing about the literature

Intercountry adoption in Western Australia

(A profile of adoptive families)

The literature was reviewed under the following themes:

- ⤳ Introduction (introductory remarks about adoption)
- ⤳ History and philosophy of adoption
- ⤳ Reasons for adoption
- ⤳ Trends in adoption (global and national)
- ⤳ Intercountry adoption
- ⤳ History of intercountry adoption in Western Australia
- ⤳ Trends in intercountry adoption in Western Australia
- ⤳ The Adoption Act in Western Australia
- ⤳ The adoption process in Western Australia
- ⤳ Problems and issues in adoption
- ⤳ Gaps in the literature (in this case it was a lack of information about those parents who had adopted children from other countries that became *the* basis of the study)

Figure 3.2a   Sample outline of a literature review

The literature review for this study was carried out around the following themes identified through the objectives of the study and the literature review.

→ Background to the introductions of the concept
→ What does community responsiveness mean?
→ Historical perspective to the introduction of community responsiveness in Western Australia
→ Philosophy underpinning the concept of community responsiveness
→ Attitudes of the stakeholders towards the community responsiveness
→ Attitudes of the stakeholders towards the community responsiveness concept
→ Strategies for achieving community responsiveness
→ Measuring effectiveness of the implementation strategies; indicators and methodologies

Figure 3.2b   Main themes from the literature review for the community responsiveness study

SUMMARY

Reviewing the literature is a continuous process. It begins before a research problem is finalised and continues until the report is finished. There is a paradox in the literature review: you cannot undertake an effective literature review unless you have formulated a research problem, yet your literature search plays an extremely important role in helping you to formulate your research problem. The literature review brings clarity and focus to your research problem, improves your research methodology and broadens your knowledge base. A literature review identifies the main themes from the literature reviewed that are of relevance to your study, whereas a summary of the literature describes the main findings from a reference reviewed without thematic integration and linkage.

Reviewing the literature involves a number of steps: searching for existing literature in your area of study; reviewing the literature selected; using it to develop a theoretical framework from which your study emerges and also to develop a conceptual framework which will become the basis of your investigation. The main sources for identifying literature are books, journals, conference papers and the Internet. There are several sources which can provide information about locating relevant material.

The literature review serves two important functions: (1) it provides a theoretical background to your study, and (2) it helps you to contextualise your findings by comparing them with what others have found out in relation to the area of enquiry. At this stage of the research process, only the first function can be addressed. You can only take steps to address the second function when you have analysed your data and are in the process of writing about your findings.

Your writing about the literature reviewed should be thematic in nature; that is, based on main themes. The sequence of these themes in the write-up should follow a logical progression; various arguments should be substantiated with specific quotations and citations from the literature, adhering to an acceptable academic referencing style.

Now that you have read the full chapter...

CHECK YOUR UNDERSTANDING

☐ Do you understand the meaning and application of all of the keywords at the start of the chapter? If not, visit the online resources and use the glossary flashcards to get to grips with their definitions.

☐ What functions does the literature review perform in a research study?

☐ Describe the differences between theoretical and conceptual frameworks.

☐ What is the difference between a review of the literature and a summary of the literature?

APPLY IT TO YOUR OWN PROJECT

☐ Undertake a keyword search for a theme or issue that interests you using (a) an Internet search engine, such as Google Scholar, and (b) a library search facility. Compare the results.

☐ Choose two or three research reports from your search and scan through the summaries noting the theories put forward, the methodologies adopted and any recommendations for further study. Do these reports point to a consensus or differences of opinion in the field?

☐ Develop a theoretical framework for the theme or issue you selected.

CONFUSED?

THE ONLINE RESOURCES ARE HERE TO HELP YOU

 https://study.sagepub.com/kumar5e

CHECKPOINT: What is a literature review? Watch this video.

CHECKPOINT: Where can you find possible credible, relevant sources for a literature review? Visit this website.

CHECKPOINT: What sort of questions should you ask of the articles I select? Visit this website.

CHECKPOINT: What are the most important things I need to include when using reviewed literature to write a theoretical background for my research? Visit this website.

NEED MORE GENERAL SUPPORT?

Get up to speed on key terms with *glossary flashcards* and test yourself on important concepts with *multiple choice questions*.

UP FOR A CHALLENGE?

THE ONLINE RESOURCES ARE HERE TO INSPIRE YOU

 https://study.sagepub.com/kumar5e

CHECKPOINT: How are some other ways you might use a literature review to benefit your project? Visit this website.

CHECKPOINT: How can you improve your search strategies to find relevant research more efficiently? Read this chapter.

CHECKPOINT: How do you read and evaluate literature more critically? Read this chapter.

CHECKPOINT: What does a well-written literature review look like? Read this chapter.

READY TO WORK ON YOUR OWN PROJECT?

Start building a portfolio of your ideas with the exercise workbook and get support tailored to your specific assignment with the assessment toolkit.

FORMULATING A RESEARCH PROBLEM

- step one -
FORMULATING A RESEARCH PROBLEM

Reviewing the literature   54

→ Formulating a research problem   76

Identifying variables   100

Constructing hypotheses   126

ESSENTIAL TERMS

You should be able to define these by the end of the chapter

→ research objectives
→ research problem

→ operational definition (working definition)

BONUS TERMS

You will learn more about these by the end of the chapter

→ qualitative research
→ quantitative research
→ validity

→ Variable
→ Study population

LEARNING OBJECTIVES

At the end of this chapter, you will be able to:

→ Formulate a research problem in qualitative and quantitative research
→ Identify sources of possible research problems
→ Understand the considerations involved in formulating a research problem
→ Form of research questions and objectives
→ Establish operational definitions

The central aim of this chapter is to detail the process of formulating a research problem, even though the specific procedure that you are likely to adopt depends upon:

- your expertise in research methodology;
- your knowledge of the subject area;
- your understanding of the issues to be examined;
- the extent to which the focus of your study is predetermined; and
- your own orientation to the research methodology – quantitative, qualitative or mixed.

If you are not very familiar with the research process and/or do not have a very specific idea about what is to be researched, you need to follow every step detailed in this chapter. However, more experienced researchers can take a number of shortcuts. The process outlined here assumes that you have neither the required knowledge of the process of formulating a research problem nor a specific idea about what is to be researched. If you have a specific idea for the basis of your enquiry, you do not need to go through this chapter. However, you should make sure that your idea is researchable as not all problems lend themselves to research methodologies.

Research problem: Any issue, problem or question that becomes the basis of your enquiry. It is what you want to find out about during your research endeavour.

Subject area: Any academic or practice field in which you are conducting your study is called the subject or study area. It could be health or other needs of a community, attitudes of people towards an issue, occupational mobility in a community, coping strategies, depression, domestic violence, etc.

THE RESEARCH PROBLEM

Broadly speaking, any question that you want answered and any assumption or assertion that you want to challenge or investigate can become a research problem or a research topic for your study. However, it is important to remember that not all questions can be transformed into research problems and some may prove to be extremely difficult to study. According to Powers et al. (1985: 38), 'Potential research questions may occur to us on a regular basis, but the process of formulating them in a meaningful way is not at all an easy task'. As a newcomer it might seem easy to formulate a problem but it requires considerable knowledge of both the subject area and research methodology. Once you examine a question more closely you will soon realise the complexity of formulating an idea into a problem which is researchable. 'First identifying and then specifying a research problem might seem like research tasks that ought to be easy and quickly accomplished. However, such is often not the case' (Yegidis & Weinback 1991: 35).

It is essential for the problem you formulate to be able to withstand scrutiny in terms of the procedures required to be undertaken. Hence you should spend considerable time in thinking it through.

THE IMPORTANCE OF FORMULATING
A RESEARCH PROBLEM

The formulation of a research problem is the first and most important step of the research process. It is like the identification of a destination before undertaking a journey. In the absence of a destination, it is impossible to identify the shortest – or indeed any – route. Similarly, in the absence of a clear research problem, a clear and economical plan is impossible. To use another analogy, a research problem is like the foundation of a building. The type and design of the building are dependent upon the foundation. If the foundation is well designed and strong you can expect the building to be also. The research problem serves as the foundation of a research study: if it is well formulated, you can expect a good study to follow. According to Kerlinger (1986: 17): 'If one wants to solve a problem, one must generally know what the problem is. It can be said that a large part of the problem lies in knowing what one is trying to do.' You must have a clear idea with regard to what it is that you want to find out about and not what you think you must find.

A research problem may take a number of forms, from the very simple to the very complex. The way you formulate a problem determines almost every step that follows: the type of study design that can be used; the type of sampling strategy that can be employed; the research instrument that can be used or developed; and the type of analysis that can be undertaken.

Suppose your broad area of interest is depression. Further suppose you want to conduct a research study on the services available to patients with depression living in a community. If your focus is on finding out the types of service available to patients with depression, your study will be mainly descriptive and qualitative in nature. A study of this type will be carried out using qualitative research methodologies. On the other hand, if you want to find out the extent of use of these services, that is the number of people using them, it will use mainly quantitative methodologies even if it is otherwise descriptive in nature. If your focus is on determining the extent of use in relation to the personal attributes of the patients, the study will be classified as correlational (and quantitative). The methodology used will be different than the one used in the case of a descriptive study. Similarly, if your aim is to find out the effectiveness of these services, the study will again be classified as correlational and the study design, data collection methods and analysis will belong to the quantitative methodology. Hence, it is important for you to understand that the way you formulate a research problem determines all the subsequent steps that you will have to follow during your research journey.

The formulation of a problem is like the 'input' to a study, and the 'output' – the quality of the contents of the research report and the validity of the associations or causation established – is entirely dependent upon it. Hence the famous saying about computers, 'garbage in, garbage out', is equally applicable to research problems.

Initially, you may become more confused, but this is normal and a sign of progression. Remember that confusion is often but a first step towards clarity. Take time over formulating your problem, for the clearer you are about your research problem/question, the easier it will be for you later on. Remember, this is the most crucial step.

SOURCES OF RESEARCH PROBLEMS

This section is of particular relevance if you have not yet selected a research topic and do not know where to start. If you have already selected your topic or question, go on to the next section.

Most research in the humanities revolves around the four Ps: people, problems, programmes and phenomena. In fact, a closer look at any academic or occupational field will show that most research revolves around these four Ps. The emphasis on a particular 'P' may vary from study to study but generally, in practice, most research studies are based upon a combination of at least two Ps. You may select a group of individuals (a group of individuals, or a community as such – people) to examine the existence of certain issues or problems relating to their lives, to ascertain their attitude towards an issue (problem), to establish the existence of a regularity or occurrence (phenomenon) or to evaluate the effectiveness of an intervention (programme). Your focus may be on the study of an issue, an association or a phenomenon per se; for example, the relationship between unemployment and street crime, smoking and cancer, fertility and mortality, delinquency and street crime, or academic achievement and home environment, carried out on the basis of information collected from individuals, groups, communities or organisations. The emphasis in these studies is on exploring, discovering or establishing associations or causation. Similarly, you can study different aspects of a programme: its effectiveness, its structure, the need for it, consumers' satisfaction with it, and so on. In order to ascertain these you collect information from people.

Every research study has two aspects: people provide you with the 'study population', while the problem, programme or phenomenon furnishes the 'subject area' about which information is collected. This is outlined further in Table 4.1, which shows the aspects of a research problem.

CHECKPOINT
*Choosing a
research topic*

Table 4.1   Aspects of a research problem

Aspects of a study	Information about	Study of	Importance to the study
Study population	People	Individuals, organisations, groups, communities	They provide you with the required information or you collect information from or about them
Subject area	Problem	Issues and problems facing a group of people; description of situations, associations, needs, attitudes; population profiles; service delivery process, etc.	Information that you need to collect to find answers to your service research questions
	Programme	Contents, services provided, administrative structure, services outcomes, consumer satisfaction, profile of consumers, profile of service providers, effectiveness, cost benefit, etc.	
	Phenomenon	Cause and effect, relationships, the study of a phenomenon itself, etc.	

You can study a problem, a programme or a phenomenon in any academic field or from any professional perspective. For example, you can measure the effectiveness of a programme in the field of health, education, social work, industrial management, public health, nursing, health promotion or welfare, or you can look at a problem from a health, business or welfare perspective. Similarly, you can gauge consumers' opinions about any aspect of a programme in the above fields.

Examine your own academic discipline or professional field in the context of the four Ps in order to identify anything that looks interesting. For example, if you are a student in the health field there are an enormous number of issues, situations and associations within each subfield of health that you could examine. Issues relating to the spread of a disease, drug rehabilitation, an immunisation programme, the effectiveness of a treatment, the extent of consumers' satisfaction or issues concerning a particular health programme can all provide you with a range of research problems. Similarly, in education there are several issues: students' satisfaction with a teacher, attributes of a good teacher, the impact of the home environment on the educational achievement of students and the supervisory needs of postgraduate students in higher education. Any other academic or occupational field such as marketing research, social work, community psychology or tourism can similarly be dissected into subfields and examined for a potential research problem. Most fields lend themselves to the above categorisation even though specific problems and programmes vary markedly from field to field.

The concept of the four Ps is applicable to both quantitative and qualitative research though the main difference at this stage is the extent of their specificity, **dissection,** precision and focus. In qualitative research these attributes are deliberately kept very loose so that you can explore more as you go along, in case you find something of relevance. You do not bind yourself with constraints that would put limits on your ability to explore. There is a separate section on 'Formulating a research problem in qualitative research' later in the chapter, which provides further guidance on the process.

CHECKPOINT
Qualitative research problems

CONSIDERATIONS IN SELECTING A RESEARCH PROBLEM

When selecting a research problem or topic there are a number of considerations to keep in mind which will help to ensure that your study will be manageable and that you remain motivated:

- **Interest** – This should be the most important consideration in selecting a research problem. A research endeavour is usually time-consuming and involves hard work and possibly unforeseen problems. If you select a topic which does not greatly interest you, it could become extremely difficult to sustain the required motivation and put in enough time and energy to complete it.

- **Magnitude** – You should have sufficient knowledge about the research process to be able to visualise the work involved in completing the proposed study. Narrow the topic down to something manageable, specific and clear. It is extremely important to select a topic that you can manage within the time and with the resources at your disposal. Even if you are undertaking a descriptive study, you need to consider its magnitude carefully.

Measurement of concepts – If you are using a concept in your study (in quantitative studies), make sure you are clear about its indicators and their measurement. For example, if you plan to measure the effectiveness of a health promotion programme or a programme to rehabilitate asylum seekers in a country or random breath testing programme, you must be clear as to what determines effectiveness and how it will be measured. Do not use concepts in your research problem that you are not sure how to measure. This does not mean you cannot develop a measurement procedure as the study progresses. While most of the developmental work will be done during your study, it is imperative that you are reasonably clear about the measurement of these concepts at this stage.

Level of expertise – Make sure you have an adequate level of expertise for the task you are proposing. Allow for the fact that you will learn during the study and may receive help from your research supervisor and others, but remember that you need to do most of the work yourself.

Relevance – Select a topic that is of relevance to you as a professional. Ensure that your study adds to the existing body of knowledge, bridges current gaps or is useful in policy formulation. This will help you to sustain interest in the study.

Availability of data – If your topic entails collection of information from secondary sources (office records, client records, census or other already published reports, etc.) make sure that this data is available and in the format you want before finalising your topic.

Ethical issues – Another important consideration in formulating a research problem is the ethical issues involved. In the course of conducting a research study, the study population may be adversely affected by some of the questions (directly or indirectly); deprived of an intervention; expected to share sensitive and private information; or expected to be simply experimental 'guinea pigs'. How ethical issues can affect the study population and how ethical problems can be overcome should be thoroughly examined at the problem formulation stage.

84

STEPS IN FORMULATING A RESEARCH PROBLEM

The formulation of a research problem is the most crucial part of the research journey as the quality and relevance of your research project entirely depend upon it. As mentioned earlier, every step that constitutes the *how* part of the research journey (Figure 2.1) depends upon the way you formulated your research problem. Despite the importance of this step, there is very little available by way of specific guidance in other books. This task is largely left either to the teachers of research methodology or to students to learn for themselves. One of the strengths of this book is that it offers the beginner a very specific set of step-by-step guidelines in one place, despite the fear of being labelled as prescriptive.

The process of formulating a research problem consists of a number of steps. Working through these steps presupposes a reasonable level of knowledge in the broad subject area within which the study is to be undertaken and the research methodology itself. A brief review of the relevant literature helps enormously in broadening this knowledge base. Without such knowledge it is difficult to 'dissect' a subject area clearly and adequately.

If you do not know what specific research topic, idea, questions or issue you want to research (which is not uncommon among students), going through the following steps will prove to be of immense help in deciding what you want to find out about. They will help you to select and narrow down a subject area that could become the basis of a research problem for your study.

- **STEP ONE Identify a broad field or subject area of interest to you**. It is imperative to do this at the very beginning, before starting out on your research journey. Ask yourself, 'What is it that really interests me as a professional?' In the author's opinion, it is a good idea to think about the field in which you would like to work after graduation. This will help you to find an interesting topic, and one which may be of use to you in the future. For example, if you are a social work student, inclined to work in the area of youth welfare, refugees or domestic violence after graduation, you might take to research in one of these areas. Or if you are studying marketing you might be interested in researching consumer behaviour. Or, as a student of public health, intending to work with patients who have HIV/AIDS, you might like to conduct research on a subject area relating to HIV/AIDS. Or you might be interested in becoming a teacher.

- **STEP TWO Dissect the broad area into subareas**. At the outset, you will realise that all the broad areas mentioned above – youth welfare, refugees, domestic violence, consumer behaviour and HIV/AIDS – have many aspects. For example, there are many aspects and issues in the area of domestic violence, illustrated in Figure 4.1.

  The more you think or read about an area the more subareas you will identify. For instance, you can go through the broad area of alcoholism (see Step 2 in Fig. 4.2). In preparing your list of subareas you should also consult others who have some knowledge of the area and the literature in your subject area. Once you have developed an exhaustive list of the subareas from various sources, you can proceed to the next stage where you select what will become the basis of your enquiry.

- **STEP THREE Select what is of most interest to you**. It is neither advisable nor feasible to study all subareas. From your list, select issues, questions or subareas about which you are passionate. Your interest should be the most important determinant for selection, even though there are other considerations as discussed in the previous section. One way to decide what interests you most is to start with a process of elimination. Go through your list and delete all those subareas, issues or questions in which you are not very interested. You will find that towards the end of this process, it will become very difficult for you to delete anything further. You need to continue until you are left with something that is *manageable*, considering the time available to you, your level of expertise and other resources needed to undertake the study. Once you are confident that you have selected something that you are passionate about and can manage, you are ready to go to the next step.

- **STEP FOUR Raise research questions**. At this step ask yourself, 'What is it that I want to find out about in this subarea?' Make a list of whatever questions come to mind relating to your chosen subarea and if you think there are too many to be manageable, go through the same process of elimination as in step 3.

→ **STEP FIVE Formulate objectives**. Both your main objectives and your subobjectives now need to be formulated, based on your research questions. The main difference between objectives and research questions is the way in which they are written. Research questions are obviously that – questions. Objectives transform these questions into behavioural aims by using action-oriented phrases such as 'to find out', 'to determine', 'to ascertain' and 'to examine'. Some researchers prefer to reverse the process; that is, they start from objectives and formulate research questions from them. Some researchers are satisfied only with research questions, and do not formulate objectives at all. If you prefer to have only research questions or only objectives, this is fine, but keep in mind the requirements of your institution for research proposals. For guidance on formulating objectives, see the next section.

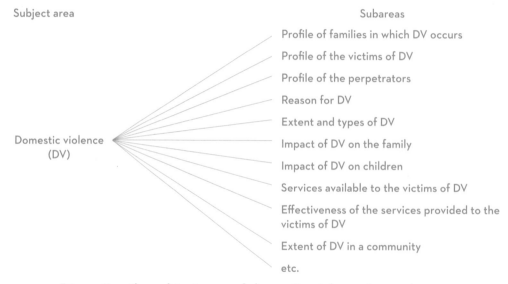

Figure 4.1   Dissecting the subject area of domestic violence into subareas

→ **STEP SIX Assess your objectives**. Now examine your objectives to ascertain the feasibility of achieving them through your research endeavour. Consider them in the light of the time, resources (financial and human) and technical expertise at your disposal.

→ **STEP SEVEN Double-check**. Go back and give final consideration to whether or not you are sufficiently interested in the study, and have adequate resources to undertake it. Ask yourself, 'Am I really enthusiastic about this study?' and 'Do I really have enough resources to undertake it?' Answer these questions thoughtfully and realistically. If your answer to one of them is 'no', reassess your objectives.

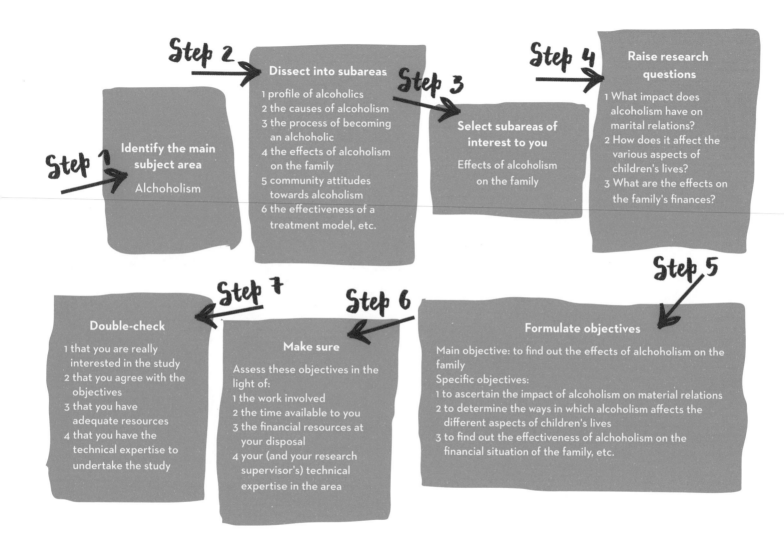

Step 1 → Identify the main subject area

Alchoholism

Step 2 → Dissect into subareas

1 profile of alcoholics
2 the causes of alcoholism
3 the process of becoming an alchoholic
4 the effects of alcoholism on the family
5 community attitudes towards alcoholism
6 the effectiveness of a treatment model, etc.

Step 3 → Select subareas of interest to you

Effects of alcoholism on the family

Step 4 → Raise research questions

1 What impact does alcoholism have on marital relations?
2 How does it affect the various aspects of children's lives?
3 What are the effects on the family's finances?

Step 5 → Formulate objectives

Main objective: to find out the effects of alchoholism on the family
Specific objectives:
1 to ascertain the impact of alcoholism on material relations
2 to determine the ways in which alcoholism affects the different aspects of children's lives
3 to find out the effectiveness of alchoholism on the financial situation of the family, etc.

Step 6 → Make sure

Assess these objectives in the light of:
1 the work involved
2 the time available to you
3 the financial resources at your disposal
4 your (and your research supervisor's) technical expertise in the area

Step 7 → Double-check

1 that you are really interested in the study
2 that you agree with the objectives
3 that you have adequate resources
4 that you have the technical expertise to undertake the study

Figure 4.2   Steps in formulating a research problem – alcoholism

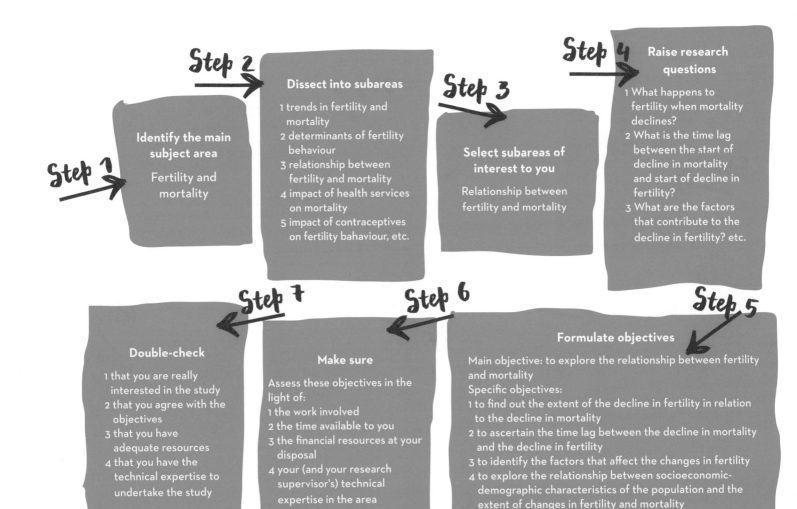

Step 1

Identify the main subject area

Fertility and mortality

Step 2

Dissect into subareas

1 trends in fertility and mortality
2 determinants of fertility behaviour
3 relationship between fertility and mortality
4 impact of health services on mortality
5 impact of contraceptives on fertility bahaviour, etc.

Step 3

Select subareas of interest to you

Relationship between fertility and mortality

Step 4

Raise research questions

1 What happens to fertility when mortality declines?
2 What is the time lag between the start of decline in mortality and start of decline in fertility?
3 What are the factors that contribute to the decline in fertility? etc.

Step 5

Formulate objectives

Main objective: to explore the relationship between fertility and mortality
Specific objectives:
1 to find out the extent of the decline in fertility in relation to the decline in mortality
2 to ascertain the time lag between the decline in mortality and the decline in fertility
3 to identify the factors that affect the changes in fertility
4 to explore the relationship between socioeconomic-demographic characteristics of the population and the extent of changes in fertility and mortality

Step 6

Make sure

Assess these objectives in the light of:
1 the work involved
2 the time available to you
3 the financial resources at your disposal
4 your (and your research supervisor's) technical expertise in the area

Step 7

Double-check

1 that you are really interested in the study
2 that you agree with the objectives
3 that you have adequate resources
4 that you have the technical expertise to undertake the study

Figure 4.3   Formulating a research problem – the relationship between fertility and mortality

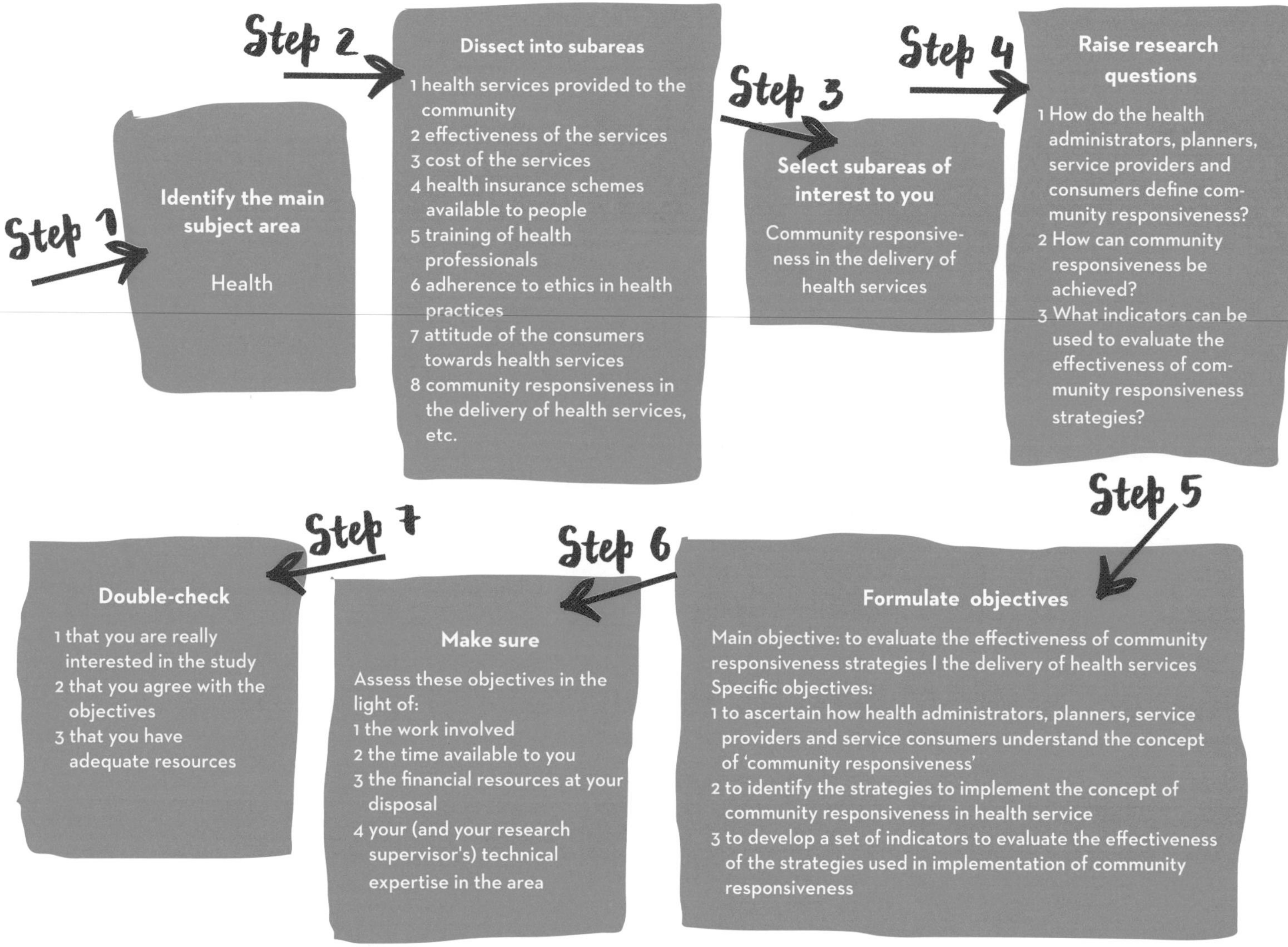

Step 1 → Identify the main subject area

Health

Step 2 → Dissect into subareas

1 health services provided to the community
2 effectiveness of the services
3 cost of the services
4 health insurance schemes available to people
5 training of health professionals
6 adherence to ethics in health practices
7 attitude of the consumers towards health services
8 community responsiveness in the delivery of health services, etc.

Step 3 → Select subareas of interest to you

Community responsiveness in the delivery of health services

Step 4 → Raise research questions

1 How do the health administrators, planners, service providers and consumers define community responsiveness?
2 How can community responsiveness be achieved?
3 What indicators can be used to evaluate the effectiveness of community responsiveness strategies?

Step 5 → Formulate objectives

Main objective: to evaluate the effectiveness of community responsiveness strategies I the delivery of health services
Specific objectives:
1 to ascertain how health administrators, planners, service providers and service consumers understand the concept of 'community responsiveness'
2 to identify the strategies to implement the concept of community responsiveness in health service
3 to develop a set of indicators to evaluate the effectiveness of the strategies used in implementation of community responsiveness

Step 6 → Make sure

Assess these objectives in the light of:
1 the work involved
2 the time available to you
3 the financial resources at your disposal
4 your (and your research supervisor's) technical expertise in the area

Step 7 → Double-check

1 that you are really interested in the study
2 that you agree with the objectives
3 that you have adequate resources

Figure 4.4   Narrowing down a research problem – health

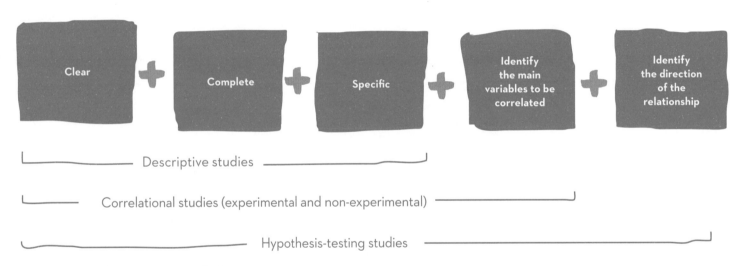

Figure 4.5   Characteristics of objectives

Figures **4.2–4.4** operationalise steps 1–7 with examples from different academic disciplines (health, social work/social sciences and community development).

THE FORMULATION OF RESEARCH OBJECTIVES

Objectives are the goals you set out to attain in your study. Since these objectives inform the reader of what you want to achieve in the study, it is extremely important to word them clearly and specifically.

It is important to distinguish between main objectives and subobjectives. The main objective relates to the overall thrust of your study. It is also concerned with the main associations and relationships that you seek to discover or establish. The subobjectives are the specific aspects of the topic that you want to investigate within the main framework of your study.

Subobjectives should be listed numerically. They should be worded clearly and unambiguously. Make sure that each subobjective contains only one aspect of the study. Use action-oriented words or verbs when writing your objectives. The objectives should start with words such as 'to determine', 'to find out', 'to ascertain', 'to measure' and 'to explore'.

The way the main objectives and subobjectives are worded determines how your research is classified (e.g. descriptive, correlational or experimental). In other words, the wording of your objectives determines the type of research design you need to adopt to achieve them. Hence, be careful about the way you word your objectives.

Irrespective of the type of research, the objectives should be expressed in such a way that the wording clearly, completely and specifically communicates your intention to your readers. There is no place for ambiguity, non-specificity or incompleteness, either in the wording of your objectives or in the ideas they communicate. Figure 4.5 displays the characteristics of the wording of objectives in relation to the type of research study.

If your study is primarily descriptive, your main objective should clearly describe the major focus of your study, even mentioning the organisation and its location unless these are to be kept confidential (e.g. to describe the types of treatment programme provided by [name of the organisation] to alcoholics in [name of the place] or to find out the opinion of the community about the health services provided by [name of the health centre/department] in [name of the place]). Identification of the organisation and its location is important as the services may be peculiar to the place and the organisation and may not represent the services provided by others to similar populations.

If your study is correlational in nature, in addition to the first three characteristics shown in Figure 4.5, the wording of the main objective should also include the main variables being correlated (e.g. to ascertain the *impact of migration* on *family roles* or to compare the effectiveness of *different teaching methods* on the *comprehension of students*).

If the overall thrust of your study is to test a hypothesis, the wording of the main objectives should also indicate the direction of the relationship being tested (e.g. to ascertain if an *increase in youth unemployment* will *increase the incidence of street crime*, or to demonstrate that the provision of maternal and child health services to Aboriginal people in rural Australia will *reduce infant mortality*).

CHECKPOINT
Researchable questions

Study population: Every study in the social sciences has two aspects: study population and study area (subject area). The people you want to find out about are collectively known as the study population or simply population; the size of the population is usually denoted by the letter N. It could be a group of people living in an area, employees of an organisation, a community, a group of people with special issues, etc. The people from whom you gather information, known as the sample, are selected from the study population; the sample size is usually denoted by n.

THE STUDY POPULATION

CHECKPOINT
Narrowing your research problem

So far we have focused on only one aspect of a study, the research problem. But every study in social sciences has a second aspect, the study population, from whom the information required to find answers to your research question is obtained. As you narrow the research problem, similarly you need to decide very specifically and clearly who constitutes your study population, in order to select the appropriate respondents.

Suppose you have designed a study to ascertain the needs of young people living in a community. In terms of the study population, one of the first questions you need to answer is 'Who do I consider to be a young person?' You need to decide, in measurable terms, which age group your respondents should come from. Is it those between 15 and 18, 15 and 20, or 15 and 25 years of age? Or you may be interested in some other age group. You need to decide this before undertaking your research journey. Having decided the age group that constitutes your 'young person', the next question you need to consider is whether you want to select young people of either gender or confine the study to one only. In addition, there is another dimension to consider: that is, what constitutes the community? Which geographical area(s) or ethnic background should you select your respondents from?

Let us take another example. Suppose you want to find out the settlement process of immigrants. As a part of identifying your study population, you need to decide who you would consider an immigrant. Is it a person who immigrated 5, 10, 15 or 20 years ago? You also need to consider the countries from where the immigrants come. Will you select your respondents irrespective of the country of origin or select only those who have come from a specific country or countries? You need to narrow your definition of the study population as you have done with your research problem. These issues are discussed in greater depth in the next section.

In quantitative research, you need to narrow both the research problem and the study population and make them as specific as possible so that you and your readers are clear about them. In qualitative research, reflecting the 'exploratory' philosophical base of the approach, both the study population and the research problem should remain loose and flexible to ensure the freedom necessary to obtain varied and rich data if a situation emerges.

Operational definition: When you define concepts used by you either in your research problem or in the study population in a measurable form, they are called working or operational definitions. It is important to understand that the operational definitions that you develop are only for the purpose of your study.

Working definition: see Operational definition

ESTABLISHING OPERATIONAL DEFINITIONS

In defining the problem you may use certain words or items that are as such difficult to measure and/or the understanding of which may vary from respondent to respondent. In a research study it is important to develop, define or establish a set of rules, indicators or yardsticks in order to establish clearly the meaning of such words/items. It is sometimes also important to define clearly the study population from which you need to obtain the required information. When you define concepts that you plan to use either in your research problem and/or in identifying the study population in a measurable form, they are called operational definitions or working definitions. You must understand that these operational definitions that you develop are only for the purpose of your study and could be quite different from legal definitions, or those used by others. The meanings you assign to the concepts are only for the purpose of your study and are designed to remove ambiguity when selecting or communicating with your respondents. As the understanding of concepts can vary markedly from person to person, your operational definitions will inform your readers what exactly you mean by the concepts that you have used in your study.

Let us take an example from studies where the main objectives are:

1. to find out the number of *children* living below the *poverty* line in Australia;
2. to ascertain the impact of immigration on *family* roles among *immigrants*;
3. to measure the *effectiveness* of a retraining programme designed to help *young people*.

Although these objectives clearly state the main thrust of the studies, they are not specific in terms of either the main variables to be studied or the study populations. You cannot count the number of children living below the poverty line until you decide what constitutes the poverty line and how to determine it; you cannot find out the impact of immigration on family roles unless you identify which roles constitute family roles; and you cannot measure effectiveness until you define what effectiveness is. On the other hand, it is equally important to decide exactly what you mean by 'children',' immigrants' or 'young'. Up to what age will you consider a person to be a child? Who would you consider young? Who would you consider to be an immigrant? In addition, will you consider immigrants from every country or only a few? In many cases you need to develop operational definitions for the variables and concepts you are studying and for the population that becomes the source of the information for your study. Table 4.2 lists the concepts and the population groups to be operationalised for the above examples. Defining these clearly by developing operational definitions will avoid ambiguity and confusion.

Table 4.2   Operationalisation of concepts and study populations

	Concept to be studied		Population to be studied	
Study	Concepts	Issues	Study populations	Issues
1	Poverty line	What constitutes the 'poverty line'?	Children	Who would you consider a child?
2	Family roles	What constitutes 'family roles'?	Immigrants	Who would you consider an immigrant?
3	Effectiveness	What constitutes 'effectiveness'?	The young	Who would you consider a young person?
You must:	operationalise the concepts – define in practical, observable and measurable terms 'poverty line', 'family roles' and 'effectiveness'		operationalise the study population – define in identifiable terms 'children', 'immigrants' and 'young'	

Operational definitions may differ from day-to-day meanings as well as dictionary or legal definitions. These meanings may not be helpful in identifying either your study population or the concepts you are studying. Though in daily life you often use words such as 'children', 'youth' and 'immigrant' loosely, you need to be more specific when using them in a research study. You should work through your own definitions.

Operational definitions give an operational meaning to the study population and the concepts used. It is only through making your procedures explicit that you can validly describe, explain, verify and test. It is important to remember that there are no rules for deciding if an operational definition is valid. Your arguments must convince others about the appropriateness of your definitions.

FORMULATING A RESEARCH PROBLEM IN QUALITATIVE RESEARCH

The difference in qualitative and quantitative studies starts with the way you formulate your research problem. In quantitative research you strive to be as specific as possible, attempt to narrow the magnitude of your study and develop a framework within which you confine your search. On the other hand, in qualitative research, this specificity in scope, methods and framework is not required. You strive instead to maintain flexibility, openness and freedom to include any new ideas or exclude any aspect that you initially included but later consider not to be relevant. At the initial stage you may only identify the main thrust of your study and some specific aspects which you want to find out about. Qualitative research primarily employs inductive reasoning. In contrast to quantitative research, where a research problem is stated before data collection, in qualitative research the problem is reformulated several times after you have begun data collection. The research problem and the data collection strategies are reformulated as necessary throughout data collection either to acquire the 'totality' of a phenomenon or to select certain aspects for greater in-depth study.

This flexibility and freedom, though providing you with certain advantages, can also create problems in terms of comparability of the information gathered. It is possible that your areas of search may become markedly different during the preliminary and final stages of data gathering. During the initial developmental phase, many researchers produce a framework of 'reminders' (a conceptual framework of enquiry) to ensure that key issues/aspects are covered during discussions with the respondents. As the study progresses, if need be, issues or themes are added to this framework. This is not a list of questions but reminders that are only used if for some reason the interaction with respondents lacks discussion.

Look at the example above that details the process of formulating a research problem in qualitative research. In qualitative research you do not formulate a research problem as you do in quantitative research. However, it is of immense importance that you develop a conceptual framework that could serve as a basis for discussing issues with the respondents, especially in cases where respondents are not very forthcoming. In qualitative research you need to be open and flexible in terms of the framework of your enquiry so that you can bring depth and richness to the data.

Once I supervised a student who was interested in attention-deficit hyperactivity disorder (ADHD). She wanted to find out, as she put it, 'What does it mean to have a child with ADHD in the family?' Of course my first question to her was 'What do you mean by "what does it mean"?' She paused for a while and then said, 'it means what it means'. I asked her to treat me as one of her respondents and ask the question. She asked me, 'What does it mean to have a child with ADHD?' to which my answer was, 'I do not understand your question. Could you please explain to me the meaning of "what does it mean"?' She found it difficult to explain and immediately realised the problem with the question. What she thought was very clear to her became quite difficult to explain. It took her a while to explain to me what she had in mind. During the discussion that followed, though she could explain some of the things she had in mind, she realised that she could not go to a respondent with her initial question.

The student knew a family who had a child with ADHD from which her interest in the topic had probably stemmed. I suggested that she have a talk with the mother. She did, and, to her surprise, the mother asked her the same question that I had.

I advised her to read some literature on ADHD and also have informal talks with two families who have a child with ADHD. We decided to select one single-mother family and another where the father and the mother both take responsibility for the child. She was advised to record all the issues and aspects that reflected her understanding of 'what it means', relating to bringing up a child with ADHD in the family. After going through the above, she developed a list, three and a half pages long, of the aspects and issues that, according to her, reflected her understanding of 'what it means'. She did not construct any specific questions around these aspects or issues. They served as background for her to raise with potential respondents in case respondents did not come up with issues or aspects for discussion in terms of 'What does it mean to have a child with ADHD in the family?'

This list brought immense clarification to her thinking about 'what it means' and served as the basis of her interviews with the families. A number of times during the supervisory sessions she had mentioned that she would not have been able to do much without the conceptual framework. You should not confuse it with the interview guide. The list is a conceptual construction of the thoughts that serve as background and become the basis of discussions in case there is insufficient dialogue with your potential respondents.

95

SUMMARY

The formulation of a research problem is the most important step in the research process. It is the foundation, in terms of design, on which you build the whole study. Any defects in it will adversely affect the validity and reliability of your study.

There are no specific guidelines, but the model suggested in this chapter could serve as a useful framework for the beginner. The seven-step model helps you to narrow your broad area of interest to enable you to decide specifically what you want to study. It is operational in nature and follows a logical sequence that takes the beginner through the complexities of formulating a research problem in a simple and easy-to-understand manner.

In quantitative research you need to determine the path of your research journey in advance. This navigational map becomes your guide. However, in qualitative research the journey is open, and free from strict adherence to any path.

In quantitative studies it is important to go through the process of narrowing down or zeroing in on the research problem. The path and the outcome are determined by a set of objectives that you formulate. It is therefore important that you articulate the objectives of your study clearly. Objectives – whether the main objective or the subobjectives – should be specific and free from ambiguity, and each one should relate to only one aspect of the study. Use action-oriented words when writing your objectives.

Formulation of a research problem in qualitative research follows a different path. You do not predetermine the exact nature and extent of the research problem you propose to find answers to. You continue to modify it as you start finding out more about it. However, it will help you if you develop a conceptual framework for the different aspects of the problem to serve as a backdrop for issues to be discussed with potential respondents.

Developing operational definitions for the concepts that you propose to study is extremely important. This enhances clarity about the issues you are trying to find out about and about the study population you plan to gather information from. It is important that you operationalise both the main variables you are proposing to study and the study population.

Now that you have read the full chapter...

CHECK YOUR UNDERSTANDING

- ☐ Do you understand the meaning and application of all of the keywords at the start of the chapter? If not, visit the online resources and use the glossary flashcards to get to grips with their definitions.

- ☐ What are some of the broad differences in formulating a research problem in quantitative and qualitative research?

- ☐ What considerations should you bear in mind in the wording of objectives?

APPLY IT TO YOUR OWN PROJECT

- ☐ Identify two or three potential research questions, related to your own academic field or professional area, that would fall under each of the four Ps (as outlined in Table 4.1): people, problems, programmes and phenomena.

- ☐ For each of the hypothetical research questions you created, identify which concepts and study populations would need to be operationally defined. Consider what problems might occur if this were not done.

CONFUSED?

THE ONLINE RESOURCES ARE HERE TO HELP YOU

 https://study.sagepub.com/kumar5e

CHECKPOINT: How do you choose a research topic? Watch this video.

CHECKPOINT: What is a qualitative research problem? Watch this video.

CHECKPOINT: What is a researchable question? Visit this website.

CHECKPOINT: How do you narrow your topic into a researchable problem? Watch this video.

NEED MORE GENERAL SUPPORT?

Get up to speed on key terms with *glossary flashcards* and test yourself on important concepts with *multiple choice questions*.

UP FOR A CHALLENGE?

THE ONLINE RESOURCES ARE HERE TO INSPIRE YOU

 https://study.sagepub.com/kumar5e

CHECKPOINT: How do you choose a relevant and interesting topic? Visit this website.

CHECKPOINT: What does a good qualitative research question look like? Visit this website.

CHECKPOINT: Is your question researchable? Review this checklist.

CHECKPOINT: What factors can you adjust if you research question is too broad? Visit this website.

READY TO WORK ON YOUR OWN PROJECT?

Start building a portfolio of your ideas with the exercise workbook and get support tailored to your specific assignment with the assessment toolkit.

IDENTIFYING VARIABLES

– step one –
FORMULATING A RESEARCH PROBLEM

Reviewing the literature   54

Formulating a research problem   76

Identifying variables   100

Constructing hypotheses   126

ESSENTIAL TERMS

You should be able to define these by the end of the chapter

- categorical variables
- concept
- dependent variables
- extraneous variables

- independent variables
- intervening variables
- measurement scales

BONUS TERMS

You will learn more about these by the end of the chapter

- active variables
- attribute variables
- causation
- constant variables
- continuous variables
- dichotomous

- interval scale
- nominal scale
- ordinal scale
- polytomous
- ratio scale
- unit of measurement

LEARNING OBJECTIVES

At the end of this chapter, you will be able to:

- Understand the place of variables in research
- Explain what variables and concepts are and how they are different
- Turn concepts into operational variables
- Assess types of variables from the viewpoint of causation, the study design and unit of measurement
- Identify types of measurement scales: nominal or classificatory, ordinal or ranking, interval and ratio

If it exists, it can be measured. (Babbie 1989: 105)

In the process of formulating a research problem in quantitative research, there are two important considerations that you should keep in mind: whether or not you are researching a concept(s) in the process of undertaking your study; and whether or not you are testing a hypothesis. Both concepts and hypotheses place additional responsibility on you in terms of their operationalisation. Concepts need to be operationalised in behavioural terms, and hypotheses need to be constructed and their outcome communicated in a specific manner. In the previous chapter, we established that concepts are highly subjective as their understanding may vary from person to person. It follows, therefore, that as such they may not be uniformly (and thus accurately) measurable. In a research study it is important that the concepts used should be operationalised in measurable terms so that the extent of variation in respondents' understanding is reduced if not eliminated. Using techniques to operationalise concepts, and knowledge about variables and their measurement, play an important role in reducing this variability and 'fine-tuning' your research problem.

WHAT IS A VARIABLE?

Whether we accept it or not, we all make value judgements constantly in our daily lives: 'This food is *excellent*'; 'I did not sleep *well* last night'; 'I do not *like* this'; and 'I think this is *wonderful*'. These are all judgements based upon our *own* preferences, indicators or assessment. Because they explain feelings or preferences, the basis on which they are made may vary markedly from person to person. There is no uniform yardstick with which to measure them. A particular food may be judged 'excellent' by one person but 'awful' by another, and something else could be wonderful to one person but ugly to another. When people express these feelings or preferences, they do so on the basis of certain criteria in their minds, or in relation to their expectations. If you were to question them you would discover that their judgement is based upon indicators and/or expectations that lead them to conclude and express a particular opinion.

Let us consider this in a professional context:

> → 'This programme is *effective*.'
> → 'This programme is *not effective*.'
> → 'We are providing a *quality service* to our clients.'
> → 'This is a *waste of time*.'
> → 'In this institution women are *discriminated* against.'
> → 'There is no *accountability* in this office.'
> → 'This product is not doing *well*.'

These are not preferences per se; they are judgements that require a sound basis on which to proclaim. For example, if you want to find out if a programme is effective, if a service is of quality or if there is discrimination, you need to be careful that such judgements have a rational and sound basis. This warrants the use of a measuring mechanism and it is in the process of measurement that knowledge about variables plays an important role.

An image, perception or concept that is capable of measurement – hence capable of taking on different values – is called a variable. According to Kerlinger (1986: 27), 'A variable is a property that takes on different values. Putting it redundantly, a variable is something that varies ... A variable is a symbol to which numerals or values are attached.' Black and Champion (1976: 34) define variables as 'rational units of analysis that can assume any one of a number of designated sets of values'. A variable, then, is a concept that can be measured on any one of the four types of measurement scale, which have varying degrees of precision in measurement (measurement scales are discussed later in this chapter).

However, there are some who believe that scientific methods are incapable of measuring feelings, preferences, values and sentiments. In the author's opinion most of these things can be measured, though there are situations where they must be measured indirectly through appropriate indicators rather than directly. These feelings and judgements are based upon observable behaviours in real life, though the extent to which the behaviours reflect their judgements may vary from person to person. In the words of Cohen and Nagel (1966: 352):

> There are, indeed, a great many writers who believe that scientific method is inherently inapplicable to such judgements as estimation or value, as 'This is beautiful', 'This is good' or 'This ought to be done' ... all judgements of the latter type express nothing but feelings, tastes or individual preferences, such judgements cannot be said to be true or false (except as descriptions of the personal feelings of the one who utters them) ... Almost all human discourse would become meaningless if we took the view that every moral or aesthetic judgement is no more true or false than any other.

THE DIFFERENCE BETWEEN A CONCEPT AND A VARIABLE

The main difference between a concept and a variable is measurability. Concepts are mental images or perceptions and therefore their meanings vary markedly from individual to individual, whereas variables are measurable, though, of course, with varying degrees of accuracy depending upon the measurement scale used. A concept as such cannot be measured, whereas a variable can be subjected to measurement by crude/refined or subjective/objective units of measurement. Concepts are subjective impressions which, if measured as such, would cause problems in comparing responses obtained from different respondents. According to Young (1966: 18):

> Each collaborator must have the same understanding of the concepts if the collaborative data are to be similarly classified and the findings pooled and tested, or reproduced. Classification and comparison demand uniform and precise definitions of categories expressed in concepts.

It is therefore important for the concepts to be converted into variables (either directly or through a set of indicators) as they can be subjected to measurement, even though the degree of precision with which they can be measured markedly varies from one measurement scale (*nominal*, *ordinal*, *interval* and **ratio**) to another. Table 5.1 gives examples of concepts and variables to illustrate the differences between them.

Variable: An image, perception or concept that is capable of measurement – hence capable of taking on different values – is called a variable. In other words, a concept that can be measured is called a variable. A variable is a property that takes on different values. It is a rational unit of measurement that can assume any one of a number of designated values.

Measurement scales: A system of classifying objects, responses, characteristics and attributes into different categories. These categorisations could be very subjective or objective depending upon the scale used. The four commonly used scales are nominal, ordinal, interval and ratio.

Concept: In defining a research problem or the study population you may use certain words that are difficult to measure as such and/or the understanding of which may vary from person to person. These words are called concepts. In order to measure them they need to be converted into indicators (not always) and then variables. Words like satisfaction, impact, young, old, happy are concepts as their understanding would vary from person to person.

Table 5.1 Examples of concepts and variables

Concepts	Variables
• Effectiveness	• Gender (male/female)
• Satisfaction	• Attitude
• Impact	• Age (x years, y months)
• Excellent	• Income ($ –– per year)
• High achiever	• Weight (–– kg)
• Self-esteem	• Height (–– cm)
• Rich	• Religion (Catholic, Protestant, Jewish, Muslim)
• Domestic violence	• etc.
• Extent and pattern of alcohol consumption	
• etc.	
– Subjective impression – No uniformity as to its understanding among different people – As such cannot be measured	– Measurable, though the degree of precision varies from scale to scale and from variable to variable (e.g. attitude – subjective, income – objective)

CONVERTING CONCEPTS INTO VARIABLES

If you are using a concept in your study, you need to consider its operationalisation – that is, how it will be measured. In most cases, to operationalise a concept you first need to go through the process of identifying indicators – a set of criteria reflective of the concept – which can then be converted into variables. The choice of indicators for a concept might vary with the researcher, but those selected must have a logical link with the concept. Some concepts, such as 'rich' (in terms of wealth), can easily be converted into indicators and then variables. For example, to decide objectively if a person is 'rich', one first needs to decide upon the indicators of wealth. Assume that we decide upon income and assets as the indicators. Income is already a variable since it can be measured in some unit of currency, say dollars; therefore, you do not need to convert this into a variable. Although the assets owned by an individual are indicators of his/her 'richness', they still belong to the category of concepts. You need to look further at the indicators of assets. For example, house, boat, car and investments are indicators of assets. Converting the value of each one into dollars will give the total value of the assets owned by a person. Next, fix a level, based upon available information on income distribution and an average level of assets owned by members of a community, which acts as the basis for classification. Then analyse the information on income and the total value of the assets to make a decision about whether the person should be classified as 'rich'. The operationalisation of other concepts, such as the 'effectiveness' or 'impact' of a programme, may prove more difficult. Table 5.2 shows some examples that will help you to understand the process of converting concepts into variables. Note that in these examples only some of the indicators have been picked up. Also, the values set for decision levels are arbitrary and have no empirical validity.

One of the main differences between quantitative and qualitative research studies is in the area of variables. In qualitative research, as it usually involves studying perceptions, beliefs or feelings, you do not make any attempt to establish uniformity in them across respondents and hence measurements and variables do not carry much significance. On the other hand, in quantitative studies, as the emphasis is on exploring commonalities in the study population, measurements and variables play an important role.

CHECKPOINT
Defining variables

TYPES OF VARIABLE

A variable can be classified in a number of ways. The classification developed here results from looking at variables in three different ways (see Figure 5.1):

→ the causal relationship;
→ the study design;
→ the unit of measurement.

From the viewpoint of causal relationship

In studies that attempt to investigate a causal relationship or association, four sets of variables may operate (see Figure 5.2):

→ variables that are responsible for *bringing about change* in a phenomenon, situation or circumstance;
→ *outcome* variables, which are the effects, impacts or consequences of a change variable;
→ variables which *affect or influence* the link between cause-and-effect variables; and
→ *connecting or linking variables*, which in certain situations are necessary to complete the relationship between cause-and-effect variables.

In research terminology, change variables are called independent variables, outcome/effect variables are called dependent variables, the unmeasured variables affecting the cause-and-effect relationship are called extraneous variables, and the variables that link a cause-and-effect relationship are called intervening variables. To give a little more detail:

1   **Independent variable** – the cause supposed to be responsible for bringing about change(s) in a phenomenon or situation.
2   **Dependent variable** – the outcome or change(s) brought about by introduction of an independent variable.

Independent variable: When examining causality in a study, there are four sets of variables that can operate. One of them is a variable that is responsible for bringing about change. This variable which is the cause of the changes in a phenomenon is called an independent variable. In the study of causality, the independent variable is the cause variable which is responsible for bringing about change in a phenomenon.

Dependent variable: When establishing causality through a study, the variable assumed to be the cause is called an independent variable and the variables in which it produces changes are called the dependent variables. A dependent variable is dependent upon the independent variable that is assumed to be responsible for changes in the dependent variable.

Extraneous variables: In studying causality, the dependent variable is the consequence of the change brought about by the independent variable. In everyday life there are many other variables that can affect the relationship between independent and dependent variables. These variables are called extraneous variables.

3 **Extraneous variable** – several other factors operating in a real-life situation may affect or effect changes in the dependent variable. These factors, not measured in the study, may increase or decrease the magnitude or strength of the relationship between independent and dependent variables.

4 **Intervening variable** – sometimes called the confounding variable (Grinnell 1988: 203), it links the independent and dependent variables. In certain situations the relationship between an independent and a dependent variable cannot be established without the intervention of another variable. The cause, or independent, variable will have the assumed effect only in the presence of an intervening variable.

Table 5.2   Converting concepts into variables

Concepts	Indicators	Variables	
		Variables	Decision level (working definitions)
Rich/poor	1 Income 2 Value of all assets	1 Total income per year 2 Total value of: home(s); car(s); boat; investments	Considered rich: 1 if income is > 200,000 p.a. 2 if total value of assets is > 2,000,000
High academic achievement	1 Performance in examinations 2 Performance in practical work/field placements 3 Performance in tutorial presentations 4 Overall performance, etc.	1 Marks in examinations 2 Marks in practical work/field placements 3 Marks in tutorial presentations 4 Overall marks	Considered high achiever: 1 if > 85% 2 if > 85% 3 if > 85% 4 if > 85%
Effectiveness (of a health programme)	1 Changes in the utilisation pattern of services 2 Changes in the morbidity pattern of the community 3 Changes in the illness episodes in a specific period 4 Changes in child mortality rates 5 Changes in the nutritional status of children (weight, height, illness episodes, etc.)	1 Increase or decrease in the number of patients per month 2 (a) Changes in the morbidity pattern (b) Changes in morbidity typology 3 Increase or decrease in the number of illness episodes in a month 4 Changes in age-specific death rate 5 Increase or decrease in the crude death rate in the community 6 Changes in the weight, height and illness episodes among children up to 5 years of age in the community	Considered effective if: 1 after a year, the number of patients increases by 25% 2 changes in the morbidity pattern are significant, as judged by a group of experts 3 after a year, the number of illness episodes falls by 30% 4 the crude death rate falls by 0.05 by the end of the year, or any change considered significant by a group of experts 5 there is a significant increase in weight and height and significant reduction in the illness episodes among children under 5 as judged by a group of experts

To explain this typology, let us consider some examples. Suppose you want to study the relationship between smoking and cancer. You assume that smoking is a cause of cancer. Studies have shown that there are many factors affecting this relationship, such as the number of cigarettes or the amount of tobacco smoked every day; the duration of smoking; the age of the smoker; dietary habits; and the amount of exercise taken by the individual. All of these factors may affect the extent to which smoking might cause cancer. These variables may either increase or decrease the magnitude of the relationship.

In this example the extent of smoking is the independent variable, incidence of cancer is the dependent variable, and all the variables that might affect this relationship, either positively or negatively, are extraneous variables. See Figure 5.3.

Let us take another example. Suppose you want to study the effects of a marriage counselling service on marital problems among clients of an agency providing such a service. Figure 5.4 shows the sets of variables that may operate in studying the relationship between counselling and marriage problems.

In studying this relationship, it is assumed that the counselling service will influence the extent of marital problems. Thus, the type of counselling service is the independent variable and the extent of marriage problems is the dependent variable. The magnitude or strength of this relationship can be affected, positively or negatively, by a number of other factors that are not the focus of the study. These extraneous variables might be the birth of a child; improvement in a couple's economic situation; the couple's motivation to change the situation; the involvement of another person; self-realisation; and pressure from relatives and friends. Extraneous variables that work both ways can increase or decrease the strength of the relationship.

The example in Figure 5.5 should help you to understand intervening variables. Suppose you want to study the relationship between fertility and mortality. Your aim is to explore what happens to fertility when mortality declines. The history of demographic transition has shown that a reduction in the fertility level follows a decline in the mortality level, though the time taken to attain the same level of reduction in fertility varies markedly from country to country. As such, there is no direct relationship between fertility and mortality. With the reduction in mortality, fertility will decline only if people attempt to limit their family size. History has shown that for a multiplicity of reasons (the discussion of which is beyond the scope of this book) people have used one method or another to control their fertility, resulting in lower fertility levels. It is thus the intervention of contraceptive methods that completes the relationship: the greater the use of contraceptives, the greater the decline in the fertility level, and the sooner the adoption of contraceptive methods by people, the sooner the decline. The extent of the use of contraceptives is also affected by a number of other factors, for example attitudes towards contraception, level of education, socioeconomic status and age, religion, and provision and quality of health services. These are classified as extraneous variables.

In this example, decline in mortality is assumed to be the cause of a reduction in fertility, hence the mortality level is the independent variable and fertility is the dependent variable. But this relationship will be completed only if another variable intervenes – that is, the use of contraceptives. A reduction in mortality (especially child mortality) increases family size, and an increase in family size creates a number of social, economic and psychological pressures on families, which in turn create attitudes favourable to a smaller family size. This change in attitudes is eventually operationalised in behaviour through the adoption of contraceptives. If people do not adopt methods of contraception, a change in mortality levels will not be reflected in fertility levels. The population explosion in developing countries is primarily due to lack of acceptance of contraceptives. The extent of the use of contraceptives determines the level of the decline in fertility. The extent of contraceptive adoption by a

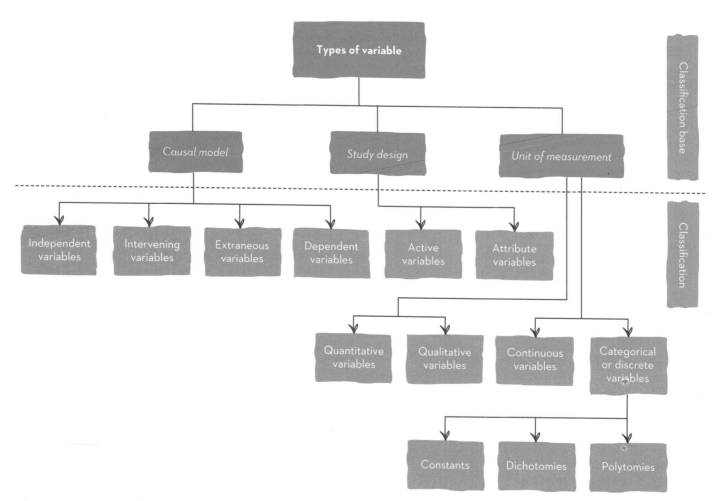

Figure 5.1   Types of variable

Note: Classification across a classification base is not mutually exclusive but classification within a classification base is. Within a study an independent variable can be an active variable, or a quantitative or a qualitative variable, and it can also be a continuous or a categorical variable, but it cannot be a dependent, an extraneous or an intervening variable.

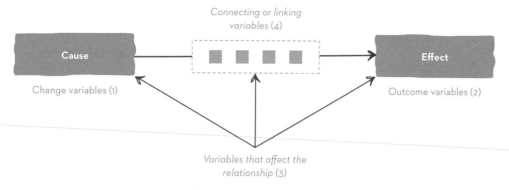

Figure 5.2   Types of variable in a causal relationship

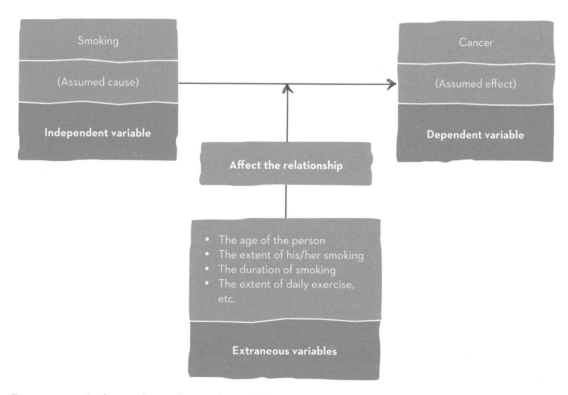

Figure 5.3   Independent, dependent and extraneous variables in a causal relationship

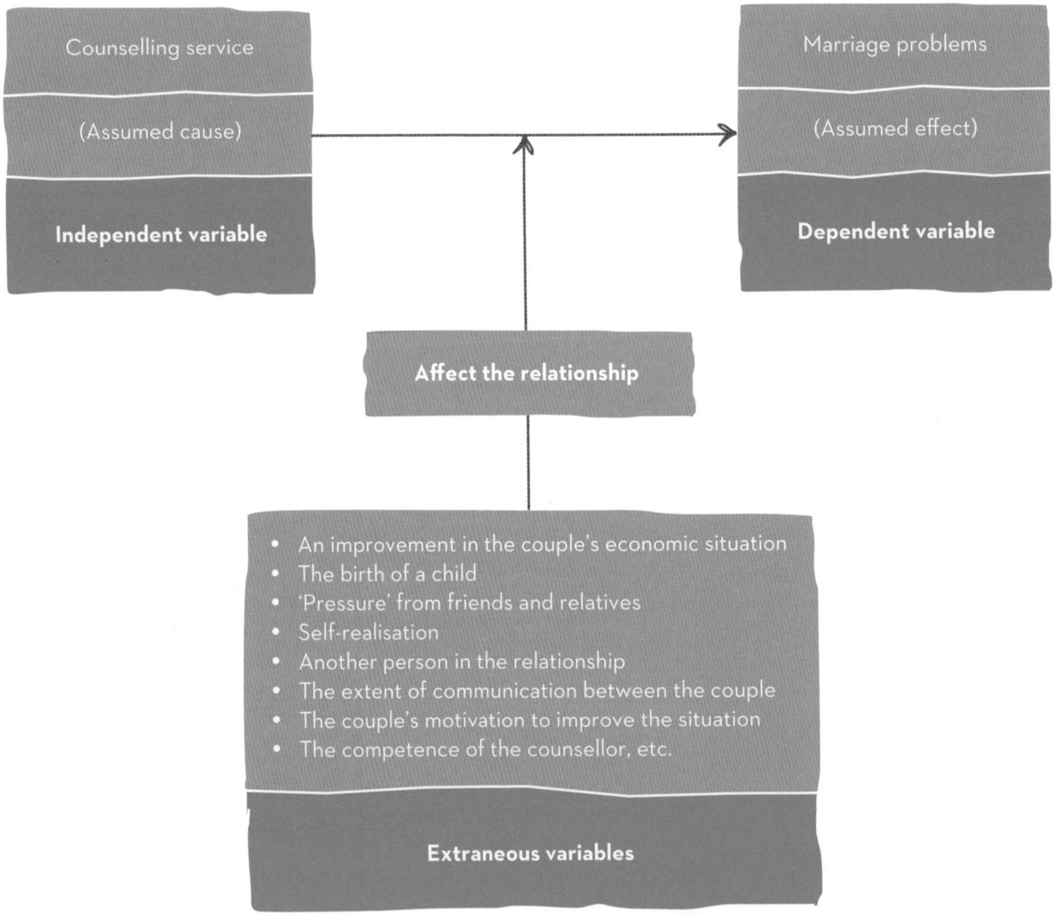
Counselling service
(Assumed cause)
Independent variable
Marriage problems
(Assumed effect)
Dependent variable
Affect the relationship
• An improvement in the couple's economic situation
• The birth of a child
• 'Pressure' from friends and relatives
• Self-realisation
• Another person in the relationship
• The extent of communication between the couple
• The couple's motivation to improve the situation
• The competence of the counsellor, etc.
Extraneous variables

Figure 5.4 Sets of variables in counselling and marriage problems

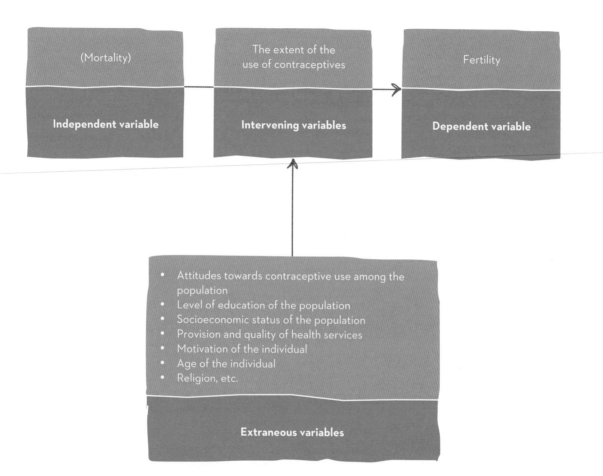

Figure 5.5   Independent, dependent, extraneous and intervening variables

CHECKPOINT
Types of variables

population is dependent upon a number of factors. As mentioned earlier, in this causal model, the fertility level is the dependent variable, the extent of contraceptive use is the intervening variable, the mortality level is the independent variable, and the unmeasured variables such as attitudes, education, age, religion and the quality of services are all extraneous variables. Without the intervening variable the relationship between the independent and dependent variables will not be complete.

From the viewpoint of the study design

A study that examines association or causation may be a controlled/contrived experiment, a quasi-experiment or an *ex post facto* or non-experimental study. In controlled experiments the independent (cause) variable may be introduced or manipulated either by the researcher or by someone else who is providing the service. In these situations there are two sets of variables (see Figure 5.6):

↝ Active variables – those variables that can be manipulated, changed or controlled.
↝ Attribute variables – those variables that cannot be manipulated, changed or controlled, and that reflect the characteristics of the study population, for example age, gender, education and income.

Suppose a study is designed to measure the relative effectiveness of three teaching models (A, B and C). The structure and contents of these models could vary and any model might be tested on any population group. The contents, structure and testability of a model on a population group may also vary from researcher to researcher. On the other hand, a researcher has no control over characteristics of the student population such as their age, gender or motivation to study. These characteristics of the study population are called attribute variables. However, a researcher does have the ability to control and/or change the teaching models. S/he can decide what constitutes a teaching model and on which group of the student population it should be tested (if randomisation is not used).

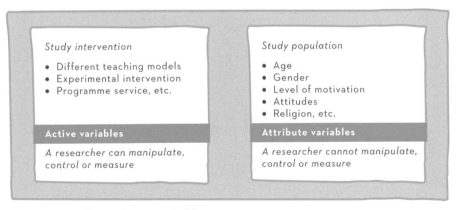

Figure 5.6   Active and attribute variables

From the viewpoint of the unit of measurement

From the viewpoint of the unit of measurement, there are two ways of categorising variables:

⤳ whether the unit of measurement is categorical (as in nominal and ordinal scales) or continuous in nature (as in interval and ratio scales);

⤳ whether it is qualitative (as in nominal and ordinal scales) or quantitative in nature (as in interval and ratio scales).

On the whole there is very little difference between categorical and qualitative, and between continuous and quantitative, variables. The slight difference between them is explained below.

Categorical variables are measured on nominal or ordinal measurement scales, whereas for continuous variables the measurements are made on either an interval or a ratio scale. There are three types of categorical variables:

⤳ constant variable – has only one category or value, for example taxi, tree and water;

⤳ dichotomous variable – has only two categories, as in male/female, yes/no, good/bad, heads/tails, up/down and rich/poor;

⤳ polytomous variable – can be divided into more than two categories, for example religion (Christian, Muslim, Hindu); political parties (Labour, Liberal, Conservative); and attitudes (strongly favourable, favourable, uncertain, unfavourable, strongly unfavourable).

Continuous variables, on the other hand, have continuity in their measurement, for example age, income and attitude score. They can take any value on the scale on which they are measured. Age can be measured in years, months and days. Similarly, income can be measured in dollars and cents.

In many ways qualitative variables are similar to categorical variables as both use either nominal or ordinal measurement scales. However, there are some differences. For example, it is possible to develop categories on the basis of measurements made on a continuous scale, such as measuring the income of a population in dollars and cents and then developing categories such as 'low', 'middle' and 'high' income. The measurement of income in dollars and cents is classified as the measurement of a continuous variable, whereas its subjective measurement in categories such as 'low', middle' and 'high' groups is a qualitative variable.

Although this distinction exists, for most practical purposes there is no real difference between categorical and qualitative variables or between continuous and quantitative variables. Table 5.3 shows similarities and differences among the various types of variable.

For a beginner it is important to understand that the way a variable is measured determines the type of analysis that can be performed, the statistical procedures that can be applied to the data, the way the data can be interpreted and the findings that can be communicated. You may not realise at the beginning that the style of your report is entirely dependent upon the way the different variables have been measured – that is, the way a question has been asked and its response recorded. The way you measure the variables in your study determines whether a study is 'qualitative' or 'quantitative' in nature. It is therefore important to know about the measurement scales for variables.

Categorical variables: Variables where the unit of measurement is in the form of categories. On the basis of presence or absence of a characteristic, a variable is placed in a category. There is no measurement of the characteristics as such. In terms of measurement scales such variables are measured on nominal or ordinal scales. Rich/poor, high/low, hot/cold are examples of categorical variables.

Continuous variables: These are variables that have continuity in their unit of measurement; for example, age, income and attitude score. They can take on any value of the scale on which they are measured. Age can be measured in years, months and days. Similarly, income can be measured in dollars and cents.

Constant variable: When a variable can have only one category or value, for example taxi, tree and water, it is known as a constant variable.

Dichotomous variable: A variable which can have only two categories (e.g. male/female, yes/no, good/bad, head/tail, up/down and rich/poor).

Polytomous variable: A variable consisting of more than two categories, for example religion (Christian, Muslim, Hindu), political parties (Labour, Liberal, Conservative), and attitudes (strongly in favour, in favour, uncertain, against, strongly against).

Table 5.3 Categorical/continuous and quantitative/qualitative variables

Categorical			Continuous	Qualitative	Quantitative
Constant	Dichotomous	Polytomous			
• water • tree • taxi	• yes/no • good/bad • rich/poor • day/night • male/female • hot/cold	**Attitudes** • strongly agree • agree • uncertain • disagree • strongly disagree **Political parties** • Labour • Liberal • Conservative **Age**[a] • old • child • young **Income**[b] • high • middle • low	Income ($) Age (years) Weight (kg)	**Gender** • female • male **Educational level** • high • average • low **Age**[a] • old • young • child **Income** • high • middle • low **Temperature**[c] • hot • cold	Educational level: no. of years completed Age:[a] ____years/ months Income:[b] $ per year Temperature:[c] _____°C or °F

[a] Can be classified in qualitative categories, e.g. old, young, child; or quantitatively on a continuous scale, e.g. in years, months and days.
[b] Can be measured quantitatively in dollars and cents as well as qualitatively in categories such as high, middle and low.
[c] Can be measured quantitatively in degrees on different scales (Celsius, Fahrenheit) or in qualitative categories such as hot and cold.

TYPES OF MEASUREMENT SCALE

> The frame into which we wish to make everything fit is one of our own construction; but we do not construct it at random, we construct it by measurement so to speak; and that is why we can fit the facts into it without altering their essential qualities. (Poincaré 1952: xxv)

Measurement is central to any enquiry. In addition to the ideology and philosophy that underpin each mode of enquiry, the most significant difference between qualitative and quantitative research studies is in the types of measurement used in collecting information from the respondents. Qualitative research mostly uses descriptive statements to seek answers to the research questions, whereas in quantitative research these answers are usually sought on one of the measurement scales (nominal, ordinal, interval or ratio). If information is not collected using one of the scales at the time of data collection, it is transformed into variables by using these measurement scales at the time of analysis. Measurement on these scales could be either in the form of qualitative categories or through a precise unit of measurement. Those scales which have a unit of measurement (interval and ratio) are considered to be more refined, objective and accurate. On the other hand, nominal and ordinal scales are considered subjective and hence not as accurate as they do not have a unit of measurement per se. The greater the refinement in the unit of measurement of a variable, the greater the confidence placed in the findings by others, other things being equal. One of the main differences between the physical and the social sciences is the units of measurement used and the degree of importance attached to them. In the physical sciences measurements have to be absolutely accurate and precise, whereas in the social sciences they may vary from the very subjective to the very quantifiable. Within the social sciences the emphasis on precision in measurement varies markedly from one discipline to another. An anthropologist normally uses very 'subjective' units of measurement, whereas an economist or an epidemiologist emphasises 'objective' measurement.

There are two main classification systems in the social sciences for measuring different types of variable. One was developed by S. S. Stevens (in 1946; see Stevens 1951) and the other by Duncan (1984). According to Smith (1991: 72), 'Duncan (1984) has enumerated, in increasing order of interest to scientists, five types of measurement: nominal classification, ordinal scaling, cardinal scaling, ratio scaling, and probability scaling'. Duncan (1984: viii) writes about Stevens's classification as follows:

> The theory of scale types proposed in 1946 by S. S. Stevens focused on nominal, ordinal, interval, and ratio scales of measurement. Some of his examples of these types – notably those concerning psychological test scores – are misleading.

However, Bailey (1978: 52) considers that 'S. S. Stevens constructed a widely adopted classification of levels of measurement'. As this book is written for the beginner and as Stevens's classification is simpler, this is what is used for discussion in this chapter. Stevens classified the different types of measurement scale into four categories:

- nominal or classificatory scale;
- ordinal or ranking scale;
- interval scale;
- ratio scale.

Table 5.4 summarises the characteristics of the four scales.

The nominal or classificatory scale

A nominal scale enables the classification of individuals, objects or responses based on a common/shared property or characteristic. Such individuals, objects or responses are divided into a number of subgroups in such a way that each member of the subgroup shares a common characteristic or a property. A variable measured on a nominal scale may have **one**, two or more subcategories depending upon the extent of variation. For example,

Table 5.4   Characteristics and examples of the four measurement scales

Measurement scale	Examples	Characteristics of the scale
Nominal or classificatory	Tree, house, taxi, etc. Gender: male/female Attitude: agree/disagree Political parties • Labour • Liberal • Democrats • Greens Psychiatric disorders • Schizophrenic • Paranoid • Manic-depressive, etc. Religions • Christian • Islam • Hindu, etc.	Each subgroup has a characteristic/property which is common to all classified within that subgroup
Ordinal or ranking	Income • above average • average • below average Socioeconomic status • upper • middle • lower Attitudes • strongly agree • agree • uncertain • disagree • disagree Likert attitudinal scale (see Chapter 10)	This has the characteristics of a nominal scale, e.g. individuals, groups, characteristics classified under a subgroup have a common characteristic PLUS • Subgroups have a relationship with one another • They are arranged in relation to their respective magnitude either in ascending or descending order
Interval	Temperature • Celsius • Fahrenheit Thurstone attitudinal scale (see Chapter 10):	This has all the characteristics of an ordinal scale (which also includes a nominal scale) PLUS • It has a unit of measurement with an arbitrary starting and terminating point
Ratio	Height: cm Income: $ Age: years/months Weight: kg Attitudinal score: Guttman scale (see Chapter 10)	This has all the properties of an interval scale PLUS • It has a fixed starting point at zero

'water' and 'taxi' have only **one** subgroup, whereas the variable 'gender' can be classified into two subcategories: male and female. Political parties in Australia can similarly be classified into four main subcategories: Labour, Liberal, Democrats and Greens. Those who identify themselves, either by membership or belief, as belonging to the Labour Party are classified as 'Labour', those identifying with the Liberals are classified as 'Liberal', and so on. The name chosen for a subcategory is notional, but for effective communication it is best to choose something that describes the characteristic of the subcategory.

Classification by means of a nominal scale ensures that individuals, objects or responses within the same subgroup have a common characteristic or property as the basis of classification. The sequence in which subgroups are listed makes no difference as there is no order relationship among subgroups.

The ordinal or ranking scale

An ordinal scale has all the properties of a nominal scale – categorising individuals, objects, responses or a property into subgroups on the basis of a common characteristic – but also ranks the subgroups in a certain order. They are arranged in either ascending or descending order according to the extent to which a subcategory reflects the magnitude of variation in the variable. For example, income can be measured either quantitatively (in dollars and cents) or qualitatively, using subcategories: 'above average', 'average' and 'below average'. (These categories can also be developed on the basis of quantitative measures, for example below $10 000 is defined as below average, $10 000–$25 000 as average, and above $25 000 as above average.) The subcategory 'above average' indicates that people so grouped have more income than people in the 'average' category, and people in the 'average' category have more income than those in the 'below average' category. These subcategories of income are related to one another in terms of the magnitude of people's income, but the magnitude itself is not quantifiable, and hence the difference between 'above average' and 'average' or between 'average' and 'below average' subcategories cannot be ascertained. The same is true for other variables such as socioeconomic status and attitudes measured on an ordinal scale.

To summarise, an ordinal scale has all the properties/characteristics of a nominal scale, in addition to its own. Subcategories are arranged in order of the magnitude of the property/characteristic. Also, the 'distance' between the subcategories is not equal as there is no quantitative unit of measurement.

The interval scale

An interval scale has all the characteristics of an ordinal scale; that is, individuals or responses belonging to a subcategory have a common characteristic and the subcategories are arranged in an ascending or descending order. In addition, an interval scale uses a unit of measurement that enables the individuals or responses to be placed at equally spaced intervals in relation to the spread of the variable. This scale has a **starting** and a terminating point and is divided into equally spaced units/intervals. The starting and terminating points and the number of units/intervals between them are arbitrary and vary from scale to scale.

Celsius and Fahrenheit scales are examples of an interval scale. In the **Celsius** system the starting point (considered as the freezing point) is 0°C and the terminating point (considered as the boiling point) is 100°C. The gap between the freezing and boiling points is divided into 100 equally spaced intervals, known as degrees. In the Fahrenheit system the freezing point is 32°F and the boiling point is 212°F, and the gap between the two points is divided into 180 equally spaced intervals. Each degree or interval is a measurement of temperature – the higher the degree, the higher the temperature. As the starting and terminating points are arbitrary, they are not absolute; that is, you cannot say that 60°C is twice as hot as 30°C or 30°F is three times hotter than 10°F. This means that while no mathematical operation can be performed on the readings, it can be performed on the differences between readings. For example, if the difference in temperature between two objects, A and B, is 15°C and the difference in temperature between two other objects, C and D, is 45°C, you can say that the difference in temperature between C and D is three times as great as that between A and B. An attitude towards an issue measured on the Thurstone scale is similar. However, the Likert scale does not measure the absolute intensity of the attitude but simply measures it in relation to another person.

To summarise, the interval scale is relative; that is, it plots the position of individuals or responses in relation to one another with respect to the magnitude of the measurement variable. Hence, an interval scale has all the properties of an ordinal scale, and it has a unit of measurement with an arbitrary starting and terminating point.

The ratio scale

CHECKPOINT
*Measurement
scales*

A ratio scale has all the properties of nominal, ordinal and interval scales and it also has a starting point fixed at zero. Therefore, it is an absolute scale – the difference between the intervals is always measured from a zero point. This means the ratio scale can be used for mathematical operations. The measurement of income, age, height and weight are examples of this scale. A person who is 40 years of age is twice as old as a 20-year-old. A person earning $60 000 per year earns three times the salary of a person earning $20 000.

SUMMARY

The understanding and interpretation of a concept or a perception may vary from respondent to respondent, hence its measurement may not be consistent. A variable has some basis of classification and hence there is far less inconsistency in its meaning and understanding. Concepts are mental perceptions, whereas variables are measurable either subjectively or objectively on one of the measurement scales. When you convert a concept into a variable you classify it on the basis of measurement into categories, thereby minimising the inherent variability in understanding. When you are unable to measure a concept directly, you need first to convert it into indicators and then into variables.

The way the required information is collected in quantitative and qualitative research is the most significant difference between them. Qualitative research mostly uses descriptive or narrative statements as the 'units of measurement', whereas quantitative research places greater emphasis of measuring responses on one of the four measurement scales. Though qualitative research places emphasis on descriptive statements in data collection, in some cases these statements are classified at the time of analysis into categories on the basis of the main themes they communicate. However, there are times when you will prefer to use verbatim descriptions and narrations to build your logic and arguments.

Knowledge of the different types of variables and the way they are measured plays a crucial role in quantitative research. Variables are important in bringing clarity and specificity to the conceptualisation of a research problem, to the formulation of hypotheses and to the development of a research instrument. They affect how the data can be analysed, what statistical tests can be applied to the data, what interpretations can be made, how the data can be presented and what conclusions can be drawn. The way you ask a question determines its categorisation on a measurement scale, which in turn affects how the data can be analysed, what statistical tests can be applied to the data, what interpretations can be made, how the data can be presented and what conclusions can be drawn. Also, the way variables are measured at the data collection stage to a great extent determines whether a study is considered to be predominantly 'qualitative' or 'quantitative' in nature.

It is important for a beginner to understand the different ways in which a variable can be measured and the implications of this for the study. A variable can be classified from three perspectives that are not mutually exclusive: causal relationship, design of the study and unit of measurement. From the perspective of causality a variable can be classified into one of four categories: independent, dependent, extraneous and intervening. From the viewpoint of study design, there are two categories of variable: active and attribute. If we examine a variable from the perspective of the unit of measurement, it can be classified into categorical and continuous or qualitative and quantitative.

There are four measurement scales used in the social sciences: nominal, ordinal, interval and ratio. Any concept that can be measured on these scales is called a variable. Measurement scales enable highly subjective responses, as well as responses that can be measured with extreme precision, to be categorised. The choice of measuring a variable on a measurement scale is dependent upon the purpose of your study and the way you want to communicate the findings to readers.

Now that you have read the full chapter...

CHECK YOUR UNDERSTANDING

- ☐ Do you understand the meaning and application of all of the keywords at the start of the chapter? If not, visit the online resources and use the glossary flashcards to get to grips with their definitions.

- ☐ What is the difference between extraneous and intervening variables?

- ☐ What are the different types of measurement scale? What purpose do they serve in a research study?

- ☐ Develop the typology of variables from different perspectives.

- ☐ Critically examine the typology of variables developed in this chapter. What changes would you like to propose?

APPLY IT TO YOUR OWN PROJECT

☐ Identify a concept and a variable in your own research and explain the differences between them.

☐ Imagine that you have been asked to evaluate your lecturer. Determine which aspects of teaching you would consider important and develop a set of indicators that might reflect these.

☐ Suppose you have chosen to research a concept that is difficult to operationalize. How might you go about developing a set of indicators to determine variation surrounding this concept? Consider, for example, if you were researching the levels of self-esteem in a group of individuals.

122

CONFUSED?

THE ONLINE RESOURCES ARE HERE TO HELP YOU

 https://study.sagepub.com/kumar5e

CHECKPOINT: What is a variable? Read this encyclopaedia entry.

CHECKPOINT: What are the different types of variables, and how do they compare? Watch this video.

CHECKPOINT: What are the four types of measurement scales, and how do they relate? Read this encyclopaedia entry.

NEED MORE GENERAL SUPPORT?

Get up to speed on key terms with *glossary flashcards* and test yourself on important concepts with *multiple choice questions*.

UP FOR A CHALLENGE?

THE ONLINE RESOURCES ARE HERE TO INSPIRE YOU

→ https://study.sagepub.com/kumar5e ←

CHECKPOINT: What do variables look like in real, published research? Visit this website.

CHECKPOINT: What is an example of research that is not examing a causal relationship? Watch this video.

CHECKPOINT: Why is it important to choose the right measurement scale for your research question or the type of data you collect? Visit this website.

READY TO WORK ON YOUR OWN PROJECT?

Start building a portfolio of your ideas with the exercise workbook and get support tailored to your specific assignment with the assessment toolkit.

CONSTRUCTING HYPOTHESES

- step one -
FORMULATING A RESEARCH PROBLEM

Reviewing the literature   54

Formulating a research problem   76

Identifying variables   100

→ Constructing hypotheses   126

CONFUSED?
UP FOR A
CHALLENGE?

OR
NEED HELP
WITH YOUR
ASSIGNMENT?

VISIT
https://study.sagepub.
com/kumar5e for
resources specially
designed to support
you and all your
research needs.

ESSENTIAL TERMS

You should be able to define these by the end of the chapter

- alternative hypotheses
- hypothesis
- null hypothesis
- research hypothesis

BONUS TERMS

You will learn more about these by the end of the chapter

- hunch
- hypothesis of point
- prevalence
- operationalisable
- Type I error
- Type II error
- Unidimensional
- valid

LEARNING OBJECTIVES

At the end of this chapter, you will be able to:

- Define what a hypothesis is
- Understand the functions of a hypothesis in your research
- Describe how hypotheses are tested
- Formulate a hypothesis
- Discuss different types of hypotheses and their applications
- Identify how errors in the testing of a hypothesis can occur
- Understand the use of hypotheses in qualitative research

Almost every great step [in the history of science] has been made by the 'anticipation of nature', that is, by the invention of hypotheses which, though verifiable, often had very little foundation to start with.
(T.H. Huxley, cited in Cohen & Nagel 1966: 197)

THE DEFINITION OF A HYPOTHESIS

Hypothesis: A hypothesis is a hunch, assumption, suspicion, assertion or idea about a phenomenon, relationship or situation, the reality or truth of which you do not know, and you set up your study to find this truth. A researcher refers to these assumptions, assertions, statements or hunches as hypotheses and they become the basis of an enquiry. In most studies the hypothesis will be based either upon previous studies or on your own or someone else's observations.

The second important consideration in the formulation of a research problem in quantitative research is the construction of a hypothesis. Hypotheses bring clarity, specificity and focus to a research problem, but are not essential for a study. You can conduct a valid investigation without constructing a single formal hypothesis. On the other hand, within the context of a research study, you can construct as many hypotheses as you consider to be appropriate. Some believe that one must formulate a hypothesis to undertake an investigation; however, the author does not hold this opinion. Hypotheses primarily arise from a set of 'hunches' that are tested through a study, and one can conduct a perfectly valid study without having these hunches or speculations. However, in epidemiological studies, to narrow the field of investigation, it is important to formulate hypotheses. The importance of hypotheses lies in their ability to bring direction, specificity and focus to a research study. They tell a researcher what specific information to collect, and thereby provide greater focus.

Let us imagine you are at the races and you place a bet. You bet on a hunch that a particular horse will win. Only after the race will you know if your hunch was right. To take another example, suppose you have a hunch that there are more smokers than non-smokers in your class. To test your hunch, you ask either all or just some of the class if they are smokers. You can then conclude whether your hunch was right or wrong.

Now let us take a slightly different example. Suppose you work in the area of public health. Your clinical impression is that a higher rate of a particular condition prevails among people coming from a specific population subgroup. You want to find out first whether or not your hunch is right, and second what are the probable causes of this condition. There could be many causes. To explore every conceivable possibility would require an enormous amount of time and resources. Hence, to narrow the choice, based on your knowledge of the field, you could identify what you assume to be the most probable cause. You could then design a study to collect the information needed to verify your hunch. If on verification you were able to conclude that there is a prevalence of the assumed condition in the population subgroup and that the assumed cause really is the reason, your assumptions would be proved right.

In these examples, you started with a superficial hunch or assumption. In one case (horse racing) you waited for the event to take place, and in the other two instances you designed a study to assess the validity of your assumption, and only after careful investigation did you arrive at a conclusion about the validity of your assumptions.

Hypotheses are based upon similar logic. As a researcher you *do not know* about a phenomenon, a situation, the prevalence of a condition in a population or the outcome of a programme, but you do have a hunch to form the basis of certain *assumptions* or guesses. You test these by collecting the information that will enable you to conclude whether or not your hunch was right. The verification process can have one of three outcomes.

Your hunch may prove to be right, partially right or wrong. Without this process of verification, you cannot conclude anything about the validity of your assumption.

Hence, a hypothesis is a hunch, assumption, suspicion, assertion or an idea about a phenomenon, relationship or situation, the reality or truth of which you do not know. A researcher refers to these assumptions, assertions, statements or hunches as hypotheses, and they become the basis of an enquiry. In most studies the hypothesis will be based upon either previous studies or your own or someone else's observations.

There are many definitions of a hypothesis. According to Kerlinger (1986: 17), 'A hypothesis is a conjectural statement of the relationship between two or more variables'. *Webster's Third New International Dictionary* (1976) defines a hypothesis as:

> a proposition, condition, or principle which is assumed, perhaps without belief, in order to draw out its logical consequences and by this method to test its accord with facts which are known or may be determined.

Black and Champion (1976: 126) define a hypothesis as 'a tentative statement about something, the validity of which is usually unknown'. In another definition, Bailey (1978: 35) defines a hypothesis as:

> a proposition that is stated in a testable form and that predicts a particular relationship between two (or more) variables. In other words, if we think that a relationship exists, we first state it as a hypothesis and then test the hypothesis in the field.

According to Grinnell (1988: 200):

> A hypothesis is written in such a way that it can be proven or disproven by valid and reliable data – it is in order to obtain these data that we perform our study.

From the above definitions it is apparent that a hypothesis has certain characteristics:

1   It is a tentative proposition.
2   Its validity is unknown.
3   In most cases, it specifies a relationship between two or more variables.

THE FUNCTIONS OF A HYPOTHESIS

While some researchers believe that to conduct a study requires a hypothesis, having a hypothesis is not essential, as already mentioned. However, a hypothesis is important in terms of bringing clarity to the research problem. Specifically, a hypothesis serves the following functions:

The formulation of a hypothesis forces you to precisely specify what you want to find out about, thus bringing specificity and clarity to your study.

The specificity and clarity needed to construct a hypothesis ensure you only collect the information you need, thereby providing focus to the study. This also enhances the validity of your study as it ensures you are measuring what you set out to measure.

As it provides a focus, the construction of a hypothesis enhances objectivity in a study.

The testing of a hypothesis enables you to specifically conclude what is true or what is false, thus enabling you to contribute towards theory formulation.

THE TESTING OF A HYPOTHESIS

To test a hypothesis you need to go through a process that comprises three phases: (1) constructing the hypothesis; (2) gathering appropriate evidence; and (3) analysing evidence to draw conclusions as to the validity of the hypothesis. Figure 6.1 shows this process diagrammatically. It is only after analysing the evidence that you can conclude whether your hunch or hypothesis was true or false. Conventionally, when drawing your conclusion about a hypothesis, you specifically make a statement about the correctness or otherwise of a hypothesis in the form of 'the hypothesis is **true**' or 'the hypothesis is false'. It is therefore imperative that you formulate your hypotheses clearly, precisely and in a form that is testable. In arriving at a conclusion about the validity of your hypothesis, the way you collect your evidence is of central importance and it is therefore essential that your study design, sample, data collection method(s), data analysis and conclusions, and communication of the conclusions be valid, appropriate and free from any bias. Testing and drawing conclusions about the validity of a hypothesis become meaningless if the study design, sampling, methods of data collection, etc. used in testing the hypothesis are inappropriate. You need to be certain about the appropriateness of the whole research process when testing a hypothesis.

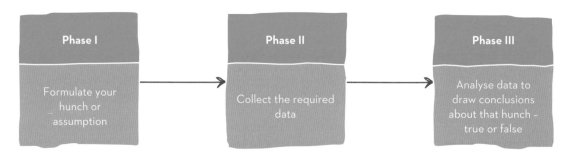

Figure 6.1   The process of testing a hypothesis

THE CHARACTERISTICS OF A HYPOTHESIS

There are a number of considerations to keep in mind when constructing a hypothesis, as they are important for valid verification. The wording of a hypothesis therefore must have certain attributes that make it easier for you to ascertain its validity.

First, a hypothesis should be *simple*, *specific* and *conceptually clear*. There is no place for ambiguity in the construction of a hypothesis, as ambiguity will make the verification of your hypothesis almost impossible. It should be 'unidimensional' – that is, it should test only one relationship or hunch at a time. To be able to develop a good hypothesis you must be familiar with the subject area (the literature review is of immense help). The more insight you have into a problem, the easier it is to construct a hypothesis. For example:

The average age of the male students in this class is higher than that of the female students.

The above hypothesis is clear, specific and easy to test. It tells you what you are attempting to compare (average age of this class), which population groups are being compared (female and male students), and what you want to explore (whether male students have higher average age).

Let us take another example:

Suicide rates vary inversely with social cohesion. (Black & Champion 1976: 126)

This hypothesis is clear and specific, but a lot more difficult to test. There are three aspects of this hypothesis: 'suicide rates'; 'vary inversely', which stipulates the direction of the relationship; and 'social cohesion'. To find out the suicide rates and to establish whether the relationship is inverse or otherwise are comparatively easy, but to ascertain social cohesion is a lot more difficult. What determines social cohesion? How can it be measured? This problem makes it more difficult to test this hypothesis.

Second, a hypothesis should be *capable of verification*. Methods and techniques must be available for data collection and analysis. There is no point in formulating a hypothesis if it cannot be subjected to verification because there are no techniques to verify it. However, this does not necessarily mean that you should not formulate a hypothesis for which there are no methods of verification. You might, in the process of doing your research, develop new techniques to verify it.

Third, a hypothesis should be *related to the existing body of knowledge*. It is important that your hypothesis emerges from the existing body of knowledge, and that it adds to it, as this is an important function of research. This can only be achieved if the hypothesis has its roots in the existing body of knowledge.

Finally, a hypothesis should be *operationalisable*. This means that it can be expressed in terms that can be measured. If it cannot be measured, it cannot be tested, and hence no conclusions can be drawn.

TYPES OF HYPOTHESIS

Theoretically there should be only one type of hypothesis, that is the research hypothesis – the basis of your investigation. However, because of the conventions in scientific enquiry and because of the wording used in the construction of a hypothesis, hypotheses can be classified into several types. Broadly, there are two categories of hypothesis:

1   research hypotheses;

2   alternative hypotheses.

The formulation of an alternative hypothesis is a convention in scientific circles. Its main function is to explicitly specify the relationship that will be considered as true in case the research hypothesis proves to be wrong. In a way, an alternative hypothesis is the opposite of the research hypothesis. Conventionally, a null hypothesis, or hypothesis of no difference, is formulated as an alternative hypothesis.

Let us take an example. Suppose you want to test the effect that different combinations of maternal and child health services (MCH) and nutritional supplements (NS) have on the infant mortality rate. To test this, you adopt a two-by-two factorial experimental design (see Figure 6.2). Within the framework of this study you can formulate a hypothesis in several ways. For example:

1   There will be no difference in the level of infant mortality among the different treatment modalities (Null hypothesis usually written as H_o).

2   The MCH and NS treatment groups will register a greater decline in infant mortality than the MCH-only treatment group, the NS-only treatment group or the control group.

3   Infant mortality in the MCH treatment group will reach a level of 30 per 1000 over 5 years.

4   Decline in the infant mortality rate will be three times greater in the MCH treatment group than in the NS group only over 5 years.

Let us take another example. Suppose you want to study the smoking pattern in a community in relation to gender differentials. The following hypotheses could be **constructed**:

1   There is no significant difference in the proportion of male and female smokers in the study population.

2   A greater proportion of females than males are smokers in the study population.

3   A total of 60 per cent of females and 30 per cent of males in the study population are smokers.

4   There are twice as many female smokers as male smokers in the study population.

In both sets of examples, the way the first hypothesis has been formulated indicates that there is no difference either in the extent of the impact of different treatment modalities on the infant mortality rate or in the proportion of male and female smokers. When you construct a hypothesis stipulating that there is no difference between two

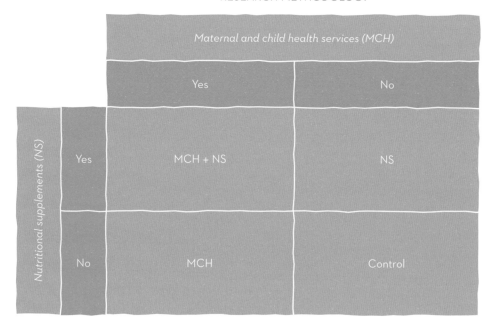

Figure 6.2   Two-by-two factorial experiment to study the relationship between MCH, NS and infant mortality

situations, groups, outcomes, or the prevalence of a condition or phenomenon, this is called a null hypothesis and is usually written as H_o.

The second hypothesis in each example implies that there is a difference either in the extent of the impact of different treatment modalities on infant mortality or in the proportion of male and female smokers among the population, though the **extent** of the difference is not specified. A hypothesis in which a researcher stipulates that there will be a difference but does not specify its magnitude is called a hypothesis of difference.

A researcher may have enough knowledge about the smoking behaviour of the community or the treatment programme and its likely outcomes to speculate about the exact prevalence of the situation or the outcome of a treatment programme in quantitative units. Examine the third hypothesis in both sets of examples: the level of infant mortality is 30 per 1000 and the proportion of female and male smokers is 60 and 30 per cent, respectively. This type of hypothesis is known as a hypothesis of point-prevalence.

CHECKPOINT
Alternative and null hypotheses

Null hypothesis: A hypothesis stipulating that there is no difference between two situations, groups, outcomes, or the prevalence of a condition or phenomenon; it is usually written as Ho.

Hypothesis of difference: A hypothesis in which a researcher stipulates that there will be a difference but does not specify its magnitude.

Hypothesis of point-prevalence: There are times when a researcher has enough knowledge about a phenomenon that he/she is studying and is confident about speculating almost the exact prevalence of the situation or the outcome in quantitative units. This type of hypothesis is known as a hypothesis of point-prevalence.

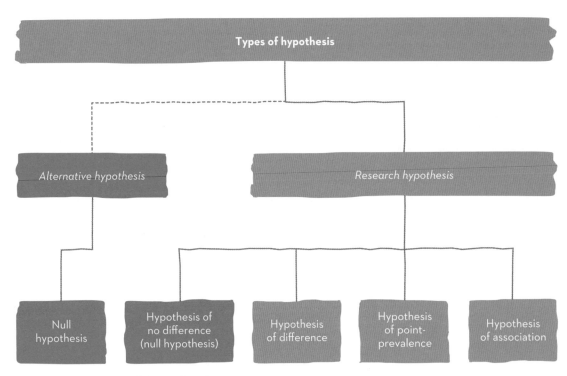

Figure 6.3   Types of hypothesis

The fourth hypothesis in both sets of examples posits a relationship between the impact of different combinations of MCH and NS programmes on the dependent variable (infant mortality) or the relationship between the prevalence of a phenomenon (smoking) among different populations (male and female). This type of hypothesis stipulates the extent of the relationship in terms of the effect of different treatment groups on the dependent variable ('three times greater in the MCH treatment group than in the NS group over 5 years') or the prevalence of a phenomenon in different population groups ('twice as many female as male smokers'). This type of hypothesis is called a hypothesis of association.

Note that in Figure 6.3 the null hypothesis is also classified as a hypothesis of no difference under 'research hypothesis'. Any type of hypothesis, including a null hypothesis, can become the basis of an enquiry. When a null hypothesis becomes the basis of an investigation, it becomes a research hypothesis.

Hypothesis of association: When as a researcher you have sufficient knowledge about a situation or phenomenon and are in a position to stipulate the extent of the relationship between two variables and formulate a hunch that reflects the magnitude of the relationship, such a hypothesis formulation is known as a hypothesis of association.

ERRORS IN TESTING A HYPOTHESIS

As already mentioned, a hypothesis is an assumption that may prove to be either correct or incorrect. It is possible to arrive at an incorrect conclusion about a hypothesis for a variety of reasons. Incorrect conclusions about the validity of a hypothesis may be drawn if:

CHECKPOINT
Errors in hypothesis testing

→ the study design selected is faulty;
→ the sampling procedure adopted is faulty;
→ the method of data collection is inaccurate;
→ the analysis is wrong;
→ the statistical procedures applied are inappropriate; or
→ the conclusions drawn are incorrect.

Any, some or all of these aspects of the research process could be responsible for the inadvertent introduction of error in your study, making conclusions misleading. Hence, in the testing of a hypothesis there is always the possibility of errors attributable to the reasons identified above. Figure 6.4 shows the types of error that can result in the testing of a hypothesis.

Hence, in drawing conclusions about a hypothesis, two types of error can occur:

→ *Rejection* of a null hypothesis when it is true. This is known as a Type I error.
→ *Acceptance* of a null hypothesis when it is false. This is known as a Type II error.

Type I error: In testing a hypothesis, for many reasons you may sometimes commit a mistake and draw the wrong conclusion with respect to the validity of your hypothesis. If you reject a null hypothesis when it is true and you should not have rejected it, this is called a Type I error.

Type II error: In testing a hypothesis, for many reasons you may sometimes commit a mistake and draw the wrong conclusion in terms of the validity of your hypothesis. If you accept a null hypothesis when it is false and you should not have accepted it, this is called a Type II error.

HYPOTHESES IN QUALITATIVE RESEARCH

One of the differences between qualitative and quantitative research is around the importance attached to and the extent of use of hypotheses when undertaking a study. As qualitative studies are characterised by an

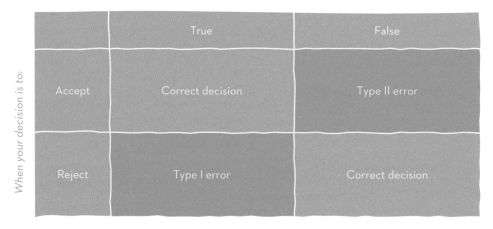

Figure 6.4   Type I and Type II errors in testing a hypothesis

emphasis on describing, understanding and exploring phenomena using categorical and subjective measurement procedures, construction of hypotheses is neither greatly advocated nor significantly practised. In addition, as the degree of specificity needed to test a hypothesis is deliberately not adhered to in qualitative research, the testing of a hypothesis becomes difficult. This does not mean that you cannot construct hypotheses in qualitative research; however non-specificity of the problem as well as methods and procedures make the convention of hypothesis formulation far less practicable and advisable. Even within quantitative studies the importance attached to and the practice of formulating hypotheses vary markedly from one academic discipline to another. For example, hypotheses are most prevalent in epidemiological research and research relating to the establishment of causality of a phenomenon, where it becomes important to narrow the list of probable causes so that a specific cause-and-effect relationship can be studied. In the social sciences formulation of hypotheses is mostly dependent on the researcher and the academic discipline, whereas within an academic discipline it varies markedly between the quantitative and qualitative research paradigms.

SUMMARY

Hypotheses, though important, are not essential for a study. A perfectly valid study can be conducted without constructing a single hypothesis. Hypotheses are important for bringing clarity, specificity and focus to a research study.

A hypothesis is a speculative statement that is subjected to verification through a research study. In formulating a hypothesis it is important to ensure that it is simple, specific and conceptually clear; can be verified; is rooted in an existing body of knowledge; and can be operationalised.

There are two broad categories of hypothesis: a research hypothesis and an alternative hypothesis. A research hypothesis can be further classified, based upon the way it is formulated, as a null hypothesis, a hypothesis of difference, a hypothesis of point-prevalence and a hypothesis of association.

One of the main differences in qualitative and quantitative research is the extent to which hypotheses are used and the importance attached to them. In qualitative research, because of the purpose of an investigation and methods used to obtain information, hypotheses are not used and almost no importance is given to them. However, in quantitative research, their use is far more prevalent though it varies markedly from one academic discipline to another and from researcher to researcher. On the whole it can be said that if the aim of a study is to explore where very little is known, hypotheses are usually not formulated; however, if a study aims to test an assertion by way of causality or association, validate the prevalence of something or establish its existence, hypotheses can be constructed.

The testing of a hypothesis becomes meaningless if any one of the aspects of your study – design, sampling procedure, method of data collection, analysis of data, statistical procedures applied or conclusions drawn – is faulty or inappropriate. This can result in erroneous verification of a hypothesis: Type I error occurs where you reject a null hypothesis when it is true and should not have been rejected; and Type II error is introduced where you accept a null hypothesis when it is false and should not have been accepted.

Now that you have read the full chapter...

CHECK YOUR UNDERSTANDING

- ☐ Do you understand the meaning and application of all of the keywords at the start of the chapter? If not, visit the online resources and use the glossary flashcards to get to grips with their definitions.

- ☐ What is a hypothesis and what functions does it serve in a research study?

- ☐ What are the different types of hypothesis? What is the main function of a null hypothesis?

- ☐ What are the two types of error in testing of a hypothesis? Explain them.

- ☐ The validity of a hypothesis test is dependent on a number of prerequisites. What are these requisites?

- ☐ To what extent do you think that the use of hypotheses is relevant to social research?

APPLY IT TO YOUR OWN PROJECT

- ☐ Formulate two or three hypotheses that relate to your own areas of interest and consider the factors that might affect their validity.

CONFUSED?

THE ONLINE RESOURCES ARE HERE TO HELP YOU

 https://study.sagepub.com/kumar5e

CHECKPOINT: What is the difference between a hypothesis and a research question? Visit this website.

CHECKPOINT: What is a null hypothesis? Watch this video.

CHECKPOINT: What are the two types of hypothesis erros, and how do they differ? Visit this website.

NEED MORE GENERAL SUPPORT?

Get up to speed on key terms with *glossary flashcards* and test yourself on important concepts with *multiple choice questions*.

UP FOR A CHALLENGE?

THE ONLINE RESOURCES ARE HERE TO INSPIRE YOU

 https://study.sagepub.com/kumar5e

CHECKPOINT: What are some of the most bizzare social science hypotheses researchers have tried to test? Visit this website.

CHECKPOINT: What are some examples of alternative and null hypotheses? Watch this video.

CHECKPOINT: How do you reduce errors in hypothesis testing? Visit this website.

READY TO WORK ON YOUR OWN PROJECT?

Start building a portfolio of your ideas with the exercise workbook and get support tailored to your specific assignment with the assessment toolkit.

DEVELOPING A RESEARCH PROJECT: A SET OF EXERCISES FOR BEGINNERS

Application is the essence of knowledge. However, there always remains a gap between theoretical knowledge and its application. It is only with practice that this gap can be narrowed. A beginner attempting to apply theoretical knowledge needs direction and guidance. This set of exercises, each one of which is attached to an operational step, has been developed with this belief in mind. Working through them will help you to develop a research project.

The main aim of these exercises is to provide you with a broad framework that is central to the operationalisation of each step of the research process. In most cases, a separate exercise is provided for quantitative and qualitative studies, so it is important that you know before you start which approach you are going to take. Within each exercise, there are brief reminders of some of the key issues relating to the process and a series of questions to help you to think through procedures and provide a framework for the development of your study.

Answers to these questions and awareness of the issues that the exercises outline will put you in a position to complete the framework suggested for writing a research proposal (Chapter 13), and therefore these will also constitute the core of your research proposal.

It is important for a beginner to work through these exercises with considerable thought and care.

Congratulations!

Now you have learnt how to take the first step towards your research journey. By this time you should have a reasonably good understanding about how to formulate a research problem. You should be ready to put your knowledge and skills into practice by actually working through the process of formulating a research problem. This exercise is designed to help you to formulate a research problem of interest to you. Good luck!

Exercise I: Formulation of a research problem
Quantitative studies

Now that you have gone through all the chapters that constitute Step I of the research process, this exercise provides you with an opportunity to apply that knowledge to formulate a research problem that is of interest to you. As you know, selecting a research problem is one of the most important aspects of social research, so this exercise will help you in formulating your research problem by raising questions and issues that will guide you to examine critically various facets and implications of what you are proposing to study. The exercise is designed to provide a directional framework that guides you through the problem formulation path. Keep in mind that the questions and issues raised in this exercise are not prescriptive but indicative and directional, hence you need to be critical and innovative while working through them. Thinking through a research problem with care can prevent a tremendous waste of human and financial resources.

A research problem should be clearly stated and be specific in nature. The feasibility of the study in terms of the availability of technical expertise, finances and time, and in terms of its relevance, should be considered thoroughly at this stage. In studies that attempt to establish a causal relationship or an association, the accuracy of the measurement of independent (cause) and dependent (effect) variables is of crucial importance

Template of Exercise I

and, hence, should be given serious consideration. If you have already selected a problem, you need not go through this process.

Start by identifying a *broad subject area* of interest to you; for example, health, education, crime, immigration, public health, tourism, recreation, parenting, crime, social justice. This exercise is designed to help you to dissect and then select the subarea(s) of interest to you to become the basis of your study. Chapter 4 of this book will help you to work through this exercise.

STEP ONE Select a broad area of study that interests you from within your academic discipline.

Having selected an area, the next step is to 'dissect' it in order to identify its various aspects and subareas. For example, suppose your broad area of interest is migration. Some aspects or subareas of migration are:

- a socioeconomic-demographic profile of immigrants;
- reasons for immigration;
- problems of immigrants;
- services provided to immigrants;
- attitudes of immigrants towards migration;
- attitudes of host communities towards immigrants;
- the extent of acculturation and assimilation;
- racial discrimination in the host country.

Or perhaps you are interested in studying a public health programme. Dissect it as finely as possible in order to identify the aspects that could be studied. List them as they come to you. For example:

- a socioeconomic-demographic profile of the target group;
- the morbidity and mortality patterns in a community;
- the extent and nature of programme utilisation;
- the effects of a programme on a community;
- the effectiveness of a particular health promotion strategy.

Or your interest may be in studying delinquents. Some aspects of delinquency are:

- delinquency as related to unemployment, broken homes or urbanisation;
- a profile of delinquents;
- reasons for delinquency;
- various therapeutic strategies.

STEP TWO 'Dissect' the broad area that you selected in Step I into subareas as discretely and finely as possible. Have a one-person (with yourself) brainstorming session.

1 _____

2 _____

3 _____

4 _____

5 _____

To investigate all these subareas is neither advisable nor feasible. Select only those subareas that would be possible for you to study within the constraints of time, finance and expertise at your disposal. One way to select your subarea is to start with a process of elimination: delete those areas you are not very interested in. Towards the end it may become difficult but you need to keep eliminating until you have selected a subarea(s) that can be managed within your constraints. Even one subarea can provide you with a valid and exhaustive study.

STEP THREE From the above subareas, select a subarea or subareas in which you would like to conduct your study.

1 _____

2 _____

3 _____

STEP FOUR Within each chosen subarea, what research questions do you hope to answer? (Be as specific as possible. You can select one or as many subareas as you want.)

Subarea	Specific research questions to be answered
1a	1 _____
	2 _____
	3 _____
1b	1 _____
	2 _____

1 (a) _____
  (b) _____
  (c) _____
  (d) _____
  (e) _____

2 (a) _____
  (b) _____
  (c) _____
  (d) _____
  (e) _____

3 (a) _____
  (b) _____
  (c) _____
  (d) _____
  (e) _____

The research questions to be answered through the study become the basis of your objectives. Now you need to formulate your study objectives. In so doing, use action-oriented words. The main difference between research questions and objectives is the way they are written. Questions are worded in question form and objectives are statements referring to the achievement of a task.

Your main objective should indicate the overall focus of your study and the subobjectives, its specific aspects. Subobjectives should be listed numerically. They should be worded clearly and unambiguously. Make sure each objective contains only one aspect of the study.

STEP FIVE On the basis of your research questions, formulate the main objective and the subobjectives of your study.

Main objective (the main focus of your study):

_____

_____

Subobjectives (specific aspects of your study):

1 _____

2 _____

3 _____

4 _____

5 _____

STEP SIX Carefully consider the following aspects of your study.

Task	What is involved	Time needed	Approx. cost	Technical expertise needed	Gaps in knowledge and skills
Literature review					
Instrument construction					
Data collection					
Data analysis					
Draft report					
Final report					

Now you have developed the objectives of your study. Take some time to think about them. Be clear about what tasks are involved, what time is realistically required and what skills you need to develop in order to conduct your study. Consider these areas carefully again.

STEP SEVEN Double-check:

→ Are you really interested in the study?

Yes ☐   No ☐   Uncertain ☐

→ Do you agree with the objectives of the study?

Yes ☐   No ☐   Uncertain ☐

→ Are you certain you want to pursue the study?

Yes ☐   No ☐   Uncertain ☐

→ Do you have adequate resources?

Yes ☐   No ☐   Uncertain ☐

→ Do you have access to an appropriate study population?

Yes ☐   No ☐   Uncertain ☐

If your answer to any of these questions is either 'no' or 'uncertain', re-examine the selected aspects carefully and make the appropriate changes in your objectives.

What, in your opinion, is the relevance of this study to theory and practice? How will your study contribute to the existing body of knowledge, help the practitioners in your profession and assist in programme development and policy formulation?

Relevance to theory:

....

Relevance to practice:

....

Now that you have formulated your research problem, it is important to examine your objective, research questions and hypotheses to identify if you have used any concepts in their formulation. When you convert concepts into variables an understanding about variables plays a very important role. Concepts are highly subjective as their understanding varies from person to person and, as such, they may not be measurable. Any concept, perception or imagination that can be measured on any one of the four measurement scales (nominal, ordinal, interval or ratio) is called a variable. It is important for concepts used in a study to be operationalised in measurable terms so that the extent of variation in a study population's understanding of them is reduced, if not eliminated.

At this stage, when you have formulated your objectives, it is important for you to think how you will operationalise any concepts used in the objectives, research questions or hypotheses formulated: what are their indicators and how will they be measured?

The following table suggests how you might operationalise the concept of 'effectiveness', in relation to a health education programme on AIDS. It lists the indicators of effectiveness (you can have other indicators), sets out the variables that measure the indicators and describes the unit of measurement for the variables.

Concept	Indicator	Variable(s)	Unit of measurement
Effectiveness	Awareness of AIDS	Extent of change in:	Change in the proportion of the population, before and after the health education programme, with respect to:
	Knowledge about AIDS	Awareness Knowledge Practice	Awareness of, and knowledge about, different aspects of AIDS
	Use of contraceptives (practice)		Use of contraceptives for safe sex

This part of the exercise is designed to help you operationalise the major concepts used in your study. Refer to Chapter 5 for additional information on variables.

STEP EIGHT Operationalise your concepts.

Objectives/ research questions/ hypotheses	Major concepts	Indicators	Variables	Unit of measurement

Objectives/ research questions/ hypotheses	Major concepts	Indicators	Variables	Unit of measurement

It is essential to develop a working or operational definition of your study population. For example, who would you consider to be a patient, an immigrant, a youth, a psychologist, a teacher, a delinquent or a Christian? Working definitions play a crucial role in avoiding ambiguities in the selection of a sample and help you to narrow your study population.

STEP NINE Operationally define your study population.

Skip this section if you are *not* constructing a hypothesis.

As discussed, some believe that one must have a hypothesis to undertake an investigation; however, in the author's opinion, hypotheses, although they bring clarity, specificity and focus to a research problem, are not essential for a study. You can conduct a valid investigation without constructing a single formal hypothesis. On the other hand, you can construct as many hypotheses as you think appropriate. In epidemiological studies, to narrow the field of investigation, one must construct a hypothesis as to the probable cause of the condition to be investigated.

A hypothesis is a hunch, assumption, suspicion, assertion or idea about a phenomenon, relationship or situation, which you intend to investigate in order to find out if you are right. If it proves to be right, your assumption was correct; hence, you prove that your hypothesis was true. Otherwise, you conclude your hypothesis to be false.

Disproving a hypothesis is as important as, or more important than, proving it. As a hypothesis is usually constructed on the basis of what is commonly believed to be right, your disproving it might lead to something new that has been ignored by previous researchers.

A hypothesis should be conceptually simple, clear and specific, and be capable of verification and being expressed operationally.

There is a specific way of writing a hypothesis, with which you need to be familiar (refer to Chapter 6).

STEP TEN Construct your hypothesis or hypotheses for each subobjective/research question.

Objectives/research questions	Hypotheses to be tested
	1
	2
	3
	1
	2
	3
	1
	2
	3

Qualitative studies

As mentioned earlier, the difference in qualitative and quantitative research studies starts with the way you think about and formulate your research problem. In qualitative studies, it is preferred that the research problem is broad, flexible and continuously formulated as the information is collected. In the process of data collection, if you find something interesting relating to your broad area of study, you add the aspect(s) and change the focus to accommodate the new vision.

This flexibility is an important strength of qualitative research but it is also important that you develop a conceptual framework of issues and questions for your study, as non-specificity about what you want to find out can often create problems for your respondents. Many do not feel comfortable or are not in a position to articulate the multiple aspects of an area without being prompted. For situations like this it is important that you are fully prepared with a framework in mind for your enquiry. No doubt you can develop this framework during data collection, while talking to your respondents, but this may create a problem in terms of completeness and comparability with the information obtained during the early phase of the study. You can minimise some of these problems by developing a conceptual framework in advance. It is also important that you communicate with respondents in specific terms without bias or influencing their thinking.

Remember, these are not the questions that you will ask of your respondents. These are just reminders for raising issues or questions if nothing much is forthcoming from a respondent.

In qualitative research the following would be considered as broad areas of interest:

→ What does it mean to have a child with ADHD in the family?

→ How resilient is this community?

→ What is community responsiveness?

→ Living with HIV/AIDS.

↳ How has a community coped after a major bush fire or tsunami?

STEP ONE Select a broad area of study that interests you or a question that you want to find answers to through the research study.

_____

_____

_____

_____

STEP TWO Having selected your main research question or broad area of study, list all questions to which you want to find answers. Also list all issues that you want to discuss with your respondents. Your literature review, discussions with others and consultation with potential respondents will be of immense help at this stage.

Questions: _____

_____

_____

_____

_____

_____

_____

_____

_____

Issues: _____

_____

_____

_____

_____

_____

_____

_____

_____

STEP TWO

CONCEPTUALISING A RESEARCH DESIGN

THE RESEARCH DESIGN

- step two -
CONCEPTUALISING A RESEARCH DESIGN

This operational step includes two chapters:

→ The research design   150

Selecting a study design   166

CONFUSED?
UP FOR A
CHALLENGE?

OR
NEED HELP
WITH YOUR
ASSIGNMENT?

VISIT
https://study.sagepub.
com/kumar5e for
resources specially
designed to support
you and all your
research needs.

ESSENTIAL TERMS

You should be able to define these by the end of the chapter

- causality
- chance variables
- control group
- experimental group

- extraneous variables
- independent variable
- research design
- study design

BONUS TERMS

You will learn more about these by the end of the chapter

- matching
- 'maxmincon' principle of variance
- random error

- randomisation
- treatment group

LEARNING OBJECTIVES

At the end of this chapter, you will be able to:

- Explain what research design means
- Consider issues when designing your own research
- Understand the relationship between the theory of causality and the research design
- Identify the functions of research design in social research
- Determine factors responsible for bringing about change in a phenomenon
- Quantify the impact of extraneous variables in impact assessment studies

If you are clear about your research problem, your achievement is worth praising. You have crossed one of the most important and difficult sections of your research journey. Having decided *what* you want to study, you now need to determine *how* you are going to conduct your study. There are a number of questions that need to be answered before you can proceed with your journey. What procedures will you adopt to obtain answers to research questions? How will you carry out the tasks needed to complete the different components of the research process? What should you do and what should you not do in the process of undertaking the study? Basically, answers to these questions constitute the core of a research design.

WHAT IS A RESEARCH DESIGN?

A research design is the road map that you decide to follow during your research journey to find answers to your research questions as validly, objectively, accurately and economically as possible. It is a procedural-cum-operational plan that details what and how different methods and procedures to be applied during the research process. According to Kerlinger (1986: 279):

> A research design is a plan, structure and strategy of investigation so conceived as to obtain answers to research questions or problems. The plan is the complete scheme or programme of the research. It includes an outline of what the investigator will do from writing the hypotheses and their operational implications to the final analysis of data.

According to Thyer (1993: 94):

> A traditional research design is a blueprint or detailed plan for how a research study is to be completed – operationalizing variables so they can be measured, selecting a sample of interest to study, collecting data to be used as a basis for testing hypotheses, and analysing the results.

According to Selltiz et al. (1962: 50):

> A research design is the arrangement of conditions for collection and analysis of data in a manner that aims to combine relevance to the research purpose with economy in procedure.

A research design is a plan through which you decide for yourself and communicate to others your decisions regarding what study design you propose to use, how you will collect information from your respondents, how you will select your respondents, how the information you will collect is to be analysed and how you will communicate your findings. In addition, you detail your rationale and justification for each decision that shapes your answers to the 'how' of the research journey. In presenting your rationale and justification you need to support them critically from the literature reviewed. You also need to assure yourself and others that the path you have proposed will yield valid and reliable results.

THE FUNCTIONS OF A RESEARCH DESIGN

The above definitions suggest that a research design has two main functions. The first relates to the identification and/or development of procedures and logistical arrangements required to undertake a study, and the second emphasises the importance of quality in these procedures to ensure their validity, objectivity and accuracy. Hence, through a research design you:

- conceptualise an operational plan to undertake the various procedures and tasks required to complete your study;

- ensure that these procedures are adequate to obtain valid, objective and accurate answers to the research questions. Kerlinger (1986: 280) calls this function the control of variance.

Let us take the first of these functions. The research design should detail for you, your supervisor and other readers all the procedures you plan to use and the tasks you will perform to obtain answers to your research questions. One of the most important requirements of a research design is to specify everything clearly so that a reader will understand what procedures to follow and how to follow them. These should be written in such detail and clarity that if someone else wants to conduct the study, he/she should be able to follow exactly the way you would have done. A research design, therefore, should include the following:

- Name the study design per se – that is, 'cross-sectional', 'before-and-after', 'comparative', 'control experiment' or 'random control' (Chapter 8 describes some of the commonly used study designs).

- Provide detailed information about the following aspects of the study (details of these are covered in the subsequent chapters of the book):

  - Who will constitute the study population?
  - How will the study population be identified?
  - Will a sample or the whole population be selected?
  - If a sample is selected, how will it be contacted?
  - How will consent be sought?
  - What method of data collection will be used and why?
  - In the case of a questionnaire, where will the responses be returned?
  - How should respondents contact you if they have queries?
  - In the case of interviews, where will they be conducted?
  - How will ethical issues be taken care of?

Control of variance: When you design a study in such a way that enables you to ensure that the independent variable has a maximum chance of affecting the dependent variable(s) and the effect of extraneous variables is designed to be minimum and quantifiable. (See also the maxmincon principle of variance.)

CHECKPOINT
Research designs

155

THE THEORY OF CAUSALITY AND THE RESEARCH DESIGN

Now let us turn to the second function of the research design – ensuring that the procedures undertaken are adequate to obtain valid, objective and accurate answers to the research questions. In the social sciences there are many causes that are responsible for changing a phenomenon as we are exposed to so many factors on which we do not have any control. These factors can affect the phenomenon in a number of ways. However, in most studies you examine one cause (independent variable) and occasionally two. As you add more independent variables, the design becomes more and more complicated, expensive and difficult to manage. All these variables which have a link with the dependent variable but are not the focus of your study, are considered extraneous variables. The theory of causality helps you to understand the different sets of variables that cause the change in the dependent variable. It also helps you to determine and isolate the impact of different categories of variables so that you validly, objectively and accurately ascertain the impact of independent variables. To explain this, let us examine a few examples.

Suppose you want to examine the effectiveness of a marriage counselling service provided by an agency – that is, the extent to which the service has been able to help its clients to resolve their marital problems. In studying such relationships you must understand that in real life there are many outside factors that can influence the outcome of your intervention. For example, during visits to your agency for counselling, your client may get a better job. If some of the marital problems came about because of economic hardship, and if the problem of money is now solved, it may be a factor in reducing the marital problems. On the other hand, if a client loses his/her job, the worsening of the economic problems may either intensify or lessen the marital problems; that is, for some couples a perceived financial threat may increase marital problems, whereas for others it may create more closeness between partners. In some situations, an improvement in a marriage may have very little to do with the counselling received, coming about almost entirely because of a change in economic circumstances. Other events such as the birth of a child to a couple or a couple's 'self-realisation', independently arrived at, may also affect the extent and nature of marital problems. Figure 7.1 lists other possible factors under the category of extraneous variables. This list is by no means exhaustive.

Continuing the example of marriage and counselling, there are sets of factors that can affect the relationship between counselling and marriage problems. These are:

1   Counselling per se (the independent variable).

2   Any reason, other than counselling, that can produce change, positive or negative, in the extent of marital problems (the extraneous variables).

3   The change or otherwise in the extent of the marital problems (the dependent variable).

4   Sometimes, the variation in response to questions about marital problems can be accounted for by either the mood of respondents or ambiguity in the questions. Some respondents may either overestimate or underestimate their marital problems because of their state of mind at the time. Some respondents, in spite of being in exactly the same situation, may respond to non-specific or ambiguous questions differently, according to how they interpret the question (the chance or random variables).

As already explained in Chapter 5, any variable that is responsible for bringing about a change is called an *independent variable*. In this example, the counselling is an independent variable. When you study a cause-and-effect relationship, usually you study the impact of only one independent variable. Occasionally you may study the impact of two independent variables, or (very rarely) more than two, but these study designs are more complex.

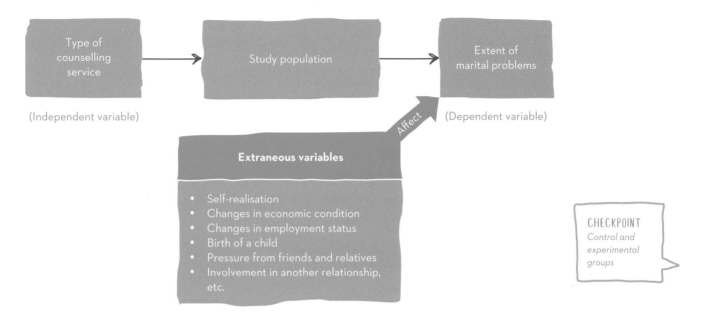

CHECKPOINT
Control and experimental groups

Figure 7.1   Factors affecting the relationship between a counselling service and the extent of marital problems

For this example *counselling* was the assumed cause of change in the *extent of marital problems*; hence, the extent of marital problems is the *dependent variable*, as the change in the degree of marital problems was dependent upon counselling.

All other factors that affect the relationship between marital problems and counselling are called *extraneous variables*. In the social sciences, extraneous variables operate in every study and cannot be eliminated. However, they can be controlled to some extent. (Some of the methods for controlling them are described later in this chapter.) Nevertheless, it is possible to examine the impact attributable to extraneous variables. This is done with the introduction of a control group in the study design. The sole function of a control group is to quantify the impact of extraneous variables on the dependent variable(s).

Changes in the dependent variable, because of the respondent's state of mood or ambiguity in the research instrument, are called random variables or chance variables. The error thus introduced is called the *chance* or *random error*. In most cases the net effect of chance variables is considered to be negligible as respondents who overreport tend to cancel out those who underreport. The same applies to responses to ambiguous questions in a research instrument.

Hence in any causal relationship, changes in the dependent variable may be attributed to three types of variable:

Control group: The group in an experimental study which is not exposed to the experimental intervention is called a control group. The sole purpose of the control group is to measure the impact of extraneous and chance variables on the dependent variable.

Random variables: When collecting information from respondents, there are times when the mood of a respondent or the wording of a question can affect the way a respondent replies. There is no systematic pattern in terms of this change. Such shifts in responses are said to be caused by random or chance variables.

Change in the dependent variable	=	Change attributable to independent variable	±	Change attributable to extraneous variables	±	Change attributable to chance or random variables

Chance variables: In studying causality or association there are times when the mood of a respondent or the wording of a question can affect the reply given by the respondent when asked again in the post-test. There is no systematic pattern in terms of this change. Such variables are called chance or random variables.

Let us take another example. Suppose you want to study the impact of different teaching models on the level of comprehension of students, and you adopt a comparative study design. In this study, the change in the level of comprehension can be attributed not only to the teaching models but also to a number of other factors, some of which are shown in Figure 7.2:

[change in level of comprehension]

= [change attributable to the teaching model]

± [change attributable to extraneous variables]

± [change attributable to **chance variables**]

In fact, in any study that attempts to establish a causal relationship, you will discover that there are three sets of variables operating to bring about a change in the dependent variable. This can be expressed as an equation:

[change in the outcome variable]

= [change because of the change variable]

± [change because of extraneous variables]

± [change because of chance or random variables]

This can also be expressed (in research terminology) as:

[change in the dependent variable]

= [change attributable to the independent variable]

± [change attributable to extraneous variables]

± [change attributable to chance variables]

or in statistical/technical terms:

[total variance]

= [variance attributable to the independent variable]

[variance attributable to extraneous variables]

[random or chance variance]

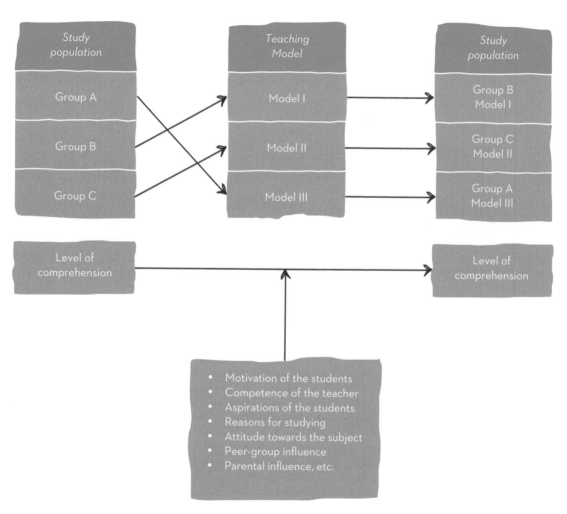

Figure 7.2 **The relationship between teaching models and comprehension**

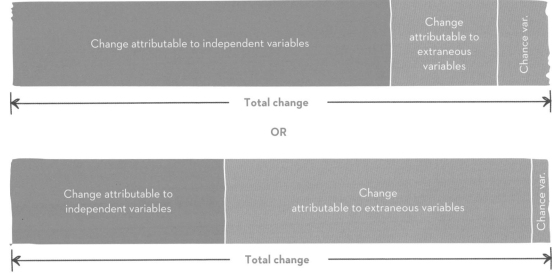

Figure 7.3   The components of total change: independent, extraneous and chance

It can also be expressed graphically (Figure 7.3).

As the total change measures the combined effects of all three components it is difficult to isolate the individual impact of each of them (see Figure 7.3). Since your aim as a researcher is to determine the change that can be attributed to the independent variable, you need to design your study to ensure that the independent variable has the *maximum* opportunity to have its full effect on the dependent variable, while the effects that are attributed to extraneous and chance variables are minimised (if possible) or quantified or eliminated. This is what Kerlinger (1986: 286) calls the maxmincon principle of variance.

One of the most important questions is: how do we minimise the effects attributable to extraneous and chance variables? The simple answer is that in most situations we cannot; however, it can be quantified. The sole purpose of having a control group, as mentioned earlier, is to measure the change that is a result of extraneous variables. The effect of chance variables is often assumed to be none or negligible because of the neutralising effect. As discussed, chance variation comes primarily from two sources: respondents and the research instrument. It is assumed that if some respondents affect the dependent variable positively, others will affect it negatively. For example, if some respondents are extremely positive in their attitude towards an issue, being very liberal or positively biased, there are bound to be others who are extremely negative (being very conservative or negatively biased). Hence, they tend to cancel each other out so the net effect is assumed to be zero. However, if in a study population most individuals are either negatively or positively biased, a systematic error in the findings will be introduced. Similarly, if a research instrument is not reliable (i.e. it is not measuring correctly what it is supposed to measure), a systematic bias may be introduced into the study.

In the physical sciences a researcher can control extraneous variables as experiments are usually done in a laboratory. By contrast, in the social sciences, the laboratory is society, over which the researcher lacks control. Since no researcher has control over extraneous variables, their effect, as mentioned, in most situations cannot be minimised. The best option is to quantify their impact through the use of a control group, though the introduction of a control group creates the problem of ensuring that the extraneous variables have a similar effect on both control and experimental groups. In some situations their impact can be eliminated (this is possible only where one or two variables are known to have a marked impact on the dependent variable). There are two methods used to ensure that extraneous variables have a similar effect on control and experimental groups and two methods for eliminating extraneous variables:

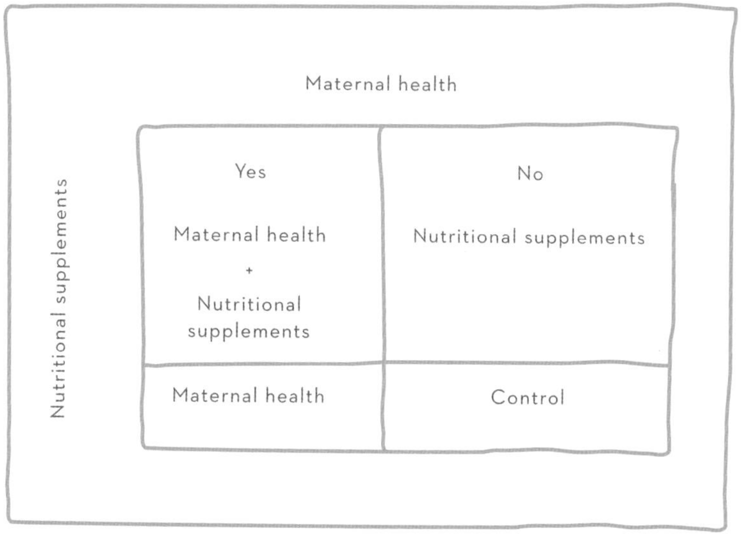

Figure 7.4   Building into the design

Randomisation: In experimental and comparative studies, you often need to study two or more groups of people. In forming these groups it is important that they are comparable with respect to the dependent variable and other variables that affect it so that the effects of independent and extraneous variables are uniform across groups. Randomisation is a process that ensures that each and every person in a group is given an equal and independent chance of being in any of the groups, thereby making groups comparable.

Matching: Is a technique that is used to form two groups of patients to set up an experiment–control study to test the effectiveness of a drug. From a pool of patients, two patients with identical predetermined attributes, characteristics or conditions are matched and then randomly placed in either the experimental or control group. The matching continues for the rest of the pool. The two groups thus formed are supposed to be comparable, thus ensuring uniform impact of different sets of variables on the patients.

1   **Ensure that extraneous variables have a similar impact on control and experimental groups**. It is assumed that if two groups are comparable, the extent to which the extraneous variables will affect the dependent variable will be similar in both groups. There are two methods that ensure that the control and experimental groups are comparable with one another: randomisation and matching (discussed in Chapter 8).

2. **Eliminate or isolate extraneous variable(s)**. Sometimes it is possible to eliminate an extraneous variable or to build it into the study design. This is usually done when there is strong evidence that the extraneous variable has a high correlation with the dependent variable. There are two methods used to achieve this:

   a. **Build the extraneous variable into the design of the study**. To explain this concept let us take an example. Suppose you want to study the impact of maternal health services on the infant mortality of a population. It can be assumed that the nutritional status of children also has a marked effect on infant mortality. To study the impact of maternal health services per se, you adopt a two-by-two factorial design as explained in Figure 7.4. In this way you can study the impact of the extraneous variable separately as well as interactively with the independent variable.

   b. **Eliminate the variable**. To understand this, let us take another example. Suppose you want to study the impact of a health education programme on the attitudes towards, and beliefs about, the causation and treatment of a certain illness among non-indigenous Australians and indigenous Australians living in a particular community. As attitudes and beliefs vary markedly from culture to culture, studying non-indigenous Australians and indigenous Australians as one group will not provide an accurate picture. In such studies it is appropriate to eliminate the cultural variation in the study population by selecting and studying the populations separately or by constructing culture-specific cohorts at the time of analysis.

SUMMARY

In this chapter you have learnt about the functions of a research design. A research design serves two important functions: (1) to detail the procedures for undertaking a study; and (2) to ensure that, in the case of causality, the independent variable has the maximum opportunity to have its effect on the dependent variable while the effect of extraneous and chance variables is minimised or quantified. In terms of the first function, a research design should outline the logistical details of the whole process of the research journey. You need to spell out in detail what type of study design you are proposing to use and why, who will be your respondents and how they will be selected, from how many you propose to get the required information, how you will collect the information and how you will analyse it. For each aspect you need to provide your rationale and justification and as far as possible support them from the literature reviewed.

Through the second function, 'control of variance', when establishing association or causality, you assure your supervisor and readers that you have set up your study in such a way that your independent variable has the maximum chance of affecting the dependent variable and that the effects of extraneous and chance variables are minimised, quantified and/or controlled (the 'maxmincon' principle of variance).

A study without a control group measures the total change (change attributable to independent variable ± change attributable to extraneous variables ± change attributable to chance variables) in a phenomenon or situation. The purpose of introducing a control group is to quantify the impact of extraneous and chance variables.

The study design is a part of the research design. The research design also includes other logistical details which are proposed to complete the study.

Now that you have read the full chapter...

CHECK YOUR UNDERSTANDING

☐ Do you understand the meaning and application of all of the keywords at the start of the chapter? If not, visit the online resources and use the glossary flashcards to get to grips with their definitions.

☐ Identify the aspects of a study that need to be described in a research design.

☐ What are the main functions of a research design? Why is it important to have a research design before undertaking a study?

☐ Explain, by providing an example, the three sets of variables that affect the dependent variable when studying association or causality.

☐ How might you quantify the impact of extraneous variables when studying the impact of a programme?

☐ Can you eliminate the impact of extraneous variables when undertaking impact assessment studies? If yes, how?

☐ Visit the companion website and read some of the materials provided on causality and qualitative research. What issues do you think choosing a qualitative method of data collection might raise when thinking about causality?

APPLY IT TO YOUR OWN PROJECT

☐ Provide examples from your own area of study to illustrate the main variables in terms of causality (you may find it useful to refer back to Chapter 5).

☐ Identify one or two examples from an area that interests you to demonstrate how the 'maxmincon' principle of variance can be applied.

CONFUSED?

THE ONLINE RESOURCES ARE HERE TO HELP YOU

 https://study.sagepub.com/kumar5e

CHECKPOINT: What is a research design, and what functions does it serve? Visit this website.

CHECKPOINT: What is the difference between a control group and an experimental group? Visit this website.

CHECKPOINT: What is the principle of variance? Visit this website.

NEED MORE GENERAL SUPPORT?

Get up to speed on key terms with *glossary flashcards* and test yourself on important concepts with *multiple choice questions*.

UP FOR A CHALLENGE?

THE ONLINE RESOURCES ARE HERE TO INSPIRE YOU

→ 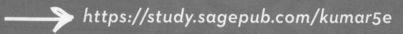 https://study.sagepub.com/kumar5e ←

CHECKPOINT: How is your research design impacted by your research question?
Read this chapter.

CHECKPOINT: How can you limit and quantify the impact of extraneous variables on your study?
Visit this website.

CHECKPOINT: How can you maximize the effectiveness of the independent variable in
your research? Visit this website.

READY TO WORK ON YOUR OWN PROJECT?

Start building a portfolio of your ideas with the exercise workbook and get support tailored to
your specific assignment with the assessment toolkit.

SELECTING A STUDY DESIGN

- step two -
CONCEPTUALISING A RESEARCH DESIGN

The research design   150

→ Selecting a study design   166

**CONFUSED?
UP FOR A
CHALLENGE?**

**OR
NEED HELP
WITH YOUR
ASSIGNMENT?**

VISIT
https://study.sagepub.
com/kumar5e for
resources specially
designed to support
you and all your
research needs.

ESSENTIAL TERMS

You should be able to define these by the end of the chapter

- action research
- after-only design
- before-and-after study design
- case studies
- collaborative enquiry
- community discussion forums
- control studies
- cross-sectional study design
- experimental study design
- feminist research

- focus studies
- holistic research
- longitudinal studies
- non-experimental studies
- oral history
- participant observation
- prospective study design
- reflective journal
- retrospective studies

BONUS TERMS

You will learn more about these by the end of the chapter

- attrition
- blind studies
- cohort studies
- conditioning effect
- double-blind studies
- experimental mortality
- maturation effect

- panel studies
- power gap
- quasi-experimental studies
- reactive effect
- regression effect
- semi-experimental studies
- trend studies

LEARNING OBJECTIVES

At the end of this chapter, you will be able to:

- Differentiate quantitative and qualitative study designs
- Identify common study designs in quantitative research and know when to use them
- Identify common study designs in qualitative research and know when to use them
- Point out the strengths and weaknesses of different study designs

DIFFERENCES BETWEEN QUANTITATIVE AND QUALITATIVE STUDY DESIGNS

In this chapter we will discuss some of the most commonly used study designs in both quantitative and qualitative research. Overall, there are many more study designs in quantitative research than in qualitative research. Quantitative study designs are specific, well structured, have been tested for their validity and reliability, and can be explicitly defined and recognised. Study designs in qualitative research either do not have these attributes or have them to a lesser degree. They are less specific and precise, and do not have the same structural depth. Qualitative designs are described in the following words by Maxwell (2013: 3):

> To design a qualitative study, you can't just develop (or borrow) a logical strategy in advance and implement it faithfully. You need, to a substantial extent, to *construct* and *reconstruct* your research design, and this is a major rationale for my design model. Qualitative research design, to a much greater extent than quantitative research, is a 'do-it-yourself' rather than an 'off-the-shelf' process, one that involves 'tacking' back and forth between the different components of the design, assessing their implications for one another. It does not begin from a predetermined starting point or proceed through a fixed sequence of steps, but involves interconnection and interaction among the different design components.

Differences in philosophical perspectives in each paradigm, combined with the aims of a study, to a large extent determine the focus, approach and mode of enquiry, which in turn determine the structural aspects of a study design. The main focus in qualitative research is to understand, explain, explore, discover and clarify situations, feelings, perceptions, attitudes, values, beliefs and experiences of a group of people. The study designs are therefore often based on deductive rather than inductive logic, are flexible and emergent in nature, and are often non-linear and non-sequential in their operationalisation. The study designs mainly entail the selection of people from whom the information, through an open frame of enquiry, is gathered and explored. The parameters of the scope of a study, and information gathering methods and processes, are often flexible and evolving; hence, most qualitative designs are not as structured and sequential as quantitative ones. On the other hand, in quantitative research, the measurement and classification requirements of the information that is to be gathered demand that study designs are more structured, rigid, fixed and predetermined to ensure validity and reliability of the information and its classification.

In qualitative studies the distinction between study designs and methods of data collection is far less clear. Quantitative study designs have more clarity and distinction between designs and methods of data collection. In qualitative research there is an overlap between the two. Some designs are basically methods of data collection. For example, in-depth interviewing is a design as well as a method of data collection, and so are oral history and participant observation.

One of the most distinguishing features of qualitative research is the adherence to the concept of respondent concordance, whereby you as a researcher make every effort to seek agreement of your respondents with your interpretation, presentation of the situations, experiences, perceptions and conclusions. In quantitative research respondent concordance does not occupy an important place. Sometimes it is assumed to be achieved by circulating or sharing the findings with those who participated in the study.

The 'power gap' between the researcher and the study population in qualitative research is far smaller than in quantitative research because of the informality in structure and situation in which data is collected.

In quantitative research enough detail about a study design is provided for it to be replicated for verification and reassurance. In qualitative research little attention is paid to study designs or the other structural aspects of a study, hence the replication of a study design and its findings becomes almost impossible.

Another difference in the designs in qualitative and quantitative studies is the possibility of introducing researcher bias. Because of flexibility and lack of control it is more difficult to check for researcher bias in qualitative studies.

Study designs in each paradigm are appropriate for finding different things. Study designs in qualitative research are more appropriate for exploring the variation and diversity in any aspect of social life, whereas in quantitative research they are more suited to finding out the extent of this variation and diversity. If your interest is in studying values, beliefs, understandings, perceptions, meanings, etc., qualitative study designs are more appropriate as they provide immense flexibility. On the other hand, if your focus is to measure the magnitude of that variation – how many people have a particular value, belief, etc. – the quantitative designs are more appropriate. For good quantitative research it is important that you combine quantitative skills with qualitative ones when ascertaining the nature and extent of diversity and variation in a phenomenon. In the author's opinion, the qualitative–quantitative–qualitative approach to research is comprehensive and worth consideration. This involves starting with qualitative methods to determine the spread of diversity, using quantitative methods to quantify the spread, and then going back to qualitative to explain the observed patterns. As already stated, the author does not recommend your locking yourself into either the qualitative or quantitative paradigm and, though you may have your preference, it is the purpose that should determine the choice between quantitative and qualitative study designs. If you already know (from previous studies or practice knowledge) the nature of diversity in the area of interest to you, knowledge about its extent can be determined only by using quantitative methods. In most cases where you want to explore both, you need to use methods that fall in the domain of both paradigms.

CHECKPOINT
Designs for different paradigms

STUDY DESIGNS IN QUANTITATIVE RESEARCH

All study designs used in quantitative studies can be classified by examining them from three different perspectives:

1   the number of contacts with the study population;
2   the reference period of the study;
3   the nature of the investigation.

These perspectives are arbitrary bases of classification; hence, the terminology used to describe them is not universal. However, the names of the designs within each classification base are universally used. Note that the designs *within* each category are mutually exclusive; that is, if a particular study is cross-sectional in nature it cannot at the same time be a before-and-after or a longitudinal study, but it can be a non-experimental or experimental study, as well as a retrospective study or a prospective study. See Figure 8.1.

The chapter concludes with a section on commonly used designs which are based on a certain philosophy or methodology, and which have acquired their own names.

Study designs based on the number of contacts

Based on the number of contacts with the study population, designs can be classified into three groups:

1   cross-sectional studies;

2   before-and-after studies;

3   longitudinal studies.

The cross-sectional study design

Cross-sectional studies: The most commonly used design in the social sciences, also known as one-shot or status studies. This design is best suited to studies aimed at finding out the prevalence of a phenomenon, situation, problem, attitude or issue, by taking a cross-section of the population. They are useful in obtaining an overall 'picture' as it stands at the time of the study.

Cross-sectional studies, also known as *one-shot* or *status studies*, are the most commonly used design in the social sciences. This design is best suited to studies aimed at finding out the prevalence of a phenomenon, situation, problem, attitude or issue, by taking a cross-section of the population. They are useful in obtaining an overall 'picture' as it stands at the time of the study. They are 'designed to study some phenomenon by taking a cross-section of it at one time' (Babbie 1989: 89). Such studies are cross-sectional with regard to both the study population and the time of investigation.

A cross-sectional study is extremely simple in design. You decide what you want to find out about, identify the study population, select a sample (if you need to) and contact your respondents to find out the required information. For example, a cross-sectional design would be the most appropriate for a study of the following topics:

→ The attitude of the study population towards uranium mining in Australia.
→ The socioeconomic-demographic characteristics of immigrants in Western Australia.
→ The incidence of HIV-positive cases in Australia.
→ The reasons for homelessness among young people.
→ The quality assurance of a service provided by an organisation.
→ The impact of unemployment on street crime (this could also be a before-and-after study).
→ The relationship between the home environment and the academic performance of a child at school.
→ The attitude of the community towards equity issues.
→ The extent of unemployment in a city.
→ Consumer satisfaction with a product.
→ The effectiveness of random breath testing in preventing road accidents (this could also be a before-and-after study).
→ The health needs of a community.
→ The attitudes of students towards the facilities available in their library.

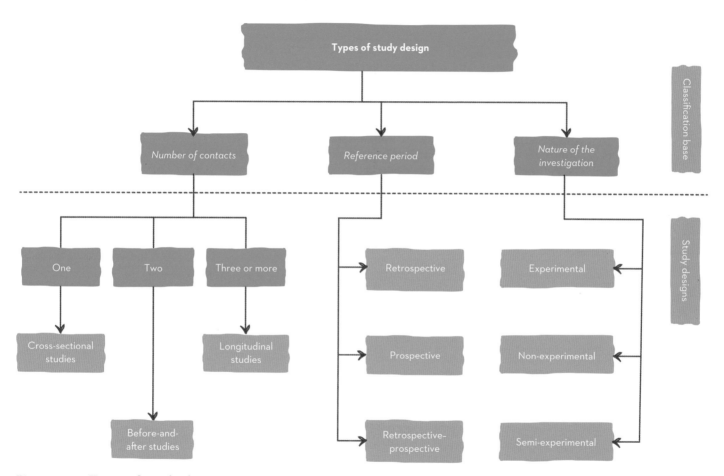

Figure 8.1   Types of study design

As these studies involve only one contact with the study population, they are comparatively cheap to undertake and easy to analyse. However, their biggest disadvantage is that they cannot measure change. To measure change it is necessary to have at least two data collection points – that is, at least two cross-sectional studies, at two points in time, on the same population.

The before-and-after study design

The main advantage of the before-and-after design (also known as the *pre-test/post-test* design) is that it can measure change in a situation, phenomenon, issue, problem or attitude. It is the most appropriate design for measuring the impact or effectiveness of a programme. A before-and-after design can be described as two sets of cross-sectional data collection points on the same population to find out the change in the phenomenon or variable(s) between two points in time. The change is measured by comparing the difference in the phenomenon or variable(s) before and after the intervention (sees Figure 8.2).

A before-and-after study is carried out by adopting the same process as a cross-sectional study, except that it comprises two cross-sectional data sets, the second being undertaken after a certain period. Depending upon how it is set up, a before-and-after study may be either an experiment or a non-experiment. It is one of the most commonly used designs in evaluation studies. The difference between the two sets of data collection points with respect to the dependent variable is considered to be the impact of the programme. The following are examples of topics that can be studied using this design:

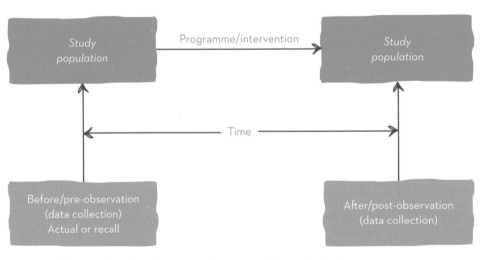

Figure 8.2   Before-and-after (pre-test/post-test) study design

- The impact of administrative restructuring on the quality of services provided by an organisation.
- The effectiveness of a marriage counselling service.
- The impact of sex education on sexual behaviour among schoolchildren.
- The effect of a drug awareness programme on the knowledge about, and use of, drugs among young people.
- The impact of incentives on the productivity of employees in an organisation.
- The impact of increased funding on the quality of teaching in universities.
- The impact of maternal and child health services on the infant mortality rate.
- The effect of random breath testing on road accidents.
- The effect of an advertisement on the sale of a product.

CHECKPOINT
Pre-test/Post-test study design

The main advantage of before-and-after design is its ability to measure change in a phenomenon or to assess the impact of an intervention. However, there can be disadvantages which may not occur, individually or collectively, in every study. The prevalence of a particular disadvantage(s) is dependent upon the nature of the investigation, the study population and the method of data collection. These disadvantages include the following:

- As two sets of data must be collected, involving two contacts with the study population, the study is more expensive and more difficult to implement. It also requires a longer time to complete, particularly if you are using an experimental design, as you will need to wait until your intervention is completed before you collect the second set of data.

- In some cases the time lapse between the two contacts may result in *attrition in the study population*. It is possible that some of those who participated in the pre-test may move out of the area or withdraw from the experiment for other reasons.

- One of the main limitations of this design, in its simplest form, is that as it measures *total change* you cannot ascertain whether independent or extraneous variables are responsible for producing change in the dependent variable. Also, it is not possible to quantify the contribution of independent and extraneous variables separately.

- Depending on the age of the study population and if there is a significant time lapse between the before-and-after sets of data collection, changes in the study population may be because it is maturing. This is particularly true when you are studying young children. The effect of this maturation, if it is significantly correlated with the dependent variable, is reflected in the 'after' observation and is known as the maturation effect.

- Sometimes the instrument itself educates the respondents. This is known as the reactive effect of the instrument. For example, suppose you want to ascertain the impact of a programme designed to create awareness of drugs in a population. To do this, you design a questionnaire listing various drugs and asking respondents to indicate whether they have heard of them. At the pre-test stage a respondent, while answering questions that include the names of the various drugs, is being made aware of them, and this will be reflected in his/her responses at the post-test stage. Thus, the research instrument itself has educated the study population and, hence, has affected the dependent variable. Another example of this effect is a study designed to measure the impact of a family planning education programme on respondents' awareness

Maturation effect: If there is a significant time lapse between the before and after data sets, the study population may change simply because it has grown older. This is particularly true when you are studying young children. The effect of this maturation, if it is significantly correlated with the dependent variable, is reflected in the after observation.

175

Reactive effect: Sometimes the way a question is worded informs respondents of the existence or prevalence of something that the study is trying to find out about as an outcome of an intervention. This effect is known as reactive effect of the instrument.

Regression effect: Sometimes people who place themselves on the extreme positions of a measurement scale at the pre-test stage may, for a number of reasons, shift towards the mean at the post-test stage. They might feel that they have been too negative or too positive at the pre-test stage. Therefore, the mere expression of the attitude in response to a questionnaire or interview has caused them to think about and alter their attitude towards the mean at the time of the post-test. This type of effect is known as the regression effect.

Longitudinal study: In longitudinal studies the study population is visited a number of times at regular intervals, usually over a long period, to collect the required information. These intervals are not fixed, so their length may vary from study to study. Intervals might be as short as a week or longer than a year. Irrespective of the size of the interval, the information gathered each time is identical.

of contraceptive methods. Most studies designed to measure the impact of a programme on participants' awareness face the difficulty that a change in the level of awareness, to some extent, may be because of this reactive effect.

Another disadvantage that may occur when you use a research instrument twice to gauge the attitude of a population towards an issue is a possible shift in attitude between the two points of data collection. Sometimes people who place themselves at the extreme positions of a measurement scale at the pre-test stage may, for a number of reasons, shift towards the mean at the post-test stage (see Figure 8.3). They might feel that they have been too negative or too positive at the pre-test stage. Therefore, the mere expression of an attitude in response to a questionnaire or interview has caused them to think about and alter their attitude at the time of the post-test. This type of effect is known as the regression effect.

The longitudinal study design

The before-and-after study design is appropriate for measuring the extent of change in a phenomenon, situation, problem, attitude, and so on, but is less helpful for studying the pattern of change. To determine the pattern of change in relation to time, a longitudinal design is used; for example, when you wish to study the proportion of people adopting a programme over a period. Longitudinal studies are also useful when you need to collect factual information on a continuing basis. You may want to ascertain the trends in the demand for labour, immigration, changes in the incidence of a disease or in the mortality, morbidity and fertility patterns of a population.

In longitudinal studies the study population is visited a number of times at regular intervals, usually over a long period, to collect the required information (see Figure 8.4). These intervals are not fixed, so their length may vary from study to study. Intervals might be as short as a week or longer than a year. Irrespective of the size of

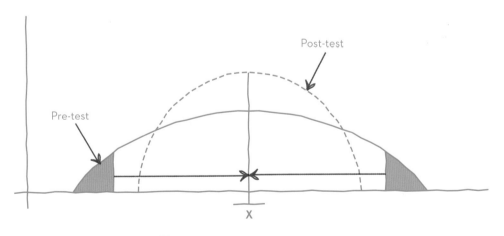

Figure 8.3 The regression effect

STEP TWO CONCEPTUALISING A RESEARCH DESIGN

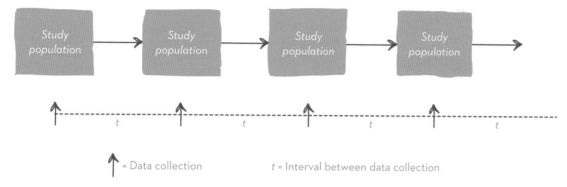

↑ = Data collection   *t* = Interval between data collection

Figure 8.4   The longitudinal study design

the interval, the type of information gathered each time is identical. Although the data collected is from the same study population, it may or may not be from the same respondents. A longitudinal study can be seen as a series of repeated cross-sectional studies.

Longitudinal studies have many of the same disadvantages as before-and-after studies, in some instances to an even greater degree. In addition, longitudinal studies can suffer from the conditioning effect. This describes a situation where, if the same respondents are contacted frequently, they begin to know what is expected of them and may respond to questions without thought, or they may lose interest in the enquiry, with the same result.

The main advantage of a longitudinal study is that it allows the researcher to measure the pattern of change and obtain factual information, requiring collection on a regular or continuing basis, thus enhancing its accuracy.

Study designs based on the reference period

The *reference period* refers to the time-frame in which a study is exploring a phenomenon, situation, event or problem. Studies are categorised from this perspective as:

⤷ retrospective;
⤷ prospective;
⤷ retrospective–prospective.

The retrospective study design

Retrospective studies investigate a phenomenon, situation, problem or issue that has happened in the past. They are usually conducted either on the basis of the data available for that period or on the basis of respondents' recall of the situation (Figure 8.5a). For example, studies conducted on the following topics are classified as retrospective studies:

CHECKPOINT
Longitudinal vs Cross-sectional designs

Conditioning effect: This describes a situation where, if the same respondents are contacted frequently, they begin to know what is expected of them and may respond to questions without thought, or they may lose interest in the enquiry, with the same result. This situation's effect on the quality of the answers is known as the conditioning effect.

Retrospective study: A retrospective study investigates a phenomenon, situation, problem or issue that has happened in the past. Such studies are usually conducted either on the basis of the data available for that period or on the basis of respondents' recall of the situation.

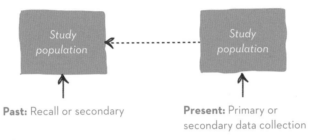

(a) **Retrospective Study Design**

Study population ←---- Study population

Past: Recall or secondary | **Present:** Primary or secondary data collection

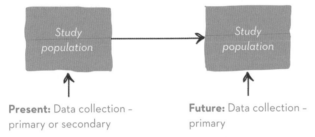

(b) **Prospective Study Design**

Study population ----→ Study population

Present: Data collection – primary or secondary | **Future:** Data collection – primary

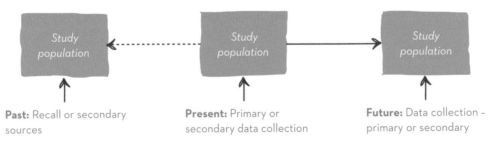

(c) **Retrospective-prospective Study Design**

Study population ←---- Study population ----→ Study population

Past: Recall or secondary sources | **Present:** Primary or secondary data collection | **Future:** Data collection – primary or secondary

Figure 8.5 **Classification of study designs based on the reference period: (a) retrospective; (b) prospective; (c) retrospective–prospective**

- The living conditions of aboriginal and Torres Strait islander peoples in Australia in the early twentieth century.
- The utilisation of land before the Second World War in Europe.
- A historical analysis of migratory movements in Eastern Europe between 1915 and 1945.
- The relationship between levels of unemployment and street crime (can be retrospective as well as prospective depending upon the way data is collected. If the data is collected from secondary sources pertaining to the past, it is a retrospective study. If it is collected on an ongoing basis to become the basis of exploring the relationship, it becomes a prospective study.)

The prospective study design

Prospective studies refer to the likely prevalence of a phenomenon, situation, problem, attitude or outcome in the future (Figure 8.5b). Such studies attempt to establish the outcome of an event or what is likely to happen. Experiments are usually classified as prospective studies as the researcher must wait for an intervention to register its effect on the study population. The following are classified as prospective studies:

- To determine, under field conditions, the impact of maternal and child health services on the level of infant mortality.
- To establish the effects of a counselling service on the extent of marital problems.
- To determine the impact of random breath testing on the prevention of road accidents.
- To find out the effect of parental involvement on the level of academic achievement of their children.
- To measure the effects of a change in migration policy on the extent of immigration in Australia.

The retrospective-prospective study design

Retrospective-prospective studies focus on past trends in a phenomenon and study it into the future. Part of the data is collected retrospectively from the existing records before the intervention is introduced and then the study population is followed to ascertain the impact of the intervention (Figure 8.5c).

A study is classified under this category when you measure the impact of an intervention without having a control group. In fact, most before-and-after studies, if carried out without having a control – where the baseline is constructed from the same population before introducing the intervention – will be classified as retrospective–prospective studies. Trend studies, which become the basis of projections, fall into this category too. Some examples of retrospective–prospective studies are:

- The effect of random breath testing on road accidents.
- The impact of incentives on the productivity of the employees of an organisation.
- The impact of maternal and child health services on the infant mortality rate.
- The effect of an advertisement on the sale of a product.

Prospective studies: refer to the likely prevalence of a phenomenon, situation, problem, attitude or outcome in the future. Such studies attempt to establish the outcome of an event or what is likely to happen. Experiments are usually classified as prospective studies because the researcher must wait for an intervention to register its effect on the study population.

Retrospective-prospective study: A retrospective-prospective study focuses on past trends in a phenomenon and studies it into the future. A study where you measure the impact of an intervention without having a control group by 'constructing' a previous baseline from either respondents' recall or secondary sources, then introducing the intervention to study its effect, is considered a retrospective-prospective study. In fact, most before-and-after studies, if carried out without having a control – where the baseline is constructed from the same population before introducing the intervention – will be classified as retrospective-prospective studies.

179

Study designs based on the nature of the investigation

On the basis of the nature of the investigation, study designs in quantitative research can be classified as:

↳ experimental;
↳ non-experimental;
↳ quasi- or semi-experimental.

To understand the differences, let us consider some examples. Suppose you want to test the following: the impact of a particular teaching method on the level of comprehension of students; the effectiveness of a programme such as random breath testing on the level of road accidents; or the usefulness of a drug such as azidothymidine (AZT) in treating people who are HIV-positive. In such situations there is assumed to be a cause-and-effect relationship.

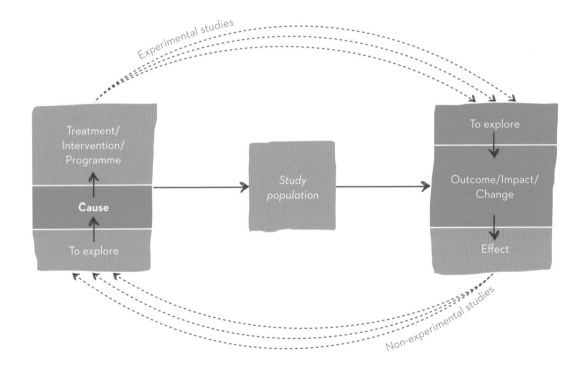

Figure 8.6   Experimental and non-experimental studies

There are two ways of studying these relationships. The first involves the researcher (or someone else) introducing the intervention that is assumed to be the 'cause' of change, and waiting until it has produced – or has been given sufficient time to produce – the change. The second consists of the researcher observing a phenomenon and attempting to establish what caused it. In this instance the researcher starts from the effect(s) or outcome(s) and attempts to determine the causes. If a relationship is studied in the first way, starting from the cause to establish the effects, it is classified as an experimental study. If the second path is followed – that is, starting from the effects to trace the cause – it is classified as a non-experimental study (see Figure 8.6).

In the former case the independent variable can be 'observed', introduced, controlled or manipulated by the researcher or someone else, whereas in the latter this cannot happen as the assumed cause has already occurred. Instead, the researcher retrospectively links the cause(s) to the outcome(s). A semi-experimental study or quasi-experimental study has the properties of both experimental and non-experimental studies; part of the study may be non-experimental and the other part experimental.

An experimental study can be carried out in either a 'controlled' or a 'natural' environment. For an experiment in a controlled environment, the researcher (or someone else) introduces the intervention or stimulus to study its effects. The study population is in a 'controlled' situation such as a room and such experiments are called controlled experiments. For an experiment in a 'natural' environment, the study population is exposed to an intervention in its own environment.

Experimental studies can be further classified on the basis of whether or not the study population is randomly assigned to different treatment groups. One of the biggest problems in comparative designs (those in which you compare two or more groups) is a lack of certainty that the different groups are in fact comparable in every

Experimental studies: In studying causality, when a researcher or someone else introduces the intervention that is assumed to be the 'cause' of change and waits until it has produced – or has been given sufficient time to produce – the change. In experimental studies a researcher starts with the cause and waits to observe its effects.

Non-experimental studies: There are times when, in studying causality, a researcher observes an outcome and wishes to investigate its causation. From the outcomes the researcher starts linking causes with them. Such studies are called non-experimental studies. In a non-experimental study you neither introduce nor control/manipulate the cause variable. You start with the effects and try to link them with the causes.

Semi-experimental studies: see Quasi-experimental studies.

Quasi-experimental studies: Studies which have the attributes of both experimental and non-experimental studies are called quasi- or semi-experiments.

Controlled experiments: In a control experiment the study population is divided into two groups, one experimental and the other control. The control group does not receive any stimulus or intervention whereas the experimental is exposed to it. The intervention or stimulus is ether introduced by the researcher or someone else.

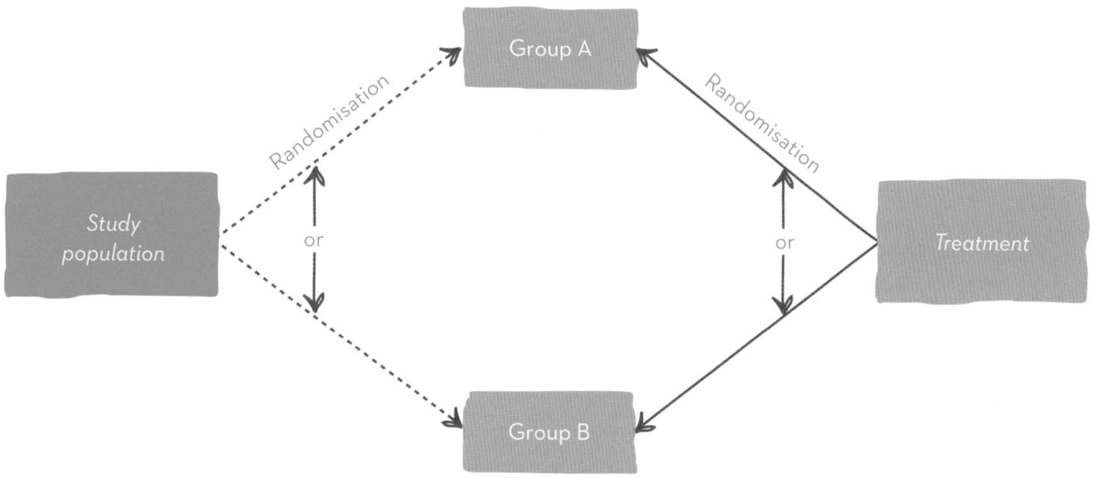

Figure 8.7   Randomisation in experiments

respect except the treatment. The process of randomisation is designed to ensure that the groups are comparable. In a random design, the study population, the experimental treatments or both are not predetermined but randomly assigned (see Figure 8.7). Random assignment in experiments means that any individual or unit of a study population group has an *equal* and *independent* chance of becoming part of an experimental or control group or, in the case of multiple treatment modalities, any treatment has an equal and independent chance of being assigned to any of the population groups. It is important to note that the concept of randomisation can be applied to any of the experimental designs we discuss.

Experimental study designs

There are so many types of experimental design that not all of them can be considered within the scope of this book. This section, therefore, is confined to describing those most commonly used in the social sciences, the humanities, public health, marketing, education, epidemiology, social work, and so on:

- the after-only experimental design;
- the before-and-after experimental design;
- the control group design;
- the double-control design;
- the comparative design;
- the matched control experimental design;
- the placebo design.

The after-only experimental design

In an after-only design the researcher knows that a population is being, or has been, exposed to an intervention and wishes to study its impact on the population. In this design, baseline information (pre-test or before observation) is usually 'constructed' on the basis of respondents' recall of the situation before the intervention, or from information available in existing records – secondary sources (Figure 8.8). The change in the dependent variable is measured by the difference between the 'before'(baseline) and 'after' data sets. Technically, this is a faulty design for measuring the impact of an intervention as there are no proper baseline data to compare the 'after' observation with. One of the major problems is that the two data sets are not strictly comparable. For example, some of the changes in the dependent variable may be attributable to the difference in the way the two sets of data were compiled. Another problem with this design is that it measures total change, including change attributable to extraneous variables; hence, it cannot identify the net effect of an intervention. However, this design is widely used in **impact assessment studies**, as in real life many programmes operate without the benefit of a planned evaluation at the programme planning stage (though this is rapidly changing) in which case it is just not possible to follow the sequence strictly – collection of baseline information, implementation of the programme and then programme evaluation. An evaluator therefore has no choice but to adopt this design.

In practice, the adequacy of this design depends on having reasonably accurate data available about the prevalence of a phenomenon before the intervention is introduced. This might be the case for situations such as

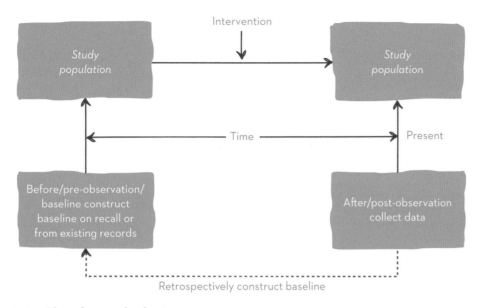

Figure 8.8   The after-only design

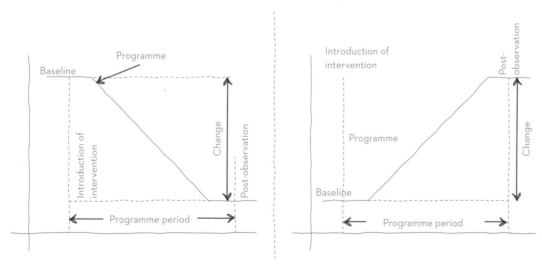

Figure 8.9   Measurement of change through a before-and-after design

the impact of random breath testing on road accidents, the impact of a health programme on the mortality of a population, the impact of an advertisement on the sale of a product, the impact of a decline in mortality on the fertility of a population or the impact of a change in immigration policy on the extent of immigration. In these situations it is expected that accurate records are kept about the phenomenon under study and so it may be easier to determine whether any change in trends is primarily because of the introduction of the intervention or change in the policy.

The before-and-after experimental design

The before-and-after design overcomes the problem of retrospectively constructing the 'before' observation by establishing it before the intervention is introduced to the study population (see Figure 8.2). Then, when the programme has been completely implemented or is assumed to have had its effect on the population, the 'after' observation is carried out to ascertain the impact attributable to the intervention (see Figure 8.9).

The before-and-after design takes care of only one problem of the after-only design – that is, the comparability of the before-and-after observations. It still does not enable one to conclude that any change – in whole or in part – can be attributed to the programme intervention. To overcome this, a *control group* is used. Before-and-after designs may also suffer from the problems identified earlier in this chapter in the discussion of before-and-after study designs. The impact of the intervention in before-and-after design is calculated as follows:

[change in dependent variable]

= [status of the dependent variable at the 'after' observation]

– [status of the dependent variable at the 'before' observation]

The control group design

In a study utilising the control design the researcher selects two population groups instead of one: a control group and an experimental group (Figure 8.10). These groups are expected to be comparable as far as possible in every respect except for the intervention (which is assumed to be the cause responsible for bringing about the change). The experimental group receives or is exposed to the intervention, while the control group is not. First, the 'before' observations are made on both groups at the same time. The experimental group is then exposed to the intervention. When it is assumed that the intervention has had an impact, an 'after' observation is made on both groups. Any difference in the 'before' and 'after' observations between the groups regarding the dependent variable(s) is attributed to the intervention.

In the experimental group, the total change in the dependent variable (Y_e) can be calculated as follows:

$$Y_e = E_a - E_b$$

where E_a is the 'after' observation on the experimental group and E_b is the 'before' observation on the experimental group. In other words,

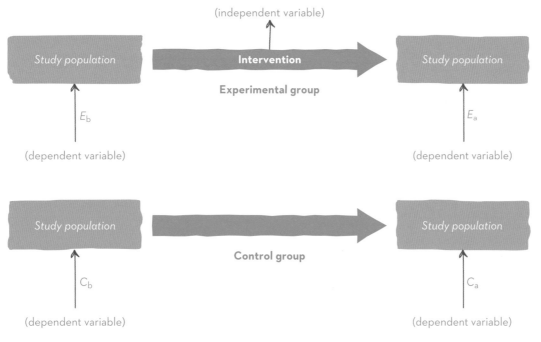

(independent variable)

Intervention

Study population | Study population

Experimental group

E_b

(dependent variable)

E_a

(dependent variable)

Study population | Study population

Control group

C_b

(dependent variable)

C_a

(dependent variable)

Figure 8.10   The control experimental design

$E_a - E_b$ = (impact of programme intervention) $\pm$ (impact of extraneous variables) $\pm$ (impact of chance variables)

In the control group, the total change in the dependent variable (Y_c) can be calculated as follows:

$$Y_c = C_a - C_b$$

where C_a is the 'after' observation on the control group and C_b is the 'before' observation on the control group. In other words,

$$C_a - C_b = \text{(impact of extraneous variables)} \pm \text{(impact of chance variables)}$$

The difference between the control and experimental groups can be calculated as

$$Y_e - Y_c = (E_a - E_b) - (C_a - C_b)$$

which is

{(impact of programme intervention) ± (impact of extraneous variables in experimental groups) ± (impact of chance variables in experimental groups)} – {(impact of extraneous variables in control group) ± (impact of chance variables in control group)}

Using simple arithmetic operations, this equals the impact of the intervention. Therefore, the impact of any intervention is equal to the difference in the 'before' and 'after' observations in the dependent variable between the experimental and control groups.

It is important to remember that the chief objective of the control group is to quantify the impact of extraneous variables. This helps you to ascertain the impact of the intervention only.

The double-control design

Double-control studies: Although the control group design helps quantify the impact that can be attributed to extraneous variables, it does not separate out other effects that may be due to the research instrument (such as the reactive effect) or respondents (such as the maturation or regression effects, or placebo effect). When you need to identify and separate out these effects, a double-control design is required. In a double-control study, you have two control groups instead of one. To quantify, say, the reactive effect of an instrument, you exclude one of the control groups from the 'before' observation.

Comparative study design: Sometimes you seek to compare the effectiveness of different treatment modalities. In such situations a comparative design is used. With a comparative design, as with most other designs, a study can be carried out either as an experiment or as a non-experiment. In the comparative experimental design, the study population is divided into the same number of groups as the number of treatments to be tested. For each group the baseline with respect to the dependent variable is established. The different treatment modalities are then introduced to the different groups. After a certain period, when it is assumed that the treatment models have had their effect, the 'after' observation is carried out to ascertain changes in the dependent variable.

Although the control design helps you to quantify the impact that can be attributed to extraneous variables, it does not separate out other effects that may be due to the research instrument (such as the reactive effect) or respondents (such as the maturation or regression effects, or placebo effect). When you need to identify and separate out these effects, a double-control design is required.

In double-control studies, you have two control groups instead of one. To quantify, say, the reactive effect of an instrument, you exclude one of the control groups from the 'before' observation (Figure 8.11).

You can calculate the different effects as follows:

$Y''_e - Y'_e$ = (impact of programme intervention) ± (impact of extraneous variables) ± (reactive effect) ± (random effect)

$Y''_{c1} - Y'_{c1}$ = (impact of extraneous variables) ± (reactive effect) ± (random effect)

$Y''_{c2} - Y'_{c1}$ = (impact of extraneous variables) ± (random effect)

(Note that the latter expression is $Y''_{c2} - Y'_{c1}$ and not $Y''_{c2} - Y'_{c2}$ as there is no 'before' observation for the second control group.) The differences are:

$Y''_e - Y'_e - (Y''_{c1} - Y'_{c1})$ = impact of programme intervention

$Y''_{c1} - Y'_{c1} - (Y'_{c2} - Y'_{c1})$ = reactive effect

The net effect of the programme intervention can be calculated in the same manner as for the control group designs as explained earlier.

The comparative design

Sometimes you seek to compare the effectiveness of different treatment modalities, and in such situations a comparative design is appropriate.

With a comparative study design, as with most other designs, a study can be carried out either as an experiment or as a non-experiment. In the comparative experimental design, the study population is divided into the same number of groups as the number of treatments to be tested. For each group the baseline with respect to the dependent variable is established. The different treatment models are then introduced to the different groups. After a certain period, when it is assumed that the treatment models have had their effect, the 'after' observation is carried out to ascertain any change in the dependent variable. The degree of change in the dependent variable in the different population groups receiving various treatment modalities is then compared to establish the relative effectiveness of the various interventions.

In the non-experimental form of comparative design, groups already receiving different interventions are identified, and only the post-observation with respect to the dependent variable is conducted. The pre-test data set is constructed either by asking the study population in each group to recall the required information relating to the period before the introduction of the treatment, or by extracting such information from existing records. Sometimes a pre-test observation is not constructed at all, on the assumption that if the groups are comparable the baseline must be identical. As each group is assumed to have the same baseline, the difference in the post-test observation is assumed to be because of the intervention.

To illustrate this, imagine you want to compare the effectiveness of three teaching models (A, B and C) on the level of comprehension of students in a class (Figure 8.12). To undertake the study, you divide the class into three groups (X, Y and Z), through randomisation, to ensure their comparability. Before exposing these groups to the teaching models, you first establish the baseline for each group's level of comprehension of the chosen subject. You then expose each group to a different teaching model to teach the chosen subject. Afterwards, you again measure the groups' levels of comprehension of the material. Suppose X_a is the average level of comprehension of group X before the material is taught, and X'_a is this group's average level of comprehension after the material is taught. The change in the level of comprehension, $X'_a - X_a$, is therefore attributed to model A. Similarly, changes in groups Y and Z, $Y'_b - Y_b$ and $Z'_c - Z_c$, are attributed to teaching models B and C, respectively. The changes in the average level of comprehension for the three groups are then compared to establish which teaching model is the most effective. (Note that extraneous variables will affect the level of comprehension in all groups equally, as they have been formed randomly.)

It is also possible to set up this study as a non-experimental one, simply by exposing each group to one of the three teaching models, following up with an 'after' observation. The difference in the levels of comprehension is attributed to the difference in the teaching models as it is assumed that the three groups are comparable with respect to their original level of comprehension of the topic.

The matched control experimental design

Comparative groups are usually formed on the basis of their overall comparability with respect to a relevant characteristic in the study population, such as socioeconomic status, the prevalence of a certain condition or the extent of a problem in the study population. In matched studies, comparability is determined on an individual-by-individual basis. Two individuals from the study population who are almost identical with respect to a selected characteristic and/or condition, such as age, gender or type of illness, are matched and then each is allocated to a separate group (the matching is usually done on an easily identifiable characteristic). In the case of a matched control experiment,

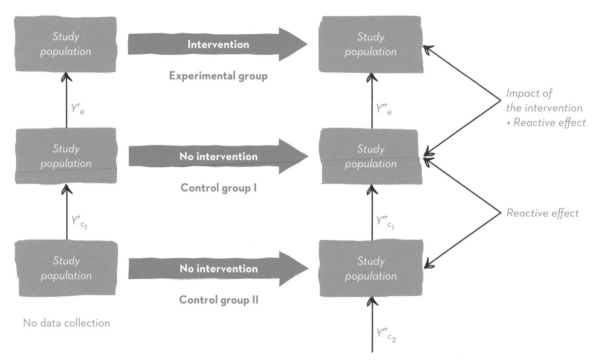

Figure 8.11   Double-control designs

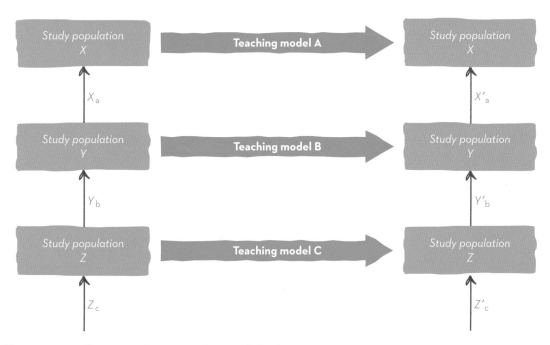

Figure 8.12 Comparative experimental design

once the two groups are formed, the researcher decides through randomisation or otherwise which group is to be considered control, and which experimental. The matched design can pose a number of challenges:

→ Matching increases in difficulty when carried out on more than one variable.

→ Matching on variables that are hard to measure, such as attitude or opinion, is extremely difficult.

→ Sometimes it is hard to know which variable to choose as a basis for matching. You may be able to base your decision upon previous findings, or you may have to undertake a preliminary study to determine your choice of variable.

Matched controlled designs are most commonly used in the testing of new drugs.

The placebo design

A patient's belief that s/he is receiving treatment can play an important role in his/her recovery from an illness even if treatment is ineffective. This psychological effect is known as the placebo effect. A placebo design

Placebo effect: A patient's belief that s/he is receiving a treatment plays an important role in his/her recovery even though the treatment may be fake or ineffective. The change occurs because a patient believes that s/he is receiving the treatment. This psychological effect that helps a patient to recover is known as the placebo effect.

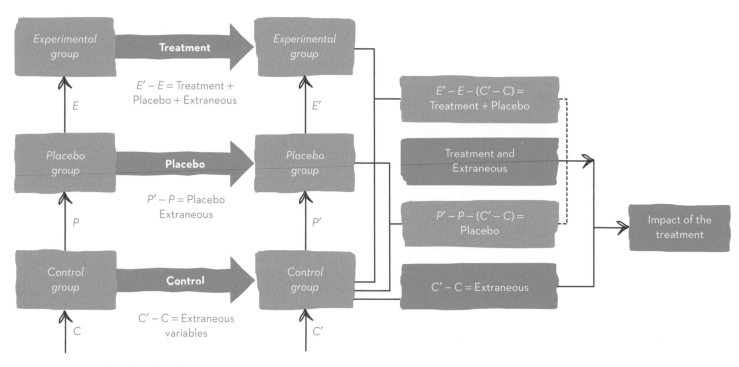

Figure 8.13　The placebo design

attempts to determine the extent of this effect. A placebo study involves two or three groups, depending on whether or not the researcher wants to have a control group (Figure 8.13). If the researcher decides to have a control group, the first group receives the treatment, the second receives the placebo treatment, and the third – the control group – receives nothing. The decision as to which group will be the treatment, the placebo or the control group can also be made through randomisation.

CHECKPOINT
Experimental designs

Other designs commonly used in quantitative research

There are some study designs that may be classified in the typology described above but, because of their uniqueness and prevalence, they have acquired their own names. They are therefore described separately below.

Online surveys

Advancements in and increased use of digital technology, in particular for communication, have created a unique opportunity for it to be used for social research. The last few years have witnessed a substantial increase in the use of online surveys for researching social issues. 'Like all research methods, online surveys research has benefits and drawbacks; the method works for some research projects but is by no means appropriate for all research objectives' (Sue & Ritter 2012: 1).

There are three common options for online surveys: e-mail, websites and mobile phones. Data collection through these follows the same developmental process as for a normal questionnaire. You develop a questionnaire through the use of software and store it on an Internet server for retrieval by a potential respondent via an Internet link. As a potential respondent, you retrieve the questionnaire via the link and answer the questions in the same way as you would have done for a normal questionnaire. The only difference is that in a normal questionnaire you complete the questionnaire by hand and in an online questionnaire you use a computer keyboard.

Sue and Ritter (2012: Chapter 1) have identified many situations in which online surveys are desirable to conduct. Online surveys are extremely useful when you have a large and geographically diverse sample. They are quicker and cheaper. However, there are a number of constraints on their use. First and foremost, not everyone has Internet or mobile phone access, so online surveys cannot be used for all population groups. In addition, the population with Internet and mobile phone access may have very different characteristics as compared to the general population so may not truly represent the general population. It is also impossible to select a random sample as there is no sampling frame for Internet users. Use of the Internet also requires the researcher to have adequate technical knowledge and skills in the development of a digital survey. But if you have the requisite technical expertise and there are no other constraints, the use of the Internet for social research could be fast, efficient and low cost.

According to Sue and Ritter (2012: 14), 'When we refer to e-mail surveys, we mean surveys created by using survey software and accessed by respondents through a link in an e-mail invitation. These are among the most common online surveys because anyone who has access to online survey software, such as SurveyMonkey, Zoomerang, or InstantSurvey, can create an e-mail survey.'

Placebo study: A study that attempts to determine the extent of a placebo effect is called a placebo study. A placebo study is based upon a comparative study design that involves two or more groups, depending on whether or not you want to have a control group to isolate the impact of extraneous variables or other treatment modalities to determine their relative effectiveness.

Online survey: Online surveys have become reasonably common in collecting data and, in some situation, its analysis. There are three common options for data collection through online: e-mail, websites and mobile phones.

191

The main difference between an e-mail and an Internet survey is the way a respondent accesses the survey questionnaire. In an e-mail survey the access is through a link provided in the e-mail, whereas in an Internet survey the questionnaire 'appears on a webpage, either as a link posted somewhere on the page or as a pop-up or crawl-in link' (Sue & Ritter 2012: 17–18).

With the development of smartphones and computer tablets the scope of mobile surveys has changed. Formerly, mobile surveys 'referred primarily to a series of text messages sent to respondents' mobile phones' (Sue & Ritter 2012: 19). Nowadays, with the advancement in technology, there are programs that enable you to do full online surveys on smartphones and tablets.

'To conduct an e-mail, website, or mobile survey, you will need software and the service of a web-based survey host' (Sue & Ritter 2012: 20). There are many web-based survey hosts in the market providing different types of survey software, and you need to do some research to determine their suitability for your situation. In addition, you also need to thoroughly consider their terms and conditions of use as set out by the application service provider that you intend to use. You should thoroughly consider all technical and logistical aspects before undertaking an online study. There is much to think about, and you are advised to read references specifically dealing with online surveys before venturing into one.

The cross-over comparative experimental design

The denial of treatment to the control group is considered unethical by some professionals. In addition, it may be unacceptable to some individuals in the control group, which could result in them dropping out of the experiment and/or going elsewhere to receive treatment. The former increases experimental mortality, and the latter may contaminate the study. The cross-over comparative experimental design makes it possible to measure the impact of a treatment without denying treatment to any group, though this design has its own problems.

In the cross-over design, also called the ABAB design (Grinnell 1993: 104), two groups are formed, the intervention is introduced to one of them and, after a certain period, the impact of this intervention is measured. Then the interventions are 'crossed over'; that is, the experimental group becomes the control and vice versa, sometimes repeatedly over the period of the study (Figure 8.14). However, in this design, population groups do not constitute experimental or control groups but only segments upon which experimental and control observations are conducted.

One of the major issues is in relation to the discontinuity in treatment. The main question is: what impact would intervention have produced had it not been withdrawn from the experimental segments; that is, how would the discontinuity in the treatment have affected the overall impact of the treatment?

The replicated cross-sectional design

In practice one usually examines programmes already in existence and ones in which clients are at different stages of an intervention. Evaluating the effectiveness of such programmes within a conventional experimental design is impossible because a baseline cannot be established as the intervention has already been introduced. This means that the usual method of selecting a group of people recently recruited to the programme and following them through until the intervention has been completed may take a long time. In such situations, it is possible to choose clients who are at different stages of the programme to form the basis of your study (Figure 8.15).

Cross-over comparative experimental design: In the cross-over design, also called the ABAB design, two groups are formed, the intervention is introduced to one of them and, after a certain period, the impact of this intervention is measured. Then the interventions are 'crossed over'; that is, the experimental group becomes the control and vice versa.

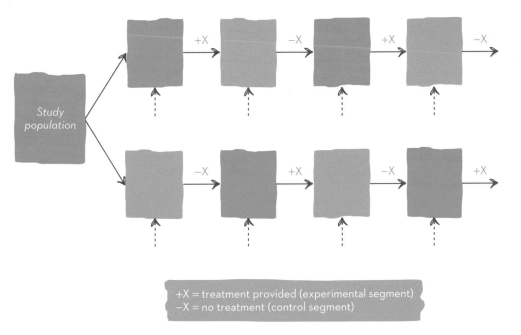

+X = treatment provided (experimental segment)
−X = no treatment (control segment)

Figure 8.14   The cross-over experimental design

The replicated cross-sectional design is based upon the assumption that participants at different stages of a programme are similar in terms of their socioeconomic-demographic characteristics and the problem for which they are seeking intervention. Assessment of the effectiveness of an intervention is done by taking a sample of clients at different stages of the intervention. The difference in the dependent variable among clients at intake and termination stage is considered to be the impact of the intervention.

Trend studies

If you want to map changes in a phenomenon, situation, attitudes or facts relating to an area of interest to you over a period, a trend study is the most appropriate method of investigation. Trend analysis enables you to find out what has happened in the past, what is happening now and what is likely to happen in the future in a population group. This design involves selecting a number of data observation points in the past, together with a picture of the present or immediate past with respect to the phenomenon under study, and then making certain assumptions as to the future trends. In a way you are collecting cross-sectional observations about the trend being

Replicated cross-sectional design: This study design is based upon the assumption that participants at different stages of a programme are similar in terms of their socioeconomic-demographic characteristics and the problem for which they are seeking intervention. Assessment of the effectiveness of an intervention is done by taking a sample of clients who are at different stages of the intervention. The difference in the dependent variable among clients at the intake and termination stage is considered to be the impact of the intervention.

Trend studies: These studies involve selecting a number of data observation points in the past, together with a picture of the present or immediate past with respect to the phenomenon under study, and then making certain assumptions as to the likely future trends. In a way you are compiling a cross-sectional picture of the trends being observed at different points in time over the past, present and future. From these cross-sectional observations you draw conclusions about the pattern of change.

observed at different points in time in the past, present and future. From these cross-sectional observations you draw conclusions about the pattern of change.

Trend studies are useful in making forecasts by extrapolating present and past trends, thus making a valuable contribution to planning. Trends regarding the phenomenon under study can be correlated with other characteristics of the study population. For example, you may want to examine the changes in political preference of a study population in relation to age, gender, income or ethnicity. This design can also be classified as a retrospective–prospective design.

Cohort studies

Cohort studies are based upon the existence of a common characteristic, such as year of birth, graduation or marriage, within a subgroup of a population. Suppose you want to study the employment pattern of a batch of accountants who graduated from a university in 1985, or study the fertility behaviour of women who were married in 1970. To study the accountants' career paths you would contact all the accountants who graduated from the university

Cohort studies: These are based upon the existence of a common characteristic such as year of birth, graduation or marriage, within a subgroup of a population that you want to study. People with the common characteristics are studied over a period of time to collect the information of interest. Studies could cover fertility behaviour of women born in 1986 or career paths of 1990 graduates from a medical school, for instance. Cohort studies look at the trends over a long period of time and collect data from the same group of people.

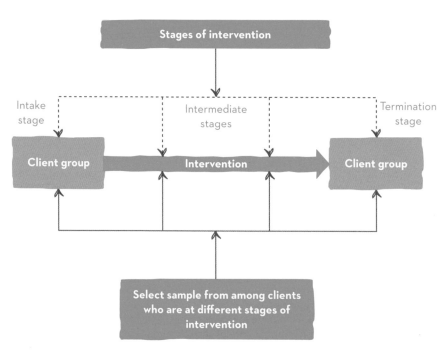

Figure 8.15   The replicated cross-sectional design

STEP TWO CONCEPTUALISING A RESEARCH DESIGN

in 1985 to find out their employment histories. Similarly, you would investigate the fertility history of those women who married in 1970. Both of these studies could be carried out either as cross-sectional or longitudinal designs. If you adopt a cross-sectional design you gather the required information in one go, but if you choose the longitudinal design you collect the required information at different points in time over the study period. Both these designs have their strengths and weaknesses. In the case of a longitudinal design, it is not important for the required information to be collected from the same respondents, though it is important that all the respondents belong to the cohort being studied; that is, in the above examples they must have graduated in 1985 or married in 1970.

Panel studies

Panel studies are similar to trend and cohort studies except that, in addition to being longitudinal, they are prospective in nature and the information is always collected from the same respondents. (In trend and cohort studies the information can be collected in a cross-sectional manner and the observation points can be retrospectively constructed.) Suppose you want to study the changes in the pattern of expenditure on household items in a community. To do this, you would select a few families to find out how much they spend (say) every fortnight on household items. You would keep collecting the same information from the same families over a period of time to ascertain the changes in the expenditure pattern. Similarly, a panel study design could be used to study the morbidity pattern in a community.

Blind studies

The concept of a blind study is used in relation to comparable and placebo designs and is applicable to studies that are designed to measure the effectiveness of a drug or an intervention. In a blind study, the study population does not know whether or not it is getting real or fake treatment or, in the case of comparative testing, which treatment. The main objective of using a blind study design is to isolate the placebo effect by not letting the participants know about the treatment.

Double-blind studies

Double-blind studies are very similar to blind studies but also try to eliminate researcher bias by concealing the identity of the experimental and placebo groups from the researcher. In other words, in a double-blind study neither the researcher nor the study participants know who is receiving real and who is receiving fake treatment or which treatment they are receiving.

STUDY DESIGNS IN QUALITATIVE RESEARCH

This section provides a brief description of some of the designs commonly used in qualitative research. The author does not like to segregate quantitative and qualitative designs, but has done so to enable the newcomer

Panel studies: These are prospective in nature and are designed to collect information from the same respondents over a period of time. The group of individuals selected becomes a panel that provides the required information. In a panel study the period of data collection can range from once only to repeated data collections over a long period.

Blind studies: In a blind study, the study population does not know whether it is getting real or fake treatment or, modality in the case of comparative studies, which treatment. The main objective of designing a blind study is to isolate the placebo effect.

Double-blind studies: A double-blind study is very similar to a blind study except that it also tries to eliminate researcher bias by not disclosing to the researcher the identities of experimental, comparative and placebo groups. In a double-blind study neither the researcher nor the study participants know which study participants are receiving real, placebo or other forms of interventions. This prevents the possibility of introducing bias by the researcher.

195

to research to gain a better understanding. Keep in mind, as has been repeated a number of times, that many qualitative study designs are quite prevalent in quantitative research studies. For an in-depth understanding you are advised to consult books on qualitative research.

Case study

Case study: The case study design is based upon the assumption that the case being studied is typical of cases of a certain type and therefore a single case can provide insight into the events and situations prevalent in a group from where the case has been drawn. In a case study design the 'case' you select becomes the basis of a thorough, holistic and in-depth exploration of the aspect(s) that you want to find out about. It is an approach in which a particular instance or a few carefully selected cases are studied intensively. To be called a case study it is important to treat the total study population as one entity. It is one of the important study designs in qualitative research.

The case study, though predominantly a qualitative study design, is also prevalent in quantitative research. A case could be an individual, a group, a community, an instance, an episode, an event, a subgroup of a population, a town or a city. To be called a case study it is important to treat the total study population as one entity.

In a case study design the case you select becomes the basis of a thorough, holistic and in-depth exploration of the aspect(s) that you want to find out about. It is an approach 'in which a particular instance or a few carefully selected cases are studied intensively' (Gilbert 2008: 36). According to Burns (1997: 364), 'to qualify as a case study, *it must be a bounded system*, an entity in itself. A case study should focus on a bounded subject/unit that is either very representative or extremely atypical.' A case study, according to Grinnell (1981: 302), 'is characterized by a very flexible and open-ended technique of data collection and analysis'.

The case study design is based upon the assumption that the case being studied is typical of cases of a certain type and therefore a single case can provide insight into the events and situations prevalent in a group from where the case has been drawn. According to Burns (1997: 365), 'In a case study the focus of attention is the case in its idiosyncratic complexity, not on the whole population of cases'. In selecting a case therefore you usually use purposive, judgemental or information-oriented sampling techniques.

It is a very useful design when exploring an area where little is known or where you want to have a holistic understanding of the situation, phenomenon, episode, site, group or community. According to Gilbert (2008: 36), 'The advantage of the case study design is that the research can be much more detailed than would be possible if one is studying a large sample, but the corresponding disadvantage is that it is much more difficult and often impossible to generalise the findings'. This design is of immense relevance when the focus of a study is on extensively exploring and understanding rather than confirming and quantifying. It provides an overview and in-depth understanding of a case(s), process and interactional dynamics within a unit of study but cannot claim to make any generalisations to a population beyond cases similar to the one studied.

In this design you are attempting not to select a random sample but a case that can provide you with as much information as possible to understand the case in its totality. When studying an episode or an instance, you attempt to gather information from all available sources so as to understand it in its entirety. If the focus of your study is a group or community you should spend sufficient time building a good rapport with its members before collecting any information about them.

Though you can use a single method, in-depth interviewing, the use of multiple methods to collect data, such as obtaining information from secondary records, gathering data through observations and collecting information through focus groups and group interviews, is an important aspect of a case study. However, it is important that at the time of analysis you continue to consider the case as a single entity.

Oral history

Oral history is more a method of data collection than a study design; however, in qualitative research, it has become an approach to the study of perceptions, experiences and accounts of an event or gathering historical knowledge as viewed by individuals. It is a picture of something in someone's own words. Oral history is a process of obtaining, recording, presenting and interpreting historical or current information, based upon personal experiences and opinions of some members of a study group or unit. These opinions or experiences could be based upon eyewitness evidence or information passed on from other sources such as older people, ancestors, folklore and stories. According to Ritchie (2003: 19), 'Memory is the core of oral history, from which meaning can be extracted and preserved. Simply put, oral history collects memories and personal commentaries of historical significance through recorded interviews.' According to Burns (1997: 368), 'these are usually first person narratives that the researcher collects using extensive interviewing of a single individual'.

In terms of design it is quite simple. You first decide what types of account, experience, perception or historical event you want to find out about. Then you need to identify the individuals or sources (which could be difficult and time-consuming) that can best provide you with the required information. You then collect information from them to be analysed and interpreted.

Focus groups/group interviews

Focus groups are a form of strategy in qualitative research in which attitudes, opinions or perceptions towards an issue, product, service or programme are explored through a free and open discussion between members of a group and the researcher. Both focus groups and group interviews are facilitated group discussions in which a researcher raises issues or asks questions that stimulate discussion among members of the group. Because of its low cost, it is a popular method for finding information in almost every professional area and academic field. Social, political and behavioural scientists, market research and product testing agencies, and urban and town planning experts often use this design for a variety of situations. For example, in marketing research this design is widely used to obtain consumers' opinion of and feedback on a product, their opinions on the quality of the product, its acceptance and appeal, price and packaging, how to improve the quality and increase the sale of the product, etc. Focus groups are also prevalent in formative and summative evaluations and for developing social programmes and services. It is a useful tool in social and urban planning for identifying issues, options, development strategies, and future planning and development directions.

In its design it is very simple. As a researcher, you select a group of people who you think are best equipped to discuss what you want to explore. The group could comprise individuals drawn from a group of highly trained professionals or average residents of a community, depending upon the objectives of the focus group. In the formation of a focus group the size of the group is an important consideration. It should be neither too large nor too small as this can impede upon the extent and quality of the discussion; about eight to ten people is usually considered optimal. You need to identify carefully the issues for discussion, providing every opportunity for additional relevant ones to emerge. You need to decide, in consultation with the group, the process of recording

Oral history: More a method of data collection than a study design; however, in qualitative research, it has become an approach for studying a historical event or for gaining information about a culture, custom or story that has been passed on from generation to generation. It is a picture of something in someone's own words. Oral histories, like narratives, involve the use of both passive and active listening. However, they are more commonly used for learning about cultural, social or historical events whereas narratives are more about a person's own experiences.

Focus group: The focus group is a form of strategy in qualitative research in which attitudes, opinions or perceptions towards an issue, product, service or programme are explored through a free and open discussion between members of a group and the researcher. The focus group is a facilitated group discussion in which a researcher raises issues or asks questions that stimulate discussion among members of the group. Issues, questions and different perspectives on them and any significant points arising during these discussions provide data to draw conclusions and inferences. It is like collectively interviewing a group of respondents.

Group interview: A group interview is both a method of data collection and a qualitative study design. The interaction is between the researcher and the group with the aim of collecting information from the group collectively rather than individually from members.

the discussion. This may include very simple things such as fixing the times that the group can meet, and more complex matters such as how to arrive at agreement if disagreement emerges in the group.

Your records of the discussions then become the basis of analysis for findings and conclusions. The main difference between a focus group and a group interview is in the degree of specificity with respect to the issues to be discussed. The issues discussed in focus groups are more specific and focused than in group interviews and they are largely predetermined by the researcher. In a group interview you let the group members discuss whatever they want. However, your role as a researcher is to bring them back to the issues of interest as identified by the group.

Compared with other designs this is less expensive and needs far less time to complete. The information generated can be detailed and rich and can be used to explore a vast variety of issues. However, the disadvantage is that if the discussion is not carefully directed it may reflect the opinion of those who have a tendency to dominate a group. This design is very useful for exploring the diversity in opinions on different issues, but will not help you if you want to find out the extent or magnitude of this diversity.

Participant observation

Participant observation is another strategy for gathering information about a social interaction or a phenomenon in qualitative studies. This is usually done by developing a close interaction with members of a group or 'living' in the situation which is being studied. Though predominantly a qualitative research design, it is also used in quantitative research, depending upon how the information has been generated and recorded. In qualitative research, an observation is always recorded in a descriptive format, whereas in quantitative research it is recorded either in categories or on a scale. It can also be a combination of both – some categorisation and some description or categorisation accompanied by a descriptive explanation. You can also change a descriptive recording into a categorical one through analysis and classification. In addition to the observation itself, where you as an observer generate information, the information can also be collected through other methods such as informal interviewing, in-depth interviewing, group discussions, previous documents and oral histories. Use of multiple methods will enhance the richness of the information collected by participant observation.

In its design it is simple. You as a researcher get involved in the activities of the group, create a rapport with group members and then, having sought their consent, keenly observe the situation, interaction, site or phenomenon. You make detailed notes of what you observe in a format that best suits you as well as the situation. You can also collect information using other methods of data collection, if need be. You analyse records of your observations and data collected by other means to draw inferences and conclusions.

The main advantage of participant observation is that as you spend sufficient time with the group or in the situation, you gain much deeper, richer and more accurate information, but the main disadvantage is that, if you are not very careful, you can introduce your own bias.

Holistic research

The **holistic approach** to research is once again more a philosophy than a study design. The 'design' is based upon the philosophy that as a multiplicity of factors interact in our lives, we cannot understand a phenomenon from just

198

one or two perspectives. To understand a situation or phenomenon you need to look at it in its totality – that is, holistically from every perspective. You can use any design when exploring a situation from different perspectives and the use of multiple methods is prevalent and desirable.

CHECKPOINT
Focus groups vs Interviews

Community discussion forums

Community discussion forums are designed to find the opinions, attitudes and/or ideas of a community with regard to community issues and problems. They are a very popular way to seek a community's participation in deciding about issues of concern to its members. Such forums are used in developing town planning options and community health programmes for a community, seeking the participation of its members in resolving issues relating to traffic management, infrastructure development and determining future directions for the area, and informing communities of new initiatives.

Community forums are very similar to group discussions but are on a bigger scale in terms of the number of participants. Also, in group discussions you may select the participants, but community forums involve self-selection of the participants as they are open to everyone with an interest in the issues or concerns. You as a researcher usually use local media to inform the residents of a local community about such forums.

This is a useful design for finding out about the spread of issues, concerns, etc., at a community level. It is economical and quick, but there are some disadvantages. For example, it is possible that a few people with a vested interest can dominate the discussion in a forum, and it is equally possible that on occasions there may be very low attendance. Such situations may result in the discussion not reflecting the community's attitudes.

Community discussion forum: A community discussion forum is a qualitative strategy designed to find opinions, attitudes and ideas of a community with regard to community issues and problems. It is one of the common ways of seeking a community's participation in deciding about issues of concern to it.

Reflective journal log

Basically, this design entails keeping a reflective journal log of your thoughts as a researcher whenever you notice anything, talk to someone, participate in an activity or observe something that helps you understand or add to whatever you are trying to find out about. These reflective records then become the basis of your findings and conclusions. You can have a reflective journal as the only method of data collection, or it can be used in combination with other methods such as interviewing, group interviews or secondary sources.

Reflective journal log: This is a method of data collection in qualitative research that entails keeping a log of your thoughts as a researcher whenever you notice anything, talk to someone, participate in an activity or observe something that helps you understand or add to whatever you are trying to find out about. This log becomes the basis of your research findings.

199

OTHER COMMONLY USED PHILOSOPHY-GUIDED DESIGNS

There are a number of other approaches to research that have acquired recognition in the research literature. While not designs per se, they do advance a particular philosophical perspective in social research. These are: action research, feminist research, participatory research and collaborative enquiry. Strictly speaking, a piece of research within each of these could be either quantitative or qualitative, though they are considered predominantly as qualitative designs. The need to place them in a separate category stems from their prominence and possible use in each paradigm. These designs are more philosophy guided than methods based. For example,

CHECKPOINT
What is netnography?

action research is guided by the philosophy that a piece of research should be followed by some form of appropriate action to achieve betterment in life or service; feminist research is influenced by the philosophy that opposes and challenges the predominant male bias in social science research, and seems to believe that issues relating to women are best understood and researched by women alone. For participatory research and collaborative enquiry, the involvement of research participants or the community in the research process is the underlying philosophy. One of the important aspects of all these 'designs' is that they attempt to involve research participants in the research process. The research findings are then used to depict the current situation with respect to certain issues or problems and help to form a sound basis for strategy development to deal with them.

Action research

Action research: In common with participatory research and collaborative enquiry, action research is based upon a philosophy of community development that seeks the involvement of community members in planning, undertaking, developing and implementing research and programme agendas. Research is a means to action to deal with a problem or an issue confronting a group or community. It follows a cyclical process that is used to identify the issues, develop strategies and implement the programmes to deal with them and then again assessing strategies in light of the issues.

As the name suggests, action research comprises two components: *action* and *research* (see Figure 8.16). Research is a means to action, either to improve your practice or to take action to deal with a problem or an issue. Since action research is guided by the desire to take action, strictly speaking it is not a design per se. Most action research is concerned with improving the quality of service. It is carried out to identify areas of concern, develop and test alternatives, and experiment with new approaches.

Action research seems to follow two traditions. The British tradition tends to view action research as a means of improvement and advancement of practice (Carr & Kemmis 1986), whereas in the US tradition it is aimed at systematic collection of data that provides the basis for social change (Bogdan & Biklen 1992).

Action research, in common with participatory research and collaborative enquiry, is based upon a philosophy of community development that seeks the involvement of community members. The two salient features of all three approaches are the involvement and participation of a community in the total process from problem identification to implementation of solutions. Data is collected through a research process that can be either quantitative, qualitative or mixed, and changes are achieved through action. This action is taken either by officials of an institution or the community itself in the case of action research, or by members of a community in the case of collaborative or participatory research.

There are two focuses of action research:

1 An existing programme or intervention is studied in order to identify possible areas of improvement in terms of enhanced efficacy and/or efficiency. The findings become the basis of bringing about changes.

2 A professional identifies an unattended problem or unexplained issue in the community or among a client group, and research evidence is gathered to justify the introduction of a new service or intervention. Research techniques establish the prevalence of the problem or the importance of an issue so that appropriate action can be taken to deal with it.

Feminist research

Feminist research: Like action research, feminist research is more a philosophy than design. Feminist concerns and theory act as the guiding framework for this research. The main characteristics of feminist research are a focus on the viewpoints of women, the aim of reducing the power imbalance between researcher and respondents, and attempts to change social inequality between men and women.

Feminist research is characterised by a feminist theory philosophical base that underpins all enquiries and feminist concerns act as the guiding framework. Feminist research differs from traditional research in three ways:

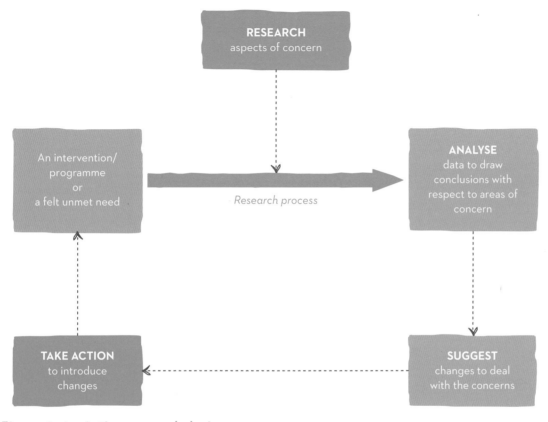

Figure 8.16   Action research design

1   Its main focus is the experiences and viewpoints of women. It uses research methods aimed at exploring these.

2   It actively tries to remove or reduce the power imbalance between the researcher and respondents.

3   The goal of feminist research is to change the social inequality between men and women. In fact, feminist research may be classified as action research in the area of gender inequality, using research techniques to create awareness of women's issues and concerns, and to foster action promoting equality between sexes.

Any study design could be used in feminist research.

Participatory research and collaborative enquiry

Participatory research: Participatory research and collaborative enquiry are not study designs per se but signify a philosophical perspective that advocates an active involvement of research participants in the research process. Participatory research is based upon the principle of minimising the 'gap' between the researcher and the research participants. The most important feature is the involvement and participation of the community or research participants in the research process to make the research findings more relevant to their needs.

Collaborative enquiry: Another name for participatory research that advocates a close collaboration between the researcher and the research participants.

As already mentioned, to the author's mind, these are not designs per se but signify a philosophical perspective that advocates the active involvement of research participants in the research process. Both participatory research and collaborative enquiry are based upon the principle of minimising the 'gap' between the researcher and the research participants and emphasis on increased community involvement and participation to enhance the relevance of the research findings to their needs. It is assumed that such involvement will increase the possibility of the community accepting the research findings and, if need be, its willingness and involvement in solving the problems and issues that confront it. You can undertake a quantitative or qualitative study in these perspectives but the main emphasis is on people's engagement, collaboration and participation in the research process. In a way these designs are based on the community development model where engagement of a community by way of consultation and participation in planning and execution of research tasks is imperative. You are not merely a researcher but also a community organiser seeking active participation of the community.

As a researcher you work at two different levels: (1) community organisation and (2) research. As community organiser you seek a community's involvement and participation in identifying community demands and needs, prioritising them, developing solutions, planning strategies and executing tasks to meet them. In terms of research, your main responsibility is to develop, in consultation with the community, the research tasks and procedures and share research findings with its members. Consultation with research participants at both these levels is a continuous and integral part of these designs.

SUMMARY

In this chapter various study designs in both quantitative and qualitative research have been examined. For each study design, details have been provided on the situations in which the design is appropriate to use, its strengths and weaknesses, and the process adopted in its operationalisation.

In quantitative research the various study designs have been examined from three perspectives. The terminology used to describe these perspectives is that of the author, but the names of the study designs are universally used. The different study designs across each category are mutually exclusive, but not so within a category.

The three perspectives are the number of contacts, the reference period and the nature of the investigation. The first includes cross-sectional studies, before-and-after studies and longitudinal studies. The second categorises the studies as retrospective, prospective and retrospective–prospective. The third classifies studies as experimental, non-experimental and semi-experimental studies. Designs such as after-only experimental designs, before-and-after experimental designs, control designs, comparative designs, matched control, the placebo design have been described in detail. The chapter also details some of the commonly used designs in quantitative research. These are online surveys, cross-over comparative design, trend studies, cohort studies, panel studies, and blind and double-blind studies.

Qualitative study designs are not as specific, precise and well defined as designs in quantitative research. Also, there is a degree of overlap between study designs and methods of data collection. Some designs can easily be considered as methods of data collection. Some of the commonly used designs in qualitative research are: case study design, oral history, focus group studies, participant observation, community discussion forums and the reflective journal log.

Four additional approaches to research have been described: action research, feminist research, participatory research and collaborative enquiry. Though these cannot really be considered designs in themselves, they have acquired their own identity. Both action and feminist research can be carried out either quantitatively or qualitatively, but participatory and collaborative enquiries are usually qualitative in nature.

Now that you have read the full chapter...

CHECK YOUR UNDERSTANDING

- ☐ Do you understand the meaning and application of all of the keywords at the start of the chapter? If not, visit the online resources and use the glossary flashcards to get to grips with their definitions.

- ☐ What are the differences between quantitative and qualitative study designs?

- ☐ Define the following:
  - ☐ Regression effect
  - ☐ Maturation effect
  - ☐ Reactive effect

- ☐ In an experimental study, what purpose does a control group serve?

- ☐ What is the difference between an experimental and non-experimental study?

- ☐ What is randomisation and what purpose does it serve in a study?

- ☐ In this book the typology of study designs is developed from three perspectives. Critically examine the validity of these perspectives.

APPLY IT TO YOUR OWN PROJECT

- ☐ Identify two or three situations relating to your own area of interest where you think qualitative study designs might be more beneficial, and consider why this might be the case.

- ☐ Take an example from your own academic field or professional area where an experimental control or placebo group might be used and explore the ethical issues relating to this.

CONFUSED?

THE ONLINE RESOURCES ARE HERE TO HELP YOU

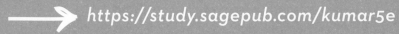 https://study.sagepub.com/kumar5e

CHECKPOINT: What are the major differences between qualitative and quantitative designs? Visit this website.

CHECKPOINT: What is a cross-sectional study? Read this encyclopaedia entry.

CHECKPOINT: What are the different types of a pre-test/post-test design? Visit this website.

CHECKPOINT: What are the differences between a longitudinal design and a cross-sectional design? Visit this website.

CHECKPOINT: What are the most common experimental designs in the social sciences? Visit this website.

CHECKPOINT: What are the main principles of an online survey? Visit this website.

CHECKPOINT: What is the difference between a focus group and an in-depth interview? Watch this video.

NEED MORE GENERAL SUPPORT?

Get up to speed on key terms with *glossary flashcards* and test yourself on important concepts with *multiple choice questions*.

UP FOR A CHALLENGE?

THE ONLINE RESOURCES ARE HERE TO INSPIRE YOU

 https://study.sagepub.com/kumar5e

CHECKPOINT: How do you determine if a qualitative research design or a quantitative research design is better suited to your research problem? Visit this website.

CHECKPOINT: What does a cross-sectional study look like? Explore this case study.

CHECKPOINT: What does a pre-test/post-test study look like? Explore this case study.

CHECKPOINT: When would you choose to use a longitudinal design instead of a cross-sectional one? Visit this website.

CHECKPOINT: Where can you find cutting-edge examples of experimental social science research? Visit this website.

CHECKPOINT: How do you conduct a valid and reliable online survey? Read this chapter.

CHECKPOINT: When would you want to conduct a focus group instead of interviews? Visit this website.

READY TO WORK ON YOUR OWN PROJECT?

Start building a portfolio of your ideas with the exercise workbook and get support tailored to your specific assignment with the assessment toolkit.

EXERCISE II: CONCEPTUALISING A STUDY DESIGN

For quantitative studies

Exercise I helped you to develop your research problem, providing you with a clear idea about *what* you want to find out about. Now the next step is to decide *how* to go about it. Exercise II is designed to help you to take this step. This includes deciding on an overall plan and selecting procedures and methods that you propose to use during your research journey. The details of your plan and procedures become the core of your study design.

Template of Exercise II

A study design describes the design per se, that is, the type of study design you propose to adopt; for example, whether the proposed study is cross-sectional, correlational or experimental. It should also provide details of the logistical procedures required for gathering information from the study population. This exercise helps you to put forward your arguments to justify the selection of the design you are proposing for your study, critically examining its strengths and weaknesses, and thus enabling you to select the best and workable study design. The exercise also challenges you to think through other logistical procedures such as outlining the process of identifying and contacting your study population and your plan to obtain the required information from your potential respondents, thus helping you to develop the road map for your journey.

For qualitative studies the process is the same though it varies in content.

The issues raised in this exercise will help you to conceptualise your study design. Chapter 8 details the various types of study design in both quantitative and qualitative research for you to refer to while working through this exercise.

A Answers to the following questions will help you to develop your study design (Step II).

1 Is the design that you propose to adopt to conduct your study cross-sectional, longitudinal, experimental or comparative in nature? If possible draw a diagram depicting the design.

----

2 Why did you select this design?

----

3 What, in your opinion, are the strengths of this design?

----

4 Do you plan to select a sample?

Yes ☐ No ☐

In either case, explain the reasons for your decision.

----

5   How will you collect data from your respondents (e.g. interview, questionnaire)?

_____

_____

_____

(a)   Why did you select this method of data collection?

_____

_____

_____

(b)   What, in your opinion, are its strengths and weaknesses?
Strengths:

_____

_____

_____

Weaknesses:

_____

_____

_____

(c)   If you are interviewing, where will the interviews be held?

_____

_____

_____

(d)   If you are using mailed questionnaires:

(i)   From where will you obtain the addresses of potential respondents?

_____

_____

_____

_____

(ii)   Are you planning to enclose a self-addressed stamped envelope with the questionnaires?
Yes ☐   No ☐

(iii)   In the case of a low response rate, will you send a reminder?
Yes ☐   No ☐

(iv)   If there are queries, how should respondents get in touch with you?

_____

_____

_____

B   On the basis of the above information, describe your study design. (For further guidance, consult Chapter 8.)

For qualitative studies

A   Answers to the following questions will help you in developing a road map for your research journey.

1   In which geographical area, community, group or population group would you like to undertake your study?

_____

_____

_____

2   How do you plan to get entry into the area, community or group? Which network, if any, are you planning to use?

_____

_____

_____

3   Why did you select this group?

_____
- -
- -

4   From whom will you gather the required information?
    (Who will be your respondents?)

- -
- -
- -

5   If you are gathering information from secondary sources,
    have you checked their availability?

    Yes ☐   No ☐   Not Applicable ☐

6   Have you checked the availability of the required informa-
    tion in them?

    Yes ☐   No ☐   Not Applicable ☐

7   If you are gathering information from individuals, how
    many will you contact?

- -
- -
- -

8   What will be the basis of selection of these individuals?

- -
- -
- -

9   How will you collect the required information? List all
    methods that you plan to use.

- -
- -

STEP THREE

CONSTRUCTING AN INSTRUMENT FOR DATA COLLECTION

SELECTING A METHOD OF DATA COLLECTION

- step three -
CONSTRUCTING AN INSTRUMENT FOR DATA COLLECTION

This operational step includes three chapters:

→ Selecting a method of data collection   210

Collecting data using attitudinal scales   248

Establishing the validity and reliability of a research instrument   266

ESSENTIAL TERMS

You should be able to define these by the end of the chapter

- non-participant observation
- observation
- participant observation
- primary data
- questionnaire
- secondary data
- secondary sources
- structured interview
- unstructured interview

BONUS TERMS

You will learn more about these by the end of the chapter

- closed questions
- content analysis
- covering letter
- double-barrelled questions
- elevation effect
- error of central tendency
- focus group
- halo effect
- Hawthorne effect
- in-depth interviews
- interview schedule
- leading questions
- narratives
- observer bias
- open-ended questions
- oral history
- response rate
- primary sources
- self-selecting bias

LEARNING OBJECTIVES

At the end of this chapter, you will be able to:

- Differentiate methods of data collection in quantitative, qualitative and mixed methods research
- Describe and evaluate major approaches to information gathering
- Collect data using primary sources: observation, interviews and questionnaires
- Outline methods of data collection used in qualitative research
- Collect data using secondary sources
- Express the differences between primary and secondary data

DIFFERENCES IN THE METHODS OF DATA COLLECTION IN QUANTITATIVE, QUALITATIVE AND MIXED METHODS RESEARCH

Most methods of data collection can be used across studies that are classified as qualitative, quantitative or mixed methods. As a matter of fact the way a specific method is employed for data collection determines the classification of a study to a large extent. The distinction is mainly determined by the restrictions imposed on the philosophy underpinning the enquiry, freedom and flexibility in the structure and approach in gathering data, and the depth and freedom given to you as a researcher in probing to obtain answers to your research questions. Quantitative studies favour these restrictions, whereas qualitative ones advocate against them. The respective restrictions or flexibilities in mixed methods studies are dependent upon what and how the specific methods are employed. The classification of a method as quantitative, qualitative or mixed depends upon your answers to the following questions:

CHECKPOINT
Epistemology

⤳ What philosophical epistemology is underpinning your approach to research enquiry?
⤳ How was the information collected? Was it through a structured or unstructured/flexible format of data collection or a combination of both?
⤳ Were the questions or issues discussed during data collection predetermined or developed during data collection?
⤳ How was the information you gathered recorded? Was it in a descriptive, narrative, categorical, quantitative form or on a scale?
⤳ How was the information analysed? Was it a descriptive, categorical or numerical analysis?
⤳ How do you propose to communicate the findings? Do you want to write in a descriptive or analytical manner?
⤳ How many different methods were used in undertaking the study?

If your answers to the above questions are that you adopted the philosophical epistemology that is embedded in empiricism, you collected the information through an unstructured and flexible format, you indentified issues for discussion during the data collection process, you recorded the information in a descriptive and narrative format and subjected it to categorical and descriptive analysis, and you communicated the findings in a non-analytical style, the research process is labelled as qualitative; otherwise it is quantitative. If you used more than one method, quantitative or qualitative or both, then it is a mixed methods study. For example, if an observation is recorded in a narrative or descriptive format, it becomes qualitative information, but if it is recorded in categorical form or on a scale, it will be classified as quantitative information, and use of both the methods would mean a mixed methods classification. Similarly for data collected through interviews. An unstructured interview, recorded in a descriptive or narrative form, becomes a qualitative method, but in a structured interview, if the information is recorded in response categories or if the categories are developed and quantified out of descriptive responses, it is a quantitative method. Descriptive responses obtained in reply to open-ended questions are all qualitative, but if the responses are numerical they will be considered quantitative. If you develop categories and quantify the categorisations as a part of the analysis of descriptive responses to an open-ended question, it becomes a quantitative analysis. Data generated by focus groups, oral histories, narratives, group interviews is always qualitative in nature; however, you can subject the data to categorical analysis which then becomes quantitative analysis.

The differences between quantitative and qualitative approaches, in brief, depend upon three things: how the data was collected; how it was analysed; and how the findings were communicated.

MAJOR APPROACHES TO INFORMATION GATHERING

There are two major approaches to gathering information about a situation, person, problem or phenomenon. When you undertake a research study, in most situations, you need to collect the required information; however, sometimes the information required is already available and need only be extracted. Based upon these broad approaches to information gathering, data can be categorised as:

- primary data;
- secondary data.

Information gathered using the first approach is said to be collected from primary sources, whereas the sources used in the second approach are called secondary sources. Examples of primary sources include finding out first-hand the attitudes of a community towards health services, ascertaining the health needs of a community, evaluating a social programme, determining the job satisfaction of the employees of an organisation, and ascertaining the quality of service provided by a worker. On the other hand, extracting data from a census to obtain information on the age–sex structure of a population, the use of hospital records to find out the morbidity and mortality patterns in a community, the use of an organisation's records to ascertain its activities, and the collection of data from sources such as articles, journals, magazines, books and periodicals to obtain historical and other types of information, are all classified as information obtained from secondary sources. In summary, primary sources provide first-hand information and secondary sources provide second-hand data. Figure 9.1 shows the various methods of data collection.

None of the methods of data collection provides 100 per cent accurate and reliable information. The quality of the data gathered is dependent upon a number of other factors, which we will identify as we discuss each method. Your skill as a researcher lies in your ability to take care of the factors that could affect the quality of your data. One of the main differences between experienced and amateur researchers lies in their understanding of, and ability to control, these factors. It is therefore important for a beginner to be aware of them.

Primary sources: Sources that provide primary data such as interviews, observations and questionnaires.

Secondary sources: Sources that provide secondary data are called secondary sources. Sources such as books, journals, previous research studies, records of an agency, client or patient information already collected and routine service delivery records all form secondary sources.

215

COLLECTING DATA USING PRIMARY SOURCES

Several methods can be used to collect primary data. The choice of a method depends upon the purpose of the study, the resources available and the skills of the researcher. There are times when the method most appropriate to achieve the objectives of a study cannot be used because of constraints such as a lack of resources and/or required skills. In such situations you should be aware of the problems that these limitations impose on the quality of the data.

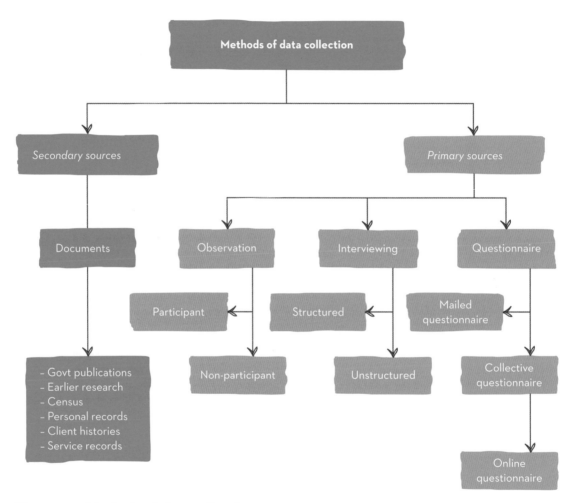

Figure 9.1   Methods of data collection

In selecting a method of data collection, the socioeconomic-demographic characteristics of the study population play an important role. You should know as much as possible about characteristics such as educational level, age structure, socioeconomic status and ethnic background. If possible, it is helpful to know the study population's interest in, and attitude towards, participation in the study. Some populations, for a number of reasons, may not feel at ease with a particular method of data collection (such as being interviewed) or comfortable with expressing opinions in a questionnaire. Furthermore, people with little education may respond differently to certain methods of data collection compared to people with more education.

Another important determinant of the quality of your data is the way the purpose and relevance of the study are explained to potential respondents. Whatever method of data collection is used, make sure that respondents clearly understand the purpose and relevance of the study. This is particularly important when you use a questionnaire to collect data, because in an interview situation you can answer a respondent's questions but in a questionnaire you will not have this opportunity.

In the following sections each method of data collection is discussed from the point of view of its applicability and suitability to a situation, and the problems and limitations associated with it.

Observation

Observation is one way to collect primary data. It is a purposeful, systematic and selective way of watching and listening to an interaction or phenomenon as it takes place. There are many situations in which observation is the most appropriate method of data collection; for example, when you want to learn about the interaction in a group, study the dietary patterns of a population, ascertain the functions performed by a worker, or study the behaviour or personality traits of an individual. It is also appropriate in situations where full and/or accurate information cannot be elicited by questioning, because respondents either are not co-operative or are unaware of the answers because it is difficult for them to detach themselves from the interaction. In summary, when you are more interested in the behaviour than in the perceptions of individuals, or when subjects are so involved in the interaction that they are unable to provide objective information about it, observation is the best approach to collecting the required information.

Types of observation

There are two types of observation:

1   participant observation;
2   non-participant observation.

Participant observation is when you, as a researcher, participate in the activities of the group being observed, in the same manner as its members, with or without their knowing that they are being observed. For example, as a student of occupational therapy, you are interested in studying reactions of the general population towards people in wheelchairs. To do so, you pretend to have a handicap that requires you to use a wheelchair. As you use the wheelchair in a public area you observe the reactions of people you encounter. You make appropriate observational notes for your study when appropriate. Or suppose you want to study what it means to be prisoner and to

Observation: is one of the methods for collecting primary data. It is a purposeful, systematic and selective way of watching and listening to an interaction or phenomenon as it takes place. Though predominantly used in qualitative research, it is also used in quantitative research.

Participant observation: This is when you, as a researcher, participate in the activities of the group being observed in the same manner as its members, with or without their knowing that they are being observed. Participant observation is principally used in qualitative research and is usually done by developing a close interaction with members of a group or 'living' in with the situation which is being studied.

217

Non-participant observation: When you, as a researcher, do not get involved in the activities of the group but remain a passive observer, watching and listening to its activities and interactions and drawing conclusions from them, this is called non-participant observation.

Hawthorne effect: When individuals or groups become aware that they are being observed, they may change their behaviour. Depending upon the situation, this change could be positive or negative – it may increase or decrease, for example, their productivity – and may occur for a number of reasons. When a change in the behaviour of persons or groups is attributed to their being observed, it is known as the Hawthorne effect.

Observer's bias: is when, as an observer, you purposely do not accurately report what you observe because of your own vested interest. It is both illegal and unethical.

do so, one way or another, you become a prisoner to achieve your aim. You live exactly the way other prisoners live and collect the information required to achieve the objectives of your study. Or suppose you want to study a tribe in some remote area and to do so you go and live with them and collect the data you need. Many anthropological studies have been conducted by using this approach.

Non-participant observation, on the other hand, is when you, as a researcher, do not get involved in the activities of the group but remain a passive observer, watching and listening to its activities and drawing conclusions from this. For example, you might want to study the functions carried out by nurses in a hospital. As an observer, you could watch, follow and record the activities as they are performed. After making a number of observations, you could draw conclusions about the functions nurses carry out in the hospital. Any occupational group in any setting can be observed in the same manner.

Problems with using observation as a method of data collection

The use of observation as a method of data collection may suffer from a number of problems, which is not to suggest that all or any of these necessarily prevail in every situation. But as a beginner you should be aware of these potential problems:

- ⤳ When individuals or groups become aware that they are being observed, they may change their behaviour. Depending upon the situation, this change could be positive or negative – it may increase or decrease, for example, their productivity – and may occur for a number of reasons. When a change in the behaviour of persons or groups is attributed to their being observed it is known as the Hawthorne effect. The use of observation in such a situation may introduce distortion: what is observed may not represent their normal behaviour.

- ⤳ There is always the possibility of observer bias. If an observer is not impartial, s/he can easily introduce bias and there is no easy way to verify the observations and the inferences drawn from them.

- ⤳ The interpretations drawn from observations may vary from observer to observer.

- ⤳ There is the possibility of incomplete observation and/or recording, which varies with the method of recording. An observer may watch keenly but at the expense of detailed recording. The opposite problem may occur when the observer takes detailed notes but in doing so misses some of the interaction.

Situations in which observations can be made

Observations can be made under two conditions:

1 natural;
2 controlled.

Observing a group without interfering in its normal activities is referred to as observation under natural conditions. Introducing a stimulus to the group for it to react to and observing the reaction is referred to as observation under controlled conditions.

Recording of observations

There are many ways of recording observations. The selection of a method of recording depends upon the purpose of the observation. The way an observation is recorded also determines whether it is a quantitative or qualitative study. Narrative and descriptive recording is mainly used in qualitative research, but if you are doing a quantitative study you would record an observation in categorical form or on a numerical scale. Keep in mind that each method of recording an observation has its advantages and disadvantages.

In *narrative* recording the researcher records a description of the interaction in his/her own words. Such recording clearly falls in the domain of qualitative research. Usually, the researcher makes brief notes while observing the interaction and then, soon after completing the observation, makes detailed notes in narrative form. In addition, some researchers may interpret the interaction and draw conclusions from it. The biggest advantage of narrative recording is that it provides a deeper insight into the interaction. However, a disadvantage is that an observer may be biased in his/her observation and, therefore, the interpretations and conclusions drawn from the observation may also be biased. In addition, interpretations and conclusions drawn are bound to be subjective, reflecting the researcher's perspectives. Also, if a researcher's attention is on observing, s/he might forget to record an important piece of interaction. Furthermore, in the process of recording, part of the interaction may be missed. Hence, there is always the possibility of incomplete recording and/or observation. In addition, when there are different observers the comparability of narrative recording can be a problem.

Some observers may sometimes prefer to develop a *scale* in order to rate various aspects of the interaction or phenomenon. The recording is done on a scale developed by the observer/researcher. A scale may be one-, two- or three-directional, depending upon the purpose of the observation. For example, in the scale in Figure 9.2 – designed to record the nature of the interaction within a group – there are three directions: positive, negative and neutral.

The main advantage of using scales in recording an observation is that you do not need to spend time on taking detailed notes and can thus concentrate on observation. On the other hand, one problem with using a scale is that it does not provide specific and in-depth information about the interaction. In addition, it may suffer from any of the following errors:

→ Unless the observer is extremely confident of his/her ability to assess an interaction, s/he may tend to avoid the extreme positions on the scale, using mostly the central part. The error that this tendency creates is called the error of central tendency.

→ Some observers may prefer certain sections of the scale in the same way that some teachers are strict markers and others are not. When observers have a tendency to use a particular part of the scale in recording an interaction, this phenomenon is known as the elevation effect.

→ Another type of error that may be introduced is when the way an observer rates an individual on one aspect of the interaction influences the way s/he rates that individual on another aspect of the interaction. Again something similar to this can happen in teaching when a teacher's assessment of the performance of a student in one subject may influence his/her rating of that student's performance in another. This type of effect is known as the halo effect.

Error of central tendency: When using scales in assessments or observations, unless an observer is extremely confident of his/her ability to assess an interaction, s/he may tend to avoid the extreme positions on the scale, using mostly the central part. The error this tendency creates is called the error of central tendency.

Elevation effect: Some observers when using a scale to record an observation may prefer to use certain section(s) of the scale in the same way that some teachers are strict markers and others are not. When observers have a tendency to use a particular part(s) of a scale in recording an interaction, this phenomenon is known as the elevation effect.

Halo effect: When making an observation, some observers may be influenced to rate an individual on one aspect of the interaction by the way s/he was rated on another. This is similar to something that can happen in teaching when a teacher's assessment of the performance of a student in one subject may influence his/her rating of that student's performance in another. This type of effect is known as the halo effect.

Sometimes an observer may decide to set down his/her observations using *categorical recording*. The type and number of categories depend upon the type of interaction and the observer's choice about how to classify the observation. Examples are passive/active (two categories); introvert/extrovert (two categories); always/sometimes/never (three categories); or strongly agree/agree/uncertain/disagree/strongly disagree (five categories). The use of categories to record an observation may suffer from the same problems as those associated with scales.

Observations can also be recorded using a video camera or other *electronic devices* and then analysed. The advantage of recording an interaction in this way is that the observer can see it a number of times before interpreting an interaction or drawing any conclusions from it and can also invite other professionals to view the interaction in order to arrive at more objective conclusions. However, one of the disadvantages is that some people may feel uncomfortable or may behave differently before a camera. Therefore the interaction may not be a true reflection of the situation.

The choice of a particular method for recording your observation is dependent upon the purpose of the observation, the complexity of the interaction and the type of population being observed. It is important to consider these factors before deciding upon the method for recording your observation.

The interview

Interviewing: One of the commonly used methods of data collection in the social sciences. Any person-to-person interaction, either face to face or otherwise, between two or more individuals with a specific purpose in mind is called an interview. It involves asking questions of respondents and recording their answers. Interviewing spans a wide spectrum in terms of its structure, from highly structured to extremely flexible.

Interviewing is a commonly used method of collecting information from people. There are many definitions of interviews, but it is essentially a person-to-person interaction, either face to face or otherwise, between two or more individuals with a specific purpose in mind. According to Monette et al. (1986: 156), 'an interview involves an interviewer reading questions to respondents and recording their answers'. According to Burns (1997: 329), 'an interview is a verbal interchange, often face to face, though the telephone may be used, in which an interviewer tries to elicit information, beliefs or opinions from another person'.

When interviewing a respondent, as a researcher, you have the freedom to decide the format and content of your questions, choose how to word them, decide how you want to ask them and in what order. The process of asking questions can be either very flexible, where you as the interviewer have the freedom to think about and formulate questions as they come to your mind around the issue being investigated, or inflexible, where you have to keep strictly to questions decided on beforehand – including their wording, sequence and the manner in which they are asked. Interviews are classified into different categories according to this degree of flexibility as in Figure 9.3.

Unstructured interviews

Unstructured interviews: Interviews in which, you as an interviewer, have every flexibility in terms of questions that you ask of your respondents, explanation you provide, wording you use and the sequence in which you ask them.

The main strength of an unstructured interview lies in having almost complete freedom in terms of its structure, contents, question wording and order. You are free to ask whatever you want, and in a format that is relevant to the situation. You also have complete freedom in terms of the wording you use and the way you explain questions to your respondents. You may formulate questions and raise issues on the spur of the moment, depending upon what occurs to you in the context of the discussion.

Unstructured interviews are extremely useful in exploring intensively and extensively and digging deeper into a situation, phenomenon, issue or problem. They provide varied and in-depth information and are best suited to identifying diversity and variety. However, their disadvantage lies in the high level of skills they require in conducting them.

A study of the nature of interaction in a group

Aspects of interaction		Positive				Neutral			Negative		

Participation   5 4 3 2 1 0 1 2 3 4 5

Rapport   5 4 3 2 1 0 1 2 3 4 5

Confidence   5 4 3 2 1 0 1 2 3 4 5

Aggressiveness   5 4 3 2 1 0 1 2 3 4 5

Withdrawnness   5 4 3 2 1 0 1 2 3 4 5

Friendliness   5 4 3 2 1 0 1 2 3 4 5

Aloofness   5 4 3 2 1 0 1 2 3 4 5

Figure 9.2   Observing/recording group interactions on a three-directional rating scale

Unstructured interviews are prevalent in both quantitative and qualitative research. The difference is in how information obtained through them in response to your questions is likely to be used. In quantitative research you develop response categorisations from responses which are then coded and quantified. In qualitative research the responses are used as descriptors, often verbatim, and can be integrated with your arguments, flow of writing and sequence of logic. As unstructured interviews are predominantly used in qualitative research, they are described in greater detail under 'Methods of data collection in qualitative research' later in this chapter.

Structured interviews

In a structured interview the researcher asks a predetermined set of questions, using the same wording and order of questions as specified in the interview schedule. An interview schedule is a written list of questions, open-ended or closed, thoroughly pre-tested for standardised wording, meaning and interpretation, prepared for use by an interviewer in a person-to-person interaction (this may be face to face, by telephone or by other electronic media). Note that an interview schedule is a research tool/instrument for collecting data, whereas interviewing is a method of data collection.

Structured interviews: Interviews in which the questions that you ask of your respondents, their wording and sequence are predetermined. Everything that forms part of the interview is fixed and predetermined and any deviation from it is not permitted.

Interview schedule: A list of questions, open-ended or closed, prepared for use by an interviewer in a person-to-person interaction (this may be face to face, by telephone or by other electronic media). Note that an interview schedule is a research tool/instrument for collecting data, whereas interviewing is a method of data collection.

221

CHECKPOINT
Interviews

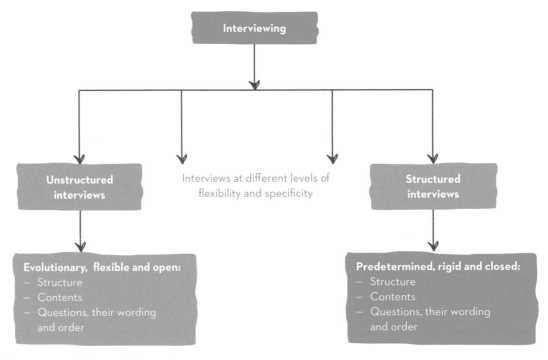

Figure 9.3 Types of interview

One of the main advantages of the structured interview is that it provides uniform information, which assures the comparability of data. Structured interviewing requires fewer interviewing skills than does unstructured interviewing.

The questionnaire

A questionnaire is a written list of questions, the answers to which are recorded by respondents. Thus, respondents read the questions, interpret what is expected and then write down the answers. The only difference between an interview schedule and a questionnaire is that in the former it is the interviewer who asks the questions (and if necessary, explains them) and records the respondent's replies on an interview schedule, and in the latter the replies are recorded by the respondents themselves. This distinction is important in accounting for the respective strengths and weaknesses of the two methods and their respective use in gathering data.

In a questionnaire, as there is no one to explain the meaning of questions to respondents, it is important that the questions are clear and easy to understand. Also, the layout of a questionnaire should be such that it is easy to read and pleasant to the eyes, and the sequence of questions should be easy to follow. A questionnaire should be developed in an interactive style. This means respondents should feel as if someone is talking to them. In a questionnaire, a sensitive question or a question that respondents may feel hesitant about answering should be prefaced by an interactive statement explaining the relevance of the question. It is a good idea to use a different font for these statements to distinguish them from the actual questions. Examples in Figures 9.4 and 9.5, taken from two surveys recently carried out by the author with the help of two students, explain some of the above points.

Ways of administering a questionnaire

A questionnaire can be administered in a number of ways. Your selection of a particular method of administration depends upon the ease in assessing your respondent population and your impressions about how they would prefer to participate in your study. The various ways in which you can administer a questionnaire are as follows:

↪ **The mailed questionnaire**. The most common approach to collecting information is to send the questionnaire to prospective respondents by mail. Obviously this approach presupposes that you have access to their addresses. It may not be easy to get addresses, so before you decide to collect your data through this method, make sure of the availability of addresses of your potential respondents. Usually it is a good idea to send a prepaid, self-addressed envelope with the questionnaire as this might increase the response rate. A mailed questionnaire must be accompanied by a *covering letter* (see below). One of the major problems with this method is the low response rate. In the case of an extremely low response rate, the findings have very limited applicability to the population studied.

↪ **Collective administration**. One of the best ways of administering a questionnaire is to obtain a captive audience such as students in a classroom, people attending a function, participants in a programme or people assembled in one place. This ensures a very high response rate as you will find few people refuse to participate in your study. Also, as you have personal contact with the study population, you can explain the purpose, relevance and importance of the study and can clarify any questions that respondents may have. The author's advice is that if you have a captive audience for your study, don't miss the opportunity – it is the quickest way of collecting data, ensures a very high response rate and saves you money on postage.

↪ **Online questionnaire**. With the advancement in communication technology, the use of the online questionnaire to collect information to answer your research questions has become quite common. You develop a questionnaire in the same way as you normally do using a program that is designed for the purpose (see Chapter 8). The main difference is that instead of personally delivering, collectively distributing or individually mailing, you post it either on a website or provide a link in your email for potential respondents to access it and respond. In the same way you could send the questionnaire to mobile phones. You can also analyse the data collected through online questionnaires using an appropriate program. There are many such programs and you need to identify the one most appropriate for your situation. Before you use this method of data collection, it is important for you to familiarise yourself with the process and program that you intend to use. In case of emailing or sending it to mobile phones you need to collect respondents' email addresses or phone numbers.

Where to go? A study of occupational mobility among immigrants

The questionnaire developed for this study opened with the following interactive statement:

Personal circumstances, and educational and occupational background, to a great extent determine the occupational mobility of an individual. This is especially true for immigrants. We would therefore like to ask you some questions about you and your family background. Knowledge of these factors is also important for assessing the representativeness of those who participated in the study and to understand the extent, nature and reasons of occupational mobility in relation to your background. We would appreciate your answering these questions as the information you provide will be very useful to us. We would like to emphasise that your responses are extremely valuable to us and we would greatly appreciate your answering all questions. However, if you feel that you do not want to answer a particular question, we will gladly accept your decision. We can assure you that your responses will be completely anonymous and will not be used for any other purpose.

Before asking questions about family background, the following interactive statement was inserted in the questionnaire:

Now, we would like to ask some questions about your family. Your family circumstances can affect your choice of an occupation after immigration. Again, we assure you of the complete anonymity of your responses.

Before ascertaining respondents' experiences with respect to recognition of their qualifications in Australia, the following interactive statement prepared them to be at ease with the area of enquiry:

Recognition of educational and professional qualifications, in addition to other factors, plays a major role in determining an individual's occupational mobility in a new country. In this section we would like to ask your opinion about the process of getting your qualifications recognised. We would also like to know how satisfied or dissatisfied you are with the outcome. if you are dissatisfied, we would like to know your reasons as this information may help decision makers to improve the process. Again, we assure you that your answers will be completely confidential. However, if you still feel that you do not want to answer a particular question, please feel free to omit it

Figure 9.4   Where to go? A study of occupational mobility among immigrants

Ways of administering a questionnaire

Occupational redeployment: a study of occupational redeployment among state government employees

The following interactive statement was inserted in the questionnaire before asking questions about the socioeconomic-demographic background of respondents:

In order to gain an understanding of the situation of employees who have experienced occupational redeployment in state government departments during the last three years, we would like to ask some questions about your background. Your answers will help us to determine the types of occupation where redeployment has occurred and the backgrounds of the employees who have been affected by it. Please do not feel obliged to answer a question if you do not wish to, though we assure you your answers to these questions are extremely important to us to ascertain the nature and extent of the shift in your career path. We again assure you that any information you provide will be treated with strict confidentiality.

Questions about occupational history were prefaced by the following statement:

We would like to ask some questions about your work history. The answers to these questions will enable us to compare the type of work you have been doing since entering the workforce with the job you have been assigned after redeployment. This will help us to establish the nature and extent of change in your job before and after redeployment. Again, there is no obligation to answer a question if you do not want to. However, answers to these questions are extremely important to us. We assure you of the anonymity of the information you provide.

Before asking questions about the impact of redeployment, the following interactive statement was incorporated into the questionnaire:

The following questions ask you to express your opinion about different aspects of your job after and before redeployment. Your answers will help us to gauge the impact of redeployment on different aspects of your work and family situation. We would appreciate your honest opinions. Be assured that your responses will be completely anonymous.

Figure 9.5   Occupational redeployment: a study among state government employees

- **Administration in a public place**. Sometimes you can administer a questionnaire in a public place such as a shopping centre, health centre, hospital, school or pub. Of course this depends upon the type of study population you are looking for and where it is likely to be found. Usually the purpose of the study is explained to potential respondents as they approach and their participation in the study is requested. Apart from being slightly more time-consuming, this method has all the advantages of administering a questionnaire collectively.

Choosing between an interview schedule and a questionnaire

The choice between a questionnaire and an interview schedule is important and should be considered thoroughly as the strengths and weaknesses of the two methods can affect the validity of the findings. The nature of the investigation and the socioeconomic-demographic characteristics of the study population are central in this choice. The selection between an interview schedule and a questionnaire should be based upon the following criteria:

- **The nature of the investigation**. If the study is about issues that respondents may feel reluctant to discuss with an investigator, a questionnaire may be the better choice as it ensures anonymity. This may be the case with studies on drug use, sexuality, indulgence in criminal activities and personal finances. However, there are situations where better information about sensitive issues can be obtained by interviewing respondents. It depends on the type of study population and the skills of the interviewer. You need to explore and decide what would be better suited for your study and respondents.
- **The geographical distribution of the study population**. If potential respondents are scattered over a wide geographical area, you have no choice but to use a questionnaire, as interviewing in these circumstances would be extremely expensive.
- **The type of study population**. If the study population is illiterate, very young or very old, or handicapped, there may be no option but to interview respondents.

Advantages of a questionnaire

A questionnaire has the following advantages:

- **It is less expensive**. As you do not interview respondents, you save time, and human and financial resources. The use of a questionnaire, therefore, is comparatively convenient and inexpensive, especially when it is administered collectively to a study population.
- **It offers greater anonymity**. As there is no face-to-face interaction between respondents and interviewer, this method provides greater anonymity. In some situations where sensitive questions are asked it helps to increase the likelihood of obtaining accurate information.

Disadvantages of a questionnaire

Although a questionnaire has several disadvantages, it is important to note that not all data collection using this method has these disadvantages. The prevalence of a particular disadvantage depends on a number of other factors. However, you need to be aware of these disadvantages to understand their possible bearing on the quality of the data. Some of these disadvantages are as follows:

- **Limited application**. One main disadvantage is that application is limited to a study population that can read and write. It also cannot be used on a population that is very young, very old or handicapped.

- **Low response rate**. Questionnaires are notorious for their low response rates; that is, people fail to return them. If you plan to use a questionnaire, keep in mind that because not everyone will return their questionnaire, your sample size will in effect be reduced. The response rate depends upon a number of factors: the interest of the sample in the topic of the study; the layout and length of the questionnaire; the quality of the letter explaining the purpose and relevance of the study; and the methodology used to deliver the questionnaire. You should consider yourself lucky to obtain a 50 per cent response rate, and sometimes it may be as low as 20 per cent. However, as mentioned, the response rate is not a problem when a questionnaire is administered in a collective situation.

- **Self-selecting bias**. Since not everyone who receives a questionnaire returns it, there is a self-selecting bias. Those who return their questionnaire may have attitudes, attributes or motivations that are different from those who do not. Hence, if the response rate is very low, the findings may not be representative of the total study population.

- **Lack of opportunity to clarify issues**. If, for any reason, respondents do not understand some questions, there is almost no opportunity for them to have the meaning clarified unless they get in touch with the researcher (which does not happen often). If different respondents interpret questions differently, this will affect the quality of the information provided.

- **No opportunity for spontaneous responses**. Mailed questionnaires are inappropriate when spontaneous responses are required, as most respondents will glance though the whole questionnaire before answering. This gives them time to reflect before answering, which may make them change their answers to some questions.

- **The response to a question may be influenced by the response to other questions**. As respondents can read all the questions before answering (which usually happens), the way they answer a particular question may be affected by their knowledge of other questions.

- **Others can influence the answers**. With mailed questionnaires respondents may consult other people before responding. In situations where an investigator wants to find out only the study population's opinions, this method may be inappropriate, though requesting respondents to express their own opinion may help.

- **A response cannot be supplemented with other information**. The information gathered by interviewing can sometimes be supplemented with information from other methods of data collection such as observation. However, a questionnaire lacks this advantage.

Advantages of the interview

- **More appropriate for complex situations**. It is the most appropriate approach for studying complex and sensitive areas as the interviewer has the opportunity to prepare a respondent before asking sensitive questions and to explain complex ones to respondents in person.

→ **Useful for collecting in-depth information**. In an interview situation it is possible for an investigator to obtain in-depth information by probing. Hence, in situations where in-depth information is required, interviewing is the preferred method of data collection.

→ **Information can be supplemented**. An interviewer is able to supplement information obtained from responses with those gained from observation of non-verbal reactions.

→ **Questions can be explained**. It is less likely that a question will be misunderstood as the interviewer can either repeat a question or put it in a form that is understood by the respondent.

→ **Has a wider application**. An interview can be used with almost any type of population: children, the handicapped, illiterate or very old.

Disadvantages of the interview

→ **Time-consuming and expensive**. This is especially so when potential respondents are scattered over a wide geographical area. However, if you have a situation such as an office, a hospital or an agency where potential respondents come to obtain a service, interviewing them in that setting may be less expensive and less time-consuming.

→ **The quality of data depends upon the quality of the interaction**. In an interview the quality of interaction between an interviewer and interviewee is likely to affect the quality of the information obtained. Also, because the interaction in each interview is unique, the quality of the responses obtained from different interviews may vary significantly.

→ **The quality of data depends upon the quality of the interviewer**. In an interview situation the quality of the data generated is affected by the experience, skills and commitment of the interviewer.

→ **The quality of data may vary when multiple interviewers are used**. Use of multiple interviewers may magnify the problems identified in the previous two points.

→ **Possibility of researcher bias**. In an interview situation a researcher's bias either in the framing of questions and/or in the interpretation of responses obtained is always possible. If the interviews are conducted by a person or persons, paid or voluntary, other than the researcher, it is also possible that they may exhibit bias in the way they interpret responses, select response categories or choose words to summarise respondents' expressed opinions.

Contents of the covering letter

It is essential that you write a covering letter with your mailed questionnaire. In it you should very briefly:

→ introduce yourself and the institution you represent;
→ describe in two or three sentences the main objectives of the study;

- explain the relevance of the study;
- convey any general instructions;
- indicate that participation in the study is voluntary – if recipients do not want to respond to the questionnaire, they have the right not to;
- assure respondents of the anonymity of the information provided by them;
- provide a contact number in case they have any questions;
- give a return address for the questionnaire and a deadline for its return;
- thank them for their participation in the study.

Types of question

The way you formulate a question (open-ended or closed) and the wording you use in its framing in an interview schedule or a questionnaire are extremely important as they influence the type and quality of information you obtain from your respondents. The wording and structure of questions should therefore be clear, succinct, appropriate, relevant and free from any of the problems discussed in the section on 'Formulating effective questions' later in this chapter. It is therefore important for you to know the types of questions commonly used in social research with their respective strengths and weaknesses. You also need to know the attributes of the wording used in their construction. This section deals with their types, characteristics, the process of formulation, and some of the common problems associated with the way they are worded.

There are two types of question commonly used in social research:

- open-ended questions; and
- closed questions.

In an open-ended question the possible response categories are *not* provided in the research instrument. In the case of a questionnaire, the respondent writes down the answers in his/her own words, but in the case of an interview schedule the investigator records the answers either verbatim or in a summary. In a closed question the possible answers are set out in the questionnaire or schedule and the respondent or investigator ticks the category that best describes the respondent's answer. It is usually wise to provide a category 'Other/please explain' to accommodate any response not listed. The questions in Figure 9.6 are examples of closed questions. The same questions could be asked as open-ended questions, as shown in Figure 9.7.

When deciding whether to use open-ended or closed questions to obtain information about a variable, visualise how you plan to use the information generated. This is important because the way you frame your questions determines the unit of measurement which could be used to classify the responses. The unit of measurement in turn dictates what statistical procedures can be applied to the data and the way the information can be analysed and displayed.

Let us take, as an example, the question about the variable 'income'. In closed questions income can be qualitatively recorded in categories such as 'above average/average/below average', or quantitatively in categories such as 'under $10 000/$10 000–$19 999/...'. Your choice of qualitative and quantitative categories affects the unit of measurement for income (qualitative uses the ordinal scale and quantitative the ratio scale of measurement), which in turn will affect the application of statistical procedures. For example, you cannot calculate the average income of

Open-ended question: In an open-ended question the possible responses are not given. In the case of a questionnaire the respondent writes down the answers in his/her words, whereas in the case of an interview schedule the investigator records the answers either verbatim or in a summary describing a respondent's answer.

Closed question: In a closed question the possible answers are set out in the questionnaire or interview schedule and the respondent or the investigator ticks the category that best describes a respondent's answer.

229

A. Please indicate your age by placing a tick in the appropriate category.

Under 15
15–19 years
20–24 years

B. How would you describe your current marital status?

Married
Single
De facto
Divorced
Separated

C. What is your average annual income?

Under $10,000
$10,000–$19,999
$30,000–$39,999
$40,000+

OR

C. (a)   How would you categorise your average annual income?

Above average
Average
Below average

D. What, in your opinion, are the qualities of a good administrator?

Able to make decisions
Fast decision maker
Able to listen
Impartial
Skilled in interpersonal communication
Other, please specify

_____
_____

Figure 9.6   Examples of closed questions

a person from the responses to question C(a) in Figure 9.6; nor can you calculate the median or modal category of income. From the responses to question C, you can accurately calculate the modal category of income, but not the mean or the median income (such calculations are usually made under certain assumptions). From the responses to question C in Figure 9.7, where the income for a respondent is recorded in exact dollars, the different descriptors

A   What is your current age?_____ years
B   How would you describe your current marital status?_____
C   What is your average annual income? $_____
D   What, in your opinion, are the qualities of a good administrator?
1   _____
2   _____
3   _____
4   _____
5   _____

Figure 9.7   Examples of open-ended questions

CHECKPOINT
*Developing
questions*

of income can be calculated very accurately. In addition, information on income can be displayed in any form. You can precisely calculate the mean, median or mode of income for a given study group. The same is true for any other information obtained in response to an open-ended question.

In closed questions, having developed categories, you cannot change them; therefore, you should be very certain about your categories when developing them. If you ask an open-ended question, you can develop any number of categories in any form at the time of analysis.

Advantages and disadvantages of open-ended and closed questions

Both open-ended and closed questions have their advantages and disadvantages in different situations. To some extent, their advantages and disadvantages depend upon whether they are being used in an interview or in a questionnaire and on whether they are being used to seek information about facts or opinions. As a rule, closed questions are extremely useful for eliciting factual information and open-ended questions for seeking opinions, attitudes and perceptions. The choice of open-ended or closed questions should be made according to the purpose for which a piece of information is to be used, the type of study population from which information is going to be obtained, the proposed format for communicating the findings and the socioeconomic background of the readership.

Open-ended questions have the following advantages and disadvantages:

↱ Open-ended questions provide in-depth information if used in an interview by an experienced interviewer. In a questionnaire, open-ended questions can provide a wealth of information provided respondents feel comfortable about expressing their opinions and are fluent in the language used. On the other hand, analysis of open-ended questions is more difficult. The researcher usually needs to go through another process – content analysis – in order to classify the data.

↱ In a questionnaire, open-ended questions provide respondents with the opportunity to express themselves freely, resulting in a greater variety of information. Thus respondents are not 'conditioned' by having to select

231

Content analysis: One of the main methods of analysing qualitative data. It is the process of analysing the contents of interviews or observational field notes in order to identify the main themes that emerge from the responses given by your respondents or the observation notes made by you as a researcher.

answers from a list. The disadvantage of free choice is that, in a questionnaire, some respondents may not be able to express themselves, and so information can be lost.

→ As open-ended questions allow respondents to express themselves freely, they virtually eliminate the possibility of investigator bias (investigator bias is introduced through the response pattern presented to respondents). On the other hand, there is a greater chance of interviewer bias in open-ended questions.

Closed questions have the following advantages and disadvantages:

→ One of the main disadvantages of closed questions is that the information obtained through them lacks depth and variety.

→ There is a greater possibility of investigator bias because the researcher may list only the response patterns that s/he is interested in or those that come to mind at the time of developing the research instrument. Even if the category of 'other' is offered, most people will usually select from the list of given responses, and so the findings may still reflect researcher bias.

→ In a questionnaire, the given response pattern for a question could condition the thinking of respondents, and so the answers provided may not truly reflect respondents' opinions. Rather, they may reflect the extent of agreement or disagreement with the researcher's opinion or analysis of a situation.

→ The ease of answering a ready-made list of responses may create a tendency among some respondents and interviewers to tick a category or categories without thinking through the issue.

→ Closed questions, because they provide 'ready-made' categories within which respondents reply to the questions asked by the researcher, help to ensure that the information needed by the researcher is obtained and the responses are also easier to analyse.

Formulating effective questions

The way you ask a question, to a great extent, determines the response that you are likely to get from your respondents. Your output in terms of the responses and their quality depends upon your input in terms of questions you ask of your respondents. The wording and tone of your questions are therefore extremely important. You should be very careful about the way you formulate questions. The following are some suggestions and considerations to keep in mind when formulating questions:

→ **Always use simple and everyday language**. Your respondents may not be highly educated, and even if they are they still may not know some of the 'simple' technical jargon that you are used to. Particularly in a questionnaire, take extra care to use words that your respondents will understand as you will have no opportunity to explain questions to them. A pre-test should show you what is and what is not understood by your respondents. For example:

Is anyone in your family a *dipsomaniac*? (Bailey 1978: 100)

In this question many respondents, even some who are well educated, will not understand 'dipsomaniac' and, hence, they either do not answer or answer the question without understanding.

→ **Do not use ambiguous questions**. An ambiguous question is one that contains more than one meaning and that can be interpreted differently by different respondents. This will result in different answers, making it difficult, if not impossible, to draw any valid conclusions from the information. The following questions highlight the problem:

Is your work made difficult because you are expecting a baby? (Moser & Kalton 1989: 323)

Yes ☐   No ☐

In the survey all women were asked this question. Those women who were not pregnant ticked 'No', meaning no they were not pregnant, and those who were pregnant and who ticked 'No' meant pregnancy had not made their work difficult. The question has other ambiguities as well: it does not specify the type of work and the stage of pregnancy.

Are you satisfied with your canteen? (Moser & Kalton 1989: 319)

This question is also ambiguous as it does not ask respondents to indicate the aspects of the canteen with which they may be satisfied or dissatisfied. Is it with the service, the prices, the physical facilities, the attitude of the staff or the quality of the meals? Respondents may have any one of these aspects in mind when they answer the question. Or the question should have been worded differently – for example, 'Overall, are you satisfied with your canteen?'

→ **Do not ask double-barrelled questions**. A double-barrelled question is a question within a question. The main problem with this type of question is that one does not know which particular question a respondent has answered. Some respondents may answer both parts of the question and others may answer only one of them.

How often and how much time do you spend on each visit?
This question was asked in a survey in Western Australia to ascertain the need for child-minding services in one of the hospitals. The question has two parts: **how often** do you visit, and how much time is spent on each visit? In this type of question some respondents may answer the first part, whereas others may answer the second part and some may answer both parts. Incidentally, this question is also ambiguous in that it does not **specify** 'how often' in terms of a period of time. Is it in a week, a fortnight, a month or a year?

Does your department have a special recruitment policy for racial minorities and women? (Bailey 1978: 97)
This question is double-barrelled in that it asks respondents to indicate whether their office has a special recruitment policy for two population groups: racial minorities and women. A 'yes' response does not necessarily mean that the office has a special recruitment policy for both groups.

→ **Do not ask leading questions**. A leading question is one which, by its contents, structure or wording, leads a respondent to answer in a certain direction. Such questions are judgemental and lead respondents to answer either positively or negatively.

Ambiguous question: An ambiguous question is one that contains more than one meaning and can be interpreted differently by different respondents.

Double-barrelled question: A double-barrelled question is a question within a question.

233

Leading question: A question which, by its contents, structure or wording, leads a respondent to answer in a certain direction.

Unemployment is increasing, isn't it?

Smoking is bad, isn't it?

The first problem is that these are not questions but statements. Because the statements suggest that 'unemployment is increasing' and 'smoking is bad', respondents may feel that to disagree with them is to be in the wrong, especially if they feel that the researcher is an authority and that if s/he is saying that 'unemployment is increasing' or 'smoking is bad', it must be so. The feeling that there is a 'right' answer can 'force' people to respond in a way that is contrary to their true position.

↝ **Do not ask questions that are based on presumptions**. In such questions the researcher assumes that respondents fit into a particular category and seeks information based upon that assumption.

How many cigarettes do you smoke in a day? (Moser & Kalton 1989: 325)

What contraceptives do you use?

Both these questions were asked without ascertaining whether or not respondents were smokers or sexually active. In situations like this it is important to ascertain first whether or not a respondent fits into the category about which you are enquiring.

Constructing a research instrument in quantitative research

The construction of a research instrument or tool is an extremely important aspect of a research project because anything you say by way of findings or conclusions is based upon the type of information you collect, and the data you collect is entirely dependent upon the questions that you ask of your respondents. The famous saying about computers – 'garbage in, garbage out'– is also applicable to data collection. The research tool provides the input to a study and therefore the quality and validity of the output, the findings, are solely dependent upon it.

In spite of its immense importance, to the author's knowledge, no specific guidelines for beginners on how to construct a research tool exist. Students are left to learn for themselves under the guidance of their research supervisor. The guidelines suggested below outline a broad approach, especially for beginners. The underlying principle is to ensure the validity of your instrument by making sure that *the questions you ask of your respondents directly relate to the objectives of your study*. Therefore, clearly stated objectives, research questions and hypotheses play an extremely important role in ensuring the validity of your research instrument as, in the suggested approach, each question in the instrument stems from them. It is suggested that a beginner should adopt the following approach in the development of a research instrument:

↝ **STEP ONE** If you have not already done so, clearly define and individually list all the specific objectives, research questions or hypotheses, if any, to be tested.

↝ **STEP TWO** For each objective, research question or hypothesis, list all the associated questions that you want to answer through your study.

STEP THREE **CONSTRUCTING AN INSTRUMENT FOR DATA COLLECTION**

→ **STEP THREE** Take each question that you identified in Step Two and list the information required to answer it.

→ **STEP FOUR** Formulate question(s) that you want to ask of your respondents to obtain the required information.

In the above process you may find that the same piece of information is required for a number of questions. In such a situation the question should be asked once only. To understand this process, study Table 9.1 for which we have already developed a set of objectives in Figure 4.4 in Chapter 4. Note that each research objective, question or hypothesis is linked to some of the questions that you ask of your respondents. In other words, each question that you ask of your respondents can be linked to one of the objectives, research questions or hypotheses, thus enhancing the validity of your research instrument. Most of the time you might need to ask more than one question to fully achieve the total intentions of an objective or research questions.

CHECKPOINT
Quantitative research instruments

Asking personal and sensitive questions

In the social sciences, sometimes one needs to ask questions that are of a personal nature. Some respondents may find this offensive. It is important to be aware of this as it may affect the quality of information or even result in an interview being terminated or questionnaires not being returned. Researchers have used a number of approaches to deal with this problem, but it is difficult to say which approach is best. According to Bradburn and Sudman (1979: 12–13), 'no data collection method is superior to other methods for all types of threatening questions. If one accepts the results at face value, each of the data gathering methods is best under certain conditions.'

In terms of the best technique for asking **sensitive** or threatening questions, there appear to be two opposite opinions, based on the manner in which the question is asked: direct or indirect. The advantage of the direct approach is that one can be sure that an affirmative answer is accurate. Those who advocate the indirect approach believe that direct questioning is likely to offend respondents and hence they are unlikely to answer even non-sensitive questions. Some ways of asking personal questions in an indirect manner are as follows:

→ by showing drawings or cartoons;
→ by asking the respondent to complete a sentence;
→ by asking the respondent to sort cards containing statements;
→ by using random devices.

A detailed description of these methods is beyond the scope of this book.

The order of questions

The order of questions in a questionnaire or in an interview schedule is important as it affects the quality of information, and the interest and even willingness of a respondent to participate in a study. Again, there are two

Table 9.1 Guidelines for constructing a research instrument (quantitative research): a study to evaluate community responsiveness in a health programme

Objectives/research questions/hypotheses Step I	Main and associated research questions Step II	Information required Step III	Questions Step IV
1 To find out the understanding of the concept 'community responsiveness' among health administrators, planners, service providers and consumers of health services	What is community responsiveness? What does it mean when people use the term 'community responsiveness'?	1 Perception of community responsiveness	Q1.1 When you use the term 'community responsiveness', what do you mean by it? Q1.2 What comes to your mind when you use the term 'community responsiveness' in the delivery of health services? Q1.3 What, in your opinion, are the characteristics of 'community responsiveness'? Q1.4 What, in your opinion, is the difference between 'community development' and 'community responsiveness'?
2 To identify the strategies needed to foster community responsiveness in the delivery of health services	What are the differences in the perception of community responsiveness among health administrators, planners, service providers and consumers of health services?	2 Occupational status, i.e. health administrator, planner, service provider or consumer	Q2.1 What would you categorise your job as? Health administrator/ planner Service provider Health consumer
3 To develop a set of indicators to evaluate the effectiveness of strategies to foster community responsiveness		3 Age, gender, education	Q3.1 How old are you? ___ Q3.2 Are you ___ female ___ male? Q3.3 What is the highest level of educational achievement you have attained?

categories of opinion as to the best way to order questions. The first is that questions should be asked in a random order, and the second is that they should follow a logical progression based upon the objectives of the study. The author believes that the latter procedure is better as it gradually leads respondents into the themes of the study, starting with simple themes and progressing to complex ones. This approach sustains the interest of respondents and gradually stimulates them to answer the questions. However, the random approach is useful in situations where the researcher wants respondents to express their agreement or disagreement with different aspects of an issue. In this case a logical listing of statements or questions may 'condition' a respondent to the opinions expressed by the researcher through the statements.

Pre-testing a research instrument

Having constructed your research instrument, whether an interview schedule or a questionnaire, it is important that you test it out before using it for actual data collection. Pre-testing a research instrument entails a critical examination of the understanding of each question by respondents. A pre-test should be carried out under actual field conditions on a group of people similar to your study population. The purpose is not to collect data but to identify problems that the potential respondents might have in understanding or interpreting a question. Your aim is to identify if there are problems in understanding the way a question has been worded, the appropriateness of the meaning it communicates, whether different respondents interpret a question differently, and to establish whether their interpretation is different from what you were trying to convey. If there are problems you need to re-examine the wording to make it clearer and unambiguous.

Prerequisites for data collection

Before you start obtaining information from potential respondents it is imperative that you make sure of their:

↳ **motivation to share the required information** – It is essential for respondents to be willing to share information with you. You should make every effort to motivate them by explaining clearly and in simple terms the objectives and relevance of the study, either at the time of the interview or in the covering letter accompanying the questionnaire and/or through interactive statements in the questionnaire.

↳ **clear understanding of the questions** – Respondents must understand what is expected of them in the questions. If respondents do not understand a question clearly, the response given may be either wrong or irrelevant, or make no sense.

↳ **possession of the required information** – It is a prerequisite that respondents must have the information sought. This is of particular importance when you are seeking factual or technical information. If respondents do not have the required information, they cannot provide it.

METHODS OF DATA COLLECTION IN QUALITATIVE RESEARCH

To draw a clear distinction between quantitative and qualitative methods of data collection is both difficult and inappropriate because of the overlap between them. The difference between them mainly lies in the manner in which a method is applied in an actual data collection situation. Use of these methods in quantitative research demands standardisation of questions to be asked of the respondents, a rigid adherence to their structure and order, an adoption of a process that is tested and predetermined, and making sure of the validity and reliability of the process as well as the questions. However, the methods of data collection in qualitative research follow a convention which is almost opposite to quantitative research. The wording, order and format of these questions are neither predetermined nor standardised. Qualitative methods are characterised by flexibility and freedom in terms of structure and order on the part of the researcher.

As mentioned in the previous chapter, most qualitative study designs are method based: that is, the method of data collection seems to determine the design. In some situations it becomes difficult to separate a study design from the method of data collection. For example, in-depth interviewing, narratives and oral history are both designs and methods of data collection. This may confuse some, but in this chapter they are detailed as methods and not designs.

The various methods of data collection in qualitative research can be classified into three categories. These are:

1   unstructured interviews;

2   observations; and

3   secondary sources.

Unstructured interviews

Unstructured interviewing is a very common method of data collection in qualitative research. Unstructured interviews are based upon most of the characteristics that underpin the philosophy of qualitative research. They are flexible in structure, in-depth in their search, free from rigid boundaries, and at liberty to deviate from their predetermined course if need be. In addition, they differ from structured interviews in the manner the raw data is generated and analysed and the style in which the findings are communicated.

Flexibility, freedom and spontaneity in content and structure underpin an interaction in all types of unstructured interview. This interaction can be at a one-to-one (researcher and respondent) or a group (researcher and a group of respondents) level. There are several types of unstructured interview that are prevalent in qualitative research: *in-depth interviewing, focus group interviewing, narratives* and *oral histories*. Below is a brief description of each of these. For a detailed understanding readers should consult the relevant references listed in the Bibliography.

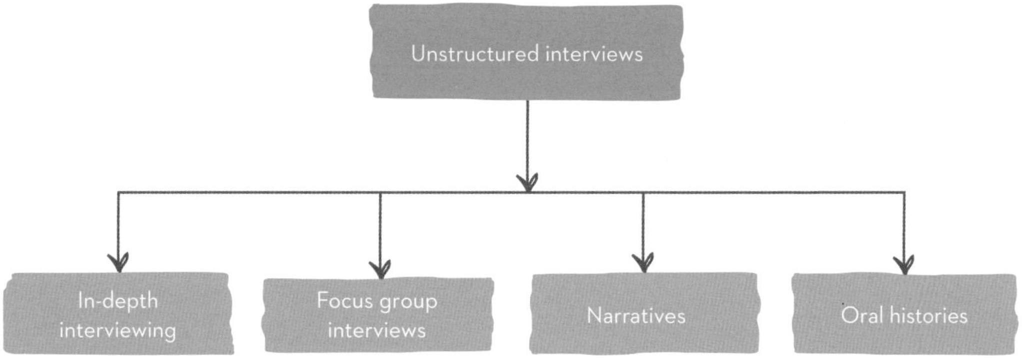

Figure 9.8   Types of unstructured interviews

In-depth interviews

The theoretical roots of in-depth interviewing are in what is known as the interpretive tradition. According to Taylor and Bogdan (1998: 77), in-depth interviewing is 'repeated face-to-face encounters between the researcher and informants directed towards understanding informants' perspectives on their lives, experiences, or situations as expressed in their own words'. This definition underlines two essential characteristics of in-depth interviewing: it involves face-to-face, repeated interaction between the researcher and his/her informant(s); and it aims to understand the perspectives of the latter. Because this method involves repeated contacts and hence an extended length of time spent with an informant, it is assumed that the rapport between researcher and informant will be enhanced, and that the corresponding understanding and confidence between the two will lead to in-depth and accurate information.

In its design, the in-depth interviewing is very simple. You select individuals who you think can provide you with the best information, and make contact with them to detail different aspects of the study, to seek their informed consent to their participation, to explain their expected involvement, and to decide where and when to carry out the interviews.

Recording the details of your discussions with your respondents is extremely important. You need to decide how and when you are going to record these details, and how the recorded material is to be given to your respondent(s) for confirmation and verification.

Focus group interviews

The only difference between a focus group interview and an in-depth interview is that the former is undertaken with a group and the latter with an individual. In a focus group interview you explore the perceptions, experiences and understandings of a group of people who have some experience in common with regard to a situation or event. For example, you may explore with relevant groups such issues as domestic violence, physical disability or

In-depth interviewing: is an extremely useful method of data collection that provides complete freedom in terms of content and structure. As a researcher you are free to order these in whatever sequence you wish, keeping in mind the context. You also have complete freedom in terms of what questions you ask of your respondents, the wording you use and the way you explain your questions to your respondents. You usually formulate questions and raise issues on the spur of the moment, depending upon what occurs to you in the context of the discussion.

239

asylum seeking in Australia. The purpose is to find out the experiences and opinions of those who have collectively experienced an event or situation.

In focus group interviews, broad areas of discussion topics are developed beforehand, either by the researcher or by the group. These only provide a broad frame for discussions which are followed by the specific discussion points that emerge as a part of the discussion. Members of a focus group express their opinions while discussing these issues.

As a researcher, you need to ensure that whatever is expressed or discussed is recorded accurately. Use the method of recording that suits you best. You may audiotape discussions, employ someone else to record them or record them yourself immediately after each session. If you are taking your own notes during discussions, you need to be careful not to lose something of importance because of your involvement in discussions. You can and should take your write-up of discussions back to your focus group for correction, verification and confirmation.

Narratives

Narratives: The narrative technique of gathering information has even less structure than the focus group. Narratives have almost no predetermined content except that the researcher seeks to hear the personal experience of a person with an incident or happening in his/her life. Essentially, the person tells his/her story about an incident or situation and you, as the researcher, listen passively, occasionally encouraging the respondent.

The narrative technique of gathering information has even less structure than the focus group. Narratives have almost no predetermined content except that the researcher seeks to hear a person's retelling of an incident or happening in his/her life. Essentially, the person tells his/her story about an incident or situation and you, as the researcher, listen passively. Occasionally, you encourage the individual by using active listening techniques; that is, you say words such as 'uh huh', 'mmmm', 'yeah', 'right' and nod as appropriate. Basically, you let the person talk freely and without interrupting.

Narratives are a very powerful method of data collection for situations which are sensitive in nature. For example, you may want to find out about the impact of child sexual abuse on people who have gone through such an experience. As a researcher, you ask these people to narrate their experiences and how they have been affected. Narratives may have a therapeutic impact; that is, sometimes simply telling their story may help a person to feel more at ease with the event. Some therapists specialise in narrative therapy. But here, we are concerned with narratives as a method of data collection.

As with focus group interviews, you need to choose the recording system that suits you best. Having completed narrative sessions you need to write up your detailed notes and give them back to the respondent to check for accuracy.

Oral histories

Oral histories, like narratives, involve the use of both passive and active listening. Oral histories, however, are more commonly used for learning about a historical event or episode or for gaining information about a culture, custom or story that has been passed from generation to generation. Narratives are more about a person's personal experiences, whereas oral histories are about historical, social or cultural events.

Suppose you want to find out about the experiences of people who were displaced after the Second World War in Europe. Talking to some of them and eliciting their stories will become the basis of your conclusions about life experiences after the war. Or suppose you want to find out about the living conditions of Aboriginal and Torres Strait Island people in the 1960s. To do so you would talk to persons who were alive during that period and ask them about life at that time.

Data collection through unstructured interviewing is extremely useful in situations where either in-depth information is needed or little is known about the area. The flexibility allowed to the interviewer in what s/he asks of a respondent is an asset as it can elicit extremely rich information. As it provides in-depth information, this technique is used by many researchers to construct a structured research instrument. On the other hand, since an unstructured interview does not list specific questions to be asked of respondents, the comparability of questions asked and responses obtained may become a problem. As the researcher gains experience during the interviews, the questions asked of respondents change; hence, the type of information obtained from those who are interviewed at the beginning may be markedly different from that obtained from those interviewed towards the end. Also, this freedom can introduce investigator bias into the study. Using an interview guide as a means of data collection requires much more skill on the part of the researcher than does using a structured interview.

Observation

Observation is another method used for data collection in qualitative research. The difference between the use of observation in quantitative and qualitative research lies in the degree of flexibility and freedom in what and how to observe, and in recording and analysing the data generated through it. In qualitative research you have almost no framework for observation, and the recording is done in descriptive and narrative form. Use of observation in quantitative studies follows a predetermined framework and the recording is either categorical or on a scale. You can have both types of observation, participant and non-participant, as a method of data collection in qualitative research. Observation as a method of data collection has been adequately covered earlier in this chapter.

CHECKPOINT
Interview guides

Secondary sources

There are many sources that can provide data for your qualitative research study. These sources are covered later in this chapter. The only difference in their use in quantitative and qualitative research is the way the information is extracted, analysed and communicated.

241

Constructing a research instrument in qualitative research

Data in qualitative research is not collected through a set of predetermined questions but by raising issues around different areas of enquiry. Hence, as such, there are no predetermined set of questions that you ask of your respondents. However, many people develop a loose list of issues and discussion points that they want to discuss with respondents or to have ready in case what they want to discuss does not surface during the discussions. This loosely developed list of issues is called an interview guide. It is a research tool that is used only as a back-up in qualitative designs. In the author's opinion, particularly for a beginner, it is important to develop an interview guide to ensure desired coverage of the areas of enquiry and comparability of information across respondents. Note that in-depth interviewing is both a method of data collection and a study design in qualitative research, and the interview guide is a research tool that is used to collect data in this design.

Interview guide: A list of issues, topics or discussion points that serves as a reminder of what you want to cover in an in-depth interview. Note that these points are not questions.

Recently the author conducted a study using in-depth interviewing and focus group methodologies to construct a conceptual service delivery model for providing child protection services through family consultation, involvement and engagement. The project was designed to develop a model that can be used by the field workers when dealing with a family in matters relating to child protection. To start with, the author conducted a number of in-depth interviews with some staff members working at different levels and the client group to gather ideas about the issues and discussion points that they thought important to raise with the staff and clients. On the basis of these in-depth interviews, a list of likely topics/issues was prepared. This list, the interview guide, became the basis for collecting the required information from individuals and focus groups in order to construct the conceptual model. Nevertheless, the focus groups were encouraged to raise any issue relating to the service delivery. And in situations where nothing much came out of the discussions, the discussion was directed around the following topics, which formed the core of the interview guide for focus groups and in-depth interviews:

- What do you understand by the concept of family engagement and involvement when deciding about a child?
- What should be the extent and nature of the involvement?
- How can it be achieved?
- What do you think are the advantages of involving families in the decision making?
- What in your opinion are its disadvantages?
- What is your opinion about this concept?
- What can a field worker do to involve a family?
- How can the success or failure of this model be measured?
- How will this model affect current services to children?
- What additional training is needed for the staff to effectively work within the framework of the model?
- What indicators can be used to measure the effectiveness of the model?

Note that these topics only served as starting points for discussions, in the absence of issues raised by the group members. The group members were encouraged to discuss whatever they wanted to in relation to the perceived model. All one-to-one in-depth interviews and focus group discussions were recorded on audiotape and were analysed to identify major themes that emerged from these discussions.

COLLECTING DATA USING SECONDARY SOURCES

So far we have discussed primary sources of data collection, where the required data is collected either by you or by someone else for the specific purpose you have in mind. There are occasions when your data has already been collected by someone else or already exists as a part of the routine record keeping by an organisation and what you need to do is to extract the required information for the purpose of your study. The following list gives some idea of possible secondary sources, grouped into categories:

- **Government or quasi-government publications** – There are many government and quasi-government organisations that collect data on a regular basis in a variety of areas and publish it for use by members of the public and interest groups. Some common examples are the census, vital statistics registration, labour force surveys, health reports, economic forecasts and demographic information.
- **Earlier research** – For some topics, a vast array of research studies that have already been done by others can provide you with the required information.
- **Personal records** – Some people write historical and personal records (e.g. diaries) that may provide the information you need.
- **Mass media** – Reports published in newspapers, in magazines, on the Internet, and so on, may be another good source of data.

CHECKPOINT
Secondary sources

All qualitative, quantitative and mixed methods research studies can use secondary sources as a method of data collection. In qualitative research you usually extract descriptive and narrative information (such as information from historical accounts of an event, descriptions of a situation, stories about beliefs and superstitions, or descriptions of a site). In quantitative studies the information is usually extracted in numerical or categorical form. In mixed methods approaches it depends upon the methods that are being used. In all situations where you are using secondary sources, you first need to decide what information you need, where it is available and how to extract it. It might be a good idea to develop a form to record the required information in the format that is best suited to your needs.

Problems with data from secondary sources

When using data from secondary sources you need to be careful as there may be problems with the availability, format and quality of data. The extent of these problems varies from source to source. While using such data some of the issues you should keep in mind are as follows:

- **Validity and reliability** – The validity of information may vary markedly from source to source. For example, information obtained from a census is likely to be more valid and reliable than that obtained from most personal diaries.
- **Personal bias** – Information from personal diaries, newspapers and magazines may have the problem of personal bias as these writers are likely to exhibit less rigour and objectivity than one would expect in research reports.
- **Availability of data** – It is common for beginning researchers to assume that the required data will be available, but you cannot and should not make this assumption. Therefore, it is important to make sure that the required data is available before you proceed further with your study.
- **Format** – Before deciding to use data from secondary sources it is equally important to ascertain that the data is available in the required format. For example, you might need to analyse age in the categories 23–33, 34–48, and so on, but, in your source, age may be categorised as 21–24, 25–29, and so on.

243

SUMMARY

In this chapter you have learnt about the various methods of data collection. Information collected about a situation, phenomenon, issue or group of people can come from either primary sources or secondary sources.

Primary sources are those where you or others collect information from respondents for the specific purpose for which a study is undertaken. These include interviewing, observation and the use of questionnaires. All other sources, where the information required is already available, such as government publications, reports and previous research, are called secondary sources.

There is a considerable overlap in the methods of data collection between quantitative and qualitative research studies. The difference lies in the way the information is generated, recorded and analysed. In quantitative research the information, in most cases, is generated through a set of predetermined questions and either the responses are recorded in categorical format or the categories are developed out of the descriptive responses at the time of analysis through the process called content analysis. The information obtained then goes through data processing and is subjected to a number of statistical procedures. In qualitative research the required information is generated through a series of questions which are not predetermined and pre-worded. In addition, the recording of information is in descriptive format and the main mode of analysis is content analysis to identify the main themes. Structured interviews, use of questionnaires and structured observations are the most common methods of data collection in quantitative research, whereas in qualitative research unstructured interviews (oral histories, in-depth interviews and narratives) and participant observation are the main methods of data collection from primary sources.

The choice of a particular method of collecting data depends upon the purpose of collecting information, the type of information being collected, the resources available, your skills in the use of a particular method of data collection and the socioeconomic-demographic characteristics of your study population. Each method has its own advantages and disadvantages and each is appropriate for certain situations. The choice of a particular method for collecting data is important in itself for ensuring the quality of the information, but no method of data collection will guarantee 100 per cent accurate information. The quality of your information is dependent upon several methodological, situational and respondent-related factors and your ability as a researcher lies in either controlling or minimising the effect of these factors in the process of data collection.

The use of open-ended and closed questions is appropriate for different situations. Both have strengths and weaknesses and you should be aware of these so that you can use them appropriately.

The construction of a research instrument is the most important aspect of any research endeavour as it determines the nature and quality of the information you gather. This is the input of your study and the output, the relevance and accuracy of your conclusions, is entirely dependent upon it. A research instrument in quantitative research must be developed in light of the objectives of your study. The method suggested in this chapter ensures that questions in an instrument have a direct link to your objectives. The wording of questions can pose several problems and you should keep them in mind while formulating your questions.

In qualitative research you do not develop a research instrument as such, but it is advisable that you develop a conceptual framework of the likely areas you plan to cover, providing sufficient allowance for new ones to emerge when collecting data from your respondents.

Now that you have read the full chapter...

CHECK YOUR UNDERSTANDING

☐ Do you understand the meaning and application of all of the keywords at the start of the chapter? If not, visit the online resources and use the glossary flashcards to get to grips with their definitions.

☐ List the different methods of data collection in quantitative research.

☐ There is a considerable overlap in the methods of data collection between quantitative and qualitative research. In spite of this they are different. List a few of the factors that differentiate them.

☐ Describe the problems that can affect the quality of data when collecting through observation.

☐ Compare the advantages and disadvantages of using questionnaire versus interviewing for data collection.

☐ What are the different forms of questions and what are their respective advantages and disadvantages?

☐ What considerations would you keep in mind when constructing a questionnaire?

☐ Detail the various methods commonly used in qualitative research to collect information from respondents.

☐ Discuss the quantitative and qualitative methods of data collection that you can use in a mixed methods approach.

APPLY IT TO YOUR OWN PROJECT

☐ Identify two or three examples from your own academic field where it may be better to use a questionnaire rather than interviewing, and vice versa.

☐ Identify three situations in your own academic area where it would be better to use open-ended questions and three where closed questions might be more useful.

CONFUSED?

THE ONLINE RESOURCES ARE HERE TO HELP YOU

 https://study.sagepub.com/kumar5e

CHECKPOINT: What is epistemology? Watch this video.

CHECKPOINT: What are the two main types of observation, and how might you undertake them? Visit this website.

CHECKPOINT: What are the two main types of interivews, and when might you use each one? Watch this video.

CHECKPOINT: What are examples of closed and open questions, and why is effective questioning important? Visit this website.

CHECKPOINT: What are some examples of quantitative research instruments, and how do they differ from qualitative instruments? Visit this website.

CHECKPOINT: How can an interview guide help you in your research? Read this encyclopaedia entry.

CHECKPOINT: Where can you find secondary data sources? Read this chapter.

NEED MORE GENERAL SUPPORT?

Get up to speed on key terms with *glossary flashcards* and test yourself on important concepts with *multiple choice questions*.

UP FOR A CHALLENGE?

THE ONLINE RESOURCES ARE HERE TO INSPIRE YOU

 https://study.sagepub.com/kumar5e

CHECKPOINT: What is the importance of epistemology in research, and how does it relate to data collection? Visit this website.

CHECKPOINT: What does an observational study look like? Explore this case study.

CHECKPOINT: How do you develop confidence in your questioning during interviews? Watch this video.

CHECKPOINT: How do you create effective questions? Visit this website.

CHECKPOINT: How do you choose a quantitative research instrument that is well suited to your research? Visit this website.

CHECKPOINT: How do you construct a useful interview guide? Visit this website.

CHECKPOINT: How can you assess the credibility and relevance of secondary data sources? Read this chapter.

READY TO WORK ON YOUR OWN PROJECT?

Start building a portfolio of your ideas with the exercise workbook and get support tailored to your specific assignment with the assessment toolkit.

COLLECTING DATA USING ATTITUDINAL SCALES

- step three -

CONSTRUCTING AN INSTRUMENT
FOR DATA COLLECTION

Selecting a method of data collection   210

→ Collecting data using attitudinal scales   248

Establishing the validity and reliability of a research instrument   266

ESSENTIAL TERMS

You should be able to define these by the end of the chapter

- attitudinal scales
- cumulative scale
- equal-appearing interval scale Guttman scale
- Likert scale
- summated rating scale
- Thurstone scale

BONUS TERMS

You will learn more about these by the end of the chapter

- attitudinal score
- attitudinal value
- attitudinal weight
- interval scale
- negative statements
- neutral items
- non-discriminative items
- numerical scale
- ordinal scale
- positive statements
- ratio scale

LEARNING OBJECTIVES

At the end of this chapter, you will be able to:

- Describe what the different attitudinal scales are and how and when to use them
- Discuss the functions of attitudinal scales in quantitative research
- Identify the difficulties in developing an attitudinal scale and how to overcome them
- Express the relationship between attitudinal and measurement scales
- Evaluate the strengths and weaknesses of each scale
- Measure attitudes through qualitative methods

MEASUREMENT OF ATTITUDES IN QUANTITATIVE AND QUALITATIVE RESEARCH

A common practice in social research is to explore the attitudes of people towards various conditions, issues, situations, policies, problems or anything that is of interest and/or concern to us in our daily lives. The importance of attitudinal scales lies in their ability to help us to find out how people feel towards these situations and issues. Knowledge about how people feel towards them plays an important role in formulating new policies and programmes to achieve improvement and betterment. For example: How do people feel towards recreational facilities in their community? What are the needs of the members of the community and how important are these needs to them? What is the attitude of people towards an urban development plan for their area? How do students feel about their lecturer's teaching? What are the attitudes of people towards a programme? How satisfied are they with the services provided by an institution? What are the problems encountered by tourists vising this town? What do consumers think of this product? These are some of the situations that are better explored by finding out attitudes towards them. The exploration of attitudes can be done in a descriptive form where you ask people to describe, discuss and explore with them their attitudes towards an issue. This description becomes the basis for ascertaining their attitudes or you can explore them through the use of the attitudinal scales.

There are a number of differences in the way attitudes are measured in quantitative and qualitative research. In quantitative research you are able to explore, measure, determine the intensity and combine attitudes to different aspects of an issue to arrive at a single indicator that is reflective of the overall attitude. In qualitative research, you can only explore the spread of attitudes and establish the types of attitudes prevalent. In quantitative research you can ascertain the types of attitudes people have in a community, how many people have a particular attitude and the intensity of those attitudes. A number of techniques have been developed to measure attitudes and their intensity in quantitative research, but such techniques are lacking in qualitative research. This is mainly because in qualitative research you do not make an attempt to measure or quantify. The concept of attitudinal scales, therefore, is more prevalent in quantitative than in qualitative research.

ATTITUDINAL SCALES IN QUANTITATIVE RESEARCH

In quantitative research there are three **scales** which have been developed to 'measure' attitudes. Each of these scales is based upon different assumptions and follows different procedures in its construction. As a beginner in research methods it is important for you to understand these procedures and the assumptions behind them so that you can make an appropriate and accurate interpretation of the findings. As you will see, it is not very easy to construct an attitudinal scale. Of the three scales, the Likert scale is the easiest to construct and therefore the most frequently used. The Thurstone scale is more difficult to construct than the Likert scale. The Guttman scale is much more complex than the Thurstone scale and therefore far less used in social research; hence, its relevance for beginners is marginal and it is not included in this book.

FUNCTIONS OF ATTITUDINAL SCALES

If you want to find out the attitude of respondents towards an issue, you can ask either a closed or an open-ended question. For example, suppose that you want to ascertain the attitude of students in a class towards their lecturer and that you have asked them to respond to the following question: 'What is your attitude towards your lecturer?' If your question is open-ended, it invites each respondent to describe the attitude that s/he holds towards the lecturer. If you have framed a closed question, with categories such as 'extremely positive', 'positive', 'uncertain', 'negative' and 'extremely negative', this guides the respondents to select a category that best describes their attitude. This type of questioning, whether framed descriptively or in a categorical form, elicits an overall attitude towards the lecturer. While ascertaining the overall attitude may be sufficient in some situations, in many others, where the purpose of attitudinal questioning is to develop strategies for improving a service or intervention, or to formulate policy, eliciting attitudes on various aspects of the issue under study is required.

But as you know, every issue, including that of the attitude of students towards their lecturers, has many aspects. For example, the attitude of the members of a community towards the provision of a particular service comprises their attitude towards the need for the service, its manner of delivery, its location, the physical facilities provided to users, the behaviour of the staff, the competence of the staff, the effectiveness and efficiency of the service, and so on. Other examples – such as the attitude of employees towards the management of their organisation, the attitude of employees towards occupational redeployment and redundancy, the attitude of nurses towards death and dying, the attitude of consumers towards a particular product, the attitude of students towards a lecturer or the attitude of staff towards the strategic plan for their organisation – can be broken down in the same manner.

Respondents usually have different attitudes towards different aspects. Only when you ascertain the attitude of respondents to an issue by formulating a question for each aspect, using either open-ended or closed questions, do you find out their attitude towards each aspect. The main limitation of this method is that it is difficult to draw any conclusion about the overall attitude of a respondent from these responses. Take the earlier example, where you want to find out the attitude of students towards a lecturer. There are different aspects of teaching: the content of lectures; the organisation of material; the lecturer's ability to communicate material; the presentation and style; knowledge of the subject; responsiveness; punctuality; and so on. Students may rate the lecturer differently on different aspects. That is, the lecturer might be considered extremely competent and knowledgeable in his/her subject but may not be considered a good communicator by a majority of students. Further, students may differ markedly in their opinion regarding any one aspect of a lecturer's teaching. Some might consider the lecturer to be a good communicator and others might not. The main problem is: how do we find out the 'overall' attitude of the students towards the lecturer? In other words, how do we combine the responses to different aspects of any issue to come up with one indicator that is reflective of an overall attitude? Attitudinal scales play an important role in overcoming this problem.

Attitudinal scales serve two main functions: they measure the intensity of respondents' attitudes towards the various aspects of a situation or issue; and they provide techniques to combine the attitudes towards different aspects into one overall indicator. This reduces the risk of an expression of opinion by respondents being influenced by their opinion on only one or two aspects of that situation or issue.

DIFFICULTIES IN DEVELOPING AN ATTITUDINAL SCALE

CHECKPOINT
Attitudinal scale functions

In the development of an attitudinal scale you are likely to face three problems:

1   Which aspects of a situation or issue should be included when seeking to measure an attitude towards an issue or problem? For instance, in the example cited above, what aspects of teaching should be included in a scale to find out the attitude of students towards their lecturer?
2   What procedure should be adopted for combining the different aspects to obtain an overall picture?
3   How can one ensure that a scale really is measuring what it is supposed to measure?

The first problem is extremely important as it largely determines the third problem: the extent to which the statements on different aspects are reflective of the main issue largely determines the validity of the scale. You can solve the third problem by ensuring that your statements on the various aspects have a logical link with the main issue under study – the greater the link, the higher the validity. The different types of attitudinal scale (Likert, Thurstone or Guttman) provide an answer to the second problem. They guide you as to the procedure for combining the attitudes towards various aspects of an issue, though the degree of difficulty in following the procedure for these scales varies from scale to scale.

Summated rating scale: see Likert scale

Likert scale: The Likert scale, also known as the summated rating scale, is one of the attitudinal scales designed to measure attitudes. This scale is based upon the assumption that each statement/item on the scale has equal attitudinal 'value', 'importance' or 'weight' in terms of reflecting attitude towards the issue in question. Comparatively it is the easiest to construct.

Attitudinal value: An attitudinal scale comprises many statements reflecting attitudes towards an issue. The extent to which each statement reflects this attitude varies from statement to statement. Some statements are more important in determining the attitude than others. The attitudinal value of a statement refers to the weight calculated or given to a statement to reflect its significance in reflecting the attitude: the greater the significance or extent: the greater the attitudinal value or weight.

TYPES OF ATTITUDINAL SCALE

There are three major types of attitudinal scale:

1   the summated rating scale, also known as the Likert scale;
2   the equal-appearing interval scale or differential scale, also known as the Thurstone scale;
3   the cumulative scale, also known as the Guttman scale.

The summated rating or Likert scale

The summated rating scale, more commonly known as the Likert scale, is based upon the assumption that each statement/item on the scale has equal attitudinal value, importance or weight in terms of reflecting an attitude towards the issue in question. This assumption is also the main limitation of this scale, as statements on a scale seldom have equal attitudinal value. For instance, in the examples in Figures 10.1 and 10.2, 'knowledge of subject' is not as important in terms of the degree to which it reflects the attitude of the students towards the lecturer as 'has published a great deal' or 'some students like, some do not', but, on the Likert scale, each is treated as having the same attitudinal weight. A student may not bother much about whether a lecturer has published a great deal, but may be more concerned about 'knowledge of the subject', 'communicates well' and 'knows how to teach'.

It is important to remember that the Likert scale does not measure attitude per se. It does help to place different respondents in relation to each other in terms of the intensity of their attitude towards an issue: it shows the strength of one respondent's view in relation to that of another and not the absolute attitude.

Considerations in constructing a Likert scale

In developing a Likert scale, there are a number of things to consider. Firstly, decide whether the attitude to be measured is to be classified into one-, two- or three-directional categories (i.e. whether you want to determine positive, negative and neutral positions in the study population) with respect to their attitude towards the issue under study. Next, consider whether you want to use categories or a numerical scale. This should depend upon whether you think that your study population can express itself better on a numerical scale or in categories. The decision about the number of points or the number of categories on a categorical scale depends upon how finely you want to measure the intensity of the attitude in question and on the capacity of the population to make fine distinctions. Figure 10.1 shows a five-point categorical scale that is three-directional and Figure 10.2 illustrates a seven-point numerical scale that is one-directional. Sometimes you can also develop statements reflecting opinion about an issue in varying degrees (Figure 10.3). In this instance the respondent is asked to select the statement which best describes his/her opinion.

CHECKPOINT
Likert scale

The lecturer:	Strongly agree	Agree	Uncertain	Disagree	Strongly Disagree
1 Knows the subject well	☐	☐	☐	☐	☐
2 Is unenthusiastic about teaching	☐	☐	☐	☐	☐
3 Shows concern for students	☐	☐	☐	☐	☐
4 Makes unreasonable demands	☐	☐	☐	☐	☐
5 Has poor communication skills	☐	☐	☐	☐	☐
6 Knows how to teach	☐	☐	☐	☐	☐
7 Can explain difficult concepts in simple terms	☐	☐	☐	☐	☐
8 Is hard to approach	☐	☐	☐	☐	☐
9 Is liked by some students and not by others	☐	☐	☐	☐	☐
10 Is difficult to get along with	☐	☐	☐	☐	☐

Figure 10.1   An example of a categorical scale

The lecturer:							
1 Knows the subject well	7	6	5	4	3	2	1
2 Is enthusiastic about teaching	7	6	5	4	3	2	1
3 Shows no concern for students	7	6	5	4	3	2	1
4 Demands too much	7	6	5	4	3	2	1
5 Communicates well	7	6	5	4	3	2	1
6 Knows how to teach	7	6	5	4	3	2	1
7 Can explain difficult concepts in simple terms	7	6	5	4	3	2	1
8 Is seldom available to the students	7	6	5	4	3	2	1
9 Is liked by some students and not by others	7	6	5	4	3	2	1
10 Has published a great deal	7	6	5	4	3	2	1

Figure 10.2   An example of a seven-point numerical scale

1   The Lecturer

a   knows the subject *extremely well*
b   knows the subject *well*
c   has an *average* knowledge of the subject
d   *does not know* the subject
e   has an *extremely poor* knowledge of the subject

Figure 10.3   An example of a scale with statements reflecting varying degrees of an attitude

Figure 10.4 shows the procedure used in constructing a Likert scale.

Calculating attitudinal scores

Suppose you have developed a questionnaire/interview schedule to measure the attitudes of a class of students towards their lecturer using a scale with five categories.

Procedure

STEP ONE   Assemble or construct statements that are reflective of the attitudes towards the main issue in question. Statements should be worded to reflect both positive and negative attitudes towards the issue; that is, they should be for as well as against, the issue. (If your scale is one-directional, you need only positive statements.) Make sure that all the statements have a logical link with the main issue. You also need to decide whether you want respondents to answer in categories or on a numerical scale.

STEP TWO   Administer the statements to a small group of people to test them for clarity.

STEP THREE   Analyse the responses by assigning a weighting — a numerical value — to the responses. Numerical values are assigned differently to positive and negative statements. For a positive statement the response indicating the most favourable attitude is to be given the highest score. For example, on a five-category or five-point scale, 5 is assigned to the response that indicates the most favourable attitude and I to the response that indicates the least favourable attitude. By contrast, a person who agrees strongly with a negative statement indicates that s/he does not have a favourable attitude; hence, the scoring is reversed, i.e. I is assigned to the response where a respondent strongly agrees with a negative statement and 5 to the response where s/he strongly disagrees with it.

STEP FOUR   Calculate each respondent's attitudinal score by adding the numerical values assigned in Step 3 to the responses slhe gave to each statement.

STEP FIVE   Compare all respondents' scores for each item to identify non-discriminative items. A non-discriminative item is where respondents with a high attitudinal score have responded in a similar manner to respondents with a low attitudinal score; that is, both groups have responded to the statement in the same manner. Non-discriminative statements do not help you to distinguish respondents with respect to attitude as almost everyone responds to them in the same way.

STEP SIX   Eliminate non-discriminative items.

STEP SEVEN   Construct a questionnaire/interview schedule comprising the selected statements/items.

Figure 10.4   The procedure for constructing a Likert scale

In Figure 10.5, statement 1 is a positive statement; hence, if a respondent ticks 'strongly agree', s/he is assumed to have a more positive attitude on this item than a person who ticks 'agree'. The person who ticks 'agree' has a more positive attitude than a person who ticks 'uncertain', and so on. Therefore, a person who ticks 'strongly agree' is given the highest score, 5, as there are five response categories. If there were four categories you would assign a score of 4. As a matter of fact, any score can be assigned as long as the intensity of the response pattern is reflected in the score and the highest score is assigned to the response with the highest positive intensity.

Statement 2 is a negative statement. In this case a person who ticks 'strongly disagree' has comparatively the most positive attitude on the aspect that is reflected by this item; hence, the highest score is assigned, 5. On the other hand, a respondent who ticks 'strongly agree' has the least positive attitude on the item and therefore is assigned the lowest score, 1. The same scoring system is followed for the other statements.

Note statement 9. There will always be some people who like a lecturer and some who do not; hence, this type of statement is neutral. There is no point in including such items in the scale; we have done so here purely for illustrative purposes.

The lecturer:	SA	A	U	o	SD
1 Knows the subject well (+)	5	4	3	2	1
2 is unenthusiastic about teaching (−)	1	2	3	4	5
3 Shows concern for students (+)	5	4	3	2	1
4 Makes unreasonable **demands (−)**	1	2	3	4	5
5 Has poor **communication skills (−)**					
6 Knows how to teach (+)					
7 Can explain difficult concepts in simple terms (+)					
8 is hard to approach (−)					
9 is liked by some students and not by others (+1−)					
10 is difficult to get along with (−)					

SA = strongly agree, A = agree, **U = uncertain, D = disagree, SD = strongly disagree**

Figure 10.5   Scoring positive and negative statements

Attitudinal score: A number that you calculate having assigned a numerical value to the response given by a respondent to an attitudinal statement or question. Different attitude scales have different ways of calculating the attitudinal score.

To illustrate how to calculate an individual's attitudinal score, let us take the example of two respondents who have ticked the different statements marked in our example by # and @ (see Figure 10.6). Let us work out their attitudinal scores:

The lecturer:	SA	A	U		SD
1 Knows the subject well (+)	@				#
2 Is unenthusiastic about teaching (—)		#			@
3 Shows concern for students (+)			©		#
4 Makes unreasonable demands (—)		#		#	@
5 Communicates poorly (-)		#			@
6 Knows how to teach (+)		@		#	
7 Can explain difficult concepts in simple terms (+)	@	#			
8 Is hard to approach (-)			@#	@#	
9 Is liked by some students and not by others (+/-)					
10 Is difficult to get along with (—)			#		@

SA = strongly agree, A = agree, U = uncertain, D = disagree, SD = strongly disagree

Figure 10.6   Calculating an attitudinal score

Statement no.	1	2	3	4	5	6	7	8	9	10
Respondent @ =	5 +	5 +	3 +	5 +	5 +	4 +	5 +	3 +	2 +	5 = 42
Respondent # =	1 +	2 +	1 +	2 +	2 +	2 +	4 +	3 +	2 +	3 = 22

The analysis shows that, overall, respondent @ has a 'more' positive attitude towards the lecturer than respondent #. You cannot say that the attitude of respondent @ is twice (42/22 = 1.91) as positive as that of respondent #. The attitudinal score only places respondents in a position relative to one another. Remember that the Likert scale does not measure the attitude per se, but helps you to rate a group of individuals in descending or ascending order with respect to their attitudes towards the issues in question.

The equal-appearing interval or Thurstone scale

Unlike the Likert scale, the Thurstone scale calculates a weight or attitudinal value for each statement. The weight (equivalent to the median value) for each statement is calculated on the basis of ratings assigned to a statement

Thurstone scale: The Thurstone scale is one of the scales designed to measure attitudes in the social sciences. Attitude is measured by this scale by means of a set of statements, the 'attitudinal value' of which has been determined by a group of judges. A respondent's agreement with the statement assigns a score equivalent to the 'attitudinal value' of the statement. The total score of all statements is the attitudinal score for a respondent.

by a group of judges. Each statement with which respondents express agreement (or to which they respond in the affirmative) is given an attitudinal score equivalent to the attitudinal value of the statement. The procedure for constructing the Thurstone scale is as given in Figure 10.7.

The main advantage of this scale is that, as the importance of each statement is determined by judges, it reflects the absolute rather than relative attitudes of respondents. The scale is thus able to indicate the intensity of people's attitudes and any change in this intensity should the study be replicated. On the other hand, the scale is difficult to construct, and a major criticism is that judges and respondents may assess the importance of a particular statement differently and, therefore, the respondents' attitudes might not be reflected.

STEP ONE	Assemble or construct statements reflective of attitudes towards the issue in question.	
STEP TWO	Select a panel of judges who are experts in the field of the attitudes being explored.	
STEP THREE	Send the statements to these judges with a request to rate each statement's importance in reflecting an attitude towards the issue being studied. Ask them to rate each statement on an 11-point scale.	
STEP FOUR	Calculate the median value of these judges' ratings for each item.	
STEP FIVE	if the judges' ratings of any item are scattered over the scale, this indicates that, even among the experts, there is no agreement as to the degree to which that statement reflects an attitude towards the issue in question. Discard such statements.	
STEP SIX	From the remaining statements select items that best reflect attitudes towards various aspects of the issue.	
STEP SEVEN	Construct a questionnaire/interview schedule comprising the selected items.	

Figure 10.7   The procedure for constructing the Thurstone scale

Guttman scale: The Guttman scale is one of the three attitudinal scales and is devised in such a way that the statements or items reflecting an attitude are arranged in perfect cumulative order. Arranging statements or items to have a cumulative relation between them is the most difficult aspect of constructing this scale.

The cumulative or Guttman scale

The Guttman scale is one of the most difficult scales to construct and therefore is rarely used. This scale does not have much relevance for beginners in research and so is not discussed in this book.

ATTITUDINAL SCALES AND MEASUREMENT SCALES

Different attitudinal scales use different measurement scales. It is important to know which attitudinal scale belongs to which measurement scale as this will help you in the interpretation of respondents' scores. Table 10.1 shows attitudinal scales in relation to measurement scales.

CHECKPOINT
Thurstone and Guttman scales

Table 10.1   The relationship between attitudinal and measurement scales

Attitudinal scales	Measurement scales
Likert scale	Ordinal scale
Thurstone scale	Interval scale
Guttman scale	Ratio scale

Attitudinal scales: Scales designed to measure attitudes towards an issue are called attitudinal scales. In the social sciences there are three types of scale: the summated rating scale (Likert scale), the equal-appearing interval scale (Thurstone scale) and the cumulative scale (Guttman scale).

ATTITUDES AND QUALITATIVE RESEARCH

As mentioned at the beginning of this chapter, in qualitative research you can only explore the spread of the attitudes. Whatever methods of data collection you use – in-depth interviewing, focus group, observation – you can explore the diversity in the attitudes but cannot find other aspects such as how many people have a particular attitude, the intensity of a particular attitude or overall what the attitude of a person is. Qualitative methods are therefore best suited to explore the diversity of attitudes rather than their intensity.

SUMMARY

261

One of the significant differences between quantitative and qualitative research is in the availability of methods and procedures to measure attitudes. In quantitative research there are a number of methods that can be used to measure attitudes, but qualitative research lacks methodology in this aspect primarily because its aim is to explain rather than to measure and quantify. Through qualitative research methodology you can find the diversity or spread of attitudes towards an issue but not their intensity and a combined overall indicator. Attitudinal scales are used in quantitative research to measure attitudes towards an issue. Their strength lies in their ability to combine attitudes towards different aspects of an issue and to provide an indicator that is reflective of an overall attitude. However, there are problems in developing an attitudinal scale. You must decide which aspects should be included when measuring attitudes towards an issue, how the responses given by a respondent should be combined to ascertain the overall attitude, and how you can ensure that the scale developed really measures attitude towards the issue in question.

There are three types of scale that measure attitude: the Likert, Thurstone and Guttman scales. The Likert scale is most commonly used because it is easy to construct. The main assumption of the scale is that each statement is equally important. The importance of each item for the Thurstone scale is determined by a panel of judges.

Now that you have read the full chapter...

CHECK YOUR UNDERSTANDING

- ☐ Do you understand the meaning and application of all of the keywords at the start of the chapter? If not, visit the online resources and use the glossary flashcards to get to grips with their definitions. What are the main advantages of attitudinal sales in social research?

- ☐ Name the different types of attitudinal scales and the assumptions made in their construction.

- ☐ Identify different situations which are appropriate for measuring attitudes by Likert and Thurstone scales in the social sciences.

- ☐ What aspects of self-esteem would you include in a five-point Likert scale to measure the self-esteem of group of unemployed youth?

APPLY IT TO YOUR OWN PROJECT

- ☐ Identify examples of how the Likert and Thurstone scales can be applied to research in your own academic field.

- ☐ Not all research topics easily lend themselves to being measured by a five-point Likert scale. What difficulties would you face in trying to develop this measurement scale for these types of projects? Consider, for example, how you would go about developing a five-point Likert scale to measure the self-esteem of a group of university students.

CONFUSED?

THE ONLINE RESOURCES ARE HERE TO HELP YOU

 https://study.sagepub.com/kumar5e

CHECKPOINT: Why would you use an additudinal scale in your research? Read this chapter.

CHECKPOINT: What is a Likert scale? Visit this website.

CHECKPOINT: What are the differences between Likert and Thurstone scales? Visit this website.

NEED MORE GENERAL SUPPORT?

Get up to speed on key terms with *glossary flashcards* and test yourself on important concepts with *multiple choice questions*.

UP FOR A CHALLENGE?

THE ONLINE RESOURCES ARE HERE TO HELP YOU

 https://study.sagepub.com/kumar5e

CHECKPOINT: What does a study using an attitudinal scale look like? Explore this case study.

CHECKPOINT: What does a Likert scale look like as a data collection instrument in published research? Explore this case study.

CHECKPOINT: What is a Guttman scale, and when can it be used? Visit this website.

READY TO WORK ON YOUR OWN PROJECT?

Start building a portfolio of your ideas with the exercise workbook and get support tailored to your specific assignment with the assessment toolkit.

ESTABLISHING THE VALIDITY AND RELIABILITY OF A RESEARCH INSTRUMENT

- step three -
CONSTRUCTING AN INSTRUMENT FOR DATA COLLECTION

Selecting a method of data collection   210

Collecting data using attitudinal scales   248

→ Establishing the validity and reliability of a research instrument   266

CONFUSED?
UP FOR A
CHALLENGE?

OR
NEED HELP
WITH YOUR
ASSIGNMENT?

VISIT
https://study.sagepub.
com/kumar5e for
resources specially
designed to support
you and all your
research needs.

ESSENTIAL TERMS

You should be able to define these by the end of the chapter

↪ reliability   ↪ validity

BONUS TERMS

You will learn more about these by the end of the chapter

↪ concurrent validity
↪ confirmability
↪ construct validity
↪ content validity
↪ credibility
↪ dependability

↪ external consistency
↪ face validity
↪ internal consistency
↪ predictive validity
↪ transferability

LEARNING OBJECTIVES

At the end of this chapter, you will be able to:

↪ Define the concept of validity
↪ Discuss different types of validity in quantitative and qualitative social research
↪ Define the concept of reliability
↪ Identify factors affecting the reliability of a research instrument
↪ Describe methods of determining the reliability of an instrument in quantitative research
↪ Ensure validity and reliability in a research study

In the previous two chapters we discussed various methods of data collection in quantitative, qualitative and mixed methods research. The questions asked of your respondents are the basis of your findings and conclusions. These questions constitute the 'input' for your conclusions (the 'output'). This input passes through a series of steps – the selection of a sample, the collection of information, the processing of data, the application of statistical procedures and the writing of a report – and the manner in which all of these are done can affect the accuracy and quality of your conclusions. Hence, it is important for you to attempt to establish the quality of your results. As a researcher you can also be asked by others to establish the appropriateness, quality and accuracy of the procedures you adopted for finding answers to your research questions. Broadly, this concept of appropriateness and accuracy as applied to a research process is called validity. As inaccuracies can be introduced into a study at any stage, the concept of validity can be applied to the research process as a whole or to any of its steps: study design, sampling strategy, conclusions drawn, the statistical procedures applied or the measurement procedures used. Broadly, there are two perspectives on validity:

1. Is the research investigation providing answers to the research questions for which it was undertaken?
2. If so, is it providing these answers using appropriate methods and procedures?

In this chapter we will discuss the concept of validity as applied to measurement procedures or the research tools used to collect the required information from your respondents.

There are prominent differences between quantitative and qualitative research in relation to the concepts of validity and reliability. Because of the defined and established structures and methods of data collection in quantitative research, the concepts of validity and reliability and the methods to determine them are well developed. However, in qualitative research it would be appropriate to say that these concepts cannot be rigorously applied in the same way as they are in quantitative research because of the flexibility, freedom and spontaneity given to a researcher in the methods and procedures of data collection. It becomes difficult to establish standardisation in the method(s) of data collection in qualitative research and, hence, their validity and reliability. Despite these difficulties, methods have been proposed to establish validity and reliability in qualitative research which are detailed in this chapter.

THE CONCEPT OF VALIDITY

To examine the concept of validity, let us take a very simple example. Suppose you have designed a study to ascertain the health needs of a community. In doing so, you have developed an interview schedule. Further suppose that most of the questions in the interview schedule relate to the attitude of the study population towards the health services being provided to them. Note that your aim was to *find out about health needs* but the interview schedule is finding out what *attitudes respondents have to the health services*; thus, the instrument is not measuring what it was designed to measure. The author has come across many similar examples among students and less skilled researchers.

In terms of measurement procedures, therefore, validity is the ability of an instrument to measure what it is designed to measure: 'Validity is defined as the degree to which the researcher has measured what he has set out to measure' (Smith 1991: 106). According to Kerlinger (1973: 457), 'The commonest definition of validity is epitomised by the question: Are we measuring what we think we are measuring?' Babbie (1989: 133) writes, 'validity refers to the extent to which an empirical measure adequately reflects the real meaning of the concept under consideration'. These definitions raise two key questions:

- Who decides whether an instrument is measuring what it is supposed to measure?
- How can it be established that an instrument is measuring what it is supposed to measure?

Obviously the answer to the first question is the person who designed the study, the readership of the report and experts in the field. The second question is extremely important. On what basis do you (as a researcher), a reader or an expert make this judgement? In the social sciences there appear to be two approaches to establishing the validity of a research instrument. These approaches are based upon either logic that underpins the construction of the research tool or statistical evidence that is gathered using information generated through the use of the instrument. Establishing validity through logic implies justification of each question in relation to the objectives of the study, whereas the statistical procedures provide hard evidence by way of calculating the correlations between the questions and the outcome variables.

Establishing a logical link between the questions and the objectives is both simple and difficult. It is simple in the sense that you may find it easy to see a link for yourself, and difficult because your justification may lack the backing of experts and the statistical evidence to convince others. Establishing a logical link between questions and objectives is easier when the questions relate to tangible matters. For example, if you want to find out about age, income, height or weight, it is relatively easy to establish the validity of the questions, but to establish whether a set of questions is measuring, say, the effectiveness of a programme, the attitudes of a group of people towards an issue or the extent of satisfaction of a group of consumers with the service provided by an organisation is more difficult. When a less tangible concept is involved, such as effectiveness, attitude or satisfaction, you need to ask several questions in order to cover different aspects of the concept and demonstrate that the questions asked are actually measuring it. Validity in such situations becomes more difficult to establish, especially in qualitative research where you are mostly exploring feelings, experiences, perceptions, motivations or stories.

It is important to remember that the concept of validity is pertinent only to a particular instrument and it is an ideal state that you as a researcher aim to achieve.

CHECKPOINT
Validity

271

TYPES OF VALIDITY IN QUANTITATIVE RESEARCH

There are three types of validity in quantitative research:

1   face and content validity;
2   concurrent and predictive validity;
3   construct validity.

Face validity: When you justify the inclusion of a question or item in a research instrument by linking it with the objectives of the study, thus providing a justification for its inclusion in the instrument, the process is called face validity.

Content validity: In addition to linking each question with the objectives of a study as a part of establishing the face validity, it is also important to examine whether the questions or items have covered all the areas you wanted to cover in the study. Examining questions of a research instrument to establish the extent of coverage of areas under study is called the content validity of the instrument.

Predictive validity: This form of validity is judged by the degree to which an instrument can correctly forecast an outcome: the higher the correctness in the forecasts, the higher the predictive validity of the instrument.

Concurrent validity: When you investigate how good a research instrument is by comparing it with some observable criterion or credible findings, this is called concurrent validity. It is comparing the findings of your instrument with those found by another which is well accepted. Concurrent validity is judged by how well an instrument compares with a second assessment done concurrently.

Construct validity: A more sophisticated technique for establishing the validity of an instrument. Construct validity is based upon statistical procedures. It is determined by ascertaining the contribution of each construct to the total variance observed in a phenomenon.

① Face and content validity

The judgement that an instrument is measuring what it is supposed to is primarily based upon the logical link between the questions and the objectives of the study. Hence, one of the main advantages of face and content validity is that it is easy to apply. Each question or item on the research instrument must have a logical link with an objective. Establishment of this link is an indication of the validity of the instrument. The greater the link, the higher the face validity of the instrument. It is equally important that the items and questions cover all the aspects of the issue or attitude being measured. Establishing that the different items of a research instrument cover various aspects of the issue is an indication of the content validity of the instrument. The greater the coverage, the higher the validity. In addition, the coverage of the issue or attitude should be balanced; that is, each aspect should have similar and adequate representation in the questions or items. Content validity is also judged on the basis of the extent to which statements or questions represent the issue they are supposed to measure, as judged by you as a researcher, your readership and experts in the field. Although it is easy to present logical arguments to establish validity, there are certain problems:

↳ The judgement is based upon subjective logic; hence, no definite conclusions can be drawn. Different people may have different opinions about the face and content validity of an instrument.

↳ The extent to which questions reflect the objectives of a study may differ. If the researcher substitutes one question for another, the magnitude of the link may be altered. Hence, the validity or its extent may vary with the questions selected for an instrument.

② Concurrent and predictive validity

'In situations where a scale is developed as an indicator of some observable criterion, the scale's validity can be investigated by seeing how good an indicator it is' (Moser & Kalton 1989: 356) by comparing the findings with the observable criterion. The greater the comparability, the greater the validity. Suppose you develop an instrument to determine the suitability of applicants for a profession. The instrument's validity might be determined by comparing it with another assessment, for example by a psychologist, or with a future observation of how well these applicants have done in the job. If both assessments are similar, the instrument used to make the assessment at the time of selection is assumed to have higher validity. These types of comparisons establish two types of validity: predictive validity and concurrent validity. Predictive validity is judged by the degree to which an instrument can forecast an outcome. Concurrent validity is judged by how well an instrument compares with a second assessment concurrently done: 'It is usually possible to express predictive validity in terms of the correlation coefficient between the predicted status and the criterion. Such a coefficient is called a validity coefficient' (Burns 1997: 220).

③ Construct validity

Construct validity is an indication of the quality of a research instrument to measure what it is supposed to. It is based upon statistical procedures. It is determined by ascertaining the contribution of each construct to the total variance observed in a phenomenon.

Suppose you are interested in carrying out a study to find the degree of job satisfaction among the employees of an organisation. You consider status, the nature of the job and remuneration as the three most important factors indicative of job satisfaction, and construct questions to ascertain the degree to which people consider each factor important for job satisfaction. After the pre-test or data analysis you use statistical procedures to establish the contribution of each construct (status, the nature of the job and remuneration) to the total variance (job satisfaction). The contribution of these factors to the overall job satisfaction (total variance) is an indication of the degree of validity of the instrument. The greater the variance attributable to the constructs, the higher the validity of the instrument.

One of the main disadvantages of construct validity is that you need to know about the required statistical procedures.

CHECKPOINT
Types of validity

THE CONCEPT OF RELIABILITY

We use the word 'reliable' very often in our lives. When we say that a person is reliable, what do we mean? We mean that s/he is dependable, consistent, predictable, stable and honest.

The concept of reliability in relation to a research instrument has a similar meaning: if a research tool is consistent and stable, hence predictable and accurate, it is said to be reliable. The greater the degree of consistency and stability in an instrument, the greater its reliability. Therefore, 'a scale or test is reliable to the extent that repeat measurements made by it under constant conditions will give the same result' (Moser & Kalton 1989: 353).

The concept of reliability can, therefore, be looked at from two sides:

1 How reliable is an instrument?
2 How unreliable is it?

The first question focuses on the ability of an instrument to produce consistent measurements. When you collect the same set of information more than once using the same instrument and get the same or similar results under the same or similar conditions, an instrument is considered to be reliable. The second question focuses on the degree of inconsistency in the measurements made by an instrument – that is, the extent of difference in the measurements when you collect the same set of information more than once, using the same instrument under the same or similar conditions. Hence, the degree of inconsistency in the different measurements is an indication of the extent of its inaccuracy. This 'error' is a reflection of an instrument's unreliability. Therefore, reliability is the degree of accuracy or precision in the measurements made by a research instrument. The lower the degree of 'error' in an instrument, the higher the reliability.

Let us take an example. Suppose you develop a questionnaire to ascertain the prevalence of domestic violence in a community. You administer this questionnaire and find that domestic violence is prevalent in, say, 5 per cent of households. If you follow this, without any time lag, with another survey using the same questionnaire on the same population under the same conditions, and discover that the prevalence of domestic violence is, say, 15 per cent, the questionnaire has not given a comparable result, which may mean it is unreliable. The less the difference between the two sets of results, the higher the reliability of the instrument.

Reliability: A research instrument that is able to provide similar results when used repeatedly under similar conditions is described as 'reliable'. Reliability indicates accuracy, stability and predictability of a research instrument: the higher the reliability, the higher the accuracy.

273

FACTORS AFFECTING THE RELIABILITY OF A RESEARCH INSTRUMENT

In the social sciences it is impossible to have a research tool which is 100 per cent accurate, not only because a research instrument cannot be so, but also because it is impossible to control the factors affecting reliability. Some of these factors are as follows:

- **The wording of questions** – A slight ambiguity in the wording of questions or statements can affect the reliability of a research instrument as respondents may interpret the questions differently at different times, resulting in different responses.

- **The physical setting** – In the case of an instrument being used in an interview, any change in the physical setting at the time of the repeat interview may affect the responses given during the initial interview by a respondent, which may affect reliability.

- **The respondent's mood** – A change in a respondent's mood when responding to questions or writing answers in a questionnaire can change and may affect the reliability of that instrument.

- **The interviewer's mood** – As the mood of a respondent could change from one interview to another so could the mood, motivation and interaction of the interviewer, which could affect the responses given by respondents, thereby affecting the reliability of the research instrument.

- **The nature of the interaction** – In an interview situation, the interaction between the interviewer and the interviewee can affect responses significantly. During the repeat interview the responses given may be different due to a change in interaction, which could affect reliability.

- **The regression effect of an instrument** – When a research instrument is used to measure attitudes towards an issue, some respondents, after having expressed their opinion, may feel that, as compared to their normal attitude, they have been either too negative or too positive towards the issue. The second time they may express their opinion differently, thereby affecting reliability.

CHECKPOINT
Validity and Reliability

274

METHODS OF DETERMINING THE RELIABILITY OF AN INSTRUMENT IN QUANTITATIVE RESEARCH

There are a number of ways of determining the reliability of an instrument, and these can be classified as either external or internal consistency procedures.

External consistency procedures

External consistency procedures compare findings from two independent processes of data collection with each other as a means of verifying the reliability of the measure. The two methods are test/retest and parallel forms of the same test.

Test/retest is a commonly used method for establishing the reliability of a research tool. An instrument is administered once (test), and then again (retest), under the same or similar conditions. The ratio or difference between the test and retest scores (these may be findings such as the prevalence of domestic violence or incidence of an illness) is an indication of the reliability of the instrument – the greater the ratio or the smaller the difference, the higher the reliability of the instrument. A test/retest ratio of 1 or a test/retest difference of 0 shows 100 per cent reliability (no difference between test and retest) and any deviation from this indicates less reliability – the smaller the ratio or the larger the difference, the less the reliability of the instrument.

The main advantage of the test/retest procedure is that it permits the instrument to be compared with itself, thus avoiding the sort of problems that could arise with the use of another instrument.

The main disadvantage of the procedure is that a respondent may recall the responses that s/he gave in the first round, which in turn may affect the reliability of the instrument. Where an instrument is reactive in nature (when an instrument educates the respondent with respect to what the researcher is trying to find out) this method will not provide an accurate assessment of its reliability. One of the ways of overcoming this problem is to increase the time span between the two tests, but this may affect reliability for other reasons, such as the maturation of respondents and the impossibility of achieving conditions similar to those under which the questionnaire or interview schedule was first administered.

In the *parallel forms of the same test* procedure you construct two instruments that are intended to measure the same phenomenon. The two instruments are then administered either to the same population or two similar populations. The results obtained from one test are compared with those obtained from the other. If they are similar, it is assumed that the instrument is reliable.

The main advantage of this procedure is that it does not suffer from the problem of recall found in the test/retest procedure. Also, a time lapse between the two tests is not required. A disadvantage is that you need to construct two instruments instead of one. Moreover, it is extremely difficult to construct two instruments that are comparable in their measurement of a phenomenon. It is equally difficult to achieve comparability in the two population groups and in the two conditions under which the tests are administered.

Internal consistency procedures

The idea behind internal consistency procedures is that items or questions measuring the same phenomenon, if they are reliable indicators, should produce similar results irrespective of their number, that is, how many questions in an instrument. Even if you randomly select a few items or questions from the total pool to test the reliability of an instrument, each segment of questions thus constructed should reflect reliability more or less to the same extent. It is based upon the logic that if each item or question is an indicator of some aspect of a phenomenon,

Credibility: Credibility in qualitative research is parallel to internal validity in quantitative research and refers to a situation where the results obtained through qualitative research are agreeable to the participants of the research. It is judged by the extent of respondent concordance whereby you take your findings to those who participated in your research for confirmation, congruence, validation and approval: the higher the outcome of these, the higher the credibility (validity) of the study.

Transferability: The concept of transferability refers to the degree to which the results of qualitative research can be generalised or transferred to other contexts or settings.

Dependability: Dependability in qualitative research is very similar to the concept of reliability in quantitative research. It is concerned with whether we would obtain the same results if we could observe the same thing twice: the greater the similarity in two results, the greater the dependability.

Confirmability: The degree to which the results obtained through qualitative research could be confirmed or corroborated by others. Confirmability in qualitative research is similar to reliability in quantitative research.

each segment constructed will still reflect different aspects of the phenomenon even though it is based upon fewer items/questions. Hence, even if we reduce the number of items or questions, as long as they reflect some aspect of a phenomenon, a lesser number of items can provide an indication of the reliability of an instrument. The internal consistency procedure is based upon this logic.

The *split-half technique* is commonly used for measuring the reliability of an instrument in this way. It is designed to correlate half of the items with the other half and is appropriate for instruments that are designed to measure attitudes towards an issue or phenomenon. The questions or statements are divided in half in such a way that any two questions or statements intended to measure the same aspect fall into different halves. The scores obtained by administering the two halves are correlated. Reliability is calculated by using the product moment correlation (a statistical procedure) between scores obtained from the two halves. Because the product moment correlation is calculated on the basis of only half the instrument, it needs to be corrected to assess reliability for the whole. This is known as *stepped-up reliability*. The stepped-up reliability for the whole instrument is calculated by a statistical procedure known as the Spearman–Brown formula.

VALIDITY AND RELIABILITY IN QUALITATIVE RESEARCH

One of the areas of difference between quantitative and qualitative research is in the use of and importance given to the concepts of validity and reliability. The debate centres on whether or not, given the framework of qualitative research, these concepts can or even should be applied in qualitative research. As you know, validity in the broader sense refers to the ability of a research instrument to demonstrate that it is finding out what you designed it to and reliability refers to consistency in its findings when used repeatedly. In qualitative research, as answers to research questions are explored through multiple methods and procedures which are both flexible and evolving, to ensure standardisation of research tools as well as processes becomes difficult. As a newcomer to research you may wonder how these concepts can be applied in qualitative research when it does not use standardised and structured methods and procedures which are the bases of testing validity and reliability as defined in quantitative research. You may ask how you can ascertain the ability of an instrument to measure what it is expected to and how consistent it is when the data collection questions are neither fixed nor structured.

However, there are some attempts to define and establish validity and reliability in qualitative research. In a chapter entitled 'Competing paradigms in qualitative research' (pp. 105–117) in the *Handbook of Qualitative Research*, edited by Denzin and Lincoln (1994), Guba and Lincoln have suggested a framework of four criteria as a part of the constructivism paradigm paralleling validity and reliability in quantitative research. According to them, the goodness or quality of an enquiry in this paradigm can be judged by its *trustworthiness* and *authenticity*. According to Guba and Lincoln, trustworthiness in a qualitative study is determined by four indicators closely related to validity and reliability: credibility (paralleling internal validity), transferability (paralleling external validity), dependability (paralleling reliability) and confirmability (paralleling objectivity).

Trochim and Donnelly (2007) compare the four criteria proposed by Guba and Lincoln with validity and reliability as defined in quantitative research:

→ **Credibility** – According to Trochim and Donnelly (2007: 149), 'credibility involves establishing that the results of qualitative research are credible or believable from the perspective of the participant in the research'. As qualitative research studies explore people's perceptions, experiences, feelings and beliefs, it is believed that the respondents are the best judge of whether or not the research findings have been able to reflect their opinions and feelings accurately. Hence, credibility, which is synonymous with validity in quantitative research, is judged by the extent of respondent concordance when you take your findings to those who participated in your research for confirmation, congruence, validation and approval. The higher the agreement of the respondents with the findings, the higher the validity of the study.

→ **Transferability** – This 'refers to the degree to which the results of qualitative research can be generalised or transferred to other contexts or settings' (Trochim & Donnelly 2007: 149). Though it is very difficult to establish transferability primarily because of the approach you adopt in qualitative research, to some extent this can be achieved if you extensively and thoroughly describe the process you adopted for others to follow and replicate.

→ **Dependability** – In the framework suggested by Guba and Lincoln this is very similar to the concept of reliability in quantitative research: 'It is concerned with whether we would obtain the same results if we could observe the same thing twice' (Trochim & Donnelly 2007: 149). Again, as qualitative research advocates flexibility and freedom, it may be difficult to establish unless you keep an extensive and detailed record of the process for others to replicate to ascertain the level of dependability.

→ **Confirmability** – This 'refers to the degree to which the results could be confirmed or corroborated by others' (Trochim & Donnelly 2007: 149). Confirmability is also similar to reliability in quantitative research. It is only possible if researchers follow the process in an identical manner for the results to be compared.

Table 11.1   Criteria for judging research

Traditional criteria for judging quantitative research	Alternative criteria for judging qualitative research
Internal Validity	Credibility
External Validity	Transferability
Reliability	Dependability
Objectivity	Confirmability

(Trochim and Donnelly 2007: 149)

To the author's mind, it is to some extent possible to establish the 'validity' and 'reliability' of findings in qualitative research in the form of the model suggested by Guba and Lincoln, but its success is mostly dependent upon the identical replication of the process and methods for data collection, which may not be easy to achieve in qualitative research.

SUMMARY

One of the differences in quantitative and qualitative research is in the use of and importance attached to the concepts of validity and reliability. These concepts, their use and methods of determination are more accepted and developed in quantitative than qualitative research. The concept of validity refers to a situation where the findings of your study are in accordance with what you designed it to find out. The notion of validity can be applied to any aspect of the research process. With respect to measurement procedures, it relates to whether a research instrument is measuring what it set out to measure. In quantitative research, there are two approaches used to establish the validity of an instrument: the establishment of a logical link between the objectives of a study and the questions used in an instrument, and the use of statistical analysis to demonstrate these links. There are three types of validity in quantitative research: face and content, concurrent and predictive, and construct validity. However, the use of the concept of validity in qualitative research is debatable and controversial. In qualitative research 'credibility' as described by Guba and Lincoln (1994) seems to be the only indicator of internal validity and is judged by the degree of respondent concordance with the findings. The methods used to establish 'validity' are different in quantitative and qualitative research.

The reliability of an instrument refers to its ability to produce consistent measurements each time. When we administer an instrument under the same or similar conditions to the same or a similar population and obtain similar results, we say that the instrument is 'reliable' – the more similar the results, the greater the reliability. You can look at reliability from two sides: reliability (the extent of accuracy) and unreliability (the extent of inaccuracy). Ambiguity in the wording of questions, a change in the physical setting for data collection, a respondent's mood when providing information, the nature of the interaction between interviewer and interviewee, and the regressive effect of an instrument are factors that can affect the reliability of a research instrument. In qualitative research 'reliability' is measured by 'dependability' and 'confirmability' as suggested by Guba and Lincoln (1994).

There are external and internal consistency procedures for determining reliability in quantitative research. Test/retest and parallel forms of the same test are the two procedures that determine the external reliability of a research instrument, whereas the split-half technique is classified under internal consistency procedures. There seem to be no set procedures for determining the various indicators of validity and reliability in qualitative research.

Now that you have read the full chapter...

CHECK YOUR UNDERSTANDING

☐ Do you understand the meaning and application of all of the keywords at the start of the chapter? If not, visit the online resources and use the glossary flashcards to get to grips with their definitions.

☐ What are the different types of validity? Explain the logic behind each of them.

☐ Explain the concept of reliability and factors affecting it.

☐ What do you see as the relevance of validity and reliability in research?

☐ Critically examine the application of the concepts of validity and reliability in qualitative studies.

☐ Compare criteria used in quantitative and qualitative research for judging validity and reliability.

APPLY IT TO YOUR OWN PROJECT

☐ Explore how the concepts of reliability and validity are applicable to research in your academic field or profession.

☐ Consider what strategies or procedures you could put in place in your own research to limit the affect on reliability of the following factors:
    ☐ wording of questions;
    ☐ physical setting;
    ☐ respondent's mood;
    ☐ interviewer's mood;
    ☐ nature of interaction;
    ☐ regression effect of an instrument.

CONFUSED?

THE ONLINE RESOURCES ARE HERE TO HELP YOU

 https://study.sagepub.com/kumar5e

CHECKPOINT: What are the two ways to measure validity? Visit this website.

CHECKPOINT: What are the three main types of validity? Watch this video.

CHECKPOINT: How do validity and reliability relate to each other? Watch this video.

CHECKPOINT: How do external consistency measures and internal consistency measures differ? Visit this website.

CHECKPOINT: How is quality in qualitative research measured? Read this chapter.

NEED MORE GENERAL SUPPORT?

Get up to speed on key terms with *glossary flashcards* and test yourself on important concepts with *multiple choice questions*.

UP FOR A CHALLENGE?

THE ONLINE RESOURCES ARE HERE TO INSPIRE YOU

→ https://study.sagepub.com/kumar5e ←

CHECKPOINT: What does a study with poor validty look like? Visit this website.

CHECKPOINT: What sort of statistical procedures are used to measure construct validity? Watch this video.

CHECKPOINT: How can you improve the validity and reliability of your research? Visit this website.

CHECKPOINT: What do reliability tests in quantitative research look like? Watch this video.

CHECKPOINT: What steps throughout the research process can you take to ensure quality in your qualitative research? Read this chapter.

READY TO WORK ON YOUR OWN PROJECT?

Start building a portfolio of your ideas with the exercise workbook and get support tailored to your specific assignment with the assessment toolkit.

EXERCISE III: DEVELOPING A RESEARCH INSTRUMENT

Template of
Exercise III

Congratulations once again! You are about to take the most important step of your research journey. Everything that follows after this depends upon how well you take this step, so you need to be extra careful about it. You need to be very wary in developing your research instrument to ensure its relevance and quality as the quality of your research outcome is entirely dependent on it.

The construction of a research instrument is the first practical step in operationalising your study. It is an important aspect of your research as it constitutes the input; the quality of your output (the findings and conclusions) is entirely dependent upon the quality and appropriateness of this input. Items in a research instrument are questions asked of respondents. Responses to these questions become the raw data that is processed to find answers to your research questions. The famous saying about computers, 'garbage in, garbage out', also equally applies to the research instrument. To a large extent, the validity of the findings depends upon the quality of the raw data which, in turn, depends upon the research instrument you have used or developed. If the latter is valid and reliable, the findings should also be valid and reliable.

The quality of a research instrument largely depends upon your experience in research. It is important for a beginner to follow the suggested steps outlined in Chapter 9.

For quantitative studies

Quantitative research is structured and predetermined in terms of what you want to find out about and how. As a part of this operational step, you need to decide what questions to ask of your respondents, the wording you are going to use and the order in which the questions will be asked. This exercise is designed to help to develop skills in constructing an instrument.

One of the ways to formulate the questions that are going to constitute your research instrument is by examining each subobjective, research question and hypothesis you have developed for your study, specifying for each the information you require, identifying the variables that are needed, and then formulating questions to be asked of your respondents to get information about those variables.

The wording of your questions should be simple and unambiguous. Do not ask leading questions or questions based upon presumptions. Avoid double-barrelled questions.

The pre-test of a research instrument is an integral part of instrument construction. As a rule, the pre-test should not be carried out on your sample but on a similar population.

STEP ONE On a separate piece of paper, draw a table as shown below, then list all your subobjectives, research questions and hypotheses in the first column and work through the other columns listing the required information.

Specific objectives/ research questions/ hypotheses	Specifically, what information do you require?	Identify the required variables	Formulate questions (on a separate piece of paper)

STEP TWO Formulate the questions, preferably on a separate piece of paper, giving particular attention to their wording and order. In your own mind you must examine the relevance and justification of each question in relation to the objectives of your study. If you cannot relate the relevance and justification of a question to the objectives of your study, it should be discarded.

STEP THREE If you are developing a questionnaire, incorporate interactive statements at appropriate places (see Chapter 9).

STEP FOUR After developing the first draft of your research instrument, answer the questions yourself; that is, interview yourself or complete the questionnaire. You need to imagine that you are a member of the study population who will be asked these questions or requested to complete the questionnaire. If you find it difficult to answer a question, re-examine it.

STEP FIVE Once you are satisfied with the research instrument, pre-test it with a few respondents from a population similar to the one you are going to study. The purpose of the pre-test/ field test is not to obtain information but to uncover problems with the instrument. If the instrument is an interview schedule, interview the pre-test respondents to find out if they understood the questions. If a question is not understood, find out what the respondent did not understand. If the same problem is identified by a number of respondents, change the wording. If your instrument is a questionnaire, ask the pre-test respondents to go through the questions with the aim of identifying any questions that are difficult to understand. Discuss the problems that they had in understanding or interpreting a question. In light of these discussions, if necessary, change the wording of questions with which pre-test respondents have difficulties.

STEP SIX Having pre-tested and, if necessary, amended the instrument, take a piece of paper and draw a table with two columns. In the first column write each subobjective, research question and hypothesis separately, and in the other, write the question number(s) that provide information for these objectives, research questions or hypotheses. In other words, make each question match the objective for which it provides information. If a question cannot be linked to a specific objective, research question or hypothesis, examine why it was included.

STEP SEVEN Prepare the final draft of your research instrument. If you plan to use a computer for data analysis, you may provide space on the research instrument for coding the data.

For qualitative studies

If you are doing a qualitative study, you do not need to develop a list of specific questions that you want to discuss with your potential respondents. However, it is important that you construct a framework of the issues that you think you should cover to achieve the objectives of your study. This interview guide or conceptual framework of questions will help you to continue with your interviews if nothing much is forthcoming from your respondents. Your aim is to let a respondent bring out the issues, but this framework is ready in case that does not happen. See Chapter 9 on developing a conceptual framework.

As part of Exercise I you wrote a list of points to discuss with your respondents. Go back to that exercise and check that list, revising it if necessary.

STEP FOUR

SELECTING A SAMPLE

SELECTING A SAMPLE

- step four -
SELECTING A SAMPLE

This operational step includes one chapter:

→ **Selecting a sample** 286

ESSENTIAL TERMS

You should be able to define these by the end of the chapter

- accidental sampling
- cluster sampling
- convenience sampling
- expert sampling
- judgemental sampling

- non-random sample
- quota sampling
- random sample
- sampling
- simple sampling

- snowball sampling
- stratified sampling
- systematic sampling

BONUS TERMS

You will learn more about these by the end of the chapter

- data saturation point
- disproportionate sampling
- equal and independent
- estimate
- information-rich
- multi-stage cluster sampling
- population mean

- population parameters
- random numbers
- sample size
- sample statistics
- sampling design
- sampling element
- sampling error

- sampling frame
- sampling population
- sampling strategy
- sampling unit
- saturation point
- study population

LEARNING OBJECTIVES

At the end of this chapter, you will be able to:

- Identify the differences between sampling in qualitative and quantitative research
- Evaluate the different sampling designs used research
- Define sampling terminology
- Explain the theoretical basis for sampling
- Discuss factors affecting the inferences drawn from a sample
- Understand different types of sampling:

- Random/probability sampling designs
- Non-random/non-probability sampling designs
- The 'mixed' sampling design
- Calculate a sample size
- Understand the concept of saturation point
- Apply your knowledge of sampling designs to your own research
- Understand the principles that guide sampling theory in quantitative studies

THE DIFFERENCES BETWEEN SAMPLING IN QUANTITATIVE AND QUALITATIVE RESEARCH

The selection of a sample in quantitative and qualitative research is guided by two opposing philosophies. In quantitative research you attempt to select a sample in such a way that it is unbiased and represents the population from which it is selected. In qualitative research, a number of considerations may influence the selection of a sample, such as: the ease in accessing the potential respondents; your judgement that the person has extensive knowledge about an episode, event or situation of interest; how typical the case is of a category of individuals; or simply that it is totally different from the others. You make every effort to select either a case that is similar to the rest of the group or one which is totally different. Such considerations in the selection of a sample are not acceptable in quantitative research.

The purpose of sampling in quantitative research is to draw inferences, with respect to the focus of your enquiry, about the group from which you have selected the sample, whereas in qualitative research it is designed to gain in-depth knowledge either about a situation, event or episode or about different aspects of an individual on the assumption that the individual is typical of the group and hence will provide insight into the group.

Similarly, the determination of sample size in quantitative and qualitative research is based upon the two different philosophies. In quantitative research you are guided by a predetermined sample size that is based upon a number of other considerations in addition to the resources available. However, in qualitative research you do not have a predetermined sample size but during the data collection phase you wait to reach a point of data saturation. When you are not getting new information or it is negligible, it is assumed you have reached a data saturation point and you stop collecting additional information from other respondents.

Considerable importance is placed on the sample size in quantitative research, depending upon the type of study and the possible use of the findings. Studies which are designed to formulate policies, to test associations or relationships or to establish impact assessments place a considerable emphasis on large sample size. This is based upon the principle that a larger sample size will ensure the inclusion of people with diverse backgrounds, thus making the sample representative of the study population. The sample size in qualitative research does not play any significant role as the purpose is to study only one or a few cases in order to identify the spread of diversity and not its magnitude. In such situations the data saturation stage during data collection determines the sample size.

In quantitative research, randomisation is used to ensure that a sample is selected in such a way that it represents the study population and to avoid bias. In qualitative research no such attempt is made in selecting a sample. You purposely select 'information-rich' respondents who will provide you with the information you need. In quantitative research, this is considered a biased sample.

Most of the sampling strategies, including some non-probability ones, described in this chapter can be used when undertaking a quantitative study provided it meets the requirements. However, when conducting a qualitative study only the non-probability sampling designs can be used.

SAMPLING IN QUANTITATIVE RESEARCH

The concept of sampling

Let us take a very simple example to explain the concept of sampling. Suppose you are interested in the **mean** age of the students in your class. There are two ways of finding this out. The first method is to contact all students in the class, find out their ages, add them up and then divide this by the number of students (the procedure for calculating sample mean). The second method is to select a few students from the class, ask them their ages, add them up and then divide by the number of students you have asked. From this you make an *estimate* of the average age of the class. Similarly, suppose you want to find out the average income of families living in a city. Imagine the amount of effort and resources required to go to every family in the city to find out their income! You could instead select a few families as the basis of your enquiry and then, from what you have found out from the few families, make an estimate of the **mean** income of families in the city. A similar procedure is used in opinion polls. These are also based upon a very small group of people who are questioned about (say) their voting preferences and, on the basis of these results, a *prediction* is made about the probable outcome of an election.

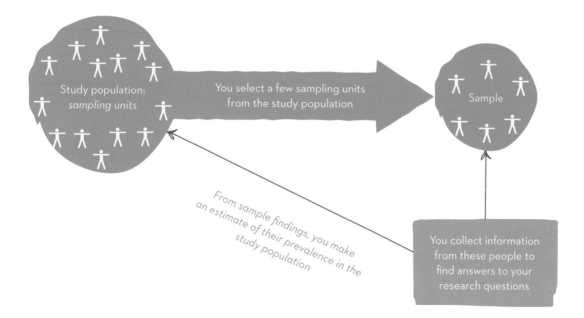

Figure 12.1   The concept of sampling

Sampling: The process of selecting a few respondents (a sample) from a bigger group (the sampling population) to become the basis for estimating the prevalence of information of interest to you.

Sampling population: The entire group, such as families living in an area, clients of an agency, residents of a community, members of a group, people belonging to an organisation about whom you want to find out about through your research endeavour, is called the sampling population or study population.

CHECKPOINT
Sampling

Study population: Every study in the social sciences has two aspects: study population and study area (subject area). The people you want to find out about are collectively known as the study population or simply population; the size of the population is usually denoted by the letter *N*. It could be a group of people living in an area, employees of an organisation, a community, a group of people with special issues, etc. The people from whom you gather information, known as the sample, are selected from the study population; the sample size is usually denoted by *n*.

Sample: A sample is a subgroup of the population which is the focus of your research enquiry and is selected in such a way that it represents the study population. A sample is composed of a few individuals from whom you collect the required information. It is done to save time, money and other resources.

Sampling, therefore, is the process of selecting a few (a sample) from a bigger group (the sampling population) as the basis for estimating or predicting the prevalence of an unknown piece of information, situation or outcome regarding the bigger group. A sample is a subgroup of the population that you are interested in. The focus of your study is to *find* answers to your research questions as they relate to the total study population and not the sample. However, through the process of sampling you attempt to *estimate* what is likely to be the situation in the total study population. (See Figure 12.1.)

This process of selecting a sample from the total population has advantages and disadvantages. The advantages are that it saves time as well as financial and human resources. However, the disadvantage is that you do not obtain information about the population's characteristics of interest to you but only *estimate* or *predict* them on the basis of what you found out in your sample. Hence, there is the possibility of an error in your estimation.

Sampling, therefore, is a trade-off between certain benefits and disadvantages. While on the one hand you save time and resources, on the other hand you may compromise the level of accuracy in your findings. Through sampling you only make an estimate about the actual situation prevalent in the total population from which the sample is drawn. If you ascertain a piece of information from the total sampling population, if your sample truly represents the study population and if your method of enquiry is correct, your findings should be reasonably accurate. But the possibility of an error is always there. Tolerance of this possibility of error is an important consideration in selecting a sample.

Sampling terminology

Let us again consider the examples used above where our main aims are to find out the mean age of the class, the average income of the families living in the city and the likely election outcome for a particular state or country. Let us assume that you adopt a sampling method – that is, you select a few students, families or voters to achieve these aims. In this process there are a number of aspects:

→ The class, families living in the city or voters from which you select your sample are called the *population* or study population. The size of this *population* is usually denoted by the letter N.

→ The small group of students, families or electors from whom you collect the required information to estimate the average age of the class, average income or the election outcome is called the sample.

→ The number of students, families or electors from whom you obtain the required information is called the sample size and is usually denoted by the letter *n*.

→ The way you select students, families or electors is called the sampling design or sampling strategy.

→ Each student, family or elector that forms the basis for selecting your sample is called a sampling unit or sampling element.

→ A list identifying each student, family or elector in the study population is called a sampling frame. If all the elements in a sampling population cannot be individually identified, you cannot have a sampling frame for that study population.

- Your findings based on the information obtained from your respondents (sample) are called sample statistics. Your sample statistics form the basis for estimating the prevalence of the characteristics of interest in the study population.

- Your main aim is to find answers to your research questions as they relate to the total study population, not to the sample you collected information from. From sample statistics we make an estimate of the possible answers to our research questions for the study population. The estimates arrived at from sample statistics are called *population parameters*. One example of a parameter is the population mean.

Principles of sampling

The theory of sampling is guided by three principles. To effectively explain these, we will take an extremely simple example. Suppose there are four individuals A, B, C and D. Further suppose that A is 18 years of age, B is 20, C is 23 and D is 25. As you know their ages, you can *find out* (calculate) their average age by simply adding 18 + 20 + 23 + 25 = 86 and dividing by 4. This gives the average (mean) age of A, B, C and D as 21.5 years.

Now let us suppose that you want to select a sample of two individuals to make an *estimate* of the average age of the four individuals. To select an unbiased sample in the statistical sense, we need to make sure that each unit has an *equal* and *independent* chance of selection in the sample. Randomisation is a process that enables you to achieve this. In order to achieve randomisation we use the theory of probability in forming pairs which will provide us with six possible combinations of two: A and B; A and C; A and D; B and C; B and D; and C and D. Let us take each of these pairs to calculate the average age of the sample:

1   A + B = 18 + 20 = 38/2 = 19.0 years;
2   A + C = 18 + 23 = 41/2 = 20.5 years;
3   A + D = 18 + 25 = 43/2 = 21.5 years;
4   B + C = 20 + 23 = 43/2 = 21.5 years;
5   B + D = 20 + 25 = 45/2 = 22.5 years;
6   C + D = 23 + 25 = 48/2 = 24.0 years.

Notice that in most cases the average age calculated on the basis of these samples of two (sample statistics) is different. Now compare these sample statistics with the average of all four individuals – the population mean (population parameter) of 21.5 years. Out of a total of six possible sample combinations, only in the case of two is there no difference between the sample statistic and the population mean. Where there is a difference, this is attributed to the sample and is known as sampling error. Again, the size of the sampling error varies markedly. Let us consider the difference in the sample statistics and the population mean for each of the six samples (Table 12.1).

Sample size: The number of individuals, usually denoted by the letter n, from whom you obtain the required information.

Sampling design: The way you select the required sampling units from a sampling population to obtain your sample is called the sampling design or sampling strategy. There are many sampling strategies in both quantitative and qualitative research.

CHECKPOINT
*Sampling
key terms*

Sampling strategy: see Sampling design

Sampling unit: see Sampling element

Sampling element: Anything that becomes the basis of selecting your sample such as an individual, family, household, members of an organisation, residents of an area, is called a sampling unit or element.

Sampling frame: When you are in a position to identify all elements of a study population, the list of all the elements is called a sampling frame.

Sample statistics: Findings based on the information obtained from your respondents (sample) are called sample statistics.

Population mean: From what you find out from your sample (sample statistics) you make an estimate of the prevalence of these characteristics for the total study population. The estimates about the total study population made from sample statistics are called population parameters or the population mean.

Randomisation: In experimental and comparative studies, you often need to study two or more groups of people. In forming these groups it is important that they are comparable with respect to the dependent variable and other variables that affect it so that the effects of independent and extraneous variables are uniform across groups. Randomisation is a process that ensures that each and every person in a group is given an equal and independent chance of being in any of the groups, thereby making groups comparable.

Sampling error: The difference in the findings (sample statistics) that is due to the selection of elements in the sample is known as sampling error.

Table 12.1   The difference between sample statistics and the population mean

Sample	Sample mean (sample statistics) (1)	Population mean (population parameter) (2)	Difference between (1) and (2)
1	19.0	21.5	−2.5
2	20.5	21.5	−1.0
3	21.5	21.5	0.0
4	21.5	21.5	0.0
5	22.5	21.5	+1.0
6	24.0	21.5	+2.5

This analysis suggests a very important principle of sampling:

↳ Principle 1. In a majority of cases where sampling is done, there will be a difference between the sample statistics and the true population mean, which is attributable to the selection of the units in the sample.

To understand the second principle, let us continue with the above example, but instead of a sample of two individuals we take a sample of three. There are four possible combinations of three that can be drawn:

1   A + B + C = 18 + 20 + 23 = 61/3 = 20.33 years;
2   A + B + D = 18 + 20 + 25 = 63/3 = 21.00 years;
3   A + C + D = 18 + 23 + 25 = 66/3 = 22.00 years;
4   B + C + D = 20 + 23 + 25 = 68/3 = 22.67 years.

Now, let us compare the difference between the sample statistics and the population mean (Table 12.2). Compare the differences calculated in Table 12.1 and Table 12.2. In Table 12.1 the difference between the sample statistic and the population mean lies between −2.5 and +2.5 years, whereas in the second it is between −1.17 and +1.17 years. The gap between the sample statistic and the population mean is reduced in Table 12.2. This reduction is attributed to the increase in the sample size. This, therefore, leads to the second principle:

↳ Principle 2. The greater the sample size, the more accurate the estimate of the true population mean.

The third principle of sampling is particularly important as a number of sampling strategies, such as stratified and cluster sampling, are based on it. To understand this principle, let us continue with the same example but use slightly different data. Suppose the ages of the four individuals are markedly different: A = 18, B = 26, C = 32 and D = 40. In other words, we are visualising a population where the individuals are markedly different with respect to age – the variable we are interested in.

Table 12.2   The difference between sample statistics and population mean

Sample	Sample mean (1)	Population man (2)	Difference between (1) and (2)
1	20.33	21.5	-1.17
2	21.00	21.5	-0.5
3	22.00	21.5	+0.5
4	22.67	21.5	+1.17

Let us follow the same procedure, selecting samples of two individuals at a time and then three. If we work through the same procedures (described above) we will find that the difference in the average age in the case of samples of two ranges between -7.00 and +7.00 years and in the case of the sample of three ranges between -3.67 and +3.67. In both cases the range of the difference is greater than previously calculated. This is attributable to the greater difference in the ages of the four individuals – the sampling population which in this instance is more heterogeneous (varied or diverse) in regard to age. In other words, if your study population is heterogeneous in terms of the variable under study, for a given level of accuracy, you need to select a larger sample as compared to if it was homogeneous.

> Principle 3. The greater the difference in the variable under study in a population, for a given sample size, the greater the difference between the sample statistics and the true population mean.

These principles are crucial to keep in mind when you are determining the sample size needed for a particular level of accuracy, and in selecting the sampling strategy best suited to your study.

Factors affecting the inferences drawn from a sample

The above principles suggest that two factors may influence the degree of certainty about the inferences drawn from a sample:

1 **The size of the sample** – Findings based upon larger samples have more certainty than those based on smaller ones. As a rule, *the larger the sample size, the more accurate the findings.*
2 **The extent of variation in the sampling population** – The greater the variation in the study population with respect to the characteristics under study, for a given sample size, the greater the uncertainty. (In technical terms, the greater the standard deviation, the higher the standard error for a given sample size in your estimates.) If a population is homogeneous (uniform or similar) with respect to the characteristics under study, a small sample can provide a reasonably good estimate, but if it is heterogeneous (dissimilar or diversified), you need to select a larger sample to obtain the same level of accuracy. Of course, if all the elements in a population are identical, then the selection of even one will provide an absolutely accurate

estimate. As a rule, *the higher the variation with respect to the characteristics under study in the study population, the greater the uncertainty for a given sample size.*

Aims in selecting a sample

When you select a sample in quantitative studies you are primarily aiming to achieve maximum precision in your estimates within a given sample size, and to avoid bias in the selection of your sample. Bias in the selection of a sample can occur if:

> sampling is done by a non-random method – that is, if the selection is consciously or unconsciously influenced by human choice;

> the sampling frame – list, index or other population records – which serves as the basis of selection, does not cover the sampling population accurately and completely;

> a section of a sampling population is impossible to find or refuses to co-operate.

Bias: A deliberate attempt either to conceal or highlight something that you found in your research or to use deliberately a procedure or method that you know is not appropriate but will provide information that you are looking for because you have a vested interest in it.

Types of sampling

The various sampling strategies in quantitative research can be categorised as follows (Figure 12.2):

> random/probability sampling designs;

> non-random/non-probability sampling designs; and

> 'mixed' sampling design.

To understand these designs, we will discuss each type individually.

Random/probability sampling designs

Random sampling: For a design to be called random or probability sampling, it is imperative that each element in the study population has an equal and independent chance of selection in the sample. Thus the probability of selection of each element in the study population is the same, and the choice of one element is not dependent upon the choice of another element in the sampling.

Probability sampling: When selecting a sample, if you adhere to the theory of probability, that is you select the sample in such a way that each element in the study population has an equal and independent chance of selection in the sample, the process is called probability sampling.

For a design to be called random sampling or probability sampling, it is imperative that each element in the study population has an *equal* and *independent* chance of selection in the sample. The concept of equality implies that the probability of selection of each element in the population is the same; that is, the choice of an element in the sample is not influenced by other considerations such as personal preference. The concept of independence means that the choice of one element is not dependent upon the choice of another element in the sampling; that is, the selection or rejection of one element does not affect the inclusion or exclusion of another. To explain these concepts let us return to our example of a class of students.

Suppose there are 80 students in the class. Assume 20 of these refuse to participate in your study. You want the entire population of 80 students in your study but, as 20 refuse to participate, you can only use a sample of 60 students. The 20 students who refuse to participate could have strong feelings about the issues you wish to explore, but your findings will not reflect their opinions. Their exclusion from your study means that each of the 80 students does not have an equal chance of selection. Therefore, your sample does not represent the total class.

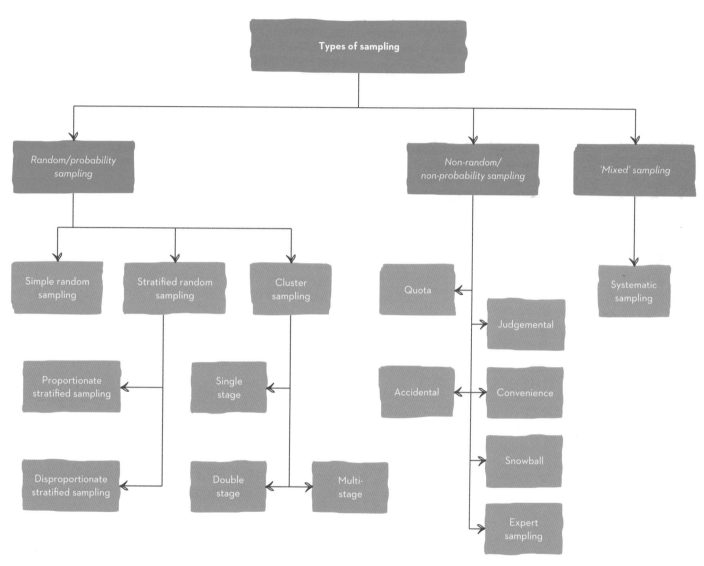

Figure 12.2 Types of sampling in quantitative research

The same could apply to a community. In a community, in addition to the refusal to participate, let us assume that you are unable to identify all the residents living in the community. If a significant proportion of people cannot be included in the sampling population because they either cannot be identified or refuse to participate, then any sample drawn will not give each element in the sampling population an equal chance of being selected in the sample. Hence, the sample will not be representative of the total community.

To understand the concept of an independent chance of selection, let us assume that there are five students in the class who are extremely close friends. If one of them is selected but refuses to participate because the other four are not chosen, and you are therefore forced to select either the five or none, then your sample will not be considered an independent sample since the selection of one is dependent upon the selection of others. The same could happen in the community where a small group says that either all of them or none of them will participate in the study. In these situations where you are forced either to include or to exclude a part of the sampling population, the sample is not considered to be independent, and hence is not representative of the sampling population. However, if the number of refusals is fairly small, in practical terms, it should not make the sample non-representative. In practice there are always some people who do not want to participate in the study, but you only need to worry if the number is significantly large.

A sample can only be considered a random/probability sample (and therefore representative of the population under study) if both these conditions are met. Otherwise, bias can be introduced into the study. There are two main advantages of random/probability samples:

CHECKPOINT
Avoiding sampling bias

1   As they represent the total sampling population, the inferences drawn from such samples can be generalised to the total sampling population.
2   Some statistical tests based upon the theory of probability can be applied only to data collected from random samples. Some of these tests are important for establishing conclusive correlations.

Methods of drawing a random sample

Of the methods that you can adopt to select a random sample the three most common are:

1   **The fishbowl draw** – If your total population is small, an easy procedure is to number each element using separate slips of paper for each element, put all the slips into a bowl and then pick them out one by one without looking, until the number of slips selected equals the sample size you decided upon. This method is used in some lotteries.
2   **A computer program** – There are a number of programs that can help you to select a random sample.
3   **A table of randomly generated numbers** – Most books on research methodology and statistics include a table of randomly generated numbers in their appendices (see, for example, Table 12.3). You can select your sample using these tables according to the procedure described in Figure 12.3.

Let us take an example to illustrate the use of Table 12.3 for random numbers. Let us assume that your sampling population consists of 256 individuals. Number each individual from 1 to 256. Randomly select the starting page, in case of multiple pages. Then select the starting column (from 1 to 10 with five columns of digits) and identify three columns of digits (as the total number of potential respondents in your study population is comprised of three digits). Run down the selected three columns of digits and select all numbers less than 256. Respondents corresponding to the selected numbers become your sample. Having gone through the selected column, if needs to, go to the adjoining columns (1–10) on either side following the same process. Or you can randomly select another column for the purpose and continue to do so till you have selected the number of respondents equivalent to your sample size. You can select your sample using the rows in the same way.

Suppose you identify the ninth column of numbers and the last three digits of this column (underlined). Assume that you are selecting 10 per cent of the total population as your sample (25 elements). Let us go through the numbers underlined in the ninth column. The first number is 049, which is below 256 (the total population); hence, the 49th element becomes a part of your sample. The second number, 319, is more than the total elements in your population (256); hence, you cannot accept the 319th element in the sample. The same applies to the next element, 758, and indeed the next five elements, 589, 507, 483, 487 and 540. After 540 is 232, and as this number is within the sampling frame, it can be accepted as a part of the sample. Similarly, if you follow down the same three digits in the same column, you select 052, 029, 065, 246 and 161, before you come to the element 029 again. As the 29th element has already been selected, go to the next number, and so on until 25 elements have been chosen. Once you have reached the end of a column, you can either move to the next column or randomly select another one in order to continue the process of selection. For example, the 25 elements shown in Table 12.4 are selected from the ninth, tenth and second columns of Table 12.3.

STEP ONE	Identify the total number of elements in the study population. Note the number of digits in this number (if your total sampling population is 9 or less, it is one digit; if it is 99 or less, it is two digits; etc.).
STEP TWO	Number each element starting from 1.
STEP THREE	If the table of random numbers is on more than one page, randomly choose the starting page. On the page thus chosen, randomly select a column or row as your starting point and proceed from there in a predetermined direction.
STEP FOUR	Corresponding to the number of digits to which the total population runs, randomly select that number of digits within each column from the table.
STEP FIVE	Decide on your sample size.
STEP SIX	Select the required number of elements for your sample from the table. If you happen to select the same number twice, discard it and go to the next. This can happen as the table for random numbers is generated by sampling with replacement.

Figure 12.3   The procedure for using a table of random numbers

Table 12.3 Selecting a sample using a table of random numbers

	1	2	3	4	5	6	7	8	9	10
1	48461	14952	72619	73689	52059	37086	60050	86192	67049	64739
2	76534	38149	49692	31366	52093	15422	20498	33901	10319	43397
3	70437	25861	38504	14752	23757	29660	67844	78815	23758	86814
4	59584	03370	42806	11393	71722	93804	09095	07856	55589	46820
5	04285	58554	16085	51555	27501	73883	33427	33343	45507	50063
6	77340	10412	69189	85171	29802	44785	86368	02583	96483	76553
7	59183	62687	91778	80354	23512	97219	65921	02035	59487	91403
8	91800	04281	39979	03927	82564	28777	59049	97532	54540	79472
9	12066	24817	81099	48940	69554	55925	48379	12866	41232	21580
10	69907	91751	53512	23748	65906	91385	84983	27915	48491	91068
11	80467	04873	54053	25955	48518	13815	37707	68687	15570	08890
12	78057	67835	28302	45048	56761	97725	58438	91529	24645	18544
13	05648	39387	78191	88415	60269	94880	58812	42931	71898	61534
14	22304	39246	01350	99451	61862	78688	30339	60222	74052	25740
15	61346	50269	67005	40442	33100	16742	61640	21046	31909	72641
16	56793	37696	27965	30459	91011	51426	31006	77468	61029	57108
17	56411	48609	36698	42453	85061	43769	39948	87031	30767	13953
18	62098	12825	81744	28882	27369	88185	65846	92545	09065	22653
19	68775	06261	54265	16203	23340	84750	16317	88686	86842	00879
20	52679	19599	13687	74872	89181	01939	18447	10787	76246	80072
21	84096	87152	20719	25215	04349	54434	72344	93008	83282	31670
22	83964	55937	21417	49944	38356	98404	14850	17994	17161	98981
23	31191	75131	72386	11689	95727	05414	88727	45583	22568	77700
24	30545	68523	29850	67833	05622	89975	79042	27142	99257	32349
25	52573	91001	52315	26430	54175	30122	31796	98842	37600	26025

	1	2	3	4	5	6	7	8	9	10
26	16586	81842	01076	99414	31574	94719	34656	80018	86988	79234
27	81841	88481	61191	25013	30272	23388	22463	65774	10029	58376
28	43563	66829	72838	08074	57080	15446	11034	98143	74989	26885
29	19945	84193	57581	77252	85604	45412	43556	27518	90572	00563
30	79374	23796	16919	99691	80276	32818	62953	78831	54395	30705
31	48503	26615	43980	09810	38289	66679	73799	48418	12647	40044
32	32049	65541	37937	41105	70106	89706	40829	40789	59547	00783
33	18547	71562	95493	34112	76895	46766	96395	31718	48302	45893
34	03180	96742	61486	43305	84183	99605	67803	13491	09243	29557
35	94822	24738	67749	83748	59799	25210	31093	62925	72061	69991
36	04330	60599	85828	19152	68499	27977	35611	96240	62747	89529
37	43770	81537	59527	95674	76692	86420	69930	10020	72881	12532
38	56908	77192	50623	41215	14311	42834	80651	93750	59957	31211
39	32787	07189	80539	75927	75475	73965	11796	72140	48944	74156
40	52441	78392	11733	57703	29133	71164	55355	31006	25526	55790
41	22377	54723	18227	28449	04570	18882	00023	67101	06895	08915
42	18376	73460	88841	39602	34049	20589	05701	08249	74213	25220
43	53201	28610	87957	21497	64729	64983	71551	99016	87903	63875
44	34919	78801	59710	27396	02593	05665	11964	44134	00273	76358
45	33617	92159	21971	16901	57383	34262	41744	60891	57624	06962
46	70010	40964	98780	72418	52571	18415	64362	90637	38034	04909
47	19282	68447	35665	31530	59838	49181	21914	65742	89815	39231
48	91429	73328	13266	54898	68795	40948	80808	63887	89939	47938
49	97637	78393	33021	05867	86520	45363	43066	00988	64040	09803
50	95150	07625	05255	83254	93943	52325	93230	62668	79529	66964

Source: *Statistical Tables*, 3rd edition, by F. James Rohlf and Robert R. Sokal. Copyright © 1969, 1981, 1994 by W.H. Freeman and Company. Used with permission.

A random sample can be selected using two different systems:

1   sampling without replacement;
2   sampling with replacement.

Suppose you want to select a sample of 20 students out of a total of 80. The first student is selected from the entire class, so the probability of selection for the first student is 1/80. When you select the second student there are only 79 left in the class and the probability of selection for the second student is not 1/80 but 1/79. The probability of selecting the next student is 1/78. By the time you select the 20th student, the probability of his/her selection is 1/61. This type of sampling is called sampling without replacement. But this is contrary to our basic definition of randomisation; that is, each element has an equal and independent chance of selection. In the second system, called sampling with replacement, the selected element is replaced in the sampling population and if it is selected again, it is discarded and the next one is selected. If the sampling population is fairly large, the probability of selecting the same element twice is fairly remote.

Table 12.4   Elements selected using the table of random numbers

Column in Table 12.3	Elements selected
9	49, 232, 52, 29, 65, 246, 161, 243, 61, 213, 34, 40,
10	63, 68, 108, 72, 25, 234, 44, 211, 156, 220, 231,
2	149, 246

Specific random/probability sampling designs

There are three commonly used types of random sampling design: simple random sampling (SRS), stratified random sampling and cluster sampling.

Simple random sampling

This is the most commonly used method of selecting a probability sample. In line with the definition of randomisation, whereby each element in the population is given an equal and independent chance of selection, a simple random sample is selected by the procedure presented in Figure 12.4.

To illustrate, let us again take our example of the class of students. There are 80 students in the class, and so the first step is to identify each student by a number from 1 to 80. Suppose you decide to select a sample of 20 using the simple random sampling technique. Use the fishbowl draw, a table for random numbers or a computer program to select the 20 students. These 20 students become the basis of your enquiry.

Sampling without replacement: When you select a sample in such a way that an element, once selected to become a part of your sample, is not placed back into the study population, this is called sampling without replacement.

Sampling with replacement: When you select a sample in such a way that each selected element in the sample is placed back into the sampling population before selecting the next, this is called sampling with replacement. Theoretically, this is done to provide an equal chance of selection to each element so as to adhere to the theory of probability to ensure randomisation of the sample. If an element is selected again, it is discarded and the next one is selected. If the sampling population is fairly large, the probability of selecting the same element twice is fairly remote.

Simple random sampling: This is the most commonly used method of selecting a random sample. It is a process of selecting the required sample size from the sampling population, providing each element with an equal and independent chance of selection by any method designed to select a random sample.

STEP ONE	Identify by a number all elements or sampling units in the population.
STEP TWO	Decide on the sample size n.
STEP THREE	Select n using the fishbowl draw, a table of random numbers or a computer program.

Figure 12.4   The procedure for selecting a simple random sample

Stratified random sampling

As discussed, the accuracy of your estimate largely depends on the extent of variability or heterogeneity of the study population with respect to the characteristics that have a strong correlation with what you are trying to ascertain (Principle 3). It follows, therefore, that if the heterogeneity in the population can be reduced by some means, for a given sample size, you can achieve greater accuracy in your estimate. Stratified random sampling is based upon this logic.

In stratified random sampling the researcher attempts to stratify the population in such a way that the population within a stratum is homogeneous with respect to the characteristic on the basis of which it is being stratified. It is important that the characteristics chosen as the basis of stratification are clearly identifiable in the study population. For example, it is much easier to stratify a population on the basis of gender than on the basis of age, income or attitude. It is also important for the characteristic that becomes the basis of stratification to be related to the main variable that you are exploring. Once the sampling population has been separated into non-overlapping groups, you select the required number of elements from each stratum, using the simple random sampling technique. There are two types of stratified sampling: proportionate stratified sampling and disproportionate stratified sampling. In proportionate stratified sampling the number of elements from each stratum is selected in relation to its proportion in the total population, whereas in disproportionate stratified sampling consideration is not given to the size of the stratum. The procedure for selecting a stratified sample is schematically presented in Figure 12.5.

Cluster sampling

Simple random and stratified sampling are based on a researcher's ability to identify each element in a population. It is easy to do this if the total sampling population is small, but if the population is large, as in the case of a city, state or country, it becomes difficult and expensive to identify each sampling unit. In such cases the use of cluster sampling is more appropriate.

Cluster sampling is based on the ability of the researcher to divide the sampling population into groups (based upon visible or easily identifiable characteristics), called clusters, and then to select elements within each cluster, using the SRS technique. Clusters can be formed on the basis of geographical proximity or a common characteristic

---

Stratified random sampling: One of the probability sampling designs in which the total study population is first classified into different subgroups based upon a characteristic that makes each subgroup more homogeneous in terms of the classificatory variable. The sample is then selected from each subgroup either by selecting an equal number of elements from each subgroup or selecting elements from each subgroup equal to its proportion in the total population.

Proportionate stratified sampling: In proportionate stratified sampling, the number of elements selected in the sample from each stratum is in relation to its proportion in the total population.

Disproportionate stratified sampling: When selecting a stratified sample, if you select an equal number of elements from each stratum without giving any consideration to its size in the study population, the process is called disproportionate stratified sampling.

Cluster sampling: Cluster sampling is based on the ability of the researcher to divide a sampling population into groups (based upon a visible or easily identifiable characteristic), called clusters, and then select elements from each cluster using simple random sampling. Clusters can be formed on the basis of geographical proximity or a common characteristic that has a correlation with the main variable of the study (as in stratified sampling). Depending on the level of clustering, sometimes sampling may be done at different levels. These levels constitute the different stages (single, double or multiple) of clustering.

that has a correlation with the main variable of the study (as in stratified sampling). Depending on the level of clustering, sometimes sampling may be done at different levels. These levels constitute the different stages (single, double or multiple) of clustering, which will be explained later.

STEP ONE   Identify all elements or sampling units in the sampling population.

STEP TWO   Decide upon the different strata (k) into which you want to stratify the population.

STEP THREE Place each element into the appropriate stratum.

STEP FOUR   Number every element in each stratum separately.

STEP FIVE   Decide the total sample size (n).

STEP SIX   Decide whether you want to select proportionate or disproportionate stratified sampling and follow the steps below.

Disproportionate stratified sampling		Proportionate stratified sampling	
STEP SEVEN	Determine the number of elements to be selected from each stratum	**STEP SEVEN**	Determine the proportion of each stratum in the study population (p)
	$= \dfrac{\text{sample size } (n)}{\text{no of strata } (k)}$		$= \dfrac{\text{elements in each stratum}}{\text{total population size}}$
STEP EIGHT	Select the required number of elements from each stratum by simple random sampling	**STEP EIGHT**	Determine the number of elements to be selected from each stratum = (sample size) x p
		STEP NINE	Select the required number of elements from each stratum by simple random sampling
As this method does not take the size of the stratum into consideration in the selection of the sample, it is called disproportionate stratified sampling.		As the sample selected is in proportion to the size of each stratum in the population, this method is called proportionate stratified sampling.	

Figure 12.5   The procedure for selecting a stratified sample

Imagine you want to investigate the attitude of post-secondary students in Australia towards problems in higher education in the country. There are higher education institutions in every state and territory of Australia. In addition, there are different types of institutions (see Figure 12.6): universities, universities of technology, colleges of advanced education and colleges of technical and further education (TAFE). Within each institution various courses are offered at both undergraduate and postgraduate levels. Each academic course could take three to four years. You can imagine the magnitude of the task. In such situations cluster sampling is extremely useful in selecting a random sample.

The first level of cluster sampling could be at the state or territory level. Clusters could be grouped according to similar characteristics that ensure their comparability in terms of student population. For example, if you can establish that certain states are comparable in terms of student socioeconomic-demographic characteristics,

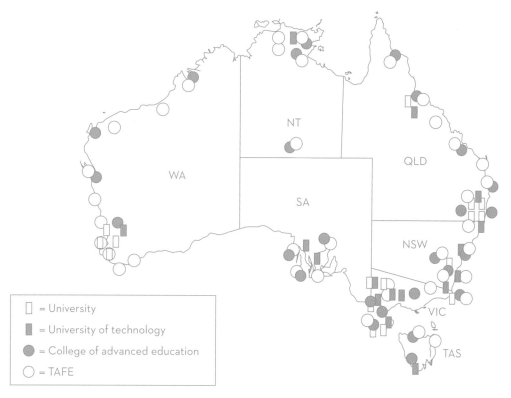

Figure 12.6   The concept of cluster sampling

instead of all, you randomly select only one or two states out of the cluster to become part of your study. If this is not easy, you may decide to select all the states and territories and then select a sample at the institutional level. You can do similar selection with respect to educational institutions. If all the universities in a state are comparable in terms of student characteristics, you might randomly select only one or two for your study. Similarly, you select one or two institutions from other categories of institutions providing higher education. For example, with a simple random technique, one or two institutions from each category within each state could be selected (say, one university, one university of technology and one TAFE college). This is based upon the assumption that institutions within a category are fairly similar with regard to student profile. Then, within an institution, one or more academic programmes could be randomly selected, depending on resources. Within each study programme selected, students studying in a particular academic year could then be selected. Further, selection of a proportion of students studying in a particular academic year could then be made using the SRS technique. The process of selecting a sample in this manner is called *multi-stage cluster sampling*.

Non-random/non-probability sampling designs in quantitative research

Non-probability sampling designs do not follow the theory of probability in the choice of elements from the sampling population. These designs are used when either the number of elements in a population is unknown or the elements cannot be individually identified. In such situations the selection of elements is dependent upon other considerations. There are six non-random designs, each based on different considerations, which are commonly used in both qualitative and quantitative research: quota sampling, accidental sampling, convenience sampling, judgemental or purposive sampling, expert sampling and snowball sampling.

What differentiates these designs being treated as quantitative or qualitative is the predetermined sample size. In quantitative research you use these designs to select a predetermined number of cases (sample size), whereas in qualitative research you do not decide the number of respondents in advance but continue to select additional cases till you reach the data saturation point. In addition, in qualitative research, you will predominantly use judgemental and accidental sampling strategies to select your respondents. Expert sampling is very similar to judgemental sampling except that in expert sampling the sampling population consists of experts in the field of enquiry. You can also use quota and snowball sampling in qualitative research but without having a predetermined number of cases in mind (sample size).

Quota sampling

The main consideration behind quota sampling is the researcher's ease of access to the sample population. In addition to convenience, you are guided by some visible characteristic, such as gender or race, of the study population that is of interest to you. You select the sample from a location convenient to you as a researcher; whenever you see a person with this visible relevant characteristic you ask that person to participate in the study. The process continues until you have been able to contact the required number of respondents (quota).

Let us suppose that you want to find out about the attitudes of Aboriginal and Torres Strait Islander students towards the facilities provided to them in your university. You might stand at a convenient location and, whenever

Non-probability sampling designs: These do not follow the theory of probability in the selection of elements from the sampling population. Non-probability sampling designs are used when the number of elements in a population is either unknown or they cannot be individually identified. In such situations the selection of elements is dependent upon other considerations. Non-probability sampling designs are commonly used in both quantitative and qualitative research.

Saturation point: The concept of saturation point refers to the stage in data collection where you, as a researcher, are discovering no or very little new information from your respondents. In qualitative research this is considered an indication of the adequacy of the sample size.

Quota sampling: The main consideration in quota sampling is the researcher's ease of access to the sample population. In addition to convenience, the researcher is guided by some visible characteristic of interest, such as gender or race, of the study population. The sample is selected from a convenient location, and whenever a person with this visible relevant characteristic is seen, that person is asked to participate in the study. The process continues until the required number of respondents (quota) have been contacted.

you see such a student, collect the required information through whatever method of data collection (such as interviewing, questionnaire) you have adopted for the study.

The advantages of using this design are: it is the least expensive way of selecting a sample; you do not need any information, such as a sampling frame, the total number of elements, their location or other information about the sampling population; and it guarantees the inclusion of the type of people you need. The disadvantages are: as the resulting sample is not a probability one, the findings cannot be generalised to the total sampling population; and the most accessible individuals selected from one location might have characteristics that are unique to them and hence might not be truly representative of the total sampling population. You can make your sample more representative of your study population by selecting it from various locations where people of interest to you are likely to be available.

Accidental sampling

Accidental sampling is also based upon convenience in accessing the sampling population. Whereas quota sampling attempts to include people possessing an obvious/visible characteristic, accidental sampling makes no such attempt. You stop collecting data when you reach the required number of respondents you decided to have in your sample.

This method of sampling is common among market research and newspaper reporters. It has more or less the same advantages and disadvantages as quota sampling but, in addition, as you are not guided by any obvious characteristics, some people contacted may not have the required information.

Convenience sampling

Accidental and convenience sampling designs are extremely similar. Convenience sampling is primarily guided by the convenience to the researcher, whatever this might be – easy accessibility, geographical proximity, known contacts, ready approval for undertaking the study, or being a part of the group. Accidental sampling is primarily selecting a place where you are likely to find your potential respondents, which place may or may not be most convenient to you, and if a person of interest comes along, you collect the required information till either you have collected the information from a specific number of respondents or have reached the saturation point.

Judgemental or purposive sampling

The primary consideration in judgemental sampling or purposive sampling is your judgement as to who can provide the best information to achieve the objectives of your study. You only go to those people who in your opinion are likely to have the required information and be willing to share it with you.

This type of sampling is extremely useful when you want to construct a historical reality, describe a phenomenon or develop something about which only a little is known. This sampling strategy is more common in qualitative research, but when you use it in quantitative research you select a predetermined number of people who, in your judgement, are best positioned to provide you with the information needed for your study.

Accidental sampling: Like quota sampling, accidental sampling is based upon your convenience in accessing the sampling population. Whereas quota sampling attempts to include people possessing an obvious/visible characteristic, accidental sampling makes no such attempt. Any person that you come across can be contacted for participation in your study. You stop collecting data when you reach the required number of respondents you decided to have in your sample.

Convenience sampling: Convenience sampling is a non-probability sampling design which is primarily guided by the convenience to the researcher in terms of selecting the potential respondents whatever this might be: easy accessibility, geographical proximity, known contacts, ready approval for undertaking the study or being a part of the group.

Accidental sampling: Like quota sampling, accidental sampling is based upon your convenience in accessing the sampling population. Whereas quota sampling attempts to include people possessing an obvious/visible characteristic, accidental sampling makes no such attempt. Any person that you come across can be contacted for participation in your study. You stop collecting data when you reach the required number of respondents you decided to have in your sample.

Judgemental sampling: The primary consideration in this sampling design is your judgement as to who can provide the best information to achieve the objectives of your study. You as a researcher only go to those people who in your opinion are likely to have the required information and are willing to share it with you. This design is also called purposive sampling.

Purposive sampling: see Judgemental sampling

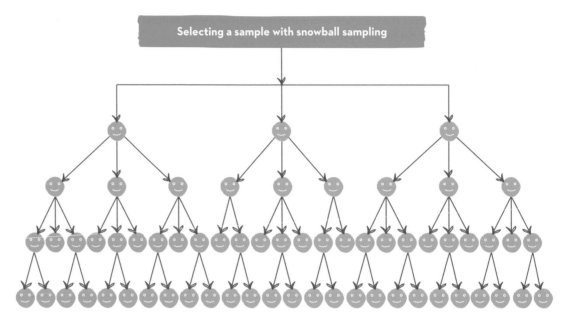

Selecting a sample with snowball sampling

Figure 12.7 Snowball sampling

Expert sampling: The selection of people with demonstrated or known expertise in the area of interest to become the basis of data collection. Your sample is a group of experts from whom you seek the required information. It is like purposive sampling where the sample comprises experts only.

Snowball sampling: A process of selecting a sample using networks. To start with, a few individuals in a group or organisation are selected using purposive, random or network sampling to collect the required information from them. They are then asked to identify other people in the group or organisation who could be contacted to obtain the same information. The people selected by them become a part of the sample. The process continues till you reach the saturation point in terms of information being collected.

Expert sampling

The only difference between judgemental sampling and expert sampling is that in the case of the former it is entirely your judgement as to the ability of the respondents to contribute to the study. In the case of expert sampling, your respondents must be known experts in the field of interest to you. This is again used in both types of research, but more so in qualitative research studies. When you use it in qualitative research the number of people you talk to is dependent upon the data saturation point, whereas in quantitative research you decide on the number of experts to be contacted without considering the saturation point.

You first identify persons with demonstrated or known expertise in an area of interest to you, seek their consent for participation, and then collect the information either individually or collectively in the form of a group.

Snowball sampling

Snowball sampling is the process of selecting a sample using networks. To start with, a few individuals in a group or organisation are selected and the required information is collected from them. They are then asked to identify other people in the group or organisation, and the people selected by them become a part of the sample.

Information is collected from them, and then these people are asked to identify other members of the group and, in turn, those identified become the basis for further data collection (Figure 12.7). This process is continued until the required number or a saturation point has been reached, in terms of the information being sought.

This sampling technique is useful if you know little about the group or organisation you wish to study, as you need only to make contact with a few individuals, who can then direct you to the other members of the group. It is useful for studying communication patterns, decision making or diffusion of knowledge within a group. There are disadvantages to this technique, however. The choice of the entire sample rests upon the choice of individuals at the first stage. If they belong to a particular faction or have strong biases, the study may be biased. Also, it is difficult to use this technique when the sample becomes fairly large.

Systematic sampling design: a mixed design

Systematic sampling is treated in this book as a 'mixed' sampling design because it has the characteristics of both random and non-random sampling designs.

To use systematic sampling design it is imperative that you have a sampling frame for your study population; it is useful in situations where records for the study population are routinely maintained as a part of service delivery. In systematic sampling the sampling frame is first divided into a number of segments called *intervals*. Then, from the first interval, using the SRS technique, one element is selected. The selection of subsequent elements from other intervals is dependent upon the position of the element selected in the first interval. If it is the fifth element in the first interval, the fifth element of each subsequent interval is chosen. Notice that from the first interval the choice of an element is on a random basis, but the choice of the elements from subsequent intervals is dependent upon the choice from the first, so this method cannot be classified as a random sample. The procedure used in systematic sampling is presented in Figure 12.8.

Saturation point: The concept of saturation point refers to the stage in data collection where you, as a researcher, are discovering no or very little new information from your respondents. In qualitative research this is considered an indication of the adequacy of the sample size.

Systematic sampling: A way of selecting a sample where the sampling frame, depending upon the sample size, is first divided into a number of segments called intervals. Then, from the first interval, using simple random sampling, one element is selected. The selection of subsequent elements from other intervals is dependent upon the order of the element selected in the first interval. If in the first interval it is the fifth element, the fifth element of each subsequent interval will be chosen.

STEP ONE	Prepare a list of all the elements in the study population (N).
STEP TWO	Decide on the sample size (n).
STEP THREE	Determine the *width of the interval (k)*

$$k = \frac{\text{total population } (N)}{\text{sample size } (n)}$$

| STEP FOUR | Using SRS, select an element from the first interval *i*th position. |
| STEP FIVE | Select the *i*th element from each subsequent interval. |

Figure 12.8 The procedure for selecting a systematic sample

You can deviate from the general procedure for selecting a sample by the systematic sampling technique by selecting a different element from each interval by the SRS technique. Systematic sampling done in this way can be classified under probability sampling designs.

To select a sample, as just mentioned, you must have a sampling frame (Figure 12.9). Sometimes this is impossible, or obtaining one may be too expensive. However, in real life there are situations where a kind of sampling frame exists, for example records of clients in an agency, enrolment lists of students in a school or university, electoral lists of people living in an area, or records of the staff employed in an organisation. All these can be used as a sampling frame to select a sample by systematic sampling. This convenience of having a 'ready-made' sampling frame may come at a price: in some cases it may not be a truly random listing. Mostly these lists are in alphabetical order, based upon a number assigned to a case, or arranged in a way that is convenient to the users of the records. If the 'width of an interval' is large, say, 1 in 30 cases, and if the cases are arranged in alphabetical order, you could exclude surnames starting with a letter that is not very common. It is also possible that some adjoining letter may not be included at all in the width of the interval.

CHECKPOINT
Sampling techniques

Suppose there are 50 students in a class and you want to select 10 students using the systematic sampling technique. The first step is to determine the width of the interval (50/10 = 5). This means that from every five you need to select one student. Using the SRS technique, from the first interval (the first five students), select one of the students. Suppose you selected the third. From the rest of the intervals you would select every third student.

The calculation of sample size

What is the appropriate sample size in quantitative research? Basically, it depends on what you want to do with the findings and what type of relationships you want to establish. Your purpose in undertaking research is the main determinant of the level of accuracy required in the results, and this level of accuracy is an important determinant of sample size. However, in qualitative research, as the main focus is to explore or describe a situation, issue, process or phenomenon, the question of sample size is less important. You usually collect data till you think you have reached saturation point in terms of discovering new information. Once you think you are not getting much new data from your respondents, you stop collecting further information. Of course, the diversity or heterogeneity in what you are trying to find out about plays an important role in how fast you will reach saturation point. As a rule: *the greater the heterogeneity or diversity in what you are trying to find out about, the greater the number of respondents you need to contact to reach saturation point.*

In determining the size of your sample for quantitative studies and in particular for cause-and-effect studies, you need to consider the following:

↣ At what *level of confidence* do you want to test your results, findings or hypotheses?
↣ With what *degree of accuracy* do you wish to estimate the population parameters?
↣ What is the estimated *level of variation* (standard deviation), with respect to the main variable you are studying, in the study population?

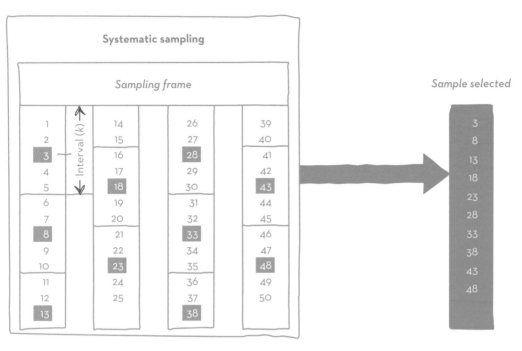

Figure 12.9   Systematic sampling

Answering these questions is necessary regardless of whether you intend to determine the sample size your-self or have an expert do it for you. The size of the sample is important for testing a hypothesis or establishing an association, but for other studies the general rule is: *the larger the sample size, the more accurate your estimates*. In practice, your budget determines the size of your sample. Your skills in selecting a sample, within the constraints of your budget, lie in the way you select your elements so that they effectively and adequately represent your sampling population.

SAMPLING IN QUALITATIVE RESEARCH

As the main aim in qualitative enquiries is to explore diversity, sample size and sampling strategy do not play a significant role in the selection of a sample. If selected carefully, diversity can be extensively and accurately described on the basis of information obtained even from one individual. All non-probability sampling designs – purposive, judgemental, expert, accidental and snowball – can also be used in qualitative research, with two differences:

1   In quantitative studies you collect information from a predetermined number of people, but in qualitative research you do not have a sample size in mind – instead you collect data until you feel you have reached the saturation point.
2   In quantitative research you are guided by your desire to select a random sample, whereas in qualitative research you are guided by your judgement as to who is likely to provide you with the 'best' information.

The concept of saturation point in qualitative research

CHECKPOINT
Sample size

As you already know, in qualitative research data is usually collected to a point where you are not getting new information or it is negligible – the data saturation point. This stage determines the sample size.

It is important for you to keep in mind that the concept of data saturation point is highly subjective. It is you who is collecting the data and who decides when you have attained the saturation point in your data collection. How soon you reach the saturation point depends upon how diverse is the situation or phenomenon that you are studying. The greater the diversity, the greater the number of people from whom you need to collect the information to reach the saturation point.

The concept of saturation point is more applicable to situations where you are collecting information on a one-to-one basis. Where the information is collected in a collective format such as focus groups, community forums or panel discussions, you strive to gather as diverse and as much information as possible. When no new information is emerging it is assumed that you have reached the saturation point.

SUMMARY

In this chapter you have learnt about sampling, the process of selecting a few elements from a sampling population. Sampling, in a way, is a trade-off between accuracy and resources. Through sampling you make an *estimate* of the information of interest. You do not find the true population mean.

Two opposing philosophies underpin the selection of sampling units in quantitative and qualitative research. In quantitative studies a sample is supposed to be selected in such a way that it represents the study population, which is achieved through randomisation. However, the selection of a sample in qualitative research is guided by your judgement as to who is likely to provide you with complete and diverse information. This is a non-random process.

Sample size does not occupy a significant place in qualitative research and it is determined by the data saturation point while collecting data instead of being fixed in advance.

In quantitative research, sampling is guided by three principles, one of which is that the greater the sample size, the more accurate the estimate of the true population mean, given that everything else remains the same.

The inferences drawn from a sample can be affected by both the size of the sample and the extent of variation in the sampling population.

Sampling designs can be classified as random/probability sampling designs, non-random/non-probability sampling designs and 'mixed' sampling designs. For a sample to be called random, each element in the study population must have an equal and independent chance of selection. Three random designs were discussed: simple random sampling, stratified random sampling and cluster sampling. The procedures for selecting a sample using these designs are detailed step by step. The use of the fishbowl technique, a table of random numbers and specifically designed computer programs are three commonly used methods of selecting a probability sample.

There are six non-probability sampling designs: quota, accidental, convenience, judgemental, expert and snowball. Each is used for a different purpose and in different situations in both quantitative and qualitative studies. In quantitative studies their application is underpinned by the sample size, and in qualitative studies by the data saturation point.

Systematic sampling is a 'mixed' design as it has the properties of both probability and non-probability sampling designs.

The last section of the chapter described determinants of calculating sample size. At your level it is sufficient to be aware of the considerations rather than calculation of the actual sample size as it entails a reasonable degree of statistical knowledge. In qualitative research, the question of sample size is less important, as your aim is to explore, not quantify, the extent of variation and you would be guided by reaching saturation point in terms of new findings.

Now that you have read the full chapter...

CHECK YOUR UNDERSTANDING

☐ Do you understand the meaning and application of all of the keywords at the start of the chapter? If not, visit the online resources and use the glossary flashcards to get to grips with their definitions.

☐ Describe the process of sampling, detailing its respective advantages and disadvantages.

☐ Explain what you understand by: study population, sample, sample size, sampling strategy, sampling unit, sampling element, sampling frame, sample statistics and population parameters.

☐ What are the different types of sampling designs and what are their advantages and disadvantages?

☐ Describe the designs that are commonly used in qualitative research.

☐ Discuss the concept of saturation point in data collection, with its advantages and disadvantages.

313

☐ In the absence of a sampling frame for employees of a large organisation, which sampling design would you use to select a sample of 219 people? Explain why you would choose this design and the process you would undertake to ensure that the sample is representative.

☐ Consider the implications of selecting a sample based upon your choice as a researcher and how you could make sure that you do not introduce bias.

APPLY IT TO YOUR OWN PROJECT

☐ From your own area of interest, identify examples of where cluster sampling could be applied.

314

CONFUSED?

THE ONLINE RESOURCES ARE HERE TO HELP YOU

 https://study.sagepub.com/kumar5e

CHECKPOINT: What is sampling, and what is its purpose in the research process? Watch this video.

CHECKPOINT: What are the key sampling terms you need to remember? Take this quiz.

CHECKPOINT: How do you avoid sampling bias? Visit this website.

CHECKPOINT: What are the most common types of sampling techniques and how do they differ? Watch this video.

CHECKPOINT: How do you ensure your sample size is large enough, but not too large? Read this chapter.

NEED MORE GENERAL SUPPORT?

Get up to speed on key terms with *glossary flashcards* and test yourself on important concepts with *multiple choice questions*.

UP FOR A CHALLENGE?

THE ONLINE RESOURCES ARE HERE TO INSPIRE YOU

 https://study.sagepub.com/kumar5e

CHECKPOINT: What is the relationship between sampling and validity? Visit this website.

CHECKPOINT: What are some types of sample populations that may be studied in social science research? Visit this website.

CHECKPOINT: How do you create a meaningful sample that is best for your research? Read this chapter.

CHECKPOINT: What do decisions relating to sampling techniques look like in real research? Explore this case study.

CHECKPOINT: What are some practical and ethical considerations involved in accessing participants and forming a sample population? Visit this website.

READY TO WORK ON YOUR OWN PROJECT?

Start building a portfolio of your ideas with the exercise workbook and get support tailored to your specific assignment with the assessment toolkit.

EXERCISE IV: SELECTING A SAMPLE

The accuracy of what you find out through your research endeavour, among many other things, depends upon the way you select your sample, the people who are going to provide you with the information you need.

The underlying premise in sampling is that a small number of respondents, if selected correctly, can provide, to a sufficiently high degree of confidence, a reasonably accurate estimate of what you are trying to ascertain in the study population.

For details on sampling designs, refer to Chapter 12.

Template of Exercise IV

For quantitative studies

The basic objective of a sampling design in quantitative research is to minimise, within a given cost, any difference between the values obtained from your sample and those actually prevalent in the study population. Sampling theory in quantitative research is thus guided by two principles:

1   the avoidance of bias in the selection of a sample;

2   the attainment of maximum precision for a given outlay of resources.

In quantitative research you can select your sample with any of the probability or non-probability sampling designs. Both have advantages and disadvantages and both are appropriate for certain situations. But whatever sampling design you choose, make sure you take steps to avoid introducing your bias in the selection of sampling units. When selecting a sample in quantitative studies you need to decide on two things: the sample size you plan to select; and how to select the required sampling units. You also need to think about your reasons for deciding the size and choosing the sampling strategy.

This exercise is designed for you to think through the issues which are important in helping you to develop your sampling strategy.

STEP ONE Answer the following about your sampling design.

1   What is the total size of your study population?_____
    _____Unknown ☐

2   Do you want to select a sample?

    Yes ☐   No ☐

    (a)   If yes, what will your sample size be? _____
    (b)   What are your reasons for choosing this sample size?

    _____
    _____
    _____
    _____

3   How will you select your sample? (What sampling design are you proposing?)

4   Why did you select this sampling design? (What are its strengths?)

5   What are the limitations of this design?

STEP TWO On the basis of the answers to the above questions, write about your sampling design, detailing the process and your justification for using it (consult Chapter 12 for details).

_____
_____
_____
_____

For qualitative studies

In qualitative research your aim is not to select a random or unbiased sample but one which can provide you, as far as possible, with the detailed, accurate and complete information that you are looking for. Hence, you are predominantly guided by your convenience and judgement in the selection of your respondents.

In qualitative research you can only use non-probability designs. You can select your sample in two ways: (i) in the light of financial constraints decide from how many respondents you can collect data; or (ii) you decide to be guided by the saturation point in data collection. If you decide to be guided by the attainment of the saturation point, you do not specify your sample but the bases that will determine the saturation point.

You also need to decide who are going to be your respondents and how they are going to be identified. You need to think about the determinants on which you are going to base your judgement as to the suitability of your respondents for being your respondents.

Answers to the following questions will help you to think through the issues you are likely to face while developing a sampling strategy for your study.

A What factors would you keep in mind when selecting a respondent?

B How would you identify your potential respondents?

C How would you determine whether you have reached the saturation point in your data collection?

STEP FIVE

WRITING A RESEARCH PROPOSAL

WRITING A RESEARCH PROPOSAL

- step five -
WRITING A RESEARCH PROPOSAL

This operational step includes one chapter:

→ **Writing a research proposal**   320

CONFUSED? UP FOR A CHALLENGE?

OR NEED HELP WITH YOUR ASSIGNMENT?

VISIT https://study.sagepub.com/kumar5e for resources specially designed to support you and all your research needs.

ESSENTIAL TERMS

You should be able to define these by the end of the chapter

→ research problem

→ research proposal

BONUS TERMS

You will learn more about these by the end of the chapter

→ conceptual framework
→ data analysis
→ data processing
→ hypothesis
→ limitations
→ literature review
→ research design

→ sampling
→ study design
→ study objectives
→ theoretical framework
→ time-frame

LEARNING OBJECTIVES

At the end of this chapter, you will be able to:

→ The purpose of the research proposal in quantitative and qualitative research
→ The contents of a research proposal
→ How to write a research proposal
→ What the differences are between quantitative and qualitative research proposals
→ What to include in a research proposal

THE RESEARCH PROPOSAL IN QUANTITATIVE AND QUALITATIVE RESEARCH

All research endeavours, in both qualitative and quantitative research, in every academic and professional field are preceded by a research proposal. It informs your academic supervisor or potential research contract provider about your conceptualisation of the total research process that you propose to undertake so that they can examine its validity and appropriateness. In any academic field, your research proposal will go through a number of committees for approval. Unless it is approved by all of them, you will not be able to start your research. Hence, it is important for you to study closely what constitutes a research proposal.

You need to write a research proposal whether your research study is quantitative or qualitative, and in both cases you use a similar structure. The main difference is in the proposed procedures and methodologies for undertaking the research endeavour. When providing details for different parts of the research proposal, for quantitative studies you will detail quantitative methods, procedures and models, and for qualitative studies your proposed process will be based upon methods and procedures that form the qualitative research methodology. If you happen to use a mixed methods approach, you need to describe them as either qualitative or quantitative procedures under their respective headings.

A research proposal serves many functions. Specifically:

→ It serves to remind you of what you are supposed to do at different steps of the research journey. It is the road map designed by you, and approved by your university, to guide you through your research journey. It is an overall plan designed to obtain answers to the research questions or problems that constitute your research project. It outlines the various tasks you plan to undertake to fulfil your research objectives, test hypotheses (if any) or obtain answers to your research questions. It should also state your reasons for undertaking the study. Broadly, a research proposal's main function is to detail the *operational plan for obtaining answers to your research questions*. In doing so it ensures and reassures the reader of the validity of the methodology for obtaining answers to your research questions accurately and objectively.

→ It serves as a document for scientific scrutiny for others to judge the appropriateness of what you are proposing and provide their seal of approval. It serves to convince your research supervisor or a reviewer that your proposed methodology is meritorious, valid, appropriate and workable in terms of obtaining answers to your research questions or objective.

In order to achieve these functions, a research proposal must tell you, your research supervisor and reviewers:

→ *what* you are proposing to do in your study;
→ *how* you plan to find answers to *what* you are proposing;
→ *why* you selected the proposed investigation strategies.

CONTENTS OF A RESEARCH PROPOSAL

A research proposal should contain the following information about your study:

- an introduction, including a brief *literature review*;
- the *theoretical framework* that underpins your study;
- the *conceptual framework* that constitutes the basis of your study;
- the *objectives* or *research questions* of your study;
- the *hypotheses* to be tested, if applicable;
- the *study design* that you are proposing to adopt;
- the *setting* for your study;
- the *research instrument*(s) you are planning to use;
- the *sampling design* and *sample size*;
- the *ethical issues* involved and how you propose to deal with them;
- the *data processing procedures*;
- the *proposed chapters* of the report;
- the *problems* and *limitations* of the study;
- the proposed *time-frame* for the project.

A research proposal should communicate the above contents clearly and specifically in such a way that anyone going through it should be able to undertake all tasks in the same manner as you would have.

Universities and other institutions may have differing requirements regarding the style and content of a research proposal. Requirements may also vary within an institution, from discipline to discipline or from supervisor to supervisor. There may be some additional specific requirements by some universities or supervisors, and you should acquaint yourself with these, but most of what is suggested here will be required by almost everyone. The framework suggested here can be easily adapted to suit your requirements and those of your university.

Your proposal should follow the suggested guidelines and be written in an academic style. It must contain appropriate references in the body of the text and a bibliography at the end. Your survey of the relevant literature should cover major publications on the topic. The theoretical framework for your study must emerge from this literature review and must have its grounding in empirical evidence. As a rule, the literature review includes:

- a conceptual framework, and theoretical and empirical information about the main issues under study;
- some of the major research findings relating to your topic, research questions raised in the literature and gaps identified by previous researchers.

Your literature review should also raise issues relating to the methodology you are proposing. For example, it may examine how other studies operationalised the major variables of relevance to your study and may include a critique of methodology relevant to your study. The critiques of methods and procedures should be included

Theoretical framework: As you start reading the literature, you will soon discover that the problem you wish to investigate has its roots in a number of theories that have been developed from different perspectives. The information obtained from different sources needs to be sorted under the main themes and theories, highlighting agreements and disagreements among the authors. This process of structuring a 'network' of these theories that directly or indirectly have a bearing on your research topic is called the theoretical framework.

Conceptual framework: A conceptual framework stems from the theoretical framework and concentrates, usually, on one section of that theoretical framework which becomes the basis of your study. The latter consists of the theories or issues in which your study is embedded, whereas the former describes the aspects you selected from the theoretical framework to become the basis of your research enquiry. The conceptual framework is the basis of your research problem.

325

under their respective headings. For example, a critique of the sampling design you adopt should be included under 'sampling' or a critique to the study design should be discussed under 'study design'.

Note that the suggested research proposal structure does not contain a section entitled 'survey of the literature' or 'literature review'. This is because references to the literature should be integrated with your arguments conceptually rather than chronologically and should become a part of all the aspects of your research report from problem conceptualisation to conclusions drawn from your findings. The literature should be reviewed under main themes that emerge from your reading of the literature and should be included in the introduction and 'research problem' section. Issues identified in the literature to do with research methodology and problems pertinent to the various aspects of research procedures should be discussed under their respective headings. For example, issues pertaining to the study design under 'study design', issues relating to sampling under 'sampling', and the literature pertaining to the research instrument under the 'measurement procedure'.

CHECKPOINT
Research proposal contents

In suggesting this format it is assumed that you are reasonably well acquainted with research methodology and an academic style of writing. That is, you know how to write a set of objectives or construct a hypothesis, you are familiar with the various study designs and you can construct a research instrument and cite a reference.

The pages that follow outline a framework for a research proposal. The contents under each heading may vary markedly from discipline to discipline, according to the academic level of the student (BA, MA, PhD) and whether your study is predominantly quantitative or qualitative. For quantitative proposals you need to be very specific in proposing how you are going to undertake each step of the research journey, whereas for qualitative research proposals such details are not expected as your methodology is flexible and unstructured to accommodate in-depth search. However, you need to provide a broad approach to your enquiry as a part of your research proposal.

It is here that your exercises, after each operational step, will help you in writing your research proposal. All you need to do is to take the relevant information from these exercises and place it at the appropriate places in your research proposal. Each section of the proposed outline for a research proposal is divided into two parts:

1   a suggested title for the section and an outline of its contents;
2   examples outlining contents for the section – the same four examples of research projects, each taken from a different discipline, are used as illustrations in each section.

Before we go into detail, note that the format of a research proposal for a qualitative study or mixed method study is very similar to that for a quantitative one, varying only in content and not structure.

Preamble/introduction

The proposal should start with an introduction to include some of the information listed below. Remember that some of the contents suggested in this section may not be relevant to certain studies, so use your discretion in selecting only what is pertinent to your study. In writing this section, the literature review (see Chapter 3 on reviewing the literature) is of central importance as it serves two main functions:

1   It acquaints you with the available literature in the area of your study, thereby broadening your knowledge base.
2   It provides you with information on the methods and procedures other people have used in similar situations and tells you what works and what does not.

The type, extent and quality of a literature review are mostly dependent upon the academic level for which you are writing the proposal. The contents of this section may also vary greatly according to the subject area under study.

Start with a very broad perspective of the main subject area, before gradually narrowing the focus to the central problem under investigation. In doing so, cover the following aspects of your study area:

- an overview of the main area under study;
- a historical perspective (development, growth, etc.) pertinent to the study area;
- philosophical or ideological issues relating to the topic;
- trends in terms of prevalence, if appropriate;
- major theories, if any;
- the main issues, problems and advances in the subject area under study;
- important theoretical and practical issues relating to the central problem under study;
- the main findings relating to the core issue(s).

Four examples of topics for the preamble/introduction for a research proposal follow.

CHECKPOINT
Appraising sources

Example A

Suppose that you are conducting a study to investigate the impact of immigration on family roles. The preamble/introduction should include a brief description of the following:

- The origins of migratory movements in the world.
- General theories developed to explain migratory behaviour.
- The reasons for migration.
- Current trends in migration (national and state).
- The impact of immigration on family roles and relationships (e.g. on husband and wife, on children and parents, on parental expectations of children, etc.).
- Occupational mobility.
- etc.

Example B

Suppose your research project is a study of the attitudes of foster carers towards foster payment in [name of the place/state/country]. The preamble/introduction would include a brief description of the following:

- The origins of foster placement, the philosophy of foster care, a historical overview of foster care and changes over the years.

- Reasons for foster care and changes over time.
- The origins of foster placement in [the country in which you are conducting your study].
- The effects of foster placement on children and parents.
- Policies with respect to foster care in [the region].
- The origins of foster care in [the region].
- Administrative procedures for foster care in [the region].
- The training of foster parents in [the region].
- The role and responsibility of foster parents.
- etc.

Example C

Suppose that you plan to study the relationship between academic achievement and social environment. The preamble/introduction would briefly include the following:

- The role of education in our society.
- Major changes in the philosophy of education over time.
- Factors affecting attitudes towards education.
- The development of education in [country].
- Trends in education participation rates in [country] with particular reference to the region in which the study is being carried out.
- Changing educational values.
- Role of parents and peers in academic achievement.
- Impact of social environment on academic achievement.
- etc.

Example D

Suppose you are undertaking a qualitative study to find out what it means to have a child with ADHD in the family. The preamble/introduction should include your thoughts and arguments, and what the literature says around the following aspects of ADHD.

- Definitions and symptoms of ADHD.
- Causes of ADHD.
- Medical perspective on ADHD.
- Effects of ADHD on family life.
- Treatment for ADHD.
- Implications for a child if untreated.
- Management of ADHD.
- etc.

The research problem

Having provided a broad introduction to the area under study, now focus on issues relating to its central theme, identifying some of the gaps in the existing body of knowledge. Identify some of the main unanswered questions. Here some of the main research questions that you would like to answer through your study should also be raised, and a rationale and relevance for each should be provided. Knowledge gained from other studies and the literature about the issues you are proposing to investigate should be an integral part of this section. Specifically, this section should:

- identify the issues that are the basis of your study;
- specify the various aspects/perspectives on these issues;
- identify the main gaps in the existing body of knowledge;
- raise some of the main research questions that you want to answer through your study;
- identify what the literature says concerning your research questions, specifying the differences of opinion, if any, in the literature regarding these questions;
- develop a rationale for your study with particular reference to how your study will fill the identified gaps in the existing body of knowledge.

The following examples outline the topics on which the literature should be reviewed and included in the section entitled 'The problem'. Keep in mind that these are just suggestions and should serve only as examples for you to develop and change as you feel appropriate for your own study. (Use information developed in Exercise I in this section.)

Example A

- What settlement process does a family go through after immigration?
- What adjustments do immigrants have to make?
- What types of change can occur in family members' attitudes? (Theory of acculturation, etc.)
- What is the possible impact of settlement on family roles and relationships?
- In terms of impact, what specific questions do you want to answer through the study? What does the literature say about these questions? What are the different viewpoints on these issues? What are your own ideas about these questions?
- What do you think will be the relevance of the findings of your study to the existing body of knowledge and to your profession?
- How will the findings add to the body of knowledge and be useful to professionals in your field?
- etc.

Example B

- What are the broad issues, debates, arguments and counter-arguments regarding foster-care payment?
- What are the attitudes of foster parents to the amount, mode and form of payment and what does the literature say about these issues?

→ What are the different viewpoints/perspectives regarding payment for foster care?
→ What main questions will your study answer?
→ How will your findings help in policy formulation and programme development?
→ etc.

Example C

→ What theories have been developed to explain the relationship between academic achievement and social environment?
→ What is the relationship between educational achievement and social environment: what theoretical model will be the basis of your study?
→ What do previous theories and researches have to say regarding the components of the theoretical model and academic achievement? For example, the relationship between academic achievement and:

→ the self-esteem and aspirations/motivation of a student;
→ peer group influence;
→ parental involvement and its relationship with their socioeconomic status;
→ the motivation and interest of students in the subject;
→ employment prospects;
→ relationship with a teacher;
→ etc.

Example D

→ What are the effects on the family of having a child with ADHD in the family, as identified in the literature?
→ According to the literature, are there any differences between these effects and the type of family?
→ What strategies have been used for the management of ADHD by a family?
→ What effects, according to the literature, does ADHD have on sibling relationships?
→ What are the perceptions of family members about the effects and management of ADHD?
→ How do families cope when they have a child with ADHD in the family?
→ etc.

Objectives of the study

In this section include a statement of both your study's main objective and subobjectives (see Chapter 4). Your main objective indicates the central thrust of your study, whereas the subobjectives identify the specific issues you propose to examine.

The objectives of the study should be clearly stated and specific in nature. Each subobjective should delineate only one issue. Use action-oriented verbs such as 'to determine', 'to find out' and 'to ascertain' in formulating subobjectives, which should be numerically listed. If the objective is to test a hypothesis, you must follow the conventions of hypothesis formulation in wording the specific objectives.

In qualitative studies the statement of objectives is not as precise as in quantitative studies. In qualitative studies you should simply mention an overall objective of the study, as your aim is to explore as much as possible as you go along. As you know, the strength of qualitative research is in flexibility of approach and the ability to incorporate new ideas while collecting data. Having structured statements that bind you to a predetermined framework of exploration is not a preferred convention in qualitative research. Statements that you intend to explore 'what it means to have a child with ADHD in the family', 'how it feels to be a victim of domestic violence', 'how people cope with racial discrimination', 'the relationship between resilience and yoga' or 'reconstructing life after a bushfire' are sufficient to communicate your intent of objectives in qualitative research. More detailed objectives, if need be, can be developed after a study is complete. (Use information developed in Exercise I in this section.)

Example A

Main objective:

↝ To ascertain the impact of immigration on the family.

Subobjectives:

↝ To determine the impact of immigration on husband/wife roles as perceived by immigrants.
↝ To find out the impact of immigration on marital relations.
↝ To ascertain perceived changes in parental expectations of children's academic and professional achievement.
↝ To determine perceived changes of attitude towards marriage in the study population.

Example B

Main objective:

↝ To determine the opinion of foster carers about the form and extent of foster payment they feel they should receive for taking care of a foster child.

Subobjectives:

↝ To determine the form and mode of payment for taking care of a foster child.
↝ To identify the factors that foster parents believe should be the basis for determining the rate of payment for fostering a child.
↝ To determine the relationship, if any, between the socioeconomic-demographic characteristics of foster parents and their views on payment.

Example C

Main objective:

⤳ To examine the relationship between academic achievement and social environment.

Subobjectives:

⤳ To find out the relationship, if any, between self-esteem and a student's academic achievement at school.
⤳ To ascertain the association between parental involvement in a student's studies and his/her academic achievement at school.
⤳ To examine the links between a student's peer group and academic achievement.
⤳ To explore the relationship between academic achievement and the attitude of a student towards teachers.

Example D

Main objective:

⤳ To explore what it means to have a child with ADHD in the family.

Hypotheses to be tested

A hypothesis is a statement of your assumptions about the prevalence of a phenomenon or about a relationship between two variables that you plan to test within the framework of the study (sees Chapter 6). If you are going to test hypotheses, list them in this section. (Use the information developed in Exercise II in this section.)

When formulating a hypothesis you have an obligation to draw conclusions about it in the text of the report. Hypotheses have a particular style of formulation. You must be acquainted with the correct way of wording them. In a study you may have as many hypotheses as you want to test. However, it is *not* essential to have a hypothesis in order to undertake a study – you can conduct a perfectly satisfactory study without formulating a hypothesis.

Example A

⤳ H_1 = In most cases there will be a change in husband/wife roles after immigration.
⤳ H_2 = In a majority of cases there will be a change in parents' expectations of their children.
⤳ H_i = etc.

Example B

⤳ H_1 = Most people become foster parents because of their love of children.
⤳ H_2 = A majority of foster parents would like to be trained to care for foster children.
⤳ H_i = etc.

Example C

H_1 = A student's self-esteem and academic achievement at school are positively correlated.

H_2 = The greater the parental involvement in a student's studies, the higher the academic achievement.

H_3 = A student's attitude towards teachers is positively correlated with his/her academic achievement in that subject.

H_i = etc.

Example D

Hypotheses are usually not constructed in qualitative research.

Study design

Describe the study design (for details see Chapter 8) you plan to use to answer your research questions. (For example, say whether it is a case study, descriptive, cross-sectional, before-and-after, experimental or non-experimental design.) Identify the strengths and weaknesses of your study design.

Include details about the various logistical procedures you intend to follow while executing the study design. One characteristic of a good study design is that it explains the details with such clarity that, if someone else wants to follow the proposed procedure, s/he will be able to do exactly as you would have done. Your study design should include information about the following:

- Who makes up the study population?
- Can each element of the study population be identified? If yes, how?
- Will a sample or the total population be studied?
- How will you get in touch with the selected sample?
- How will the sample's consent to participate in the study be sought?
- How will the data be collected (e.g. by interview, questionnaire or observation)?
- In the case of a mailed questionnaire, to what address should the questionnaire be returned?
- Are you planning to send a reminder regarding the return of questionnaires?
- How will confidentiality be preserved?
- How and where can respondents contact you if they have queries?

(Use information developed in Exercise III in this section.)

Example A

The study is primarily designed to find out from a cross-section of immigrants from [names of countries] the perceived impact of immigration on family roles. Initial contact with the ethnic associations for these countries will

CHECKPOINT
Design rationale

be made through the elected office bearers to obtain a list of members. Five immigrants will be selected from the list at random, and will be contacted by phone to explain the purpose of the study and its relevance, and to seek their agreement to participate in the study. Those who give their consent will be interviewed at their homes or any other convenient place. To select a further sample, a snowball sampling technique will be used until the desired sample size is obtained.

Example B

The study design is cross-sectional in nature, being designed to find out from a cross-section of foster parents their opinions about foster payment. All foster parents currently registered with [department name] constitute the study population. From the existing records of this department it seems that there are 457 foster parents in [name of region]. As it is impossible for the researcher, within the constraints of time and money, to collect information from all the foster parents, it is proposed to select a sample of 50 per cent of the study population with the proposed sampling strategy. The questionnaire, with a supporting letter from the department, will be sent with a prepaid envelope. The respondents will be requested to return the questionnaire by [date]. The letter from the researcher attached to the questionnaire will explain the objectives and relevance of the study, assure the respondents of anonymity and give them the option of not participating in the study if they wish. A contact number will be provided in case a respondent has any questions. In the case of a low response rate (less than 25 per cent), a reminder will be sent to respondents.

Example C

It is proposed that the study will be carried out in two government high schools in the metropolitan area. The principals of the schools most accessible to the researcher will be contacted to explain the purpose of the study and the help needed from the school, and to seek their permission for the students to participate in the study. As the constraints of time and resources do not permit the researcher to select more than two schools, negotiations with other schools will cease when two schools agree to participate in the study.

It is proposed to select year 9 students as the academic achievement of students in years 8 and 10 could be affected by factors unique to them. Year 8 students may be experiencing anxiety as a result of having just made the transition to a new system. The motivation of students in year 10 could be affected by their being at the stage in their education where they must decide if they will stay on at school.

In order to control the variance attributable to the gender of a student it is proposed to select only male students.

Once the principal of a school agrees to allow the study to be carried out, the researcher will brief the teacher in charge about the study and its relevance, and will arrange a date and time for administering the questionnaire.

When the students are assembled, ready to participate in the study, the researcher will explain its purpose and relevance, and then distribute the questionnaire. The researcher will remain with the class to answer any questions the students might have.

The researcher is known to a family that has a child with ADHD and that belongs to an ADHD support group which meets every month. The researcher proposes to make initial contact with the group through the known family. The researcher will attend one of the monthly meetings and brief the group on the purpose and relevance of the study, criteria for inclusion in the study, what it entails to be involved in the study, and other aspects of the study. The respondents will also be assured of the anonymity of the information shared by them and its ethical use. The members of the group will be encouraged to ask questions about any aspect of the study. Having sought their consent, the researcher will seek opinions of group members to decide who should participate in the study in light of the inclusion criteria.

It is proposed to select six families, three where both parents are involved in the treatment and management of an ADHD child and three from families where the mother is the sole carer. This is primarily to see if there are differences in looking after a child with ADHD among different types of family.

The potential respondents will be individually contacted by the researcher to seek their consent for participation in the study. Once consent has been obtained the place and timings for interviews will be fixed with each family. Depending upon the type of family, the issues will be discussed either collectively with the father and mother or with the mother only. Before starting an interview, their permission to tape-record the interview will be sought. Having completed the interviews, the researcher will transcribe the responses and a copy will be given to the respondents for confirmation and validation.

The setting

Briefly describe the organisation, agency or community in which you will conduct your study. If the study is about a group of people, highlight some of the salient characteristics of the group (e.g. its history, size, composition and structure) and draw attention to any available relevant information.

If your research concerns an agency, office or organisation, include the following in your description:

→ the main services provided by the agency, office or organisation;
→ its administrative structure;
→ the type of clients served;
→ information about the issues that are central to your research.

If you are studying a community, briefly describe some of the main characteristics, such as:

→ the size of the community;
→ a brief social profile of the community (i.e. the composition of the various groups within it);
→ issues of relevance to the central theme of your study.

Note that, due to the nature of the content, it would be difficult to provide examples.

Measurement procedures

This section should contain a discussion of your instrument (see Chapters 9 and 10) and the details of how you plan to operationalise your major variables (Chapter 5).

To start with, justify your choice of research tool, highlighting its strengths and pointing out its weaknesses. Then outline the major segments of your research tool and their relevance to the main objectives of the study. If you are using a standard instrument, briefly discuss the availability of evidence on its reliability and validity. If you adapt or modify it in any way, describe and explain the changes you have made.

You should also discuss how you are going to operationalise the major concepts. For example, if measuring effectiveness, specify how it will be measured. If you plan to measure the self-esteem of a group of people, mention the main indicators of self-esteem and the procedures for its measurement (e.g. the Likert or Thurstone scale, or any other procedure).

Ideally, for quantitative studies you should attach a copy of the research instrument to your proposal.

(Information developed in Exercise III should be incorporated here.)

Note that, due to the nature of the content, it would be difficult to provide examples for this section.

Ethical issues

CHECKPOINT
*Ethical
considerations*

All academic institutions are particular about any ethical implications of research. To deal with them, all institutions have some form of policy on ethics. You need to be acquainted with your institution's policy. It is imperative that in your proposal you identify any ethical issues and describe how you propose to deal with them. You need to look at the ethical issues particularly from the viewpoint of your respondents and, in case of any potential 'harm', psychological or otherwise, you need to detail the mechanism in place to deal with it. Further information on ethical issues is provided in Chapter 14. (Use information provide in Exercise III here.)

Sampling

Under this section of the proposal include the following:

- the size of the sampling population (if known) and from where and how this information will be obtained;
- the size of the sample you are planning to select and your reasons for choosing this size;
- an explanation of the sampling design you are proposing to use in the selection of the sample (simple random sampling, stratified random sampling, quota sampling, etc.).
- (Your Exercise IV will provide you all the information you need to complete this section. Also consult Chapter 12 on sampling.)

Example A

Because the lack of information as to the exact location of migrant families makes it difficult to use a probability sampling design, it is proposed that the researcher will employ a snowball sampling technique. The researcher will make initial contact with five families who have emigrated from [name of country] during the past seven to ten years, who are either known to him/her or on the basis of information obtained from the office bearers of the formal associations representing the migrant groups. From each respondent the researcher will obtain names and addresses of other immigrants who have come from the same country during the same period. The respondents thus identified will then be interviewed and asked to identify other respondents for the researcher. This process will continue until the researcher has interviewed 70 respondents.

Example B

Because of the constraints of time and resources it is proposed to select 50 per cent of the foster parents currently registered (457) with the department using the systematic random sampling technique. Every other foster parent registered with the department will be selected, thus 229 individuals will constitute the sample for the study.

Example C

The selection of schools will be done primarily through quota sampling. Schools will be selected on the basis of their geographical proximity to the researcher. The researcher will prepare a list of schools, in rank order, of accessibility. Once two schools agree to participate in the study, negotiations with other schools will cease.

All year 9 male students will constitute the study population. It is expected that the sample will not exceed 100 students.

Example D

It is proposed to use the judgemental/purposive sampling technique to select six families from the group, three where both parents look after an ADHD child and three where only the mother has the main responsibility (single parent families). On the basis of informal discussions with the group members, those families who are expected to be information-rich in treating and managing a child with ADHD will be selected to be interviewed.

Analysis of data

Describe in general terms the strategy you intend to use for data analysis (Chapter 15). Specify whether the data will be analysed manually or by computer. For computer analysis, identify the program and where appropriate the statistical procedures you plan to perform on the data. For quantitative studies also identify the main variables for cross-tabulation.

For qualitative studies, describe how you plan to analyse your interviews or observation notes to draw meaning from what your respondents have said about issues discussed or observation notes made. One of the common techniques is to identify main themes by analysing the content of the information gathered in the field. You first need to decide whether you want to analyse this information manually or use a computer program for the purpose.

There are three ways to proceed with content analysis:

1   From your field notes develop a framework for your write-up and, as you go through your notes, directly integrate that information within the structure developed. If you adopt this method, you need to be reasonably clear about the structure. It does not mean that you cannot develop the structure as you go on analysing; still, a clear vision will be of immense help in slotting information gathered in the field by you into the write-up.
2   The second method is to transcribe your field notes so that you can read them over and over again to identify the main themes. These themes become the basis of your write-up.
3   There are computer programs such as NUD*IST, Ethnograph and NVivo specifically designed to handle descriptive data. You may prefer to use one of these programs. These programs are also based upon the principle of content analysis. The only difference is that instead of your searching manually, they identify where a particular text identifying the theme appears.

You need to specify which particular strategy you are proposing for data analysis for your study.

Example A

Frequency distributions in terms of:

→ age;
→ education;
→ occupation;
→ number of children;
→ duration of immigration;
→ etc.

Cross-tabulations of impact of husband/wife roles by:

→ age;
→ number of children;
→ education;
→ occupation;
→ etc.

Example B

Frequency distributions in terms of:

→ age;
→ income;

- education;
- occupation;
- marital status;
- duration of foster care;
- number of foster children;
- etc.

Cross-tabulations of attitude towards foster payment by:

- age;
- number of children;
- education;
- occupation;
- etc.

Statistical tests to be applied:

- chi-square;
- regression analysis;
- etc.

Example C

Frequency distributions in terms of:

- age;
- parents' occupation;
- parents' educational levels;
- students' occupational aspirations;
- parental involvement in students' studies;
- self-esteem;
- peer group influence;
- number of hours spent on studies;
- etc.

Cross-tabulations of academic achievement by:

- peer group influence;
- parental involvement in students' studies;
- self-esteem;

- occupational aspirations;
- attitude towards teachers;
- etc.

Example D

The in-depth interviews carried out with the families will be transcribed using Microsoft Word. These transcribed interviews will be closely studied to identify the main themes they communicate. These themes will be sorted by issues relating to management and treatment of a child with ADHD. The themes will then become part of the write-up.

Structure of the report

As clearly as possible, state how you intend to organise the final report (see Chapter 17 and refer to your Exercise VII). In organising your material for the report, the specific objectives of your study are of immense help. Plan to develop your chapters around the main themes of your study. The title of each chapter should clearly communicate the main thrust of its contents.

The first chapter, possibly entitled 'Introduction', should be an overall introduction to your study, covering most of your project proposal and pointing out deviations, if any, from the original plan.

The second chapter should provide some information about the study population itself – that is, some of its socioeconomic-demographic characteristics. The main aim of this chapter is to give readers some background on the population from which you collected the information. The chapter may therefore be entitled 'Socioeconomic-demographic characteristics of the study population' or 'The study population' or any other title that communicates this theme to readers. Titles for the rest of the chapters will vary from study to study but, as mentioned, each chapter should be written around a main theme. Although the wording of chapter titles is an individual choice, each must communicate the main theme of the chapter. In developing these themes the specific objectives of the study should be kept in the front of your mind.

If your study is qualitative, the main issues identified during data collection and analysis stages should become the basis for developing the various chapters. Having developed significant issues, the next step is to organise the main themes under each issue and develop a structure that you will follow to communicate your findings to your readers.

> CHECKPOINT
> *Structuring your proposal*

Example A

It is proposed that the report will be divided into the following chapters:

- Chapter 1: Introduction
- Chapter 2: The socioeconomic-demographic characteristics of the study population
- Chapter 3: The impact on husband/wife roles
- Chapter 4: The impact on marital relations

- Chapter 5: The impact on expectations of children
- Chapter 6: The impact on attitudes towards marriage
- Chapter 7: Summary, conclusions and recommendations

Example B

The study will be divided into the following chapters:

- Chapter 1: Introduction
- Chapter 2: A profile of the study population
- Chapter 3: Foster carers' perceptions of their role
- Chapter 4: Attitudes of foster carers towards foster-care payment
- Chapter 5: The preferred method of payment
- Chapter 6: General comments made by respondents about foster care
- Chapter 7: Summary, conclusions and recommendations

Example C

It is proposed that the report will have the following chapters:

- Chapter 1: Introduction
- Chapter 2: The study population
- Chapter 3: Occupational aspirations, self-esteem and academic achievement
- Chapter 4: The extent of parental involvement and academic achievement
- Chapter 5: Peer group influence and academic achievement
- Chapter 6: Academic achievement and student attitudes towards teachers
- Chapter 7: Summary, conclusions and recommendations

Example D

It is proposed that the report will have the following chapters:

- Chapter 1: Introduction
- Chapter 2: ADHD: A theoretical perspective
- Chapter 3: Issues and difficulties faced by family members in bringing up a child with ADHD
- Chapter 4: ADHD and its perceived effects on the child
- Chapter 5: ADHD and its perceived impact on sibling relationships

- Chapter 6: Managing ADHD treatment
- Chapter 7: Perceived effects of ADHD on schooling of the child
- Chapter 8: Perceived effects of ADHD on relationships with other children
- Chapter 9: A case history
- Chapter 10: Summary and conclusions

Problems and limitations

This section should list any problems you think you might encounter concerning, for example, the availability of data, securing permission from the agency/organisation to carry out the study, obtaining the sample, or any other aspect of the study.

You will not have unlimited resources and, as this may be primarily an academic exercise, you may have to do less than an ideal job. However, it is important to be aware of – and communicate – any limitations that could affect the validity of your conclusions and generalisations.

Here, the word *problems* refers to difficulties relating to logistical details; *limitations*, on the other hand, are structural problems relating to methodological aspects of the study – for example, if in your opinion the study design you proposed may not be the best but you adopted it for a number of considerations. This is also true for sampling or measurement procedures. Such limitations should be communicated to readers.

Appendix

Your proposal must include a list of references as an appendix. For a quantitative study, also attach your research instrument.

WORK SCHEDULE

You must set yourself deadlines to reflect the fact that you need to complete the research within a certain time-frame. List the various operational steps you need to undertake and indicate against each the date by which you aim to complete it, having carefully considered how long you will need. Remember to keep some time towards the end as a 'cushion' in case the research process does not go as smoothly as planned. Develop a chart as shown in Table 13.1.

BUDGET

CHECKPOINT
Planning a timeline

It is a good idea to have some estimate as to what the study is going to cost and ensure the availability of funds. Though most of the work that you will do is 'free', there are aspects of a study on which money will have to be spent. Think through and identify where you need to spend the money and how much. Where you need to spend, to a large extent, depends upon the type of study you are undertaking. The main difference in the cost is dependent upon two things: the method of data collection and the sample size. All other aspects of a study, irrespective of its design, would more or less entail similar expenses. Table 13.2 applies to most studies, but you can add others that are specific to yours.

CHECKPOINT
Funding and budgeting

Table 13.1 Developing a time-frame for your study

Tasks (Any tasks which you consider important)	To be completed by (weeks or months)														
	1	2	3	4	5	6	7	8	9	10	11	12	13	14	15
Proposal writing		→													
Instrument finalisation			→												
Data collection					→										
Coding							→								
Data analysis									→						
Report/first/second/third									→						
Report/final									→						
Typing										→					

Table 13.2 Estimated cost of the study

Aspects of the study	Approximate cost
Printing of the interview schedule or questionnaire	$ ...
Use of telephone	$...
Travel	$ ...
Preparation of the report	$ ...
Stationery	$ ....
etc.	$ ....
Total	

SUMMARY

A research proposal details the operational plan for obtaining answers to research questions. It must tell your supervisor and others what you propose to do, how you plan to proceed and why the chosen strategy has been selected. It thus assures readers of the validity of the methodology used to obtain answers accurately and objectively.

The guidelines set out in this chapter provide only a framework within which a research proposal for both quantitative and qualitative studies should be written and assume that you are reasonably well acquainted with research methodology and an academic style of writing. The contents of your proposal are arranged under the following headings: preamble/introduction, the broad research problem or issue under study, objectives of the study, hypotheses to be tested, study design, setting, measurement procedures, sampling, analysis of data, structure of the report, and problems and limitations. The specifics, under each heading, will vary with the type of study you are proposing to undertake. The write-up for qualitative studies will be based upon qualitative methodology, and quantitative methodology will determine the contents of quantitative studies.

The 'preamble' or 'introduction' introduces the main area of the study. Start with a broad literature review, gradually narrowing it down to the specific problem you are investigating. The theoretical framework should be a part of this section. The next section, 'the problem', details the specific problem under study. The research questions for which you are planning to find answers are raised in this section. 'Objectives of the study' contains your main objectives and your subobjectives. Hypotheses, if any, should be listed in the 'hypotheses to be tested' section. The logistical procedures you intend to follow are detailed under 'study design'. 'The setting' consists of a description of the organisation or community in which you plan to conduct your study. The procedure for obtaining information and the measurement of major variables are explained in the 'measurement procedures' section. You need to write about ethical issues that your study might have and how you propose to deal with them. How you will select your sample is described under 'sampling'. The procedure for data analysis is discussed under 'analysis of data'. The way you plan to structure your report is outlined under 'structure of the report'. Anticipated problems in conducting the study and limitations with its design are described under 'problems and limitations'. As an appendix to your proposal attach a copy of the research instrument and a list of the references. The differences in research proposals for quantitative and qualitative studies are mostly in content and not in structure. Their contents should be methodology-specific.

A work schedule provides a time-frame for your study.

Now that you have read the full chapter...

CHECK YOUR UNDERSTANDING

- ☐ Do you understand the meaning and application of all of the keywords at the start of the chapter? If not, visit the online resources and use the glossary flashcards to get to grips with their definitions.

- ☐ What are the differences in a research proposal written for quantitative and qualitative studies?

- ☐ Critically examine the contents, as suggested in this chapter, of a research proposal.

- ☐ How has working through the exercises at the end of the each step helped you to complete your research proposal?

APPLY IT TO YOUR OWN PROJECT

☐ Compare the research proposal contents suggested in this chapter with those recommended by your university or department. If they are different, what are the differences?

☐ Find out the process that a research proposal goes through in your university before approval is granted.

CONFUSED?

THE ONLINE RESOURCES ARE HERE TO HELP YOU

 https://study.sagepub.com/kumar5e

CHECKPOINT: What are the most important elements you need to include in your research proposal? Watch this video.

CHECKPOINT: How can you appraise your sources critically? Visit this website.

CHECKPOINT: Why is it important to present a clear rationale behind your study design choices? Visit this website.

CHECKPOINT: What are some of the most important considerations to factor in to your ethics discussion? Watch this video.

CHECKPOINT: What is a good research proposal structure? Visit this website.

CHECKPOINT: How much time should you allow yourself to write your proposal? Visit this website.

NEED MORE GENERAL SUPPORT?

Get up to speed on key terms with *glossary flashcards* and test yourself on important concepts with multiple choice questions.

UP FOR A CHALLENGE?

THE ONLINE RESOURCES ARE HERE TO INSPIRE YOU

 https://study.sagepub.com/kumar5e

CHECKPOINT: What factors separate a passable and an excellent research proposal? Read this journal article.

CHECKPOINT: How do you present contrasting arguments between different scholars? Visit this website.

CHECKPOINT: How can you improve the language of your rationale to provide a persuasive justification for your study design choices? Visit this website.

CHECKPOINT: What do ethical guideline procedures look like? Visit this website.

CHECKPOINT: What does a complete research proposal look like? Visit this website.

CHECKPOINT: What are some time management techniques you can use to help you write your proposal? Watch this video.

READY TO WORK ON YOUR OWN PROJECT?

Start building a portfolio of your ideas with the exercise workbook and get support tailored to your specific assignment with the assessment toolkit.

EXERCISE V: WRITING A RESEARCH PROPOSAL

Template of Exercise V

In your research journey, you have now reached a point where you can think of putting together your research proposal even though you have not yet covered everything that needs to be included in the proposal.

In this exercise you need, in the light of the contents proposed in Chapter 13, to decide on an outline specifically for your research proposal and start putting together the material already developed in other exercises.

As suggested, the outline for a research proposal for quantitative, qualitative or mixed methods studies is the same. The difference is only in the contents which are already described in this book. Look at Chapter 13 again and extract the relevant information from the various exercises you have already done to complete your research proposal.

Your proposal should be written in an academic style, incorporating appropriate references in the body of the text, integrating your literature review at relevant places in a thematic rather than chronological manner, raising your research questions, specifying the objectives of your study and detailing the whole procedure that you propose to go through in undertaking your research journey in a clear and succinct manner.

Follow the outline below in completing this exercise. Keep in mind that you have already completed most of the tasks when completing the exercises attached to each operational step.

The points given in the following outline are merely prompts. You need to work through them with a lot more depth and understanding. As mentioned, you have already done most of the work; here you only need to put it together.

Good luck, you are nearly there!!!

Introduction

_____
_____
_____
_____

Objectives of the study

_____
_____
_____
_____

Hypotheses to be tested (if applicable)

_____
_____
_____
_____

Study design

_____
_____
_____
_____

Setting of the study

_____
_____
_____
_____

Research instrument

Sampling design

Ethical issues

Data processing

Proposed chapters of the report

Problems and limitations of the study

Proposed time-frame

Proposed budget

STEP SIX

COLLECTING DATA

CONSIDERING ETHICAL ISSUES IN DATA COLLECTION

- step six -
COLLECTING DATA

This operational step includes one chapter:

→ Considering ethical issues in data collection   352

ESSENTIAL TERMS

You should be able to define these by the end of the chapter

- bias
- confidentiality
- harm

- informed consent
- sensitive information
- stakeholders

BONUS TERMS

You will learn more about these by the end of the chapter

- code of conduct
- deprivation of treatment
- ethos
- principles of conduct

- research participants
- sponsoring organisations
- subjectivity

LEARNING OBJECTIVES

At the end of this chapter, you will be able to:

- Describe the concept of ethics
- Identify stakeholders in research
- Consider ethical issues concerning research participants
- Consider ethical issues relating to the researcher
- Consider ethical issues regarding the sponsoring organisation

ETHICS: THE CONCEPT

Code of conduct: A set of principles based upon ethical considerations that govern the professional practice in a profession.

Ethics: The moral values of professional conduct that are considered desirable for good professional practice.

Ethical practice: Professional practice undertaken in accordance with the principles of accepted codes of conduct for a given profession or group.

Unethical: Any professional activity that is not in accordance with the accepted code of conduct for that profession is considered unethical.

All professions are guided by a code of ethics that has evolved over the years to accommodate the changing ethos, values, needs and expectations of those who hold a stake in the professions. Some professions are more advanced than others in terms of the level of development of their code of ethics. Some have very strict guidelines, monitor conduct effectively and take appropriate steps against those who do not abide by the guidelines.

Most professions have an overall code of conduct that also governs the way they carry out research. In addition, many research bodies have evolved a code of ethics separately for research. Medicine, epidemiology, business, law, education, psychology and other social sciences have well-established codes of ethics for research.

Let us first examine what we mean by 'ethics' or 'ethical behaviour'. According to the *Collins Dictionary* (1979: 502), ethical means 'in accordance with principles of conduct that are considered correct, especially those of a given profession or group'. The key phrases here, 'principles of conduct' and 'considered correct', raise certain questions:

- What are these principles of conduct?
- Who determines them?
- In whose judgement must they be considered correct?

Closely related questions are as follows:

- Are there universal principles of conduct that can be applied to all professions?
- Do these change with time and should they change?
- What happens when a professional does not abide by them?

The subject of ethics needs to be considered in light of these questions.

The way each profession serves society is continuously changing in accordance with society's needs and expectations and with the technology available for the delivery of a service. The ethical codes governing the manner in which a service is delivered also need to change. What has been considered ethical in the past may not be so judged at present, and what is ethical now may not remain so in the future. Any judgement about whether a particular practice is ethical is made on the basis of the code of conduct prevalent at that point in time.

As the service and its manner of delivery differ from profession to profession, no code of conduct can be uniformly applied across all professions. Each profession has its own code of ethics, though there are commonalities. If you want guidelines on ethical conduct for a particular profession, you need to consult the code of ethics adopted by that profession or discipline.

'What are these principles of conduct?' is the most important question as it addresses the issue of the contents of ethical practice in a profession. As the code of conduct varies from profession to profession, it is not possible to provide a universal answer to this question. However, in research, any dilemma stemming from a moral quandary is a basis of unethical conduct. There are certain behaviours in research – such as causing harm to individuals, breaching confidentiality, using information improperly and introducing bias – that are considered unethical in any profession.

356

The next question is: in whose judgement must a code of conduct be considered correct? Who decides whether a particular practice is wrong? If a procedure is carried out wrongly, what penalties should be imposed? It is the overall body of professionals or government organisations that collectively develops a professional code of conduct and forms a judgement as to whether or not it is being followed.

As mentioned, most professions have established an overall code of ethics and also a code of ethics for conducting research in their respective fields. As this book is designed for researchers in the social sciences, we will examine ethical issues relating to research in general and issues that are applicable to most social science disciplines.

STAKEHOLDERS IN RESEARCH

There are many stakeholders in research, whether it is quantitative, qualitative or mixed methods. It is important to look at ethical issues in relation to each of them. The various stakeholders in a research activity are:

1   the research participants or subjects;
2   the researcher;
3   the funding body.

Who should be considered as a research participant varies from profession to profession. Generally, all those with direct and indirect involvement in a research study are considered as research participants, hence stakeholders. In addition, those who are likely to be affected by the findings of a study are also considered as stakeholders. In the fields of medicine, public health, epidemiology and nursing, patients and non-patients who become part of a study and those who participate in an experiment to test the effectiveness of a drug or treatment are considered as research participants. Even the participants of a control group in an experiment are considered to be stakeholders. Service providers, service managers and planners who are involved in either providing the service or collecting information relating to the service are also stakeholders in the research. In the social sciences, the participants include individuals, groups and communities providing information to help a researcher to gain understanding of a phenomenon, situation, issue or interaction. In social work and psychology, participants include clients as well as non-clients of an agency from whom information is collected to find out the magnitude of a problem, the needs of a community or the effectiveness of an intervention; and service providers, social workers and psychologists, when they provide information for a study. In marketing, consumers as well as non-consumers of a product provide information about consumption patterns and behaviour. In education, subjects include students, teachers and perhaps the community at large who participate in educational research activities. Similarly, in any discipline in which a research activity is undertaken, those from whom information is collected or those who are studied by a researcher become participants of the study.

Researchers constitute the second category of stakeholders. Anyone who collects information for the specific purpose of understanding, consolidation, enhancement and development of professional knowledge, adhering to the accepted code of conduct, is a researcher. S/he may represent any academic discipline.

Stakeholders in research: Those people or groups who are likely to be affected by a research activity or its findings. In research there are three stakeholders: the research participants, the researcher and the funding body.

Research participants: Those respondents or subjects who participate in a research study.

357

Funding organisations responsible for financing a research activity fall into the third category of stakeholders. Most research is carried out using funds provided by business organisations, pharmaceutical companies, service institutions (government, quasi-government or voluntary), research bodies and/or academic institutions. The funds are given for specific purposes.

Each category of stakeholders in a research activity may have different interests, perspectives, purposes, aims and motivations that could affect the way in which the research activity is carried out and the way results are communicated and used. Because of this, it is important to ensure that research is not affected by the self-interest of any party and is not carried out in a way that harms any party. It is therefore essential to examine ethical conduct in research concerning different stakeholders under separate categories.

ETHICAL ISSUES TO CONSIDER CONCERNING RESEARCH PARTICIPANTS

There are many ethical issues to consider in relation to the participants in a research activity.

Collecting information

One might ask: why should a respondent give any information to a researcher? What right does a researcher have to knock on someone's door or to send out a questionnaire? Is it ethical to disturb an individual, even if you ask permission before asking questions? Why should a person give you his/her time? Your request for information may create anxiety or put pressure on a respondent. Is this ethical?

But these questions display a naive attitude. It is an attitude that prevents all progress in the world. Research is required in order to improve conditions. Provided any piece of research is likely to help society directly or indirectly, it is acceptable to ask questions, if you first obtain the respondents' informed consent. Before you begin collecting information, you must consider the relevance and usefulness of the research you are undertaking and also be able to convince others of this. If you cannot justify the relevance of the research you are conducting, you are wasting your respondents' time, which is unethical.

Seeking informed consent

In every discipline it is considered unethical to collect information without the knowledge of participants, and their expressed willingness and informed consent. Seeking informed consent 'is probably the most common method in medical and social research' (Bailey 1978: 384). Informed consent implies that subjects are made adequately aware of the type of information you want from them, why the information is being sought, what purpose it will be put to, how they are expected to participate in the study and how it will directly or indirectly affect them. It is important that the consent should also be voluntary and without pressure of any kind. Schinke and Gilchrist (1993: 83) write:

Informed consent: implies that respondents are made adequately and accurately aware of the type of information you want from them, why the information is being sought, what purpose it will be put to, how they are expected to participate in the study, and how it will directly or indirectly affect them. It is important that the consent should also be voluntary and without pressure of any kind. The consent given by respondents after being adequately and accurately made aware of or informed about all aspects of a study is called informed consent.

Under standards set by the National Commission for the Protection of Human Subjects, all informed-consent procedures must meet three criteria: participants must be competent to give consent; sufficient information must be provided to allow for a reasoned decision; and consent must be voluntary and uncoerced.

CHECKPOINT
Informed consent

Competency, according to Schinke and Gilchrist (1993: 83), 'is concerned with the legal and mental capacities of participants to give permission'. For example, some very old people, those suffering from conditions that exclude them from making informed decisions, people in crisis, people who cannot speak the language in which the research is being carried out, people who are dependent upon you for a service, and children are not considered to be in a position to give informed consent.

Providing incentives

Is it ethical to provide incentives to respondents for sharing information with you? Some researchers provide incentives to participants for their participation in a study, feeling this to be quite proper as participants are giving their time. Others think that the offering of inducements is unethical.

In the author's experience most people do not participate in a study because of incentives, but because they realise the importance of the study. Therefore, giving a small gift after having obtained your information, as a token of appreciation, is in the author's opinion not unethical. However, giving a present before data collection is unethical.

Seeking sensitive information

Information sought can pose an ethical dilemma in research. Certain types of information can be regarded as sensitive or confidential by some people, and thus seeking it constitutes an invasion of privacy. Asking for this information may upset or embarrass a respondent. However, if you do not ask for the information, it may not be possible to pursue your interest in the area and contribute to the existing body of knowledge.

For most people, questions on sexual behaviour, drug use and shoplifting are intrusive. Even questions on marital status, income and age may be considered to be an invasion of privacy by some. In collecting data you need to be careful about the sensitivities of your respondents.

The dilemma you face as a researcher is whether you should ask sensitive and intrusive questions. In the author's opinion it is not unethical to ask such questions provided that you clearly and frankly tell your respondents the type of information you are going to ask, assure them of the confidentiality of the information, keep the information confidential and give them sufficient time to decide if they want to share the information with you, without any major inducement.

The possibility of causing harm to participants

Is the research going to harm participants in any way? Harm includes 'not only hazardous medical experiments but also any social research that might involve such things as discomfort, anxiety, harassment, invasion of privacy, or demeaning or dehumanising procedures' (Bailey 1978: 384).

When you collect data from respondents or involve subjects in an experiment, you need to examine carefully whether their involvement is likely to harm them in any way. If it is, you must make sure that the risk is minimal. Minimum risk means that the extent of harm or discomfort in the research is not greater than that ordinarily encountered in daily life. It is unethical if the way you seek information creates anxiety or harassment, and if you think it may happen, you need to take steps to prevent it.

CHECKPOINT
*Participant
risk*

Maintaining confidentiality

Sharing information about a respondent with others for purposes other than research is unethical. Sometimes you need to identify your study population to put your findings into context. In such a situation you need to make sure that at least the information provided by respondents is kept anonymous. It is unethical to identify an individual respondent and the information provided by him/her. Therefore, you need to ensure that after the information has been collected, its source cannot be identified. In certain types of study you might need to visit respondents repeatedly, in which case you will have to identify them until the completion of your visits. In such situations you need to be extra careful that others do not have access to the information. It is unethical to be negligent in not protecting the confidentiality and anonymity of the information gathered from your respondents. If you are doing research for someone else, you need to make sure that confidentiality is maintained by this party as well.

ETHICAL ISSUES TO CONSIDER RELATING TO THE RESEARCHER

Avoiding bias

Bias on the part of the researcher is unethical. Bias is different from subjectivity. Subjectivity, as mentioned earlier, is a way of thinking that you develop due to such factors as your educational background, training, professional background, competence in research, overall intellectual capabilities and philosophical perspective. Because of these you develop a way of looking at and interpreting things which could be different from that of others. You do not deliberately alter but interpret them differently, much as an economist will look at things differently than a psychologist or a doctor. Bias is a deliberate attempt either to hide what you have found in your study, or to highlight something disproportionately to its true existence. It is absolutely unethical to introduce bias into a research activity. If you are unable to control your bias, you should not be engaging in the research. Remember, it is the bias that is unethical and not the subjectivity.

Provision or deprivation of a treatment

Both the provision and deprivation of a treatment may pose an ethical dilemma for the researcher. When testing an intervention or a treatment, a researcher usually adopts a control experiment design. In such studies, is it ethical to provide a study population with an intervention or treatment that has not yet been conclusively proven effective or beneficial? But if you do not test a treatment/intervention, how can you prove or disprove its effectiveness or benefits? On the other hand, you are providing an intervention that may not be effective. Is this ethical? Is it ethical to deprive the control group of a treatment even if it may prove to be only slightly effective? And beyond the issue of control groups, is it ethical to deprive people who are struggling for life of the possible benefit, however small, which may be derived from a drug that is only under trial? As a researcher you need to be aware of these ethical issues. There are arguments and counter-arguments about these issues. However, it is usually accepted that deprivation of a trial treatment to a control group is not unethical as, in the absence of this, a study can never establish the effectiveness of a treatment which may deprive many others of its possible benefits. This deprivation of the possible benefits, on the other hand, is considered by some as unethical.

There are no simple answers to these dilemmas. Ensuring informed consent, 'minimum risk' and frank discussion as to the implications of participation in the study may help to resolve some of these ethical issues.

Using inappropriate research methodology

A researcher has an obligation to use appropriate methodology, within his/her knowledge base, in conducting a study. It is unethical to use deliberately a method or procedure you know to be inappropriate, such as by selecting a highly biased sample, using an invalid instrument or drawing wrong conclusions.

Incorrect reporting

To report the findings in a way that changes or slants them to serve your own or someone else's interest is unethical. Correct and unbiased reporting of the findings is an important characteristic of ethical research practice.

Inappropriate use of information

How will the information obtained from respondents be used by the researcher? The use of information in a way that directly or indirectly affects respondents adversely is unethical. Can information be used adversely to affect the study population? If so, how can the study population be protected? As a researcher you need to consider and resolve these issues. Sometimes it is possible to harm individuals in the process of achieving benefits for organisations. An example would be a study to examine the feasibility of restructuring an organisation. Restructuring may be beneficial to the organisation as a whole but may be harmful to some individuals. Should you ask respondents for information that is likely to be used against them? If you do, the information may be used against them, and if you do not, the organisation may not be able to derive the benefits of restructuring. In the author's opinion, it is ethical to ask questions provided you tell respondents of the potential use of the information, including the possibility of its being used against some of them, and you let them decide if they want to participate. Some may participate for the betterment of the organisation even though it may harm them, and others may decide against it. However, to identify either of them is unethical in research.

CHECKPOINT
Protecting data

ETHICAL ISSUES REGARDING
THE SPONSORING ORGANISATION

Restrictions imposed by the sponsoring organisation

Most research in the social sciences is carried out using funds provided by sponsoring organisations for a specific purpose. The funds may be given to develop a programme or evaluate it; to examine its effectiveness and efficiency; to study the impact of a policy; to test a product; to study the behaviour of a group or community; or to study a phenomenon, issue or attitude. Sometimes there may be direct or indirect controls exercised by sponsoring organisations. They may select the methodology, prohibit the publication of findings or impose other restrictions on the research that may stand in the way of obtaining and disseminating accurate information. Both the imposition and acceptance of these controls and restrictions are unethical, as they constitute interference and could amount to the sponsoring organisation tailoring research findings to meet its vested interests.

The misuse of information

How will the sponsoring body use the information? How is this likely to affect the study population? Sometimes sponsoring organisations use research as a pretext for promoting management's agenda. It is unethical to let your research be used as a reason for justifying management decisions when the research findings do not support them. However, it is recognised that it may be extremely difficult or even impossible for a researcher to prevent this from happening.

ETHICAL ISSUES IN COLLECTING DATA
FROM SECONDARY DATA

While it is important to consider ethical issues in collecting data from primary sources, it is equally important to consider them when collecting data from secondary sources. Some of the ethical considerations that you should keep in mind when collecting data from secondary sources are discussed in this section (see also www.lancs.ac.uk/researchethics).

Plagiarism is one of the important ethical issues in using data from secondary sources. It is the use of someone else's work, claiming it to be yours. It is absolutely unethical as well as illegal in research to plagiarise. It could also have severe academic consequences. All borrowed ideas and citations should be properly acknowledged and cited.

It is also unethical to use a substantial piece of work by someone else without his/her informed consent. You must seek permission from the copyright holder and/or the author to use the data.

Plagiarism: Use of someone else's work, academic or non-academic, claiming it to be yours, is called plagiarism and is considered unethical in research.

The mispresentation of data – changing its format, context or content to suit your purpose – is both illegitimate and unethical. Any change, if it leads to a different interpretation of the original data, is unethical. The misinterpretation of data is another ethical issue in social research. The data must be presented in the same format and context. If these are changed make sure they do not communicate a different presentation.

You must take care to avoid disclosing data sources. Until expressed consent is given by the author or copyright holder, you must protect the identity of the participants, places and institutions. Make sure you anonymise the identifying information by using pseudonyms. Disclosing the anonymity and confidentiality of the source without permission is unethical.

Use of data collected by covert means – without the consent of participants, without adhering to the principle of client self-determination or through any other unethical means – cannot be considered legitimate and hence its use is unethical.

CHECKPOINT
Using secondary data

SUMMARY

This chapter is designed to make you aware of the ethical issues to be considered when conducting research. The ethical issues to be considered are the same in both quantitative and qualitative research. How you resolve them depends on you and the conditions under which you are working.

Being ethical means adhering to the code of conduct that has evolved over the years for an acceptable professional practice. Any deviation from this code of conduct is considered unethical and the greater the deviation, the more serious the breach. For most professions ethical codes in research are an integral part of their overall ethics, and some research bodies have evolved their own codes.

Ethical issues in research can be examined in relation to research participants, researchers and sponsoring organisations. With regard to research participants, the following areas could pose ethical issues if not dealt with properly: collecting information; seeking consent; providing incentives; seeking sensitive information; the possibility of causing harm to participants; and maintaining confidentiality. It is important to examine these areas thoroughly for any unethical practice. With regard to the researcher, areas of ethical concern include the following: introducing bias; providing and depriving individuals of treatment; using unacceptable research methodology; inaccurate reporting; and the inappropriate use of information. Ethical considerations in relation to sponsoring organisations concern restrictions imposed on research designs and the possible use of findings. There are unethical issues that you need to be aware of when collecting data from secondary sources. Some of them are: plagiarism, collection without formed consent, misinterpretation or misquotation of the information used, disclosing data sources and using data collected by covert means. As a newcomer to research you should be aware of what constitutes unethical practice and be able to put appropriate strategies in place to deal with any harm that may be done to any stakeholder.

Proposing to study and the study population.

363

Now that you have read the full chapter...

CHECK YOUR UNDERSTANDING

☐ Do you understand the meaning and application of all of the keywords at the start of the chapter? If not, visit the online resources and use the glossary flashcards to get to grips with their definitions.

☐ What specific practices in a research study would you consider as unethical? In the light of your own position, critically examine these practices.

☐ In this chapter ethical issues have been looked at from three perspectives. If you were asked to add another perspective, what would you add?

☐ What would you consider as unethical from the perspectives of research participants?

☐ Some might suggest that asking for any kind of information from an individual is unethical as it is an invasion of his/her privacy. Consider how you might argue for and against this suggestion.

☐ Ethical issues may arise at any point in the research process. Reflecting on the principles raised in this chapter, make a list of ethical issues that you think should be considered at each step in the eight-step model.

APPLY IT TO YOUR OWN PROJECT

☐ Find a copy of your university's or department's code of ethics for research (or examples of codes of conduct for your chosen profession). Can you identify any areas of research or approaches that might come into conflict with these guidelines?

☐ Imagine you are planning to undertake a hypothetical research study in an area of interest to you. Identify the various stakeholder groups and list the possible ethical concerns you need to be aware of from the perspective of each one of the groups.

☐ How would you ensure that the research you undertake is ethical from your perspective as a researcher?

☐ What would be your position if your sponsoring organisation put pressure on you to change some of the findings you included in your study? Give reasons for your position.

CONFUSED?

THE ONLINE RESOURCES ARE HERE TO HELP YOU

 https://study.sagepub.com/kumar5e

CHECKPOINT: What is a consent form, and why do you need one? Read this encyclopaedia entry.

CHECKPOINT: What are some ways participants might be harmed during studies? Read this chapter.

CHECKPOINT: How do you reassure participants about how their data will be used? Visit this website.

CHECKPOINT: How do you present and reference secondary data accurately? Read this chapter.

NEED MORE GENERAL SUPPORT?

Get up to speed on key terms with *glossary flashcards* and test yourself on important concepts with *multiple choice questions*.

UP FOR A CHALLENGE?

THE ONLINE RESOURCES ARE HERE TO INSPIRE YOU

 https://study.sagepub.com/kumar5e

CHECKPOINT: What does a consent form look like? Visit this website.

CHECKPOINT: What are some examples of classic unethical studies? Visit this website.

CHECKPOINT: What regulations and policies are in place to protect data? Visit this website.

CHECKPOINT: How can you unpick secondary data and find the relevance to your own research questions? Explore this case study.

READY TO WORK ON YOUR OWN PROJECT?

Start building a portfolio of your ideas with the exercise workbook and get support tailored to your specific assignment with the assessment toolkit.

Well done for completing the previous steps, where you have given some thorough thoughts to your research project and by now you should have a pretty clear idea and plan on what you want to research, who your participants are and what data collection method(s) are appropriate to generate data that will answer your research question. Before you collect your data you need to consider ethical issues to ensure that all stakeholders are satisfied that your research is conducted ethically. In many social science disciplines you have to go through an ethical approval process before you can collect your data and it is suggested that you refer to your specific discipline's ethical code of conduct as only general ethical issues are examined here.

Use the key information about your study that you have already provided in your proposal for this exercise to demonstrate how you address any ethical considerations for your project before you collect the data. The following steps will help you to identify and address any ethical issues.

STEP ONE Information about your study

1   Is your study Quantitative ☐   Qualitative ☐
    Mixed methods ☐

If you are drawing on a range of different methods ensure you are clear about all that you will apply as there may be different ethical issues for you to consider depending on the qualitative and/or qualitative processes involved.

2   Who are your participants?

----

3   What are participants' key characteristics? For example, will you use any inclusion/exclusion criteria? What is the sample size?

----

4   What information are you collecting from your participants or what are your participants expected to do in your study?

----

5   What is your recruitment strategy? How will you obtain the sample, e.g. how will you advertise?

STEP TWO Identifying ethical issues

What particular ethical issues arise from the method(s) chosen?
Be as detailed as possible and address all aspects in STEP I.

STEP THREE Ethical issues to consider concerning research
participants

1   How will you seek informed consent? What information will
    you provide to participants that they can decide to take part
    in the study?

----

2   Will you use a consent form?   Yes ☐   No ☐
3   What will the consent form cover/or how can you justify not
    using a consent form?

----

4   Are you providing incentives?   Yes ☐   No ☐
If yes, what is the incentive given and how can you justify it?

----

5   Are you collecting sensitive information?   Yes ☐   No ☐
If yes, how are you communicating this to the participants?

----

6   Is the research going to harm participants in any way? Is the
    risk to take part in the study greater than risks experienced
    every day? What steps have you taken to keep potential
    risks to a minimum?

----

7   How will you ensure confidentiality to participants' data?

STEP FOUR Ethical issues relating to you as the researcher

1   Consider whether there are any potential risks to you as the
    researcher:

----

2   How will you avoid researcher bias? Also consider your
    relationship to the participants and how will this influence
    their participation?

----

3   Is the provision or deprivation of a treatment relevant to your study? (E.g. are you using a control group?)
    Yes ☐   No ☐
If yes, provide a justification that there is no advantage/disadvantage for part of the study population.

STEP FIVE Ethical issues to consider regarding a sponsoring organization

1   Can you think of any restrictions that a sponsoring organization imposed that may affect your study? How will you deal with those?

----

2   How will the sponsoring organization use the research findings? (Also consider whether this is likely to affect the study population?)

----

3   If you use secondary data for your study, do you have consent to use the data?

Yes ☐   No ☐
List the copyright/author, reference of the data:

STEP SEVEN

PROCESSING AND DISPLAYING DATA

PROCESSING
DATA

- step seven -
PROCESSING AND DISPLAYING DATA

This operational step includes two chapters:

→ Processing data   372

Displaying data   418

CONFUSED? UP FOR A CHALLENGE?

OR NEED HELP WITH YOUR ASSIGNMENT?

VISIT https://study.sagepub.com/kumar5e for resources specially designed to support you and all your research needs.

ESSENTIAL TERMS

You should be able to define these by the end of the chapter

- content analysis
- data processing
- frame of analysis

BONUS TERMS

You will learn more about these by the end of the chapter

- analysis
- closed questions
- code book
- coding
- concepts
- cross-tabulation
- data display
- editing
- frequency distribution
- multiple responses
- open-ended questions
- pre-test

LEARNING OBJECTIVES

At the end of this chapter, you will be able to:

- Process data in quantitative studies
- Edit data and prepare it for coding
- Code data, including knowing how to code qualitative data in quantitative studies
- Process data in qualitative studies
- Analyse data in qualitative and quantitative studies
- Discuss the role of computers in data analysis
- Understand the role of statistics in research
- Develop themes from open-ended responses, descriptions or narrations

If you were actually doing a research study, you would by now have reached the stage of having either extracted or collected the required information for your study. But what to do with this information? What steps do you need to take beyond data collection to find answers to your research questions? How do you make sense of the information collected? How do you draw meaning from the data gathered? If you have a hypothesis, how do you accept or reject it? How should the information be analysed to achieve the objectives of your study? To answer these questions you need to subject your data to a number of procedures that constitute the core of data processing (Figure 15.1).

These procedures are the same whether your study is quantitative or qualitative, but what you do within each procedure is different. For both types of study you need to visualise how you are going to present your findings to your readership in the light of its background and the purpose of the study. You need to decide what type of analysis would be appropriate for the readers of your report. It is in the light of the purpose of your study and your impression about the level of understanding of your readership that you decide the type of analysis you should undertake. For example, there is no point in doing a sophisticated statistical analysis if your readers are not familiar with statistical procedures. In quantitative research the main emphasis in data analysis is to decide how you are going to analyse information obtained in response to each question that you asked of your respondents. In qualitative research the focus is on what should be the basis of analysis of the information obtained; that is, is it contents, discourse, narrative or event analysis? Because of the different techniques used in processing data in quantitative and qualitative research, this chapter deals separately with data processing in quantitative and qualitative studies.

DATA PROCESSING IN QUANTITATIVE STUDIES

Editing

Irrespective of the method of data collection, the information collected is called *raw data* or simply *data*. The first step in processing your data is to ensure that the data is 'clean' – that is, free from inconsistencies and incompleteness. This cleaning process is called editing.

Editing consists of scrutinising the completed research instruments to identify and minimise, as far as possible, errors, incompleteness, misclassification and gaps in the information obtained from the respondents. Sometimes even the best investigators can:

→ forget to ask a question;
→ forget to record a response;
→ wrongly classify a response;
→ write only half a response;
→ write illegibly.

Similar problems can arise in questionnaires. These problems to a great extent can be reduced simply by (1) checking the contents for completeness, and (2) checking the responses for internal consistency.

Editing: Data editing involves scrutinising the completed research instruments to identify and minimise, as far as possible, errors in completeness, misclassification and gaps in the information obtained from respondents.

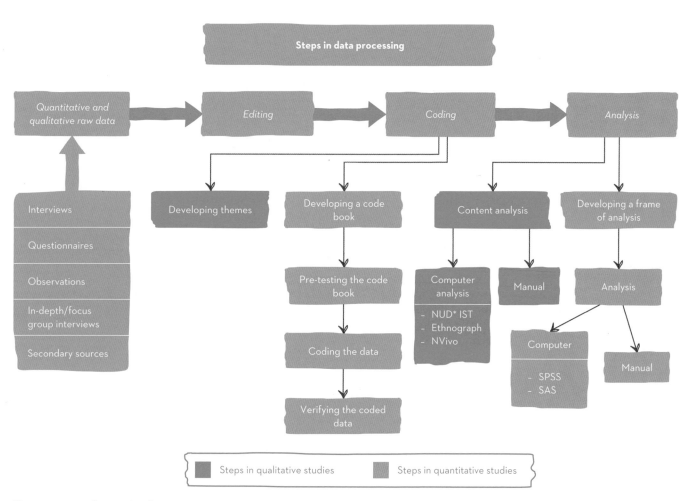

Figure 15.1   Steps in data processing

The way you check the contents for completeness depends upon the way the data has been collected. In the case of an interview, just checking the interview schedule for the above problems may improve the quality of the data. It is good practice for an interviewer to take a few moments after completing an interview to peruse responses for possible incompleteness and inconsistencies. In the case of a questionnaire, again, just by carefully checking the responses some of the problems may be reduced. There are several ways of minimising such problems:

- **By inference** – Certain questions in a research instrument may be related to one another, and it might be possible to find the answer to one question from the answer to another. Of course, you must be careful about making such inferences or you may introduce new errors into the data.

- **By recall** – If the data is collected by means of interviews, sometimes it might be possible for the interviewer to recall a respondent's answers. Again, you must be extremely careful.

- **By going back to the respondent** – If the data has been collected by means of interviews or the questionnaires contain some identifying information, it is possible to visit or phone a respondent to confirm or ascertain an answer. This is, of course, expensive and time-consuming.

There are two ways of editing the data:

CHECKPOINT
Data cleaning

1   examine all the answers to one question or variable at a time;
2   examine all the responses given to all the questions by one respondent at a time.

The author prefers the second method as it provides a total picture of the responses, which also helps you to assess their internal consistency.

Coding

Having cleaned the data, the next step is to code it. The method of coding is largely dictated by two considerations:

1   the way a variable has been measured (measurement scale) in your research instrument (e.g. if a response to a question is descriptive, categorical or quantitative);
2   the way you want to communicate the findings about a variable to your readers.

Coding: The process of assigning numerical values to different categories of responses to a question for the purpose of analysing them.

For coding, the first level of distinction is whether a set of data is qualitative or quantitative in nature. For qualitative data a further distinction is whether the information is descriptive in nature (e.g. a description of a service to a community, a case history) or is generated through discrete qualitative categories. For example, the following information about a respondent is in discrete qualitative categories: income (above average, average, below average); gender (male, female); religion (Christian, Hindu, Muslim, Buddhist, etc.); and attitude towards an issue (strongly favourable, favourable, uncertain, unfavourable, strongly unfavourable). Each of these variables is measured either on a nominal scale or an ordinal scale. Some of them could also have been measured on a ratio scale or an interval scale. For example, income can be measured in dollars (ratio scale), or an attitude towards an issue can be measured on an interval or a ratio scale. The way you proceed with the coding depends upon the measurement scale used in the measurement of a variable at the time of collecting information and whether a question is open-ended or closed.

In addition, the types of statistical procedures that can be applied to a set of information to a large extent depend upon the measurement scale on which a variable was measured in the research instrument. For example, you can calculate different statistical descriptors such as mean, mode and median if income is measured on a ratio scale, but not if it is measured on an ordinal or a nominal scale. It is extremely important to understand that the way you are able to analyse a set of information is dependent upon the measurement scale used in the research instrument for measuring a variable. It is therefore important to visualise – particularly at the planning stage when constructing the research instrument – the way you are going to communicate your findings.

How you can analyse information obtained in response to a question depends upon how a question was asked, and how a respondent answered it. In other words, it depends upon the measurement scale on which a response can be measured or classified. If you study answers given by your respondents in reply to a question, you will real-ise that almost all responses can be classified into one of the following three categories:

1 quantitative responses;
2 categorical responses (which may be quantitative or qualitative);
3 descriptive responses (which are invariably qualitative – keep in mind that this is qualitative data collected as part of quantitative research and not qualitative research).

For the purpose of analysis, quantitative and categorical responses need to be dealt with differently from descriptive ones. Both quantitative and categorical information go through a process that is primarily aimed at transforming the information into numerical values, called codes, so that the information can be easily analysed, either manually or by computer. On the other hand, descriptive information first goes through a process called content analysis, whereby you identify the main themes that emerge from the descriptions given by respondents in answer to questions. Having identified the main themes, there are three ways that you can deal with them: (1) you can examine verbatim responses and integrate them into the text of your report to either support or contradict your argument; (2) you can assign a code to each theme and count how frequently each has occurred; and (3) you can combine both methods to communicate your findings. This is your choice, and it is based on your impression of the preference of your readers.

For coding quantitative and qualitative data in quantitative studies you need to go through the following steps:

STAGE ONE	developing a code book;
STAGE TWO	pre-testing the code book;
STAGE THREE	coding the data;
STAGE FOUR	verifying the coded data.

Nominal scale: The nominal scale is one of the ways of measuring a variable in the social sciences. It enables the classification of individuals, objects or responses based on a common/ shared property or characteristic. These people, objects or responses are divided into a number of subgroups in such a way that each member of the subgroup has the common characteristic.

Ordinal scale: An ordinal scale has all the properties of a nominal scale plus one of its own. Besides categorising individuals, objects, responses or a property into subgroups on the basis of a common characteristic, it ranks the subgroups in a certain order. They are arranged in either ascending or descending order according to the extent that a subcategory reflects the magnitude of variation in the variable.

Ratio scale: A ratio scale has all the properties of nominal, ordinal and interval scales plus a property of its own: the zero point of a ratio scale is fixed, which means it has a fixed starting point. Therefore, it is an absolute scale. As the difference between the intervals is always measured from a zero point, arithmetical operations can be performed on the scores.

Interval scale: The interval scale is one of the measurement scales in the social sciences where the scale is divided into a number of intervals or units. An interval scale has all the characteristics of an ordinal scale. In addition, it has a unit of measurement that enables individuals or responses to be placed at equally spaced intervals in relation to the spread of the scale. This scale has a starting and a terminating point and is divided into equally spaced units/intervals. The starting and terminating points and the number of units/intervals between them are arbitrary and vary from scale to scale as it does not have a fixed zero point.

Code: The numerical value that is assigned to a response at the time of analysing the data.

Content analysis: One of the main methods of analysing qualitative data. It is the process of analysing the contents of interviews or observational field notes in order to identify the main themes that emerge from the responses given by your respondents or the observation notes made by you as a researcher.

Code book: A listing of a set of numerical values (set of rules) that you decide to assign to answers obtained from respondents in response to each question.

A code book provides a set of rules for assigning numerical values to answers obtained from respondents. Let us take an example. Figure 15.2 lists some questions taken from a questionnaire used in a survey conducted by the author to ascertain the impact of occupational redeployment on an individual. The questions selected should be sufficient to serve as a prototype for developing a code book, as they cover the various issues involved in the process.

There are two formats for data entry: 'fixed' and 'free'. In this chapter we will be using the fixed format to illustrate how to develop a code book. The fixed format stipulates that a piece of information obtained from a respondent is entered in a specific column. Each column has a number and the 'Col. no.' in the code book refers to the column in which a specific type of information is to be entered. The information about an individual is thus entered in a row(s) comprising these columns.

For a beginner it is important to understand the structure of a code book. The example in Table 15.1 is based on the responses given to the questions listed in Figure 15.2.

In Table 15.1, *column 1* refers to the columns in which a particular piece of information is to be entered. Allocation of columns in a fixed format is extremely important because, when you write a program, you need to specify the column in which a particular piece of information is entered so that the computer can perform the required procedures.

Column 2 identifies the question number in the research instrument for which the information is being coded. This is primarily to identify coding with the question number in the instrument.

Column 3 refers to the name of the variable. Each variable in a program is given a unique name so that the program can carry out the requested statistical procedures. Usually there are restrictions on the way you can name a variable (e.g. the number of characters you can use to name a variable and whether you use the alphabet or numerals). You need to check the program you are using for this. It is advisable to name a variable in such a way that you can easily recognise it from its name.

Column 4 lists the possible responses to the various questions. Developing a response pattern for the questions is the most important, difficult and time-consuming part of developing a code book. The degree of difficulty in developing a response pattern differs with the types of questions in your research instrument (open-ended or closed). If a question is closed, the response pattern has already been developed as part of the instrument construction and all you need to do at this stage is to assign a numerical value to each response category. In terms of analysis, this is one of the main advantages of closed questions. If a closed question includes 'other' as one of the response categories, to accommodate any response that you may not have listed when developing the instrument, you should analyse the responses and assign them to non-overlapping categories in the same way as you would do for open-ended questions. Add these to the already developed response categories and assign each a numerical value.

If the number of responses to a question is less than nine, you need only one column to code the responses, and if it is more than nine but less than 99, you need two columns (column 1 in the code book). But if a question asks respondents to give more than one response, the number of columns assigned should be in accordance with the number of responses to be coded. If there are, say, eight possible responses to a particular question and a respondent is asked to give three responses, you need three columns to code the responses to the question.

1. Please indicate:

   (a) Your current age in completed years: _____
   (c) Your marital status: (Please tick)
   Currently married _____   Divorced _____
   Living in a de facto relationship _____   Never married _____
   Separated _____

2. (b) If tertiary/university, please specify the level achieved and area of study. (Please specify all postgraduate qualifications.)

Level of achievement	Area of study: e.g. engineering, accounting
Associate diploma	
Diploma	
Bachelor	
Graduate diploma	
Masters	
PhD	

11   What, in your opinion, are the main differences between your jobs prior to and after redeployment?

_____

12   We would like to know your perception of the two jobs *before* and *after* redeployment with respect to the following aspects of your job. Please rate them on a five-point scale using the following guide: 5 = extremely satisfied, 4 = very satisfied, 3 = satisfied, 2 = dissatisfied, 1 = extremely dissatisfied

Before redeployment					Areas	After redeployment				
1	2	3	4	5		1	2	3	4	5
					Job status					
					Job satisfaction					
					Motivation to work					
					Interest in the job					
					Self-esteem					
					Professional competence					
					Peer interaction					
					Morale					
					Work environment					
					Social interaction					

Figure 15.2   Example of questions from a survey

Such questions are called multiple response questions. Let us assume there are 12 possible responses to a question. To code each response you need two columns and, therefore, to code three responses you need six columns.

The coding of open-ended questions is more difficult. Coding of open-ended questions requires the response categories to be developed first through a process called content analysis. One of the easier ways of analysing open-ended questions is to select a number of interview schedules/questionnaires randomly from all the completed interview schedules/questionnaires received. Select an open-ended question from one of these schedules/questionnaires and write down the response(s) on a sheet of paper. If the person has given more than one response, write them separately on the same sheet. Similarly, from the same questionnaire/schedule select another open-ended question and write down the responses given on a separate sheet. In the same way you can select other open-ended questions and write down the response(s). Remember that the response to each question should be written on a separate sheet. Now select another questionnaire/interview schedule and go through the same process, adding response(s) given for the same question on the sheet for that question. Continue the process until you feel that the responses are being repeated and you are getting no or very few new ones – that is, when you have reached a saturation point.

Now, one by one, examine the responses to each question to ascertain the similarities and differences. If two or more responses are similar in meaning though not necessarily in language, try to combine them under one category. Give a name to the category that is descriptive of the responses. Remember, when you code the data you code categories, *not* responses per se. It is advisable to write down the different responses under each category in the code book so that, while coding, you know the type of responses you have grouped under a category. In developing these categories there are three important considerations:

1   The categories should be *mutually exclusive*. Develop non-overlapping categories. It should not be possible to place a response in two categories.
2   The categories should be *exhaustive*; that is, it should be possible to place almost every response in one of the categories. If too many responses cannot be so categorised, it is an indication of ineffective categorisation. In such a situation you should examine your categories again.
3   The use of the 'other' category, effectively a 'waste basket' for those odd responses that cannot be put into any category, must be kept to the absolute minimum because, as mentioned, it reflects the failure of the classification system. This category should not include more than 5 per cent of the total responses and should not contain more responses than any other category.

CHECKPOINT
Data coding

Column 5 lists the actual codes of the code book that you decide to assign to a response. You can assign any numerical value to any response so long as you do not repeat it for another response within the same question. Two responses to questions are commonly repeated: 'not applicable' and 'no response'. You should select a number that can be used for these responses for all or most questions. For example, responses such as 'not applicable' and 'no response' could be given a code of 8 and 9 respectively, even though the responses to a question may be limited to only 2 or 3. In other words, suppose you want to code the gender of a respondent and you have decided to code female = 1 and male = 2. For 'no response', instead of assigning a code of 3, assign a code of 9. This suggestion helps in remembering codes, which will help to increase your speed in coding.

Table 15.1   An example of a code book

Col. no.	Q. no.	Variable name	Response pattern	Code
1	2	3	4	5
1–3	S. no.	ID	Actual serial number	Code actual
4	Record no.	RNO	First record	1
			Second record	2
			Third record	3
5	1(a)	Age	20–24	1
			25–29	2
			30–34	3
			35–39	4
			40–44	5
			45–49	6
			No response	9
6	1(c)	MS	Currently married	1
			Living in a de facto relationship	2
			Separated	3
			Divorced	4
			Never married	5
			No response	9
	2(b)	TEDU	Assoc. Dip.	1
			Diploma	2
			Bachelors	3
			Grad. Dip.	4
			Masters	5
			PhD	6
			Not applicable	8
			No response	9

(Continued)

Table 15.1 (Continued)

Col. no.	Q. no.	Variable name	Response pattern	Code
7		TEDU1	Same as in TEDU	Code
8		TEDU2	Same as in TEDU	as in
9		TEDU3	Same as in TEDU	TEDU
		STUDY	Behavioural Sciences	1
			Business	2
			Economics/Commerce	3
			Communication	4
			Engineering	5
			Geography	6
			History	7
			Graphics	8
			Librarianship	9
			Nursing	10
			Performing Arts	11
			Secretarial	12
			Social Work	13
			Psychology	14
			Education	15
			Chartered Acct.	16
			Zoology	17
			Anthropology	18
			Social Sciences	19
			Public/Health Admin.	20
			English	21
			Audio-visual Aids Education	22
			Not applicable	88
			No response	99

Col. no.	Q. no.	Variable name	Response pattern	Code
10–11	2(b)	STUDY 1	Same as in STUDY	Code
12–13		STUDY 2	Same as in STUDY	as in
				STUDY
14–15		STUDY3	Same as in STUDY	
	11	DIFWK	Lack of job satisfaction	
			– current job	01
			– previous job	02
			Less responsibility	
			– current job	03
			– previous job	04
			Low morale	
			– current job	05
			– previous job	06
			Lack of recognition of hard work	
			– current job	07
			– previous job	08
			Skills irrelevant	
			– current job	09
			– previous job	10
			Repetitious nature	
			– current job	11
			– previous job	12
			Job more segmented	
			– current job	13
			– previous job	14
			Reduction in occup. status	15
			Greater involvement in total process	

(Continued)

Table 15.1 (Continued)

Col. no.	Q. no.	Variable name	Response pattern	Code
			– current job	16
			– previous job	17
			More restricted duties	
			– current job	18
			– previous job	19
			Less flexibility	
			– current job	20
			– previous job	21
			More people contact	
			– current job	22
			– previous job	23
			Less people contact	
			– current job	24
			– previous job	25
			More responsibility	
			– current job	26
			– previous job	27
			Better work environment	
			– current job	28
			– previous job	29
			Better work morale	
			– current job	30
			– previous job	31
			Working in a team	
			– current job	32
			– previous job	33
			Work as an individual	
			– current job	34

Col. no.	Q. no.	Variable name	Response pattern	Code
			– previous job	35
			Lack of job security	
			– current job	36
			– previous job	37
			Current job full-time	38
			Better career prospects	
			– current job	39
			– previous job	40
			No commonality	41
			Different working conditions	42
			Change in occup. status (not specified)	43
			High occup. level	
			– current job	44
			– previous job	45
			More job security in present job	46
			More professional environment in	
			– current job	47
			– previous job	48
			Different skills to learn in current job	49
			Higher workload	
			– current job	50
			– previous job	51
			Less supervision in	
			– current job	52
			– previous job	53
			Current job more relevant to my training	54
			Current job more rewarding	55
			Better morale in current job	56
			Greater variety of duties in	

(Continued)

Table 15.1   (Continued)

Col. no.	Q. no.	Variable name	Response pattern	Code
			– current job	57
			– previous job	58
			Current job more	
			rewarding	59
			Better morale in	
			– current job	60
			Less variety of tasks	
			in current job	61
			Fewer skills required in	
			– current job	62
			– previous job	63
			Change in job title	64
			Previous job very demanding	65
			Opportunity to use initiative in previous job	66
			Current job does not require initiative	67
			Different skills required in current job	68
			No career prospects	
			– current job	69
			– previous job	70
			More professional environment in current job	71
			Different skills to learn in current job	72
			Different working conditions	73
			Change in occup. status (change not specified)	74
			Change in job resp. (change not specified)	75
			Current job is more structured	76
			Now part of the team	77
			No change	78
			Irrelevant response	79

Col. no.	Q. no.	Variable name	Response pattern	Code
			Other	80
			Not applicable	88
			No response	99
16–17	11	DIFWK1	Same as in DIFWK	Code as
18–19		DIFWK2	Same as in DIFWK	in
20–21		DIFWK3	Same as in DIFWK	DIFWK
22–23		DIFWK4		
24–25		DIFWK5		
			Extremely dissatisfied	1
			Dissatisfied	2
	12	BEAFTER	Satisfied	3
			Very satisfied	4
			Extremely satisfied	5
			Same as in BEAFTER	
26		JOBSTA	Same as in BEAFTER	Code as
27		JOBSTB	Same as in BEAFTER	in
				BEAFTER
28		JOBSTA	Same as in BEAFTER	Code as in
29		JOBSTA	Same as in BEAFTER	BEAFTER
			and so on	

To explain how to code, let us take each of the questions listed in the example in Figure 15.2.

Question 1(a)

Your current age in completed years: _____

This is an open-ended quantitative question. In questions like this it is important to determine the range of responses – the respondent with the lowest and the respondent with the highest age. To do this, go through a number of questionnaires/interview schedules. Once the range is established, divide it into a number of categories. The categories developed are dependent upon a number of considerations such as the purpose of analysis, the way you want to communicate the findings of your study and whether the findings are going to be compared with those of another study. Let us assume that the range in the study is 23 to 49 years and assume that you decide on the following categories to suit your purpose: 20-24, 25-29, 30-34, 35-39, 40-44 and 45-49. If your range is correct you should need no other categories. Let us assume that you decide to code 20-24 = 1, 25-29 = 2, 30-34 = 3, and so on. To accommodate 'no response' you decide to assign a code of 9. Let us assume you decided to code the responses to this question in column 5 of the code sheet.

Question 1(c)

→ Your marital status: (Please tick)
→ Currently married_____
→ Living in a de facto relationship__
→ Separated_____
→ Divorced_____
→ Never married_____

This is a closed categorical question. That is, the response pattern is already provided. In these situations you just need to assign a numerical value to each category. For example, you may decide to code 'currently married' = 1, 'living in a de facto relationship' = 2, 'separated' = 3, 'divorced' = 4 and 'never married' = 5. You may add 'no response' as another category and assign it a code of 9. The response to this question is coded in column 6 of the code sheet.

Question 2(b)

If tertiary/university, please specify the level achieved and the area of study. (Please specify all postgraduate qualifications.)

In this question a respondent is asked about tertiary qualifications. The question asks for two aspects: (1) level of achievement, which is categorical; and (2) area of study, which is open-ended. Also, a person may have more than one qualification, which makes it a multiple response question. Both aspects of the question are to be coded – the level of achievement (e.g. associate diploma, diploma) and the area of study (e.g. engineering, accounting). When coding multiple responses, decide on the maximum possible number of responses to be coded. Let us assume you code a maximum number of three levels of tertiary education. (This would depend upon the maximum number of levels of achievement identified by the study population.) Firstly, code the levels of achievement TEDU (= tertiary education) and then the area of study STUDY. In the above example, let us assume that you decided to code three levels of achievement. To distinguish them from each other we call the first level TEDU1, the second TEDU2 and the third TEDU3, and decide to code them in columns, 7, 8 and 9, respectively. Similarly, the names given to the three areas of study are STUDY1, STUDY2 and STUDY3 and we decide to code them in columns 10-11, 12-13 and 14-15. The codes (01 to 22) assigned to different qualifications are listed in the code book. If a respondent has only one qualification, the question of second and third qualifications is not applicable and you need to decide on a code for 'not applicable'. Assume you assigned a code of 88. 'No response' would then be assigned a code of 99 for this question.

What, in your opinion, are the main differences between your jobs prior to and after redeployment?

_____
_____
_____

This is an open-ended question. To code this you need to go through the process of content analysis as explained earlier. Within the scope of this chapter it is not possible to explain the details, but response categories that have been listed are based upon the responses given by 109 respondents to the survey on occupational redeployment. In coding questions like this, on the one hand you need to keep the variation in the respondents' answers, and on the other you want to break them up into meaningful categories to identify the commonalities. Because this question is asking respondents to identify the differences between their jobs before and after redeployment, for easy identification let us assume this variable was named DIFWK (*dif*ference in *work*). Responses to this question are listed in Figure 15.3. These responses have been selected at random from the questionnaires returned.

A close examination of these responses reveals that a number of themes are common; for example: 'learning new skills in the new job'; 'challenging tasks are missing from the new position'; 'more secure in the present job'; 'more interaction in the present job'; 'less responsibility'; 'more variety'; 'no difference'; 'more satisfying'. There are many similar themes that hold for both the before and after jobs. Therefore, we developed these themes for 'current job' and 'previous job'.

One of the main differences between qualitative and quantitative research is the way responses are used in the report. In qualitative research the responses are normally used either verbatim or are organised under certain themes and the actual responses are provided to substantiate them.

In quantitative research the responses are examined, common themes are identified, the themes are named (or categories are developed) and the responses given by respondents are classified under these themes. The data then can also be analysed to determine the frequency of the themes if so desired. It is also possible to analyse the themes in relation to some other characteristics such as age, education and income of the study population. The code book lists the themes developed on the basis of responses given. As you can see, many categories may result. The author's advice is not to worry about this as categories can always be combined later if required. The reverse is impossible unless you go back to the raw data.

Let us assume you want to code up to five responses to this question and that you have decided to name these five variables as DIFWK1, DIFWK2, DIFWK3, DIFWK4 and DIFWK5. Let us also assume that you have coded them in columns 16-17, 18-19, 20-21, 22-23 and 24-25, respectively.

391

CHECKPOINT
Data themes

We would like to know your perception of the two jobs before and after redeployment with respect to the following aspects of your job. Please rate them on a five-point scale using the following guide:

5 = extremely satisfied, 4 = very satisfied, 3 = satisfied, 2 = dissatisfied, 1 = extremely dissatisfied

Respondent 3
Hours now FT; totally different skills required; deal with public; busier, more structured day and duties; now a part of the team instead of an independent worker.

Respondent 20
That I am happy and made to feel as though I am a valuable part of a team.

Respondent 41
This one is great, other one was lousy due to mismanagement, poor morale and feelings that dedication and hard work counted for nothing. Department of ... is well managed and morale is good and the graphic design work is fun and I am supported by my supervisors and subordinates.

Respondent 48

Before	After
15 hours per week	24 hours per week
Monday to Friday	Very satisfactory
On the go the whole time	Dealing with the public
No sitting	Dealing with severe psychiatric
Dealing with the public	patients can be very stressful.

Respondent 52
No difference.

Respondent 54
My substantive position has been the same before and after the redeployment, but before the redeployment I was acting as Project Manager (level 5) and after being redeployed I was assigned to programming duties (level e).

Respondent 63
This position has more day-to-day administration (it includes corporate services, finance, PR, IT, etc.).

Respondent 69
Had to find my own job.

Respondent 72
The job I was doing I looked after the needs of a workshop where in this job I process Pies and deliver them.

Respondent 78
Challenging tasks are missing from the new position now that I am familiar with it. Many routine activities (that I have been glad to learn in terms of career development) but that I am becoming bored with. My previous job was much more difficult and interesting than this one.

Respondent 79
I am more secure in my present job and it is better paid as I work longer hours now. I only *worked 61.h hours as a tea attendant.*

Respondent 81
My previous job required me to be involved in the whole area of government/community and *nongovernment requiring assistance in relation to settlement needs of migrants. My current* position does not provide job satisfaction, particularly in relation to the offenders that I currently deal with.

Respondent 97
Less responsibility, more specific job, restricted job.

Respondent 105
More variety, more flexibility, more responsibility in the present job, but less confidence, more *caution and some resentment.*

Figure 15.3 Some selected responses to the open-ended question (no. 11) in Figure 15.2

This is a highly structured question asking respondents to compare on a five-point ordinal scale their level of satisfaction with various areas of their job before and after redeployment. As we are gauging the level of satisfaction before and after redeployment, respondents are expected to give two responses to each area. In this example let us assume you have used the name JOBSTA for job status after redeployment (*job status after redeployment*) and JOBSTB for before redeployment (*job status before redeployment*). Similarly, for the second area, job satisfaction, you have decided that the variable name JOBSATA, will stand for the level of job satisfaction after redeployment (*job satisfaction after redeployment*) and JOBSATB for the level before redeployment (*job satisfaction before redeployment*). Other variable names have been similarly assigned. In this example the variable JOBSTA is entered in column 26, JOBSTB in column 27, and so on.

Stage II: Pre-testing the code book

Once a code book is designed, it is important to pre-test it for any problems before you code your data. A pre-test involves selecting a few questionnaires/interview schedules and actually coding the responses to ascertain any problems in coding. It is possible that you may not have provided for some responses and therefore will be unable to code them. Change your code book, if you need to, in light of the pre-test.

Stage III: Coding the data

Once your code book is finalised, the next stage is to code the raw data. There are three ways of doing this:

1   coding on the questionnaire/interview schedule itself, if space for coding was provided at the time of constructing the research instrument;
2   coding on separate code sheets that are available for purchase;
3   coding directly into the computer using a program such as SPSS or SAS.

To explain the process of coding let us take the same questions that were used in developing the code book. We select three questionnaires at random from a total of 109 respondents (Figures 15.4–15.6). Using the code book as a guide, we code the information from these sheets onto the coding sheet (Figure 15.7). Let us examine the coding process by taking respondent 3 (Figure 15.4).

Respondent 3

The total number of respondents is more than 99 and this is the third questionnaire, so the identification number 003 was entered in columns 1–3 (Figure 15.7). Because it is the first record for this respondent, 1 was entered in column 4. This respondent is 49 years of age and falls in the category 45–49, which was coded as 6. As the information on age belongs in column 5, 6 was entered in this column of the code sheet. The marital status of this person is 'divorced', hence 4 was entered in column 6. This person has a bachelor's degree in librarianship. The code chosen for a bachelor's degree is 3, which was entered in column 7. Three tertiary qualifications have been provided for, and as this person does not have any other qualifications, so TEDU2 and TEDU3 are 'not applicable', and therefore a code of 8 is entered in columns 8 and 9. This person's bachelor's degree is in librarianship, for which code 09 was

Pre-test: In quantitative research, pre-testing is a practice whereby you test something that you have developed before its actual use to ascertain the likely problems with it. Mostly, the pre-test is done on a research instrument or on a code book. The pre-test of a research instrument entails a critical examination of each question as to how clear it is and how it is understood by potential respondents with a view to removing possible problems with it. It ensures that a respondent's understanding of each question is in accordance with your intentions. The pre-test of an instrument is only done in structured studies. Pre-testing a code book entails actually coding a few questionnaires/interview schedules to identify any problems with the code book before coding the data.

393

assigned and entered in columns 10-11. Since there is only one qualification, STUDY2 and STUDY3 are 'not applicable'; therefore, a code of 88 was entered in columns 12-13 and 14-15. This person has given a number of responses to question no. 11 (DIFWK), which asks respondents to list the main differences between their jobs before and after redeployment. In coding such questions much caution is required.

Examine the responses named DIFWK1, DIFWK2, DIFWK3, DIFWK4 AND DIFWK5, to identify the codes that can be assigned. A code of 22 (now deal with public) was assigned to one of the responses, which we enter in columns 16-17. The second difference, DIFWK2, was assigned a code of 69 (totally different skill required), which is coded in columns 18-19. DIFWK3 was assigned a code of 77 (current job more structure) and coded in columns 20-21. Similarly, the fourth (DIFWK4) and the fifth (DIFWK5) difference in the jobs before and after redeployment are coded as 78 (now part of the team instead of independent worker) and 38 (hours – now full-time), which are entered in columns 22-23 and 24-25, respectively. Question 12 is extremely simple to code. Each area of a job has two columns, one for before and the other for after. Job status (JOBST) is divided into two variables, JOBSTA for a respondent's level of satisfaction after redeployment and JOBSTB for his/her level before redeployment. JOBSTA is entered in column 26 and JOBSTB in column 27. For JOBSTA the code 5 (as marked by the respondent) was entered in column 26 and for JOBSTB the code 4 is entered in column 27. Other areas of the job before and after redeployment are similarly coded.

The other two examples are coded in the same manner. The coded data is shown in Figure 15.7. In the process of coding you might find some responses that do not fit your predetermined categories. If so, assign them a code and add these to your code book.

Stage IV: Verifying the coded data

Once the data is coded, select a few research instruments at random and record the responses to identify any discrepancies in coding. Continue to verify coding until you are sure that there are no discrepancies. If there are discrepancies, re-examine the coding.

Developing a frame of analysis

Although a frame of analysis needs to evolve continuously while writing your report, it is desirable to broadly develop it before analysing the data. A frame of analysis should specify:

Frame of analysis: The proposed plan for analysing the data to operationalise your major concepts and the statistical procedures you intend to use.

↝ which variables you are planning to analyse;
↝ what type of analysis they should be subjected to;
↝ what cross-tabulations you are planning;
↝ which variables you need to combine to construct your major concepts or to develop indices (in formulating a research problem concepts are changed to variables – at this stage change them back to concepts);
↝ which variables are to be subjected to which statistical procedures.

To illustrate, let us take the example from the survey used in this chapter.

1. Please indicate:
    (a) Your current age in completed years: 49
    (c) Your marital status: (Please tick)

    Currently married _____   Divorced __✓____
    Living in a de facto relationship _____   Never married _____
    Separated _____

2. (b) If teritiary/university, please specify the level achieved and area of study. (Please specify all postgraduate qualifications.)

Level of achievement	Area of study: e.g. engineering, accounting
Associate diploma	
Diploma	
Bachelor	Librarianship
Graduate diploma	
Masters	
PhD	

11 What, in your opinion, are the main differences between your jobs prior to and after redeployment?

Hours now FT; totally different skills required; now deal with public busier, more structured day and duties; now part of the team instead of independent worker

12 We would like to know your perception of the two jobs *before* and *after* redeployment with respect to the following aspects of your job. Please rate them on a five-point scale, using the following guide:

5 = extremely satisfied, 4 = very satisfied, 3 = satisfied, 2 = dissatisfied, 1 = extremely dissatisfied

Before redeployment					Areas	After redeployment				
1	2	3	4	5		1	2	3	4	5
			✓		Job status					✓
			✓		Job satisfaction					✓
			✓		Motivation to work					✓
			✓		Interest in the job					✓
			✓		Self-esteem					✓
			✓		Professional competence				✓	
			✓		Peer interaction					✓
			✓		Morale				✓	
			✓		Work environment				✓	
				✓	Social interaction			✓		

Figure 15.4 Some questions from a survey – respondent 3

RESPONDENT = 59

1. Please indicate:

    (a) Your current age in completed years: 45
    (c) Your marital status: (Please tick)

    Currently married ____✓____   Divorced _____

    Living in a de facto relationship _____   Never married _____

    Separated _____

2. (b) If tertiary/university, please specify the level achieved and area of study. (Please specify all postgraduate qualifications.)

Level of achievement	Area of study: e.g. engineering, accounting
Associate diploma	
Diploma	
Bachelor	Behavioural Sciences
Graduate diploma	
Masters	
PhD	

11 What, in your opinion, are the main differences between your jobs prior to and after redeployment? *Less responsibility, more specific jobs, restricted scope.*

_____

12 We would like to know your perception of the two jobs *before* and *after* redeployment with respect to the following aspects of your job. Please rate them on a five-point scale using the following guide:

5 = extremely satisfied, 4 = very satisfied, 3 = satisfied, 2 = dissatisfied, 1 = extremely dissatisfied

Before redeployment					Areas	After redeployment				
1	2	3	4	5		1	2	3	4	5
			✓		Job status		✓			
			✓✓		Job satisfaction			✓		
			✓✓		Motivation to work		✓			
				✓	Interest in the job			✓		
				✓	Self-esteem			✓		
				✓	Professional competence			✓		
				✓	peer interaction				✓	
				✓	Morale		✓			
				✓	Work environment			✓		
			✓		Social interaction				✓	

Figure 15.5   Some questions from a survey – respondent 59

RESPONDENT = 81

1. Please indicate:
   (a) Your current age in completed years: 42
   (c) Your marital status: (Please tick)
   Currently married _____   Divorced _____
   Living in a de facto relationship_____   Never married
   Separated _____

2. (b) If tertiary/university, please specify the level achieved and area of study. (Please specify all postgraduate qualifications.)

Level of achievement	Area of study: e.g. engineering, accounting
Associate diploma	
Diploma	
Bachelor	*Social work*
Graduate diploma	
Masters	
PhD	

11 What, in your opinion, are the main differences between your jobs prior to and after redeployment?

My previous job required me to be involved in the whole area of government/community and nongovernment requiring assistance in relation to settlement needs of migrants. My current position does not provide job satisfaction particularly in relation to the offenders that If currently deal with.

12 *We* would like to know your perception of the two jabs *before* and *after* redeployment with respect to the following aspects of your job. Please rate them an a five-point scale using the following guide:

5 = extremely satisfied, 4 = very satisfied, 3 = satisfied, 2 = dissatisfied, 1 = extremely dissatisfied

Before redeployment					Areas	After redeployment				
1	2	3	4	5		1	2	3	4	5
		✓			Job status		✓			
			✓		Job satisfaction		✓			
				✓	Motivation to work			✓		
			✓		Interest in the job		✓			
			✓		Self-esteem		✓			
		✓			Professional competence		✓			
		✓			Peer interaction					
			✓		Morale		✓			
			✓		Work environment		✓			
		✓			Social interaction		✓			

Figure 15.6   Some questions from a survey – respondent 81

Program

Programmer | Date

Identification number

Statement Number					Count	Marital status			Study area						Difference in work										Level of satisfaction										Fortran S				
1	2	3	4	5	6	7	8	9	10	11	12	13	14	15	16	17	18	19	20	21	22	23	24	25	26	27	28	29	30	31	32	33	34	35	36	37	38	39	40
	0	3	1	6	4	3	8	8	0	9	8	8	8	8	2	2	6	9	7	7	7	8	3	8	5	4	5	4	5	4	5	4	5	4					
	5	9	1	6	1	3	8	8	0	1	8	8	8	8	0	3	1	9	7	7	8	8	8	8	2	4	3	4	2	4	3	5	3	5					
0	8	1	1	5	1	2	8	8	1	3	8	8	8	8	1	7	0	1	8	8	8	8	8	8	2	3	2	4	3	5	2	4	2	4					

Record no. — Age — Achievement level

Figure 15.7   An example of coded data on a code sheet

Frequency distributions

A frequency distribution groups respondents into the subcategories into which a variable can be divided. Unless you are not planning to use answers to some of the questions, you should have a frequency distribution for all the variables. Each variable can be specified either separately or collectively in the frame of analysis. To illustrate, they are identified here separately by the names used in the code book. For example, the frame of analysis should include frequency distributions for the following variables:

- → AGE;
- → MS;
- → TEDU (TEDU1, TEDU2, TEDU3 – multiple responses, to be collectively analysed);
- → STUDY (STUDY1, STUDY2, STUDY 3 – multiple responses, to be collectively analysed);
- → DIFWK (DIFWK1, DIFWK2, DIFWK3, DIFWK4, DIFWK5 – multiple responses, to be collectively analysed);
- → JOBSTA, JOBSTB;
- → JOBSATA, JOBSATB;
- → MOTIVA, MOTIVB.
- → etc.

Frequency distribution: The frequency distribution is a statistical procedure in quantitative research that can be applied to any variable that is measured on any one of the four measurement scales. It groups respondents into the subcategories in which a variable has been measured or coded.

Cross-tabulations

Cross-tabulations analyse two variables, usually independent and dependent or attribute and dependent, to determine if there is a relationship between them. The subcategories of both the variables are cross-tabulated to ascertain if a relationship exists between them. Usually, the absolute number of respondents in each cell, and the row and column percentages, give you a reasonably good idea as to the possible association.

In the study we cited as an example in this chapter, one of the main variables to be explained is the level of satisfaction with jobs before and after redeployment. We developed two indices of satisfaction:

1   satisfaction with the job before redeployment (JOBSATB);
2   satisfaction with the job after redeployment (JOBSATA).

Differences in the level of satisfaction can be affected by a number of personal attributes such as the age, education, training and marital status of the respondents. Cross-tabulations help to identify which attributes affect the levels of satisfaction. Theoretically, it is possible to correlate any variables, but it is advisable to be selective or an enormous number of tables will result. Normally only those variables that you think have an effect on the dependent variable should be correlated. The following cross-tabulations are an example of the basis of a frame of analysis: JOBSATA and JOBSATB by AGE, MS, TEDU, STUDY and DIFWK (these determine whether job satisfaction before and after redeployment is affected by age, marital status, education, and so on); and JOBSATA by JOBSATB (this will reveal whether there is a relationship between job satisfaction before and after redeployment). You can specify as many variables as you want.

Cross-tabulation: A statistical procedure that analyses two variables, usually independent and dependent or attribute and dependent, to determine if there is a relationship between them. The subcategories of both the variables are cross-tabulated to ascertain if a relationship exists between them.

Reconstructing the main concepts

There may be places in a research instrument where you look for answers through a number of questions about different aspects of the same issue, for example the level of satisfaction with jobs before and after redeployment (JOBSATB and JOBSATA). In the questionnaire there were 10 aspects of a job about which respondents were asked to identify their level of satisfaction before and after redeployment. The level of satisfaction may vary from aspect to aspect. Though it is important to know respondents' reactions to each aspect, it is equally important to gauge an overall index of their satisfaction. You must therefore decide, before you actually analyse data, how you will combine responses to different questions.

In this example the respondents indicated their level of satisfaction by selecting one of the five response categories. A satisfaction index was developed by assigning a numerical value to the response given by a respondent. The numerical values corresponding to the categories ticked were added to determine the satisfaction index. The satisfaction index score for a respondent varies between 10 and 50. The interpretation of the score is dependent upon the way the numerical values are assigned. In this example the higher the score, the higher the level of satisfaction.

Statistical procedures

CHECKPOINT
Quantitative analysis

In this section you should list the statistical procedures that you want to subject your data to. You should identify the procedures followed by the list of variables that will be subjected to those procedures – for example, regression analysis (JOBSATA on JOBSATB); multiple regression analysis (JOBSATA on AGE, EDUCATION and MS; JOBSATB on AGE, EDUCATION and MS); and analysis of variance. Similarly, it may be necessary to think about and specify the different variables to be subjected to the various statistical procedures. There are a number of user-friendly programs such as SPSS and SAS that you can easily learn.

Analysing quantitative data manually

Coded data can be analysed manually or with the help of a computer. If the number of respondents is reasonably small, there are not many variables to analyse, and you neither are familiar with a relevant computer program nor wish to learn one, you can analyse the data manually. However, manual analysis is useful only for calculating frequencies and for simple cross-tabulations. If you have not entered data into a computer but want to carry out statistical tests, they will have to be calculated manually, which may become extremely difficult and time-consuming. However, the use of statistics depends upon your expertise and desire/need to communicate the findings in a certain way.

Be aware that manual analysis is extremely time-consuming. The easiest way to analyse data manually is to code it directly onto large graph paper in columns in the same way as you would enter it into a computer. On the graph paper you do not need to worry about the column number. Detailed headings can be used or question numbers can be written on each column to code information about the question (Figure 15.8).

To analyse data manually (frequency distributions), count various codes in a column and then decode them. For example, in Figure 15.8, the age of two respondents is coded 6 and one is coded 5. This shows that out of the three respondents, one was between 40 and 44 years of age and the other two were between 45 and 49. Similarly, responses for each variable can be analysed. For cross-tabulations two columns must be read simultaneously to analyse responses in relation to each other.

ID	Age	MS	Education			Study area			Difference in work					Status		Satisfaction	
			1	2	3	1	2	3	1	2	3	4	6	Before	After	Before	After
03	6	4	3	8	8	09	88	88	22	69	77	78	38	5	4	5	4
59	6	1	3	8	8	01	88	88	03	18	77	88	88	2	4	3	4
81	5	1	2	8	8	13	88	88	17	01	88	88	88	2	3	2	4

Figure 15.8   Manual analysis using graph paper

If you want to analyse data using a computer, you should be familiar with the appropriate program. You should know how to create a data file, how to use the procedures involved, what statistical tests to apply and how to interpret them. Obviously in this area knowledge of computers and statistics plays an important role.

DATA PROCESSING IN QUALITATIVE STUDIES

How you process and analyse data in a qualitative study depends upon how you plan to communicate the findings. Broadly, there are three ways in which you can write about your findings in qualitative research:

1   developing a narrative to describe a situation, episode, event or instance;
2   identifying the main themes that emerge from your field notes or transcription of your in-depth interviews and writing about them, quoting extensively verbatim; and
3   in addition to (2) above, also quantifying, by indicating their frequency of occurrence, the main themes in order to provide their prevalence.

Editing, as understood for quantitative studies, is inappropriate for qualitative research. However, it is possible that you may be able to go through your notes to identify if something does not make sense. In such an event, you may be able to recall the context and correct the contents, but be careful in doing so as inability to recall precisely may introduce inaccuracies (due to recall error) in your description. Another way of ensuring whether you are truly reflecting the situation is to transcribe the interviews or observational notes and share them with the respondents or research participants for confirmation and approval. Validation of the information by a respondent is an important aspect of ensuring the accuracy of data collected through unstructured interviews.

For writing in narrative form there is no analysis per se; however, you need to think through the sequence in which you need or want to narrate. For the other two ways of writing about the findings, you need to go through content analysis, as mentioned earlier. Content analysis means analysing the contents of interviews or observational field notes in order to identify the main themes that emerge from the responses given by your respondents or the observation notes made by you. This process involves a number of steps:

↘   STEP ONE **Identify the main themes**. You need to carefully go through descriptive responses given by your respondents to each question in order to understand the meaning they communicate. From these responses you develop broad themes that reflect these meanings. You will notice that people use different words and language to express themselves. It is important for you to select the wording of your themes in a way that accurately represents the meaning of the responses categorised under a theme. These themes become the basis for analysing the text of unstructured interviews. Similarly, you need to go through your field notes to identify the main themes.

Recall error: Error that can be introduced in a response because of a respondent's inability to recall its various aspects correctly.

402

STEP TWO **Assign codes to the main themes**. Whether or not you assign a code to a main theme is dependent upon whether or not you want to count the number of times a theme has occurred in an interview. If you decide to count these themes you should, at random, select a few responses to an open-ended question or from your observational or discussion notes and identify the main themes. You continue to identify these themes from the same question till you have reached saturation point. Write these themes and assign a code to each of them, using numbers or keywords, otherwise just identify the main themes.

STEP THREE **Classify responses under the main themes**. Having identified the themes, the next step is to go through the transcripts of all your interviews or your notes and classify the responses or contents of the notes under the different themes. You can also use a computer program such as NVivo, ATLAS.ti or MAXQDA for undertaking this thematic analysis. You will benefit from learning one of these programs if your data is suitable for such analysis.

STEP FOUR **Integrate themes and responses into the text of your report**. Having identified responses that fall within different themes, the next step is to integrate them into the text of your report. How you do so is mainly your choice. Some people, while discussing the main themes that emerged from their study, use verbatim responses to keep the 'feel' of the responses. Others count how frequently a theme has occurred, and then provide a sample of the responses. It entirely depends upon the way you want to communicate the findings to your readers.

CHECKPOINT
Qualitative analysis

Content analysis in qualitative research – an example

The above four-step process was applied to a study recently carried out by the author to develop an operational service model, based upon the principle of family engagement. The information was predominantly gathered through in-depth and focus group discussions with clients, service providers and service managers. After informal talks with a number of stakeholders, a list of possible issues was drawn up to form the basis of discussions in these in-depth interviews and group discussions. The list was merely a guiding framework and was open to inclusion of any new issue that emerged during the discussions. Out of the several issues that were identified to examine various aspects of the model, here the author has taken only one to show the process of identifying themes that emerged. Note that these themes have not been quantified. They are substantiated by verbatims, which is one of the main differences between qualitative and quantitative research. The following example shows perceived strengths of the family engagement model (FEM) as identified by the stakeholders during in-depth interviews and focus groups. Information provided in Figure 15.8 serves as an example of the outcome of this process.

DEVELOPING THEMES THROUGH CONTENT ANALYSIS

PERCEIVED STRENGTHS OF THE MODEL

The framework developed for the perceived strengths of the model is based upon the analysis of the information gathered, which suggested that the various themes that emerged during the data collection stage reflecting strengths of the model can be classified under four perspectives. The following diagram shows the framework that emerged from the analysis.

PERCEIVED STRENGTHS FROM THE PERSPECTIVE OF THE FAMILY

This section details the perceived strengths of the model from the perspective of the family. Keep in mind that the sequential order of the perceived strengths is random and does not reflect any order or preference. Also, the naming of these themes is that of the author, which to the best of his knowledge captured the 'meanings' of the intentions of the research participants.

Empowerment of families

Almost everyone expressed the opinion that one of the main strengths of the model is that it empowers families and clients to deal with their own problems. The model provides an opportunity to families to express their feelings about issues of concern to them and, to some extent, to take control of their situations themselves. It seems that in 'preparing a plan for a child under this model, the family of the child will play an extremely important role in deciding about the future of the child, which is the greatest strength of the model'. One of the respondents expressed his/her opinion as follows:

> Oh, the family engagement model actually gives the power back to the family but with the bottom line in place, like the Department's bottom lines, they have to meet them. Oh ... the old model would have been black and white; kids remain in Mum's care, he [the father] would have supervised contacts with kids and it all would have been set up ... the family engagement model was about pulling them in the whole family then coming up with the solutions as long as they reach the Department's bottom line. They actually have to come up and nominate what they were willing to do ... He [the father] returned home, which was much better ... If they have relapse we bring them back in and we talk about it, get them back on track, make sure they were engaging with the services ... In the old method, kids just would have been removed and kids would have gone into the Department's care ... It is more empowering to the family, and it is much easier to work with the family at that level than you are standing over and telling them that you have to do this and this, and holding it against them that if you do not do, well, the kids are out. It is much, much better for the families. You've got more opportunity to work with the family at that level, rather than being on the outside dictating.

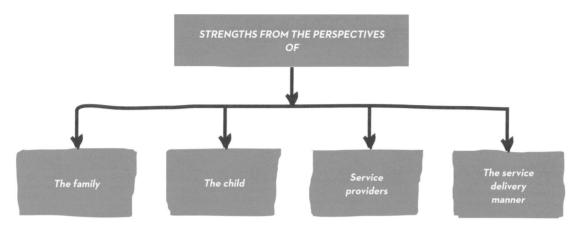

Different perspectives classifying perceived strengths of the model.

Another participant said:

> I think this model empowers the family a lot more … you are having meetings all the time. You give them the bottom line, and they develop their own strategy … I think it empowers the family when they come back … because they are developing their plan, they are using their own network and resources … I think it is empowering.

Yet, according to another respondent: 'it allows them to feel that they can make some decisions … They are able to work with the Department and that their voices or views are as valid as the Department's.'

Building of capacity of families

Another advantage that came out of the discussions is that the process adopted as a part of the FEM makes clients aware of community resources which, in turn, help them to build their capacity to deal with a situation effectively and independently. As one participant pointed out:

> They know that, ok, if something goes wrong in this aspect of their life, they know they can go there for support, they do not need to be calling us … they may have resolved their own issues … that is really empowering.

Another participant said: 'under this model, a family has taken a much stronger role in bringing about change as compared to the case conference approach.'

Acknowledgement of positives in families

One of the strengths of the approach is that it acknowledges the strengths of families. The model is primarily based upon designing interventions based on the strengths and positives of a situation rather than on the negatives. 'In the old model the strengths were not acknowledged to a large degree and certainly not of the parents.' During one of the focus groups, a participant expressed the view that:

> The family engagement model starts with the strengths of the family, so bringing the family in at an earlier stage, and trying to get them to help make decisions about what is going to happen to children who are in crisis … so … it is involving more people, their extended family, and getting them to come up with a plan.

In another focus group, a respondent said:

> It is only because you actually do work with that strength-based approach and you acknowledge it. It is a huge part of what happens. You can actually say to somebody that you are doing so well, it is great to see the change in you, and even though you personally have nothing to do with those changes, you say, well done … it is so good to see you looking so well … You get to a point in a process where you are no longer seen as an outsider, you are no longer seen as a prescriptive organisation, but you are seen as a supportive organisation which is actually assisting that person in the process … This Department has not been good in acknowledging change, we have not been.

Collaborative decision making and solutions

Another strength pointed out by many is that solutions pertaining to a child are now developed in close collaboration with the family, extended family and other appropriate stakeholders, which makes them (decisions and solutions) more acceptable and workable. In one of the focus group interviews a participant expressed this strength of the model as follows:

> They come up with answers, they got it. You are up front with the family. It gives the family a very clear idea what exactly is expected of them … this is what they have done, what are the concerns of the Department … So by having family support meetings, you are telling the family this is what we feel is happening with the child and these are the things that cannot happen to your children, what we intend to do about it in the future to be able to have them back or to improve their environment … it is straight in front of them, not behind their back … Previously I know of a case where a family was not involved in any of the discussions and they did not understand why their children were removed from them.

Many participants felt very positive about this collaborative approach. They felt that 'having a family support meeting clearly tells them what has happened, what are the intentions of the Department, and how the Department is going to work with them'. Another participant in one of the focus group discussions added:

> There are differences between how the meetings are held but, I guess, oh, sometimes to get the family to develop, and remind them of the bottom line, rather than us saying, 'This is what I want to happen'. I mean, obviously in the

406

discussion of the general situation, you make things clear, but you let the family take the responsibility to develop their own plan.

A respondent in an in-depth interview expressed the opinion that, now, 'We are identifying the members of the extended family. Once upon-a-time we just had parents; now you have to go around and search and get them all together to make a decision.'

Yet another respondent, talking about the strengths of the model, said 'now we approach very differently'. According to him/her:

> We inform you, we advise you, that the children are at risk ... whatever with the children, we want to sit down and work with you. Throughout this process we want to work with you, and also, plans have been set up. We want you to be a part of that.

It appears that, under this model, decisions are made not by a single individual, but by all those involved. According to one respondent, 'you are sharing responsibility with other agencies and family members; it is not only your decision, it is the decision of everybody'.

Keeps families intact

Some respondents also felt, that in certain cases, 'The children may not even be taken from the family so quickly'. It seems there is a greater attempt to keep the children in the family. One participant said: 'I am actually working with quite a few kids where they are trying to keep the family together.' Another participant added that 'The apprehension rate has come down substantially'.

PERCEIVED STRENGTHS FROM THE PERSPECTIVE OF THE CHILD

A greater focus on children

Many family workers as well as team leaders felt that the whole approach is a lot more focused on children. The approach is child centred and, at every step, concerns for children form the core of an intervention: 'it is a lot more child-focused as well. Rather than focusing on the parents, it is focusing on how we are going to make this child safe, and how we are going to achieve that.'

Returns children to their parents quicker

Some respondents felt that the new approach helped children to get back to their parents quicker. In one of the focus group discussions, one participant said:

> I think it gets the children back to their parents quicker because at the meeting it identifies strong people in the family that can support the parents to keep their kids. So what I found in the office is that some of the kids get back to their parents quicker than through the Case Conference. The Case Conference is every year ...

what the families have to jump through by the end of the twelve months at the next meeting ... here it is none of that. It is a strong person, how you are going to support the Mum to keep getting the kids back ... what you do need ... sometimes the kids go back, just like that.

Prevention of removal of children

Some respondents felt that the model actually prevented kids from being removed from their families. According to one participant, 'that is the big advantage of this model; to prevent kids from being removed'.

PERCEIVED STRENGTHS FROM THE PERSPECTIVE OF SERVICE PROVIDERS

Greater job satisfaction

Almost every service provider said that their work after the introduction of the model had become 'much more satisfying' because 'it is enabling workers and clients'.

Easier for the workers to work under the model

Many respondents felt that 'initially it is more work for a worker but, in the long run, it is less work because of the shared responsibility'. According to one participant:

> As a case worker, I remember the days when I had to really work so hard to meet so many people and do so many things individually and all the responsibility was on my shoulders ... but now there is a shared responsibility ... you have to do the ground work but when it is done the long term engagement is easier because there are more people involved and they in part make the decisions.

Decline in hostility towards the Department

Another advantage that some respondents pointed out was a decline in hostility among families towards the Department. It was pointed out that though it depended upon the circumstances, there was a feeling that, on the whole, hostility among clients towards the Department had declined. They also felt that though, in the beginning, there might have been hostility, working under the new model, in most situations, made that hostility disappear. In some situations, an increase in hostility was possibly attributable to a situation such as the apprehension of a child. Most respondents were of the opinion that, as compared to the Case Management model, they had experienced far less hostility towards them while working under the new approach.

Increased trust in the staff by clients

Another advantage some workers saw in the new approach was that they felt that clients had started trusting them a lot more. A participant in one of the focus groups described his/her feelings as follows:

They call us now, I do not have to go and look for them. They are calling me now and asking what is this?... which means they are taking an interest. They are not sitting back and saying, oh well, they are going to tell us or not tell us.

Better rapport with families

Because of the increased number of contacts, it appears that staff were able to build more congenial and trusting relationships with families. In a focus group, one of the respondents said, 'I think the relationship is more respectful and trustful'. Another respondent said:

Family relationships are a little bit better, and a family also understands that a DCD worker is not someone who goes to homes and removes their children ... how horrible people we are, but, by interacting with them they actually understand that we are people at work, and that we are not going to do these things, that is the old way of doing. We are not going to remove a child without saying anything. We have communication with them.

Develops better understanding by workers of the family dynamics

'One of the strengths that I have seen is that it allows the social worker to feel the family dynamics, to think about the dynamics and it allows the families to participate in whatever they want to', said a participant of a focus group.

Fewer aggressive clients

Another obvious difference between the two models, according to some respondents, was fewer aggressive clients. One respondent said:

There are far less aggressive clients here as compared to other places. I think it is partly because of the approach. Here you very rarely see people who get agitated, it is much more controlled, and it is a calmer atmosphere.

Develops a sense of ownership of a case

One of the advantages of the FEM as pointed out by various respondents was that under the model, 'you feel the case belongs to you; you "own" a child'. Because of this, according to some participants, there was a greater affiliation between the family worker and the child.

Greater community interaction

Another advantage pointed out by family workers was that the model resulted in their having a greater interaction with community agencies and, consequently, had more knowledge of their community and the services available in it. This was primarily because of restructuring under the family engagement model whereby family workers were allocated particular geographical areas, called, 'patches': 'you also develop really nice working relations with those people. You are working together collaboratively towards the goals, and I think, that is really a great benefit', said one participant. There was 'a lot more linking with other agencies' under the model. Not only was the interaction between community agencies increased but, it appears, clients had also started making more use of community agencies.

Greater knowledge about community members

Another benefit of working under the FEM and within a 'patch' was that family workers got to know a lot more community members. According to one respondent, 'The relationship with people in your community is much stronger and widespread'. Another respondent said:

> After a certain time you get to know who lives on what street, family links between people, especially, when you are working with Aboriginal families. Family links are so important, and knowing who is dealing with whom ... knowing who is in the area, what resources you have, makes your job a lot more effective.

Greater control over personal values by workers

Another advantage identified by some respondents was that, with the new model, 'case workers own values and morals cannot be imposed'.

PERCEIVED STRENGTHS FROM THE PERSPECTIVE OF THE SERVICE DELIVERY MANNER

An open, honest and transparent process

The whole process is open to all stakeholders. 'All the cards are on the table', said one participant, and another expressed the opinion that: 'The case worker may be honest, but, I guess, the process, how it was done, was not.' One respondent said that one of the good things about this model was that 'everyone knows what is going on'. According to a respondent:

> Another good thing about these family meetings is that there is the parents, there is the family. The parents might have been telling us one thing or a part of the story and Jaime, another part of the story, not telling Uncle Jimmy ... so it is good in a way that everyone knows what is going on. The whole information is there for everyone that is there. So they cannot push it to us and push it to the family. That is another good thing: they all get the same information, and we get and give the same information to them ... and it is amazing the plan they want to come up with ... it is based upon the information given to them.

Another respondent in a focus group said:

> And you are actually fighting the parents about the guardianship of the child: at the end of the day that is what you are doing, and, I think, just to have the transparent working relationship within the family engagement model actually makes that process a lot easier because everything is out in the open and when it comes up in the court, they are not going to be surprised.

Greater informality in meetings

Family meetings under the FEM are far less formal: 'The family members and others are encouraged to say whatever they want to. They can interrupt and stop the chairperson any time, if they disagree. They can even come back later.' 'What is important is that the minutes are written up, and the family gets a copy of the minutes so that they can go back home and read the minutes. They can come back to us.'

More frequent review of cases

Many people felt that the model provided an opportunity to review cases more frequently which helped them to achieve goals more quickly and, if an intervention was not working, it helped them to change the intervention. As one participant pointed out, 'Changes in the plan to reflect the changes in the family dynamics are undertaken frequently'. Hence, under the model, 'The plan for a child is continually being reviewed'. There seemed to be a lot more flexibility in terms of changing a plan under the model.

Increased honesty, transparency and accountability

Some respondents also felt that, because of the transparency and accountability of the process, simply working within the parameters of the model had helped to keep workers honest and accountable. According to one participant, 'From a practice viewpoint, it allows the social worker to be honest, accountable and to be transparent'.

A fairer approach

Many respondents felt that the FEM was fairer, as it was open, participatory and empowered a family.

Goals set for clients are more attainable and workable

According to one of the participants of a focus group: 'I think the plan of family engagement meetings is more attainable and more workable ... what they are actually capable of doing. We are not setting what they are not going to achieve, so they are not going to fail.' In addition, it seems, because families were involved in developing a plan, they had a feeling of ownership, and hence they attained the tasks set out in it. Another participant was of the opinion that: 'if you are a part of the solution, then you actually have an investment in making the change.'

Equality in relation to expression of opinion

Some respondents felt that the model provided freedom of expression to parties. All involved were free to express their opinions, and they were encouraged to share their views. As long as the bottom line was met, their opinions were taken into consideration in developing a strategy.

A less chaotic process

As one participant observed: 'it is far less chaotic, just the perception of what was going on. They [referring to workers in the CMM] felt a bit chaotic because work was coming in all the time and they were holding on to cases. Here it is more organised', one participant observed. With the old structure, 'case workers were very stressed; they were not operating particularly well'.

A less stressful approach

Many participants felt that the new approach was less stressful because of its many benefits. It was less stressful for them, and for families, as well as children. In one of the focus groups, a participant expressed his/her feeling in the following words:

> You do not feel that I hate to go to this home ... how are they going to react, what are they going to say to me, or how should I leave or how should I protect myself? You do not have to have those stresses now; it is a calmer situation, it is a happier situation and that is good for the kids, not only for us, but for the kids ... it is actually the kids who also benefit from the approach.

Fewer conflicts with families

Many respondents felt that ongoing conflicts with families were far fewer after the introduction of the new model.

Equality regarding choice of a facilitator for meetings

Another strength was that some participants thought that under the new model facilitation work was not only confined to case managers. Under the model, anyone could become a facilitator.

Increased reflection on practice

Some people also felt that the model provided an opportunity to reflect on practice, thus helping them to improve it.

Total responsibility for cases

Some also pointed out that workers have the total responsibility for cases which seemed to be much better from a number of viewpoints. As pointed out by one person, 'under the model, a field worker is responsible for the total intervention, from A to Z. You do everything in a patch.'

Compliance with government's child placement policy

One of the participants pointed out that the model actually complied with the government's legislative obligation to place Aboriginal and Torres Strait Islander children with their families. According to this participant:

> The model actually meets, for Aboriginal and Torres Strait Islanders child placement principle which is now enshrined in our legislation, where it actually states that children will be placed with family, extended family, immediate community and extended community and a non-Aboriginal person is a last resort ... So this model actually meets that.

DATA ANALYSIS IN MIXED METHODS STUDIES

In mixed methods studies you need to combine a number of data analysis procedures depending upon the way data was collected and the way you want to communicate your findings. Suppose you are interested in finding out the changes in the number of tourists coming to an area or country and how do they feel about their visit. To do so you might collect data either from secondary sources, that is from the records kept by, say, the Department of Immigration, or through cross-sectional surveys over a period of time to provide information on the number of tourists coming in a year. By analysing these numbers you can estimate the change in the number of tourists over a period of time. This type of analysis that helps you to study the trend in the number of students is quantitative in nature. Further, suppose you found out about their attitudes towards the facilities and stay in the area from some respondents through in-depth interviewing. The data collected through in-depth interviewing can be better subjected to content analysis which is qualitative in nature. In mixed/multiple methods studies, as you use two or more methods either belonging to the same or different research paradigms, mostly the methods used in data collection and your intention about the way you want to communicate your findings determine the way the data should be analysed. If the data is collected by two methods which belong to the two paradigms, you need to use different methods for its analysis appropriate to the way the data was collected.

CHECKPOINT
Mixed methods analysis

THE ROLE OF STATISTICS AND COMPUTERS IN RESEARCH

The role of statistics in research is sometimes exaggerated as you do not have to have a sound statistical knowledge in the designing of a research study (though it may help indirectly). Knowledge of statistics plays a significant role only when you have collected the required information, adhering to the requirements of each operational step of the research process. Up to data collection the role of statistics is limited; it acquires its importance thereafter. This does not mean that without statistics you cannot conduct a research study. You can conduct a perfectly valid study without using any statistics. The use of statistics depends entirely upon the type of study you are conducting, how you want to communicate your findings, who are going to be your readership, the convention in your academic area (some departments place a lot of emphasis on the use of statistical procedures and others do not) and the requirements of your department. Once data is collected you encounter two questions:

1   How do I organise this data to understand it?
2   How to understand what the data means?

    In a way, the answer to the first question forms the basis for the answer to the second. Statistics can play a very important role in answering your research questions in such a manner that you are able to quantify, measure, place a level of confidence on the findings, assess the contribution each variable has made in bringing out change, measure the association and relationship between various variables, and help predict what is likely to happen in the light of current trends.

From individual responses, particularly if there are many, it becomes extremely difficult to understand the patterns in the data, so it is important for the data to be aggregated and summarised. It is in this process of aggregation and summarisation that the statistics play a very important role. Simple aggregations such as frequency distribution and cross-tabulation tables and some simple statistical measures such as percentages, means, standard deviations and coefficients of correlation can reduce the volume of data, making it easier to understand. In computing summary measures, it is possible that some information is lost, making it possible to misinterpret the findings. Hence, caution is required when interpreting data.

Statistics also play a vital role in understanding the relationship between variables, particularly when there are more than two. With experience, it is easy to 'read' the relationship between two variables from a table, but not to quantify this relationship. Statistics help you to ascertain the strength of a relationship. They confirm or contradict what you read from a piece of information, and provide an indication of the strength of the relationship and the level of confidence that can be placed in findings. When there are more than two variables, statistics are also helpful in understanding the interdependence between them and their contribution to a phenomenon or event.

Indirectly, knowledge of statistics helps you at each step of the research process. Knowledge of the problems associated with data analysis, the types of statistical test that can be applied to certain types of variable, and the calculation of summary statistics in relation to the measurement scale used play an important role in a research endeavour. However, you can also carry out a perfectly valid study without using any statistical procedures. This depends upon the objectives of your study.

Computers in research can play a very significant role in many ways. In the modern age you can hardly imagine anyone who is computer illiterate. Almost everyone would use a computer for word-processing. All your research activities, from writing a research proposal to completion of dissertation, can be typed and saved on a computer. You will often need to go through a number of drafts to incorporate the development of new thoughts and improvement of your written communication, and computers can help you make additional changes without redoing everything.

There are a number of statistical packages, such as IBM SPSS Statistics, SAS, and R, that will make it very easy for you to carry out simple or complex data analyses.

Another advantage of computers is in displaying your data the way you want and changing the presentation to better suit your written communication style. Most programmes can help you to present you data the way you want it with extreme ease.

It will pay you to learn the program(s) you are likely to use. In the long run it will save you a great deal of time and money.

SUMMARY

In this chapter you have learnt about data processing. Irrespective of the method of data collection, qualitative or quantitative, the information is called 'raw data' or simply 'data'. The processing of data includes all operations undertaken from collection to analysis either manually or by computer. Data processing in quantitative studies starts with editing, which is basically 'cleaning' your data. This is followed by coding, which entails developing a code book, pre-testing it, the actual coding and verifying the coded data. In this chapter we have provided a prototype for developing a code book, detailing descriptions of how to develop codes for open-ended and closed questions, and a step-by-step guide to coding data, taking an example from a survey. The chapter also includes detailed information about content analysis. An extended example of content analysis is provided. The chapter also deals with how to treat data for narrative and thematic styles of writing.

Though the development of a frame of analysis continues until you have finished the report, it helps immensely in data analysis to develop this before you begin analysing data. In the frame of analysis the type of analysis to be undertaken (e.g. frequency distribution, cross-tabulation, content analysis), and the statistical procedures to be applied, should be specified.

Computers primarily help by saving labour associated with analysing data manually. Their application in handling complicated statistical and mathematical procedures, word processing, displaying and graphic presentation of the data analysed saves time and increases speed. Statistics are desirable but not essential for a study. The extent of their application depends upon the purpose of the study. Statistics primarily help you to make sense of data, 'read' the data, explore relationships and the interdependence between variables, ascertain the magnitude of an existing relationship or interdependence and place confidence in your findings.

Now that you have read the full chapter...

CHECK YOUR UNDERSTANDING

- ☐ Do you understand the meaning and application of all of the keywords at the start of the chapter? If not, visit the online resources and use the glossary flashcards to get to grips with their definitions.

- ☐ In terms of data processing, what are the advantages and disadvantages of closed and open-ended questions?

- ☐ In undertaking content analysis for descriptive information, what considerations would you keep in mind when developing themes?

- ☐ Critically examine the applications of statistics with particular reference to quantitative and qualitative research.

- ☐ What procedures can you set in place to ensure the accuracy of the information obtained in both quantitative and qualitative studies?

APPLY IT TO YOUR OWN PROJECT

- ☐ Thinking of examples from your own area of study, consider the advantages and disadvantages of having used open-ended or closed questions when you come to process your data.

- ☐ Assess the role of statistics for a study in your area of interest.

CONFUSED?

THE ONLINE RESOURCES ARE HERE TO HELP YOU

 https://study.sagepub.com/kumar5e

CHECKPOINT: What steps can you take to improve the quality of your raw data? Watch this video.

CHECKPOINT: What does it mean to 'code' your data and create a code book? Read this journal article.

CHECKPOINT: How do you examine the responses and code the themes of your data? Watch this video.

CHECKPOINT: What are the most common types of quantitative data analysis software for social science research, and how do they compare? Visit this website.

CHECKPOINT: What is qualitative content analysis? Read this encyclopaedia entry.

CHECKPOINT: When might a mixed methods approach be appropriate? Visit this website.

NEED MORE GENERAL SUPPORT?

Get up to speed on key terms with *glossary flashcards* and test yourself on important concepts with *multiple choice questions*.

UP FOR A CHALLENGE?

THE ONLINE RESOURCES ARE HERE TO INSPIRE YOU

 https://study.sagepub.com/kumar5e

CHECKPOINT: How can you clean your data quickly and efficiently? Read this chapter.

CHECKPOINT: How do you determine which and how many codes to use for your data? Read this chapter.

CHECKPOINT: How can you ensure your analysis of your data's themes is in line with your research aims? Visit this website.

CHECKPOINT: How do you pick a statistical test that will work best for your data? Watch this video.

CHECKPOINT: How do you integrate qualitative data themes into your report? Visit this website.

CHECKPOINT: How do you synthesize qualitative and quantitative data in an integrated type of analysis? Visit this website.

READY TO WORK ON YOUR OWN PROJECT?

Start building a portfolio of your ideas with the exercise workbook and get support tailored to your specific assignment with the assessment toolkit.

DISPLAYING DATA

- step seven -
PROCESSING AND DISPLAYING DATA

Processing data	372
→ Displaying data	418

ESSENTIAL TERMS

You should be able to define these by the end of the chapter

↳ graph   ↳ table

BONUS TERMS

You will learn more about these by the end of the chapter

↳ area chart   ↳ line diagram
↳ bar diagram   ↳ pie chart
↳ bivariate   ↳ polygon
↳ cumulative frequency polygon   ↳ polyvariate
↳ data display   ↳ scattergram
↳ frequency graph   ↳ univariate

LEARNING OBJECTIVES

At the end of this chapter, you will be able to:

↳ Discuss methods of communicating and displaying analysed data in quantitative and qualitative research
↳ Describe the anatomy of a table and types of tables
↳ Identify different graphics presentations

METHODS OF COMMUNICATING AND
DISPLAYING ANALYSED DATA

Having analysed the data that you collected through either quantitative, qualitative or mixed/multiple method(s), the next task is to present your findings to your readers. The main purpose of using data display techniques is to make the findings easy and clear to understand, and to provide extensive and comprehensive information in a succinct and effective way. Broadly, there are two styles of writing in research: firstly, a descriptive and narrative style; and secondly, an analytical style with factual information incorporated in the text. The descriptive and narrative style is more prevalent in qualitative studies and the analytical in quantitative studies. However, in practice you may mix them if the data permits. The choice of a particular style should be determined primarily by the type of writing style the data gathered lends itself to, your impressions/knowledge of your likely readership's preference, your familiarity with research methodology and statistical procedures, your own writing style and your impression as to which style of writing would communicate the findings more effectively to the readership.

Because of the nature and purpose of investigation in qualitative research, text becomes the dominant and usually the sole mode of communication. In quantitative studies the text is very commonly combined with other forms of data display, the extent of which depends upon your familiarity with them, the purpose of the study and what you think would make it easier for your readership to understand the content and sustain their interest in it. Hence as a researcher it is entirely up to you to decide the best way of communicating your findings to your readers. Within these two approaches there are many ways of presenting information. If your readers are likely to be familiar with 'reading' data, you can use complicated methods of data display; if not, it is wise to keep to simple techniques.

Although there are many ways of displaying data, this chapter is limited to those more commonly used. There are many computer programs that can help you with this task. In this chapter we confine the communication and display of analysed data to the following four methods: text; tables; graphs; and statistical measures.

Text

Text is by far the most common method of communication in both quantitative and qualitative research studies, and perhaps the only method in the latter. It is, therefore, essential that you know how to communicate effectively, keeping in mind the level of understanding, interest in the topic and need for academic and scientific rigour of those for whom you are writing. Your style should strike a balance between academic and scientific rigour on the one hand, and attracting and sustaining the interest of your readers on the other. Of course, it goes without saying that a reasonable command of the language and clarity of thought are imperative for good communication.

Your writing should be thematic: that is, written around the various themes of your report; findings should be integrated into the literature citing references using an acceptable system of citation; your writing should follow a logical progression of thought; and the layout should be attractive and pleasing to the eye. Language, in terms of clarity and flow, plays an important role in communication. According to the Commonwealth of Australia *Style Manual* (2002: 49):

The language of well-written documents helps to communicate information effectively. Language is also the means by which writers create the tone or register of a publication and establish relationships with their readers. For these relationships to be productive, the language the writer uses must take full account of the diversity of knowledge, interests and sensitivities within the audience.

CHECKPOINT
Effective language

Tables

Structure

Other than text, tables are the most common method of presenting analysed data in quantitative studies. According to the *Chicago Manual of Style* (1993: 21), 'Tables offer a useful means of presenting large amounts of detailed information in a small space'. According to the Commonwealth of Australia *Style Manual* (2002: 46), 'tables can be a boon for readers. They can dramatically clarify text, provide visual relief, and serve as quick point of reference.' It is, therefore, essential for beginners to know about their structure and types. Figure 16.1 shows the structure of a table.

A table has five parts:

1. **Title** – This normally indicates the table number and describes the type of data the table contains. It is important to give each table its own number as you will need to refer to the tables when interpreting and discussing the data in the text of the report. The tables should be numbered sequentially as they appear in the text. The procedure for numbering tables is a personal choice. If you are writing an article, simply identifying tables by number is sufficient. In the case of a dissertation or a report, one way to identify a table is by the chapter number followed by the number of the table within the chapter – the procedure adopted in this book. The main advantage of this procedure is that if it becomes necessary to add or delete a table when revising the report, you only need to change the table numbers for that chapter rather than for the whole report.

   The description accompanying the table number must clearly specify the contents of that table. In the description identify the variables about which information is contained in the table, for example 'Respondents by age' or 'Attitudes towards uranium mining'. If a table contains information about two variables, the dependent variable should be identified first in the title, for example 'Attitudes towards uranium mining [dependent variable] by gender [independent variable]'.

2. Stub – The subcategories of a variable, listed at the head of each row (the left-hand column of the table). According to the *McGraw-Hill Style Manual* (Longyear 1983: 97), 'the stub, usually the first column on the left, lists the items about which information is provided in the horizontal rows to the right'. The *Chicago Manual of Style* (1993: 331) describes the **stub** as 'a vertical listing of categories or individuals about which information is given in the columns of the table'.

3. **Column headings** – The subcategories of a variable, listed along the top of the table. In univariate tables (tables displaying information about one variable) the column heading is usually the 'number of respondents' and/or the 'percentage of respondents' (Tables 16.1 and 16.2). In bivariate tables (tables displaying information about two variables) it is the subcategories of one of the variables displayed in the column headings (Table 16.3).

Tables: A useful way of presenting analysed data in a small space that brings clarity to the text and serves as a quick point of reference. There are different types of tables for data pertaining to one, two or more variables.

Stub: The stub is a part of the structure of a table. It is the subcategories of a variable, listed down the left-hand column of the table. Information about these subcategories is provided to the right of the stub.

423

4   **Body** – The cells housing the analysed data.

5   **Supplementary notes or footnotes** – There are four types of footnote: source notes; other general notes; notes on specific parts of the table; and notes on the level of probability (*Chicago Manual of Style* 1993: 333). If the data is taken from another source, you have an obligation to acknowledge this. The source should be identified at the bottom of the table, and labelled by the word 'source', as in Figure 16.1. Similarly, other explanatory notes should be added at the bottom of a table.

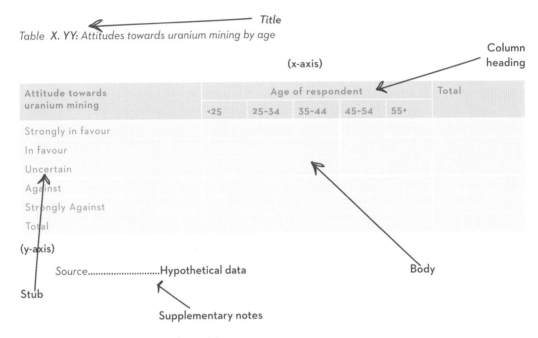

Figure 16.1   The structure of a table

Types of table

Depending upon the number of variables about which information is displayed, tables can be categorised as:

↝   univariate (also known as frequency tables) – containing information about one variable, for example Tables 16.1 and 16.2;

STEP SEVEN **PROCESSING AND DISPLAYING DATA**

- bivariate (also known as cross-tabulations) – containing information about two variables, for example Table 16.3; and
- polyvariate or multivariate – containing information about more than two variables, for example Table 16.4.

Table 16.1 Respondents by age (frequency table for one population – hypothetical data)

Age	No. of respondents
<20 years	2 (2.0)
20–24	12 (12.0)
25–29	22 (22.0)
30–34	14 (14.0)
35–39	17 (17.0)
40–44	10 (10.0)
45–49	11 (11.0)
50–54	9 (9.0)
55+	3 (3.0)
Total	100 (100.0)

Note: Figures in parentheses are percentages.

Table 16.2 Respondents by age (frequency table comparing two populations – hypothetical data)

Age	Population A	Population B
<20	2 (2.0)	1 (0.6)
20–24	12 (12.0)	17 (10.9)
25–29	22 (22.0)	23 (14.7)
30–34	14 (14.0)	18 (11.5)
35–39	17 (17.0)	26 (16.7)
40–44	10 (10.0)	16 (10.3)
45–49	11 (11.0)	18 (11.5)
50–54	9 (9.0)	27 (17.3)
55+	3 (3.0)	10 (6.4)
No response	0 (0.0)	0 (0.0)
Total	100 (100.0)	156 (100.0*)

Note: Figures in parentheses are percentages (*these sum to 99.9 due to rounding).

Table 16.3   Respondents by attitude towards uranium mining and age (cross-tabulation – hypothetical data)

Attitude towards uranium mining	Age					Total
	<25	25-34	35-44	45-54	55+	
Strongly in favour	(0.0)*	(5.5)	(14.8)	(35.0)	(100.0)	
	0	2	4	7	3	16
	(0.0)†	(12.5)†	(25.0)†	(43.6)†	(18.6)†	(100.0)†
	(0.0)*	(8.3)	(18.5)	(20.0)	(0.0)	
In favour	0	3	5	4	0	12
	(0.0)	(25.0)	(41.7)	(33.3)	(0.0)	(100.0)
	(0.0)*	(0.0)	(7.4)	(20.0)	(0.0)	
Uncertain	0	0	2	4	0	6
	(0.0)	(0.0)	(33.3)	(66.7)	(66.7)	(100.0)
	(14.3)*	(19.4)	(3.7)	(0.0)	(0.0)	
Against	2	7	1	0	0	10
	(20.0)	(70.0)	(10.0)	(0.0)	(0.0)	(100.0)
	(85.7)*	(66.7)	(55.6)	(25.0)	(0.0)	
Strongly against	12	24	15	5	0	56
	(21.4)	(42.9)	(26.8)	(8.9)	(0.0)	(100.0)
Total	(100.0)*	(100.0)	(100.0)	(100.0)	(100.0)	(100.0)
	14	36	27	20	3	100

* = column percentage;
† = row percentage.

Types of percentage

The abilities to interpret data accurately and to communicate findings effectively are important skills for a researcher. For accurate and effective interpretation of data, you may need to calculate measures such as percentages, cumulative percentages or ratios. It is also sometimes important to apply other statistical procedures to data. The use of percentages is a common procedure in the interpretation of data. There are three types of percentage: 'row', 'column' and 'total'. It is important to understand the relevance, interpretation and significance of each. Let us take some examples.

STEP SEVEN **PROCESSING AND DISPLAYING DATA**

Table 16.4   Attitude towards uranium mining by age and gender (hypothetical data)

Attitude towards uranium mining	Number of respondents												
	25		25-34		35-44		45-54		55+		Total		
	F	M	F	M	F	M	F	M	F	M	F	M	T
Strongly in favour	0	0	1	1	3	1	5	2	3	0	12	4	16
In favour	0	0	1	2	3	2	3	1	0	0	7	5	12
Uncertain	0	0	0	0	1	1	2	2	0	0	3	3	6
Against	1	1	4	3	1	0	0	0	0	0	6	4	10
Strongly against	4	8	17	7	8	7	2	3	0	0	31	25	56
Total	5	9	23	13	16	11	12	8	3	0	59	41	100

Tables 16.1 and 16.2 are univariate or frequency tables. In any univariate table, percentages calculate the magnitude of each subcategory of the variable out of a constant number (100). Such a table shows what would have been the expected number of respondents in each subcategory had there been 100 respondents. Percentages in a univariate table play a more important role when two or more samples or populations are being compared (Table 16.2). As the total number of respondents in each sample or population group normally varies, percentages enable you to standardise them against a fixed number (100). This standardisation against 100 enables you to compare the magnitude of the two populations within the different subcategories of a variable.

In a cross-tabulation such as in Table 16.3, the subcategories of both variables are examined in relation to each other. To make this table less congested, we have collapsed the age categories shown in Table 16.1. For such tables you can calculate three different types of percentage – row, column and total – as follows:

Row percentage – This is calculated from the total of *all* the subcategories of one variable that are displayed along a row in different columns, in relation to only *one* subcategory of the other variable. For example, in Table 16.3 figures in parentheses marked † are the **row percentages** calculated out of the total (16) of all age subcategories of the variable age in relation to only one subcategory of the second variable (i.e. those who are strongly in favour of uranium mining) – in other words, one subcategory of a variable displayed on the stub by all the subcategories of the variable displayed on the column heading of a table. Out of those who are strongly against uranium mining, 21.4 per cent are under the age of 25 years, none is above the age of 55 and the majority (42.9 per cent) are between 25 and 34 years of age (Table 16.3). This row percentage has thus given you the variation in terms of age among those who are strongly against uranium mining. It has shown how the 56 respondents who are strongly against uranium mining differ in age from one another. Similarly, you can select any other subcategory of the variable (attitude towards uranium mining) to examine its variation in relation to the other variable, age.

427

Row percentages: are calculated from the total of all the subcategories of one variable that are displayed along a row in different columns.

→ Column percentage – In the same way, you can hold age at a constant level and examine variations in attitude using **column percentages**. For example, suppose you want to find out differences in attitude among 25–34-year-olds towards uranium mining. The age category 25–34 (column) shows that of the 36 respondents, 24 (66.7 per cent) are strongly against while only 2 (5.5 per cent) are strongly in favour of uranium mining. You can do the same by taking any subcategory of the variable age, to examine differences with respect to the different subcategories of the other variable (attitudes towards uranium mining).

→ **Total percentage** – This standardises the magnitude of each cell; that is, it gives the per cent age of respondents who are classified in the subcategories of one variable in relation to the subcategories of the other variable. For example, what percentage of the total population is constituted by those who are under the age of 25 years and are strongly against uranium mining?

It is possible to sort data for three variables. Table 16.4 (percentages not shown) examines respondents' attitudes in relation to their age and gender. As you add more variables to a table it becomes more complicated to read and more difficult to interpret, but the procedure for interpreting it is the same.

The introduction of the third variable, gender, helps you to find out how the observed association between the two subcategories of the two variables, age and attitude, is distributed in relation to gender. In other words, it helps you to find out how many males and females constitute a particular cell showing the association between the other two variables (attitude towards uranium mining and age of the respondents). For example, Table 16.4 shows that of those who are strongly against uranium mining, 24 (42.9 per cent) are 25–34 years of age. This group comprises 17 (70.8 per cent) females and 7 (29.2 per cent) males. Hence, the table shows that a greater proportion of female than male respondents between the ages of 25 and 34 are strongly against uranium mining. Similarly, you can take any two subcategories of age and attitude and relate these to either subcategory (male/female) of the third variable, gender.

CHECKPOINT
Table designs

Graphs

Graphic presentations constitute the third way of communicating analysed data. Graphic presentations can make analysed data easier to understand and effectively communicate what it is supposed to show. One of the choices you need to make is whether a set of information is best presented as a table, a graph or text. The main objective of a graph is to present data in a way that is easy to interpret and interesting to look at. Your decision to use a graph should be based mainly on this consideration: 'A graph is based entirely on the tabled data and therefore can tell no story that cannot be learnt by inspecting a table. However, graphic representation often makes it easier to see the pertinent features of a set of data' (Minium 1978: 45).

Graphs can be constructed for every type of data – quantitative and qualitative – and for any type of variable (measured on a nominal, ordinal, interval or ratio scale). There are different types of graph, and your decision to use a particular type should be made on the basis of the measurement scale used in the measurement of a variable. It is equally important to keep in mind the measurement scale used in the measurement of a variable when it comes to interpretation. It is not uncommon to find people misinterpreting a graph and drawing wrong conclusions simply because they have overlooked the measurement scale used in the measurement of a variable.

The type of graph you choose depends upon the type of data you are displaying. For categorical variables you can construct only bar charts, histograms or pie charts, whereas for continuous variables, in addition to the above, line or trend graphs can also be constructed. The number of variables shown in a graph is also important in determining the type of graph you can construct.

When constructing a graph of any type it is important to bear the following points in mind:

→ A graphic presentation is constructed on two axes: horizontal and vertical. The horizontal axis is called the 'abscissa' or, more commonly, the x-axis, and the vertical axis is called the 'ordinate' or, more commonly, the y-axis (Minium 1978: 45).

→ If a graph is designed to display only one variable, it is customary, but not essential, to represent the subcategories of the variable along the x-axis and the frequency or count of each subcategory along the y-axis. The point where the axes intersect is considered as the zero point for the y-axis. When a graph presents two variables, one is displayed on each axis and the point where they intersect is considered as the starting or zero point.

→ A graph, like a table, should have a title that describes its contents. The axes should also be labelled.

→ A graph should be drawn to an appropriate scale. It is important to choose a scale that enables your graph to be neither too small nor too large, and your choice of scale for each axis should result in the spread of axes being roughly proportionate to one another. Sometimes, to fit the spread of the scale (when it is too spread out) on one or both axes, it is necessary to break the scale and alert readers by introducing a break (usually two slanting parallel lines) in the axes.

The histogram

A histogram consists of a series of rectangles drawn next to each other without any space between them, each representing the frequency of a category or subcategory (Figure 16.2). Their height is in proportion to the frequency they represent. The height of the rectangles may represent the absolute or proportional frequency or the percentage of the total. As mentioned, a histogram can be drawn for both categorical and continuous variables. When a histogram is based upon a continuous variable you can interpret the trend exhibited by it, but the same cannot be done if it is based on a categorical variable as you can arrange categorical variables in any order. Therefore when interpreting a histogram you need to take into account whether it is representing categorical or continuous variables. Figure 16.2 provides three examples of histograms using data from Tables 16.1 and 16.4. The histogram in Figure 16.2b is effectively the same as that in Figure 16.2a but is presented in a three-dimensional style.

The bar chart

The bar chart or bar diagram is used for displaying categorical data (Figure 16.3). A bar chart is identical to a histogram, except that in a bar chart the rectangles representing the various frequencies are spaced, thus indicating that

Histogram: A histogram is a graphic presentation of analysed data presented in the form of a series of rectangles drawn next to each other without any space between them, each representing the frequency of a category or subcategory.

Bar chart: The bar chart or diagram is one of the ways of graphically displaying categorical data. A bar chart is identical to a histogram, except that in a bar chart the rectangles representing the various frequencies are spaced, thus indicating that the data is categorical. The bar diagram is used for variables measured on nominal or ordinal scales.

the data is categorical. The bar chart is used for variables measured on nominal or ordinal scales. The discrete categories are usually displayed along the x-axis and the number or percentage of respondents on the y-axis. However, as illustrated, it is possible to display the discrete categories along the y-axis. The bar chart is an effective way of visually displaying the magnitude of each subcategory of a variable.

The stacked bar chart

Stacked bar chart: A stacked bar chart is similar to a bar chart except that in the former each bar shows information about two or more variables stacked onto each other vertically. The sections of a bar show the proportion of the variables they represent in relation to one another. Such a chart can be drawn only for categorical data.

A stacked bar chart is similar to a bar chart except that in the former each bar shows information about two or more variables stacked onto each other vertically (Figure 16.4). The sections of a bar show the proportion of the variables they represent in relation to one another. The stacked bars can be drawn only for categorical data.

The 100 per cent bar chart

100 per cent bar chart: The 100 per cent bar chart is very similar to the stacked bar chart. The only difference is that in the former the subcategories of a variable for a particular bar total 100 per cent and each bar is sliced into portions in relation to their proportion out of 100.

The 100 per cent bar chart (Figure 16.5) is very similar to the stacked bar chart. In this case, the subcategories of a variable are converted into percentages of the total population of the subcategory and drawn as a stacked bar chart. Each bar, which totals 100, is sliced into portions relative to the percentage of each subcategory of the variable.

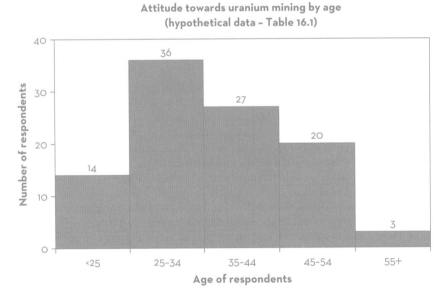

Figure 16.2a   Two-dimensional histogram

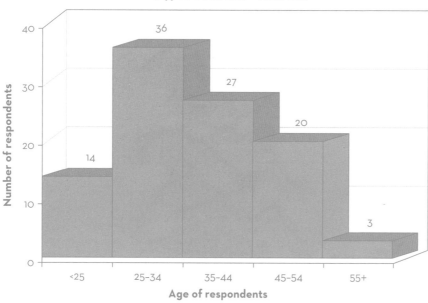

Attitude towards uranium mining by age
(hypothetical data – Table 16.1)

Figure 16.2b   Three-dimensional histogram

The frequency polygon

The frequency polygon is very similar to a histogram. A frequency polygon is drawn by joining the midpoint of each rectangle at a height commensurate with the frequency of that interval (Figure 16.6). However, there is one problem in constructing a frequency polygon, that is, what to do with the two categories at either extreme if they are open-ended (e.g. if one is less than 15 and the other over 60). How do we draw a trend line for these extremes? To overcome this you imagine that the two extreme categories have an interval similar to the rest and assume the frequency in these categories to be zero. From the midpoint of these intervals, you extend the polygon line to meet the x-axis at both ends. A frequency polygon can be drawn using either absolute or proportionate frequencies.

Frequency polygon: The frequency polygon is very similar to a histogram. A frequency polygon is drawn by joining the midpoint of each rectangle at a height commensurate with the frequency of that interval.

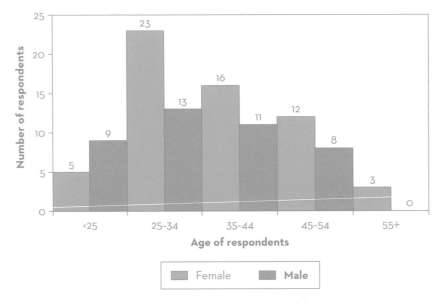

Attitude towards uranium mining by age and gender
(hypothetical data – Table 16.4)

Figure 16.2c   Two-dimensional histogram with two variables

The cumulative frequency polygon

The cumulative frequency polygon or cumulative frequency curve (Figure 16.7) is drawn on the basis of cumulative frequencies. The main difference between a frequency polygon and a cumulative frequency polygon is that the former is drawn by joining the midpoints of the intervals, whereas the latter is drawn by joining the end points of the intervals because cumulative frequencies interpret data in relation to the upper limit of an interval. As a cumulative frequency distribution tells you the number of observations less than a given value and is usually based upon grouped data, to interpret a frequency distribution the upper limit needs to be taken.

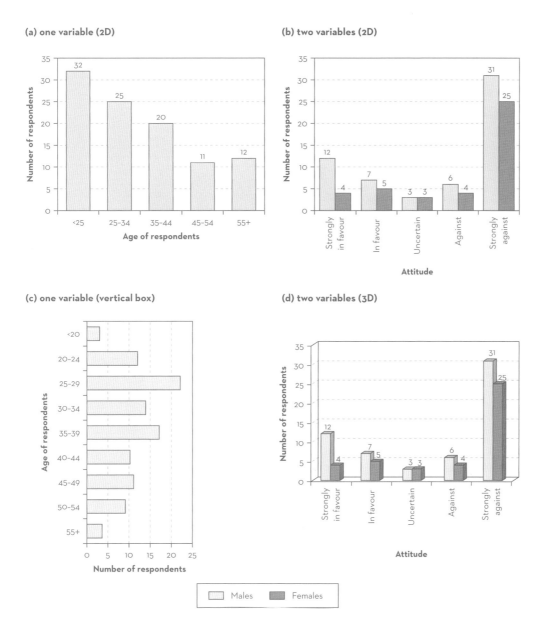

(a) one variable (2D)

(b) two variables (2D)

(c) one variable (vertical box)

(d) two variables (3D)

☐ Males   ■ Females

Figure 16.3   Different types of bar chart

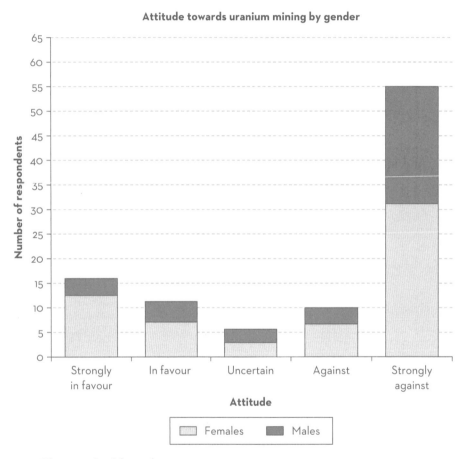

Figure 16.4   The stacked bar chart

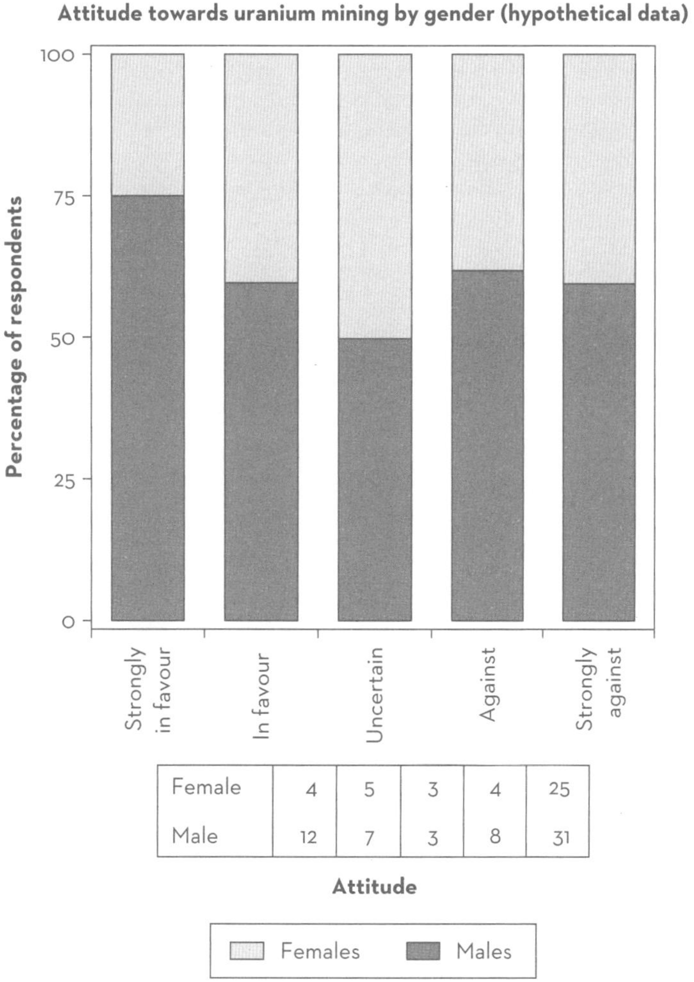

Attitude towards uranium mining by gender (hypothetical data)
Percentage of respondents
100
75
50
25
0
Strongly in favour
In favour
Uncertain
Against
Strongly against
Attitude
Females
Males

Female	4	5	3	4	25
Male	12	7	3	8	31

Figure 16.5 The 100 per cent bar chart

The stem-and-leaf display

The stem-and-leaf display is an effective, quick and simple way of displaying a frequency distribution (Figure 16.8). The stem-and-leaf diagram for a frequency distribution running into two digits is plotted by displaying digits 0 to 9 on the left of the y-axis, representing the tens of a frequency. The figures representing the units of a frequency (i.e. the right-hand figure of a two-digit frequency display) are displayed on the right of the y-axis. Note that the stem-and-leaf display does not use grouped data but absolute frequencies. If the display is rotated 90 degrees in an anti-clockwise direction, it effectively becomes a histogram. With this technique some of the descriptive statistics relating to the frequency distribution, such as the mean, the mode and the median, can easily be ascertained; however, the procedure for their calculation is beyond the scope of this book. Stem-and-leaf displays are also possible for frequencies running into three and four digits (hundreds and thousands).

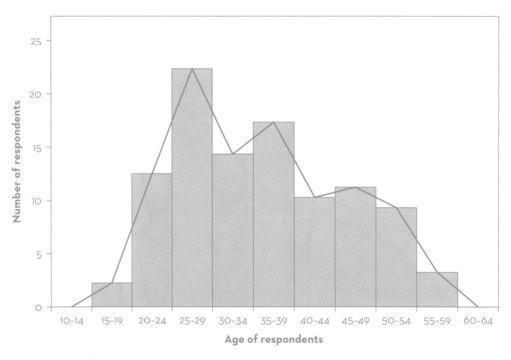

Figure 16.6   The frequency polygon

STEP SEVEN PROCESSING AND DISPLAYING DATA

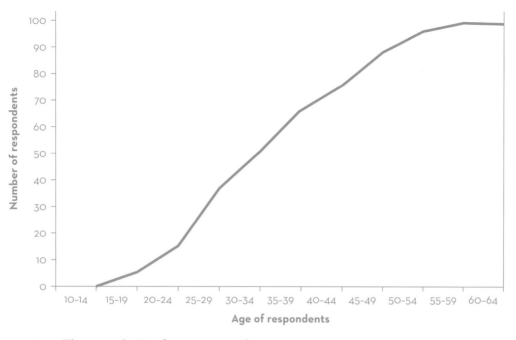

Figure 16.7   The cumulative frequency polygon

1	89
2	0001112222223344555556667777788899
3	00111222333333445555566677777889
4	112223333444555566779
5	000113355667

Figure 16.8   The stem-and-leaf display

The pie chart

The pie chart is another way of representing data graphically (Figure 16.9), this time as a circle. There are 360 degrees in a circle, and so the full circle can be used to represent 100 per cent, or the total population. The circle or pie is divided into sections in accordance with the magnitude of each subcategory, and so each slice is in proportion to the size of each subcategory of a frequency distribution. The proportions may be shown either as absolute numbers or as percentages. Manually, pie charts are more difficult to draw than other types of graph because of the difficulty in measuring the degrees of the pie/circle. They can be drawn for both qualitative data and variables measured on a continuous scale but grouped into categories.

The line diagram or trend curve

A set of data measured on a continuous interval or a ratio scale can be displayed using a line diagram or trend curve. A trend line can be drawn for data pertaining to both a specific time (e.g. 1995, 1996, 1997) or a period (e.g. 1985–1989, 1990–1994, 1995–). If it relates to a period, the midpoint of each interval at a height commensurate with each frequency – as in the case of a frequency polygon – is marked as a dot. These dots are then connected with straight lines to examine trends in a phenomenon. If the data pertains to exact time, a point is plotted at a height commensurate with the frequency. These points are then connected with straight lines. A line diagram is a useful way of visually conveying the changes when long-term trends in a phenomenon or situation need to be studied.

Pie chart: The pie chart is a way of representing data graphically. A full circle of 360 degrees can be used to represent 100 per cent or the total population. The circle is divided into sections in accordance with the magnitude of each subcategory comprising the total population. Hence each section is in proportion to the size of each subcategory of a frequency distribution.

Trend curve: A set of data measured on an interval or a ratio scale can be displayed using a line diagram or trend curve. A trend line can be drawn for data pertaining to both a specific time and a period. If it relates to a period, the midpoint of each interval at a height commensurate with each frequency is marked as a dot. These dots are then connected with straight lines to examine trends in a phenomenon. If the data pertains to an exact time, a point is plotted at a height commensurate with the frequency and a line is then drawn to examine the trend.

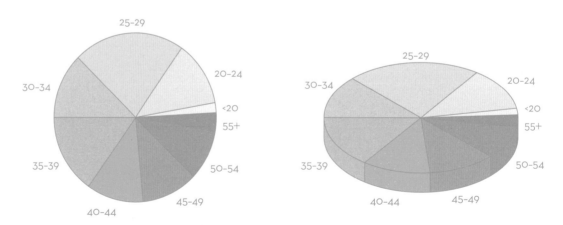

Respondents by age
Attitude towards uranium mining (hypothetical data)

Figure 16.9   Two- and three-dimensional pie charts

For example, Figure 16.10 clearly shows the trends in the number of current uses of methods for contraception over a period of five years among four study populations receiving four treatment modalities comprising different combinations of maternal and child health, nutritional supplements and family planning services. The same information could not have been depicted with such clarity by a table.

The area chart

For variables measured on an interval or a ratio scale, information about the subcategories of a variable can also be presented in the form of an area chart. This is plotted in the same way as a line diagram but with the area under each line shaded to highlight the total magnitude of the subcategory in relation to other subcategories. For example, Figure 16.11 shows the number of male and female respondents by age.

Area chart: For variables measured on an interval or a ratio scale, information about the subcategories of a variable can also be presented in the form of an area chart. This is plotted in the same way as a line diagram with the area under each line shaded to highlight the magnitude of the subcategory in relation to other subcategories. Thus an area chart displays the area under the curve in relation to the subcategories of a variable.

439

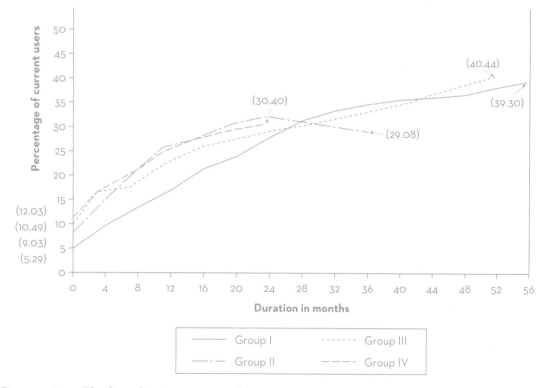

Figure 16.10 The line diagram or trend curve

When you want to show visually how one variable changes in relation to a change in the other variable, a scatter-gram is extremely effective. Both the variables must be measured either on interval or ratio scales and the data on both the variables needs to be available in absolute values for each observation – you cannot plot a scattergram for categorical variables. Data for both variables is taken in pairs and displayed as dots in relation to their values on both axes. Let us take the data on age and income for 10 respondents of a hypothetical study in Table 16.5. The relationship between age and income based upon hypothetical data is shown in Figure 16.12.

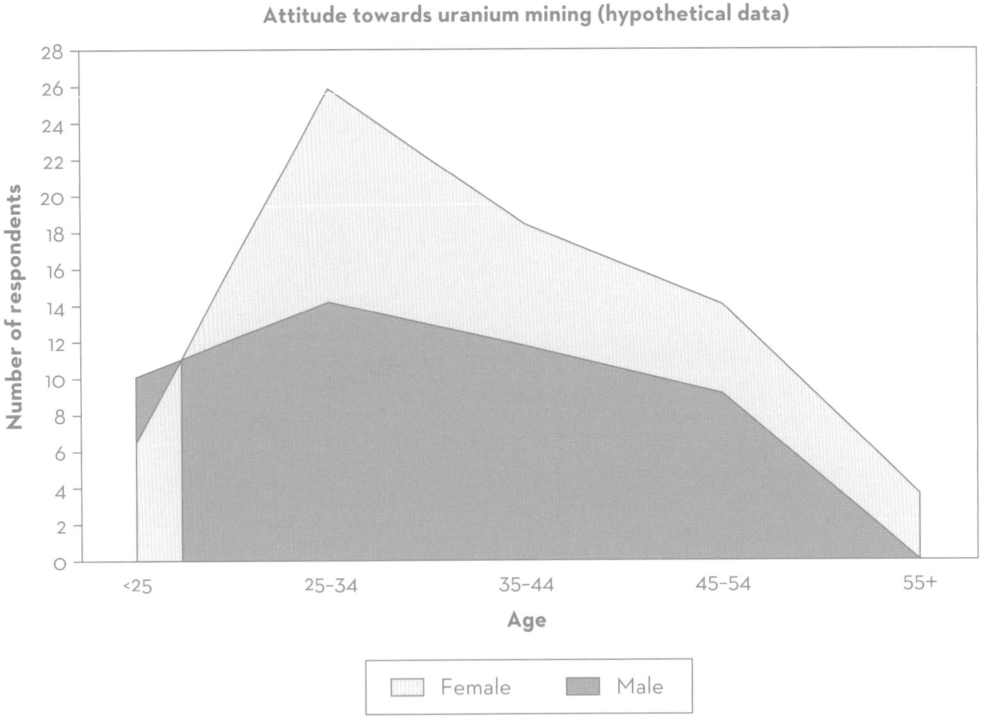

Scattergram: When you want to show graphically how one variable changes in relation to a change in another, a scattergram is extremely effective. For a scattergram, both the variables must be measured either on an interval or ratio scale and the data on both the variables needs to be available as absolute values for each observation. Data for both variables is taken in pairs and displayed as points in relation to their values on both axes. The resulting graph is known as a scattergram.

Figure 16.11   The area chart

Table 16.5   Age and income data

Respondent	Income	Age
A	25,500	24
B	46,000	50
C	30,500	36
D	55,000	45
E	27,000	29
F	35,000	38
G	40,000	37
H	52,000	48
I	47,000	41
J	38,000	47

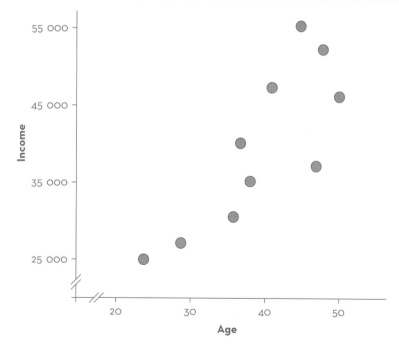

Figure 16.12   The scattergram

Statistical measures

CHECKPOINT
Graph designs

The importance of statistics in research, particularly in quantitative studies, is unquestionably immense. The role of statistics lies in first describing data in aggregated and summary form to enhance its understanding and meaning, to establish whether or not there is a relationship between two variables and, if so, to quantify the magnitude of the relationship. Placing a degree of confidence in the findings is another function of statistics. Many academic disciplines are extremely particular about the integration of statistics into research reports and place immense importance on the application of statistical measures to research findings.

The exclusion of statistics from this book is not an indication of the author's lack of appreciation for statistics, but of the difficulty in accommodating such a vast area in one text. Because of its vastness, the author thought it better for the reader to refer to texts specifically written on statistics.

Though statistical measures are extremely effective in communicating findings in a precise and succinct manner, you can conduct a perfectly valid study without using any statistical measure. However, their use in certain situations is desirable and in some it is essential.

There are many statistical measures, ranging from very simple to extremely complicated. At one end of the spectrum you have simple descriptive measures such as the mean, mode, median, and at the other there are inferential statistical measures such as analysis of variance, factorial analysis and multiple regressions.

CHECKPOINT
Exploring statistics

Because of its vastness, statistics is considered a separate academic discipline, and before you use these measures you need to learn about them.

Use of statistical measures is dependent upon the type of data collected, your knowledge of statistics, the purpose of communicating the findings and the knowledge base in statistics of your readership.

SUMMARY

Research findings in both quantitative and qualitative research are usually conveyed to readers through text. In qualitative research this is more or less the sole method of communication. However, in quantitative studies, though text is still the dominant method of communicating research findings, it is often combined with other forms such as tables, graphs and statistical measures, which can make the research easier to understand. What type of presentation use should be determined by what you feel comfortable with and what you think will be easiest for readers to understand. Tables have the advantage of containing a great deal of information in a small space, while graphs make it easy for readers to absorb information at a glance.

Usually, a table will have five parts: title, stub, column headings, body and supplementary notes or footnotes. Depending upon the number of variables about which information in a table is stored, there are three types of table: univariate (frequency), bivariate (cross-tabulation) and multivariate.

To interpret a table, simple arithmetic procedures such as percentages, cumulative frequencies or ratios can be used. You can also calculate simple descriptive statistical procedures such as the mean, the mode, the median, the chi-square test, the t-test and the coefficient of correlation. If you have statistical knowledge, advanced statistics can be applied.

Statistics are not included in this book for two reasons: to maintain a sharp focus on research study design; and because the vastness of the subject of statistics would have made this book difficult for beginners in research.

While there are many types of graphs, the common ones are: the histogram, the bar diagram, the stacked bar chart, the 100 per cent bar chart, the frequency polygon, the stem-and-leaf display, the pie chart, the line or trend diagram, the area chart and the scattergram. The choice among these depends upon your purpose and the measurement scale used to measure the variable(s) being displayed. Some graphs are difficult to draw by hand but can be readily done by computer.

Now that you have read the full chapter...

CHECK YOUR UNDERSTANDING

- ☐ Do you understand the meaning and application of all of the keywords at the start of the chapter? If not, visit the online resources and use the glossary flashcards to get to grips with their definitions.

- ☐ What are the different ways you can communicate your research findings?

- ☐ Ideally, a table has a number of parts. Explain them.

- ☐ What are the different types of percentage? What functions do they perform in data interpretation?

- ☐ What are the different types of graph? Discuss their application in relation to measurement scales.

- ☐ Identify two specific examples where you could use a table rather than just text to communicate findings and two examples where graphs would be better.

APPLY IT TO YOUR OWN PROJECT

- ☐ Construct a hypothetical bivariate table, within the context of an area of interest. Calculate different types of percentages and interpret the data

- ☐ Look at your discussion of your data. Where could you use a table rather than just text to communicate your findings? Where would a graph be better?

CONFUSED?

THE ONLINE RESOURCES ARE HERE TO HELP YOU

 https://study.sagepub.com/kumar5e ←

CHECKPOINT: How can you use language to present data in an engaging way? Visit this website.

CHECKPOINT: What do you need to consider to create an accurate and clear table? Visit this website.

CHECKPOINT: What software can help you with simple means of displaying your data graphically? Visit this website.

CHECKPOINT: Where can I find out about basic statistical principles? Visit this website.

NEED MORE GENERAL SUPPORT?

Get up to speed on key terms with *glossary flashcards* and test yourself on important concepts with *multiple choice questions*.

UP FOR A CHALLENGE?

THE ONLINE RESOURCES ARE HERE TO INSPIRE YOU

 https://study.sagepub.com/kumar5e

CHECKPOINT: How do you make your language more decisive and use it to present your results effectively? Visit this website.

CHECKPOINT: What are some examples of good and bad table designs? Watch this video.

CHECKPOINT: How do you choose a graph type that is well suited to your data? Read this chapter.

CHECKPOINT: Where can I get help if I need to know more about specific types of statistical methods? Visit this website.

READY TO WORK ON YOUR OWN PROJECT?

Start building a portfolio of your ideas with the exercise workbook and get support tailored to your specific assignment with the assessment toolkit.

EXERCISE VII: PROCESSING AND DISPLAYING DATA

Template of Exercise VII

When you have collected the relevant data for your study you need to process it, and that means preparing and then analysing the data. Finally you want to show what you have found in your study by presenting the results to answer the research question of the study. This exercise breaks this process down into operational steps for qualitative and quantitative studies.

This exercise breaks this process down into operational steps for qualitative and quantitative studies.

QUANTITATIVE STUDIES

STEP ONE Preparing data for analysis in quantitative studies

The following points can be used as a checklist:

1   Check your raw data for any inconsistencies, missing data and errors. You can make any changes (edit the data) if you are certain that you will not distort the data. It is best to examine the answers to one question/variable at a time or check the responses given to all the questions by one respondent at a time. If you electronically save your dataset always keep a copy of the raw data and a copy of your edited version which you will work with.

    Data cleaned ☐

2   In quantitative studies you also want to code your data by providing numbers for answer options in closed questions, e.g. the variable gender could be coded as males (1), females (2) and other (3). Numbers given to the categories have to be mutually exclusive for each variable. Remember each number stands for a value

or an information label. For open questions you can create categories and assign a different number to each category, for example you could put the actual age into age bands (20-24 is coded 1; 25-29 is coded 2; 30-34 is coded 3 and so on). For open text questions you may need to read through the responses provided by respondents to decide on the categories that will summarise the responses best.

3   It is suggested that you keep a code book detailing all variables and its codes as a reference. If you have a questionnaire you can number the questions and also write the number codes next to the tick boxes for each question. It could be that you have variables that have no categories or codes because you record a number for it (e.g. age in number of years).

    Code book created ☐

4   Variables can be measured in different scales. Which of your variables are:

    nominal scale (in discrete categories, e.g. male/female)?

    _____

    _____

    _____

    ordinal scale (categories that are in an order, e.g. income measured as above average/average/below average)?

    _____

    _____

    _____

Ratio or interval scale (e.g. age in years, or income in dollars)

----

5   When you are satisfied with your variable measures and code book you can code the data accordingly. For each participant record the codes for each question/variable. E.g. if participant number 1 is female and 29 years old, you would record gender: 2, age band: 2 (if using the codes introduced above).

The data can be coded manually or directly into a computer program such as Excel, SPSS or SAS. Typically each line of data will represent a participant or observation and the column will represent the question/variable.

Data coded ☐

1   Before you analyse your data, you need to decide on your analysis methods. Start by planning which variables will be analysed. List all variables you are planning to analyse and their answer options you have coded in the previous step:

----

2   Produce a frequency distribution of all variables listed above in nominal and ordinal scales. This provides for each variable how many responses were given for each subcategory and is best reported in counts (frequency) and percentages. (E.g. how many of your respondents were male and how many female? Is it a 50/50% split?)

Frequency distributions produced ☐

3   You may also want to describe data using means/median for interval scale variables (e.g. the average age of respondents). Describing two categorical variables can be done in a cross-tabulation (also see next step). Make a note of variables this applies to:

----

4   Typically you want to analyse two variables to understand the relationship between them and may have expressed this in your hypothesis. Make a list of the variable pairing you want to analyse and indicate the independent variable (the variable that has an effect on the other variable, e.g. gender) and the dependent variable (the actual data, e.g. job satisfaction measured as 1 – satisfied, 2 – not satisfied) for each pair.

----

5   It is recommended that you use a statistical program such as SPSS or SAS to analyse your data, but you need to decide on statistical procedures first. Select an appropriate statistical analysis (e.g. chi square, regression analysis, analysis of variance) that is suitable for your variables. Justify your choices and provide details before you carry the analysis.

STEP THREE Communication and displaying analysed data

1   **Text**: There are conventions on how to present statistical data depending on the procedure you have chosen. If you

decide to present your results using text describe the results in a clear manner by stating percentages or means. This is most effective if there are just two values to compare (e.g. 52% were female and 48% male).

2 **Tables** are the most common method to present numbers. The structure of the table includes a title (a clear description of what the table shows), the stub (the subcategories of the variable listed at the head of each row), the column headings (number of respondents/ percentages of respondents or subheadings of the second variable), the body (cells that display the analysed data) and optional footnotes (e.g. the source or general notes). Check list for your table:

☐ Includes all elements of a table outlined above
☐ Only numbers are presented in cells, headings explain the units
☐ Accurate data (a number typo could change the result drastically)
☐ Reader friendly and neatly formatted
☐ Includes a unique table number

3 **Graphs** can be used to visually show the analysed data. A graph often displays frequencies of one variable. There is a range of graphs to choose from depending on the data that should be displayed. The measurement scale is important for interpreting graphs but also on how it looks like in proportion to the two axes. Choose an appropriate scale and clearly label the two axes, typically the horizontal x-axis displays the subcategories of a variable and the vertical y-axis the number or percentage of respondents. The point where the axes intersect is the zero point for the y-axis. Check list for your graph:

☐ Appropriate graph for the data (e.g. bar chart) chosen
☐ Axes are labelled clearly
☐ Appropriate scale for axes chosen
☐ Colour and shading can be distinguished (consider optical effect and printing)

☐ Values are displayed for clarity (also consider vertical lines)
☐ The graph title summarises what the graph shows
☐ Unique graph number included to refer to in the text

QUALITATIVE STUDIES

STEP ONE Preparing data for analysis in qualitative studies

How you process and analyse data in a qualitative study depends upon how you plan to communicate the findings. For writing a narrative form you need to familiarise yourself with the data and decide on the sequence of the narration. However, if you decide to identify main themes that emerge from the data (which can also be quantified) you would typically transcribe audio recordings of interview, focus groups or observational field notes. In any case know your data as this may require reading the transcript several times.

How will you analyse your qualitative data?

☐ A: Developing a narrative to describe a particular situation/event/instance
☐ B: Identifying the main themes that emerge from the data
☐ C: In addition to identifying themes to also quantify the frequency of their occurrences

STEP TWO Identifying main themes

When deciding on identifying the main themes you need to organise and sort your data in a systematic way. Start by coding the transcript(s) in order to find new insights (the themes of the data). Read through the transcript and assign a descriptive label, a keyword or number to relevant sections of the text. To do this it is suggested you use different coloured highlighter pens and write in the margins of the transcript. Note that some text may be allocated to more than one description. Look for actions, relationships, emotion, ideas and meanings when coding. You may have to read through the transcripts several times, adding or collapsing codes each time. A question to ask during coding is: What is happening?

Assigned codes/descriptive labels to the text ☐

STEP THREE Assign codes to main themes

Next you need to assign codes to main themes. By reading through the codes you can attach meaning to the data and the codes can be analytical as well. What patterns, themes and trends can you see from the codes (you may want to count them too)? Now decide on themes by grouping codes. What information (code) contributed to the understanding of the themes? Each theme can have multiple layers or be seen from different perspectives. What are the main themes that emerged from the data and how did you derive at them? Write them down or alternatively draw a mind map.

Theme 1

Theme 2

Theme 3

Theme 4

STEP FOUR Classify your responses under the main themes

Having identified new ideas you need to support each theme with appropriate excerpts from the transcripts. Select relevant sections from the data to explain a certain aspect of the theme. Here you may draw on answers from different participants. Organising the data can be carried out using computer programs such as NVivo, ATLAS.ti or MAXQDA and this is advisable if you have large amounts of data (e.g. you interviewed many participants). Doing this manually you will search through all responses for relevant data quotes. Make sure you keep track of what you select and perhaps list relevant passages in a document for each theme.

Selected responses/quotes form the data for each theme

STEP FIVE Integrate themes and responses into the text of your report

Finally you have to report your findings (themes) in your report. Here you have some freedom to use narratives to explain what was found, verbatim quotes to support a particular point to say it in the words of the respondent. You can also count how frequently a theme has occurred and provide a sample of responses. It is suggested that your writing expresses the findings clearly and integrates them into the literature. Also keep the audience/reader in mind so that they can follow how you arrived at the new meanings and therefore answered the research question. To perfect this it may require several drafts.

Practise writing up themes/findings:

STEP EIGHT

WRITING A RESEARCH REPORT

WRITING A RESEARCH REPORT

- step eight -
WRITING A RESEARCH REPORT

This operational step includes one chapter:

→ **Writing a research report** 452

CONFUSED? UP FOR A CHALLENGE?

OR NEED HELP WITH YOUR ASSIGNMENT?

VISIT

https://study.sagepub.com/kumar5e for resources specially designed to support you and all your research needs.

ESSENTIAL TERMS

You should be able to define these by the end of the chapter

- outline
- referencing
- research report
- variable

BONUS TERMS

You will learn more about these by the end of the chapter

- association
- bibliography
- intellectual rigour
- non-spurious relationship
- spurious relationship
- verifiability

LEARNING OBJECTIVES

At the end of this chapter, you will be able to:

- Develop an outline of a research report
- Integrate the hard data into your report
- Write about variables
- Draw inferences and conclusions
- Use different referencing systems
- Create a bibliography

WRITING A RESEARCH REPORT

The last step in the research process is writing the research report. Each step of the process is important for a valid study, as negligence at any stage will affect the quality of not just that part but the whole study. This last step is the most crucial as it is through the report that the findings of the study and their implications are communicated to your supervisor and readers. Most people will not be aware of the amount and quality of work that has gone into your study. While much hard work and care may have been put into every stage of the research, all readers see is the report. Therefore, the whole enterprise can be spoiled if the report is not well written. As Burns (1997: 229) writes, 'extremely valuable and interesting practical work may be spoiled at the last minute by a student who is not able to communicate the results easily'.

In addition to your understanding of research methodology, the quality of the report depends upon such things as your written communication skills and clarity of thought, your ability to express thoughts in a logical and sequential manner, and your subject knowledge base. Another important determinant is your experience in research writing: the more experience you acquire, the more effective you will become at writing a research report. The use of statistical procedures will reinforce the validity of your conclusions and arguments as they enable you to establish if an observed association is due to chance or otherwise (i.e. whether a relationship is spurious or non-spurious) and indicate the strength of an association so readers can place confidence in your findings. The use of graphs to present the findings, though not essential, will make the information more easily understood by readers. As stated in the previous chapter, whether or not graphs are used depends upon the purpose for which the findings are to be used.

CHECKPOINT
*Academic
writing
conventions*

The main difference between research and other writing is in the degree of control, rigour and caution required. Research writing is controlled in the sense that you need to be extremely careful about what you write, the words you choose, the way ideas are expressed, and the validity and verifiability of the conclusions you draw. What most distinguishes research writing from other writing is the high degree of intellectual rigour required for research writing. Research writing must be absolutely accurate, clear, unambiguous, logical and concise. Your writing should not be based upon assumptions about knowledge of your readers regarding the study. Bear in mind that you must be able to defend whatever you write should anyone challenge it. Do not use ornamental and superficial language. Even the best researchers make a number of drafts before writing up their final one, so be prepared to undertake this task.

The way findings are communicated differs in quantitative and qualitative research. As mentioned earlier, in qualitative research the findings are mostly communicated in a descriptive or narrative form written around the major themes, events or discourses that emerge from your findings. The main purpose is to describe the variation in a phenomenon, situation, event or episode without making an attempt to quantify it. One way of writing a qualitative report is described in Chapter 15 as a part of the content analysis process. On the other hand, the writing in quantitative research, in addition to being descriptive, also includes its quantification and numerical analysis of data. Depending upon the purpose of the study, statistical measures and tests can also become a part of the research writing to support the findings.

DEVELOPING A DRAFT OUTLINE

Before you start writing your report, it is good practice to develop an outline ('chapterisation'). This means deciding how you are going to divide your report into different chapters and planning what will be written in each one. In developing the chapterisation, the subobjectives of your study or the major significant themes that emerged from content analysis can provide immense guidance. Develop the chapters around the significant subobjectives or themes of your study. Depending upon the importance of a theme or subobjective, either devote a complete chapter to it or combine it with related themes to form one chapter. The title of each chapter should be descriptive of the main theme, communicate its main thrust and be clear and concise. This is applicable to both types of research.

The following approach is applicable to both qualitative and quantitative types of research, but keep in mind that it is merely suggestive and may be of help if you have no idea where to start. Feel free to change the suggested format in any way you like, or if you prefer a different one, follow that.

The first chapter of your report, possibly entitled 'Introduction', should be a general introduction to the study, covering most of your research proposal and pointing out the deviations, if any, from the original plan. This chapter covers all the preparatory tasks undertaken prior to conducting the study, such as the literature review, the theoretical framework, the objectives of the study, the study design, the sampling strategy and the measurement procedures.

To illustrate this, two examples are provided below for projects referred to previously in this book: the study on foster-care payments and the family engagement model. The first chapters of these reports could be written around the subheadings below. The subsequent structure of these reports is quite different. Keeping in mind the purpose for which family engagement evaluation was commissioned, the report was divided into three parts: the Introduction, the perceived model, and conclusions and recommendation.

CHECKPOINT
Research report content

Attitudes towards foster-care payments: suggested contents of Chapter 1
Chapter I Introduction

- Introduction
- The development of foster care
- Foster care in Australia
- Foster care in Western Australia
- The Department of Community services
- The out-of-home and community care programme
- Current trends in foster-care placement in Western Australia
- Becoming a foster carer
- Foster-care subsidies

- → Issues regarding foster-care payment
- → Rationale for the study
- → Objectives of the study
- → Study design
- → Sampling
- → Measurement procedure
- → Problems and limitations
- → Working definitions

Family engagement – A service delivery model: suggested contents of Chapter 1
Part one: Introduction

- → Background: the origin of the family engagement idea
- → Historical perspective
- → The perceived model
  - → Conceptual framework
  - → Philosophical perspective underpinning the model
  - → Intended outcomes
- → Objectives of the evaluation
- → Evaluation methodology

(Note: In this section, the conceptual framework of the model, its philosophical basis, perceived outcomes as identified by the person(s) responsible for initiating the idea and what was available in the literature were included. It also included details about evaluation objectives and evaluation methodology.)

The second chapter in quantitative research reports should provide information about the study population. Here, the relevant social, economic and demographic characteristics of the study population should be described. This chapter serves two purposes:

1 It provides readers with some background information about the population from which you collected the information so they can relate the findings to the type of population studied.
2 It helps to identify the variance within a group; for example, you may want to examine how the level of satisfaction of the consumers of a service changes, e.g. with their age, gender or education.

The second chapter in a quantitative research report, therefore, could be entitled 'Socioeconomic-demographic characteristics of the study population' or just 'The study population'. Taking the example of the foster-care payment study, this chapter could be written around the subheadings below.

As qualitative studies are mostly based upon a limited number of in-depth interviews or observations, you may find it very difficult to write about the study population.

Attitude towards foster–care payments: suggested contents of Chapter 2
Chapter 2 The study population

- Introduction
- Respondents by age (Information obtained in response to the question on age should be presented here. Consult 'Writing about variables', the next section of this chapter.)
- Respondents by gender (Follow the suggestions made under 'Writing about variables' (see below) for the rest of the variables.)
- Marital status of the study population
- Ethnicity of respondents
- Study population by number of children
- Average annual income of the study population
- Study population by type of dwelling
- etc.

The title and contents of subsequent chapters depend upon what you have attempted to describe, explore, examine, establish or prove in your study. As the content of each project is different, these chapters will be different. As indicated earlier, the title of each chapter should reflect the main thrust of its contents.

The outline should specify the subsections of the chapter. These subsections should be developed around the different aspects of the theme being discussed in the chapter. If you plan to correlate the information obtained from one variable with another, specify the variables. Plan the sequence for discussion of the variables. In deciding this, keep in mind the linkage and logical progression between the sections. This does not mean that the proposed outline cannot be changed when writing the report – it is possible for it to be significantly changed. However, an outline, even if extremely rough, will be of immense help to you. Again, let us take the study on foster-care payment and the family engagement model as examples:

Attitudes towards foster-care payments: suggested contents of Chapter 3
Chapter 3 Attitudes towards the present level of payment for foster care

- Introduction
- Attitudes towards adequacy of payment for foster care (Responses to questions on the adequacy of foster-care payment should be presented here.)

  - adequacy by age (Cross-tabulation, i.e. responses to the question on adequacy of foster-care payment is examined in relation to the responses to questions on age.)
  - adequacy by marital status (Cross-tabulation, i.e. responses to the question on adequacy of foster-care payment is examined in relation to the responses to questions on marital status.)
  - adequacy by income of the family (Cross-tabulation, i.e. responses to the question on adequacy of foster-care payment is examined in relation to the responses to questions on income.)

- Aspects of foster care not covered by the payment
- Major costs borne by foster carers
- Effects of the current level of payment on the family
- Reasons for increasing the payment
    - proposed level of payment
- Conclusions

(Note: Cross-tabulations can be included for any variable where appropriate.)

Family engagement model: suggested contents of Chapter 2

Part Two: The perceived model

- The philosophy underpinning the model
- Development of the model
- The model in practice
- Perceived differences in practice before and after the introduction of the model
- Perceived strengths of the model
- Perceived weaknesses of the model
- Skills required for effective functioning under the model
- Replication of the model
- Reasons for change to the new model
- Training
    - How should staff be trained?
    - Training provided

- Name of the model
- Determinants of successful implementation of the model
- Indicators of success of the model
- What could have been done differently?
- What needs to be done to improve the model?
- Role of Community Development Funding officers
- Advantages and disadvantages of the Case Management model
- Satisfaction of staff with the model
- The model and departmental vision, philosophy, ethos, principles
- Attitude of clients towards the model
- Attitude of community agencies towards the model
- The model and changes in the selected indicators

(Note: In this section, findings about different aspects of the model as identified through in-depth interviews and focus group discussions were detailed.)

Family engagement model: suggested contents of Chapter 3

Part Three: Conclusions and recommendations

↝ Conclusions

  ↝ General
  ↝ Specific to the model

↝ Recommendations

  ↝ General
  ↝ Specific to the ... office

This type of outline provides direction in your writing. As mentioned earlier, as you start writing you will certainly change it, but you will find it none the less helpful in your write-up.

WRITING ABOUT VARIABLES

Having developed a chapter outline, the next step is to start writing. Although researchers vary greatly in the ways in which they organise their writing, the following guidelines and format may prove helpful for beginners.

When writing about the information obtained in response to a question (variable), write as if you were providing answers to the following questions:

↝ Why did you think it important to study the variable? What effects, in your opinion, may this variable have on the main variable you are explaining? (*This is where you provide your own rationale for studying the variable.*)

↝ In the case of a cross-tabulation, what relationships have other studies found between the variables you are analysing? (*This is where the literature review is integrated into the findings of the study.*)

↝ What did you expect to find out in terms of the relationship between the two variables? (*If you have formulated a hypothesis, state it here.*)

↝ What has your study found out? (*Provide the hard data from your study here, as tables, graphs or text.*)

↝ What does the data show? (*Interpret the findings of your analysis.*)

↝ What conclusions can you draw? How do the conclusions drawn from your study compare with those from similar studies in the past? Does your study support or contradict them?

↝ What explanation can you provide for the findings of your study?

The above is only a suggested format for ordering your thoughts, not a list of subheadings. You may wish to change the suggested order to make the reading more interesting. Below is an example of writing about a variable, 'Adequacy of payment for foster care', from Chapter 13:

- Why did you think it important to find out if foster-care payments are adequate? What effects, in your opinion, could the adequacy or otherwise of payment for foster care have on the quality of foster care?

- What have other studies in your literature review said about the adequacy of foster-care payments?

- What did you expect to find out from your study population in terms of its feelings about the adequacy of foster-care payments? If you formulated a hypothesis, you should specify that here. For example, H_o: Most foster parents would consider the current level of foster-care payments to be adequate.

- What did you find out about the adequacy of foster-care payments? What proportion of the study population said they were adequate? What proportion said they were inadequate? Provide a table or graph showing the distribution of respondents by their response to the question regarding the adequacy of foster-care payments.

- What does your data show about the adequacy of foster-care payments? What are the main findings of your study? How do these findings compare with those of other studies you found in your literature review? Does your study support or contradict them?

- What conclusions can you draw about the adequacy of the amount of payment for foster care?

- What explanation can you provide for the observed findings? Why do you think those who said that foster payments are either adequate or inadequate feel that way?

In the suggested format for writing about information obtained from questions, notice that the literature review is integrated with the findings and conclusions. The extent of the integration of the literature with findings mostly depends upon the level at which you are writing your dissertation (bachelor's, master's or PhD) – the higher the level, the more extensive the literature review, the greater its integration with your findings, and the more careful and confident you need to be about your conclusions.

Writing in qualitative research is more descriptive and narrative than analytical, hence you need to use your imagination in terms of placement of information, linkage between the thoughts and flow of language to make the writing interesting to read and meaningful in conveying the findings.

The suggested format is organised around the main themes of the study. There are other formats. Some researchers write everything under one heading, 'The findings'. This format is appropriate for a research paper, because it is short, but not for a research report or dissertation. Other writers follow the same order as in the research instrument; for example, findings are discussed under each question that was asked of the respondents in an interview or a questionnaire. However, this means that the reader needs to refer continuously to the instrument for each question. This format is segmental, lacks linkage and integration, and may not place findings into perspective.

CHECKPOINT
Drawing conclusions and maintaining arguments

REFERENCING

Your report must follow an acceptable academic style of referencing. There are many styles in use in academic circles and the choice of a referencing system varies from one academic discipline to another. You need to know which system is preferred by your department and the university. You should spend some time learning about it. Whichever system you decide to use, make sure you are consistent in its use. According to Butcher (1981: 226), there are four referencing systems from which to choose:

1 the short-title system;
2 the author–date system (also known as the name–year system, Harvard system or parenthetical referencing system);
3 the reference by number system (also known as the Vancouver system);
4 the author–number system.

According to Butcher (1981: 167), 'The first of these is used in most general books, the second mainly in science and social science books; the third and the fourth less frequently'. Butcher (1981) and the various style guides mentioned in this book provide plenty of examples for you to follow.

WRITING A BIBLIOGRAPHY

Again, there are several well-established systems for writing a bibliography and your choice is dependent upon the preference of the discipline and university. In the social sciences some of the most commonly used ones are (Longyear 1983: 83):

→ the Harvard system;
→ the American Psychological Association system;
→ the American Medical Association system;
→ the McGraw-Hill system;
→ the Modern Languages Association system;
→ the footnote system.

To learn about these systems and styles, consult the references provided at the end of this book or consult your library.

463

CHECKPOINT
References and citations

SUMMARY

Writing your report is the most crucial step in the research process as it communicates the findings to your research supervisor and readers. A badly written report can spoil all the hard work you have put into your research study.

Styles of research writing vary markedly among researchers but all research reports must be written clearly and concisely. Furthermore, scientific writing requires intellectual rigour and there are certain obligations in terms of accuracy and objectivity. Reports can be written in different formats, and this chapter has suggested one that research students have found to be helpful.

Writing in quantitative and qualitative research differs to the extent that in qualitative research your style is descriptive and narrative, whereas in quantitative research, in addition to being descriptive, it is also analytical and every assertion is supported by empirical evidence gathered through the investigation.

There are different ways of referencing and of writing a bibliography. You need to choose a system that is acceptable to your discipline and university.

Before you start writing the research report, develop an outline of the different chapters and their contents. The chapters should be written around the main themes of the study and for this your subobjectives are of immense help. When providing specific information about variables, the write-up should integrate the rationale for studying the variables; the literature review; the hypothesis, if any; findings; conclusions drawn; and possible explanations for the findings.

The suggested format can be described as thematic writing – writing organised around the significant themes of your study. Within a theme the information is provided in an integrated manner following a logical progression of thought.

Now that you have read the full chapter...

CHECK YOUR UNDERSTANDING

☐ Do you understand the meaning and application of all of the keywords at the start of the chapter? If not, visit the online resources and use the glossary flashcards to get to grips with their definitions.

☐ Describe some of the differences in writing a report in quantitative and qualitative research.

☐ What are the different referencing systems? Detail the referencing of the system that is used in your academic field or at your university.

☐ What are the different styles of writing a bibliography? Detail the one used in your discipline or at your university.

APPLY IT TO YOUR OWN PROJECT

☐ A literature review is an integral part of research writing. Reflecting on examples from your own area of interest, explore how you might be able to integrate your research findings with your literature review when it comes to writing your report.

CONFUSED?

THE ONLINE RESOURCES ARE HERE TO HELP YOU

 https://study.sagepub.com/kumar5e

CHECKPOINT: What are the qualities of good written communication? Read this chapter.

CHECKPOINT: What do I need to include (or not include) in my report, and in how much detail? Watch this video.

CHECKPOINT: How do you maintain focus on the 'big picture' of your research and present consistent arguments and conclusions across sections of the report? Visit this website.

CHECKPOINT: What are the most common types of referencing systems, and why is correct referencing important? Watch this video.

NEED MORE GENERAL SUPPORT?

Get up to speed on key terms with *glossary flashcards* and test yourself on important concepts with *multiple choice questions*.

UP FOR A CHALLENGE?

THE ONLINE RESOURCES ARE HERE TO INSPIRE YOU

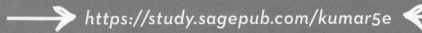 https://study.sagepub.com/kumar5e

CHECKPOINT: What are the most common academic convention errors, and how I do avoid them in my report? Watch this video.

CHECKPOINT: What does a good report outline look like? Visit this website.

CHECKPOINT: How do find the right writing style and voice for the type of report you are doing? Visit this website.

CHECKPOINT: How do I create my own citations? Visit this website.

READY TO WORK ON YOUR OWN PROJECT?

Start building a portfolio of your ideas with the exercise workbook and get support tailored to your specific assignment with the assessment toolkit.

EXERCISE VIII: REPORT WRITING

The final step in the research process is writing the research report, and this is what the reader sees of your study. Therefore it is important that you communicate the purpose of the study, its methodology, results and conclusion in an accurate, clear, unambiguous, logical and concise manner.

In this exercise you need to decide how to present your study to the reader of the report. It is suggested that you start with a draft outline using the information provided in previous exercises. By planning the order and the relevant information for each chapter before you actually write the report you will ensure that you do not neglect essential information and that it flows in a logical sequence. And having a written plan will make the process of writing straight forward when you come to it. As your research proposal, the report should be written in an academic style, integrating the literature review as appropriate where all points are supported by references and argued well. It may take several drafts before you arrive at the final version of the report. Remember findings for quantitative and qualitative studies are communicated differently, as you practised in an earlier exercise.

STEP ONE Developing a draft outline

You have the freedom to choose how you will communicate your study and its findings in the report. Start by dividing the report into different chapters. In a qualitative study the chapters could be developed from the themes that emerged from the findings. All reports should have a title and an introduction. There should be a chapter outlining the research process, participants and the findings then the report should finish with a conclusion. Draft a list of chapters for your report:

Title of report: _____

Chapter 1: Introduction _____

Chapter 2: _____

Chapter 3: _____

Chapter 4: _____

Final chapter: Conclusions (and recommendations (if appropriate)) _____

Remember – you decide on the number of chapters, so you can have more or less than above.

STEP TWO Developing a draft outline for each chapter

The list of chapters is a guideline for you and you can still make changes to it. In this next step, plan and decide what you want to write about in each chapter. This can be done in bullet points or brief notes. Again, keep in mind that you can move points around until you are satisfied with the outline of your chapters. Also see Chapter 17 which provides some examples and suggestions.

1.   What will you include in your introduction? Briefly outline aspects that should be covered in this section of the report, e.g. the purpose of the study, definitions of any concepts, background information of what is already known of the study area, a rationale for the study, how the study was conducted, etc.

Ideas for subheadings in the Introduction:

_____

_____

_____

_____

Template of Exercise VIII

2   The second chapter should provide information about the study population. If not already reported in detail, the second chapter could outline the research process giving information about the participants, how they were selected, what they had to do in the research or in other words how the data was collected, what materials were used and how the data was analysed. In quantitative studies this would also ensure that another researcher could replicate the study from this information.

Outline of contents for chapter 2:

.

3   The title and contents of subsequent chapter(s) depends upon what you have attempted to describe, explore, examine, establish or prove in your study, so these chapters will differ by project. Chapter 3 contents (e.g. it could be reporting the findings of the study):

---

4   Chapter 4 contents (if applicable):

---

5   The final chapter in a report is usually entitled 'Conclusions'. What are the general and specific conclusions? If your study had some practical implications you can also add recommendations in this chapter which can be grouped in general and specific recommendations:

STEP THREE Writing about variables

Now that you have a draft structure of your report and know what you are writing about you can start with the actual writing process.

In qualitative research the writing will be more descriptive and organised around the main themes using a narrative for the reader to find out about your study.

In quantitative studies you need to be more analytical in your writing and the following questions should help to write about variables in your study:

1   Why did you think it important to study the variable? What effects may this variable have on the main variable you are explaining? (This is where you show an understanding of the literature and provide your rationale for studying the variable.)

----

2   In the case of a cross-tabulation, what relationships have other studies found between the variables you are analysing? (This is where the literature review is integrated into the findings of the study.)

----

3   What did you expect to find out in terms of the relationship between the two variables? (If you have formulated a hypothesis, state it here.)

----

4   What has your study found out? (Provide the hard data from your study here, as tables, graphs or text.)

----

5   What does the data show? (Interpret the findings of your analysis. Here you need to show that you understand the findings using words rather than numbers.)

----

6   What conclusions can you draw? How do the conclusions drawn from your study compare with those from similar studies in the past? Does your study support or contradict them?

----

7   What explanation can you provide for the findings of your study? (Relate to the existing literature or practice in the field of study.)

....

....

....

....

STEP FOUR Referencing and writing a bibliography

In your report you are expected to reference all resources you have used in a consistent and accurate way. This means that you need to allocate some time to compile a reference list or bibliography of the literature at the end of your report. There are different referencing/bibliography systems and it is suggested that you use the system your university or discipline prefers. Indicate which system you will use for your report:

☐   the Harvard system

☐   the American Psychological Association system

☐   the American Medical Association system

☐   the McGraw-Hill system

☐   the Modern Languages Association system

☐   the footnote system

Now take some time to familiarize yourself with the system and style you have selected and use it in your report.

GLOSSARY

100 per cent bar chart: The 100 per cent bar chart is very similar to the stacked bar chart. The only difference is that in the former the subcategories of a variable for a particular bar total 100 per cent and each bar is sliced into portions in relation to their proportion out of 100.

Accidental sampling: Like quota sampling, accidental sampling is based upon your convenience in accessing the sampling population. Whereas quota sampling attempts to include people possessing an obvious/visible characteristic, accidental sampling makes no such attempt. Any person that you come across can be contacted for participation in your study. You stop collecting data when you reach the required number of respondents you decided to have in your sample.

Action research: In common with participatory research and collaborative enquiry, action research is based upon a philosophy of community development that seeks the involvement of community members in planning, undertaking, developing and implementing research and programme agendas. Research is a means to action to deal with a problem or an issue confronting a group or community. It follows a cyclical process that is used to identify the issues, develop strategies and implement the programmes to deal with them and then again assessing strategies in light of the issues.

Active variable: In studies that seek to establish causality or association there are variables that can be changed, controlled and manipulated either by a researcher or by someone else. Such variables are called active variables.

After-only design: In an after-only design the researcher knows that a population is being, or has been, exposed to an intervention and wishes to study its impact on the population. In this design, baseline information (pre-test or before observation) is usually 'constructed' either on the basis of respondents' recall of the situation before the intervention, or from information available in existing records (i.e. secondary sources).

Alternative hypothesis: The formulation of an alternative hypothesis is a convention in scientific circles. Its main function is to specify explicitly the relationship that will be considered as true in case the research hypothesis proves to be wrong. In a way, an alternative hypothesis is the opposite of the research hypothesis.

Ambiguous question: An ambiguous question is one that contains more than one meaning and can be interpreted differently by different respondents.

Applied research: Most research in the social sciences is applied in nature. Applied research is one where research techniques, procedures and methods that form the body of research methodology are applied to collect information about various aspects of a situation, issue, problem or phenomenon so that the information gathered can be utilised for other purposes such as policy formulation, programme development, programme modification and evaluation, enhancement of the understanding about a phenomenon, establishing causality and outcomes, identifying needs and developing strategies.

Area chart: For variables measured on an interval or a ratio scale, information about the subcategories of a variable can also be presented in the form of an area chart. This is plotted in the same way as a line diagram with the area under each line shaded to highlight the magnitude of the subcategory in relation to other subcategories. Thus an area chart displays the area under the curve in relation to the subcategories of a variable.

Attitudinal scales: Scales designed to measure attitudes towards an issue are called attitudinal scales. In the social sciences there are three types of scale: the summated rating scale (Likert scale), the equal-appearing interval scale (Thurstone scale) and the cumulative scale (Guttman scale).

Attitudinal score: A number that you calculate having assigned a numerical value to the response given by a respondent to an attitudinal statement or question. Different attitude scales have different ways of calculating the attitudinal score.

Attitudinal value: An attitudinal scale comprises many statements reflecting attitudes towards an issue. The extent to which each statement reflects this attitude varies from statement to statement. Some statements are more important in determining the attitude than others. The attitudinal value of a statement refers to the weight calculated or given to a statement to reflect its significance in reflecting the attitude: the greater the significance or extent, the greater the attitudinal value or weight.

Attribute variables: Those variables that cannot be manipulated, changed or controlled, and that reflect the characteristics of the study population. Examples are age, gender, education and income.

Bar chart: The bar chart or diagram is one of the ways of graphically displaying categorical data. A bar chart is identical to a histogram, except that in a bar chart the rectangles representing the various frequencies are spaced, thus indicating that the data is categorical. The bar diagram is used for variables measured on nominal or ordinal scales.

Before-and-after design: A before-and-after design can be described as two sets of cross-sectional data collection points on the same population to find out the change in a phenomenon or variable(s) between two points in time. The change is measured by comparing the difference in the phenomenon or variable(s) between before and after observations.

Bias: A deliberate attempt either to conceal or highlight something that you found in your research or to use deliberately a procedure or method that you know is not appropriate but will provide information that you are looking for because you have a vested interest in it.

Blind studies: In a blind study, the study population does not know whether it is getting real or fake treatment or, with modality in the case of comparative studies, which treatment. The main objective of designing a blind study is to isolate the placebo effect.

Case study: The case study design is based upon the assumption that the case being studied is typical of cases of a certain type and therefore a single case can provide insight into the events and situations prevalent in a group from where the case has been drawn. In a case study design the 'case' you select becomes the basis of a thorough, holistic and in-depth exploration of the aspect(s) that you want to find out about. It is an approach in which a particular instance or a few carefully selected cases are studied intensively. To be called a case study it is important to treat the total study population as one entity. It is one of the important study designs in qualitative research.

Categorical variables: Variables where the unit of measurement is in the form of categories. On the basis of presence or absence of a characteristic, a variable is placed in a category. There is no measurement of the characteristics as such. In terms of measurement scales such variables are measured on nominal or ordinal scales. Rich/poor, high/low, hot/cold are examples of categorical variables.

Chance variable: In studying causality or association there are times when the mood of a respondent or the wording of a question can affect the reply given by the respondent when asked again in the post-test. There is no systematic pattern in terms of this change. Such variables are called chance or random variables.

Closed question: In a closed question the possible answers are set out in the questionnaire or interview schedule and the respondent or the investigator ticks the category that best describes a respondent's answer.

472

Cluster sampling: Cluster sampling is based on the ability of the researcher to divide a sampling population into groups (based upon a visible or easily identifiable characteristic), called clusters, and then select elements from each cluster using simple random sampling. Clusters can be formed on the basis of geographical proximity or a common characteristic that has a correlation with the main variable of the study (as in stratified sampling). Depending on the level of clustering, sometimes sampling may be done at different levels. These levels constitute the different stages (single, double or multiple) of clustering.

Code: The numerical value that is assigned to a response at the time of analysing the data.

Code book: A listing of a set of numerical values (set of rules) that you decide to assign to answers obtained from respondents in response to each question.

Code of conduct: A set of principles based upon ethical considerations that govern the professional practice in a profession.

Coding: The process of assigning numerical values to different categories of responses to a question for the purpose of analysing them.

Cohort studies: These are based upon the existence of a common characteristic such as year of birth, graduation or marriage, within a subgroup of a population that you want to study. People with the common characteristics are studied over a period of time to collect the information of interest. Studies could cover fertility behaviour of women born in 1986 or career paths of 1990 graduates from a medical school, for instance. Cohort studies look at the trends over a long period of time and collect data from the same group of people.

Collaborative enquiry: is another name for participatory research that advocates a close collaboration between the researcher and the research participants.

Column percentages: are calculated from the total of all the subcategories of one variable that are displayed along a column in different rows.

Community discussion forum: A community discussion forum is a qualitative strategy designed to find opinions, attitudes and ideas of a community with regard to community issues and problems. It is one of the common ways of seeking a community's participation in deciding about issues of concern to it.

Comparative study design: Sometimes you seek to compare the effectiveness of different treatment modalities. In such situations a comparative design is used. With a comparative design, as with most other designs, a study can be carried out either as an experiment or as a non-experiment. In the comparative experimental design, the study population is divided into the same number of groups as the number of treatments to be tested. For each group the baseline with respect to the dependent variable is established. The different treatment modalities are then introduced to the different groups. After a certain period, when it is assumed that the treatment models have had their effect, the 'after' observation is carried out to ascertain changes in the dependent variable.

Concept: In defining a research problem or the study population you may use certain words that are difficult to measure as such and/or the understanding of which may vary from person to person. These words are called concepts. In order to measure them they need to be converted into indicators (not always) and then variables. Words like satisfaction, impact, young, old, happy are concepts as their understanding would vary from person to person.

Conceptual framework: A conceptual framework stems from the theoretical framework and concentrates, usually, on one section of that theoretical framework which becomes the basis of your study. The latter consists of the theories or issues in which your study is embedded, whereas the former describes the aspects you selected from the theoretical framework to become the basis of your research enquiry. The conceptual framework is the basis of your research problem.

Concurrent validity: When you investigate how good a research instrument is by comparing it with some observable criterion or credible findings, this is called concurrent validity. It is comparing the findings of your instrument with those found by another which is well accepted. Concurrent validity is judged by how well an instrument compares with a second assessment done concurrently.

Conditioning effect: This describes a situation where, if the same respondents are contacted frequently, they begin to know what is expected of them and may respond to questions without thought, or they may lose interest in the enquiry, with the same result. This situation's effect on the quality of the answers is known as the conditioning effect.

Confirmability: The degree to which the results obtained through qualitative research could be confirmed or corroborated by others. Confirmability in qualitative research is similar to reliability in quantitative research.

Constant variable: When a variable can have only one category or value, for example taxi, tree and water, it is known as a constant variable.

Construct validity: A more sophisticated technique for establishing the validity of an instrument. Construct validity is based upon statistical procedures. It is determined by ascertaining the contribution of each construct to the total variance observed in a phenomenon.

Consumer-oriented evaluation: The core philosophy of this evaluation rests on the assumption that assessment of the value or merit of an intervention – including its effectiveness, outcomes, impact and relevance – should be judged from the perspective of the consumer. Consumers, according to this philosophy, are the best people to make a judgement on these aspects. An evaluation done within the framework of this philosophy is known as consumer-oriented evaluation or client-centred evaluation.

Content analysis: One of the main methods of analysing qualitative data. It is the process of analysing the contents of interviews or observational field notes in order to identify the main themes that emerge from the responses given by your respondents or the observation notes made by you as a researcher.

Content validity: In addition to linking each question with the objectives of a study as a part of establishing the face validity, it is also important to examine whether the questions or items have covered all the areas you wanted to cover in the study. Examining questions of a research instrument to establish the extent of coverage of areas under study is called the content validity of the instrument.

Continuous variables: These are variables that have continuity in their unit of measurement; for example, age, income and attitude score. They can take on any value of the scale on which they are measured. Age can be measured in years, months and days. Similarly, income can be measured in dollars and cents.

Control design: In experimental studies that aim to measure the impact of an intervention, it is important to measure the change in the dependent variable that is attributed to the extraneous and chance variables. To quantify the impact of these sets of variables another comparable group is selected that is not subjected to the intervention. Study designs where you have a control group to isolate the impact of extraneous and change variables are called control design studies.

Control group: The group in an experimental study which is not exposed to the experimental intervention is called a control group. The sole purpose of the control group is to measure the impact of extraneous and chance variables on the dependent variable.

Control of variance: When you design a study in such a way that enables you to ensure that the independent variable has a maximum chance of affecting the dependent variable(s) and the effect of extraneous variables is designed to be minimum and quantifiable. (See also the maxmincon principle of variance.)

Controlled: In order to reliably establish a cause-and-effect relationship, it is sometimes important to design a study in such a way that enables you to link cause(s) with the effect(s) and vice versa so that you can study the extent of the impact of the cause on the effect(s). 'Controlling' refers to desiging a study in such a way that enables you to control/quantify the effects of all other variables on the dependent variable so that the effect of the independent variable can accurately be assessed.

Controlled experiments: In a control experiment the study population is divided into two groups, one experimental and the other control. The control group does not receive any stimulus or intervention whereas the experimental is exposed to it. The intervention or stimulus is ether introduced by the researcher or someone else.

Convenience sampling: Convenience sampling is a non-probability sampling design which is primarily guided by the convenience to the researcher in terms of selecting the potential respondents whatever this might be: easy accessibility, geographical proximity, known contacts, ready approval for undertaking the study or being a part of the group.

Correlational studies: Studies which are primarily designed to investigate whether or not there is a relationship between two or more variables.

Cost-benefit evaluation: The central aim of a cost–benefit evaluation is to put a price tag on an intervention in relation to its benefits.

Cost-effectiveness evaluation: The central aim of a cost-effectiveness evaluation is to put a price tag on an intervention in relation to its effectiveness.

Credibility: Credibility in qualitative research is parallel to internal validity in quantitative research and refers to a situation where the results obtained through qualitative research are agreeable to the participants of the research. It is judged by the extent of respondent concordance whereby you take your findings to those who participated in your research for confirmation, congruence, validation and approval: the higher the outcome of these, the higher the credibility (validity) of the study.

Cross-over comparative experimental design: In the cross-over design, also called the ABAB design, two groups are formed, the intervention is introduced to one of them and, after a certain period, the impact of this intervention is measured. Then the interventions are 'crossed over'; that is, the experimental group becomes the control and vice versa.

Cross-sectional studies: The most commonly used design in the social sciences, also known as one-shot or status studies. This design is best suited to studies aimed at finding out the prevalence of a phenomenon, situation, problem, attitude or issue, by taking a cross-section of the population. They are useful in obtaining an overall 'picture' as it stands at the time of the study.

Cross-tabulation: A statistical procedure that analyses two variables, usually independent and dependent or attribute and dependent, to determine if there is a relationship between them. The subcategories of both the variables are cross-tabulated to ascertain if a relationship exists between them.

Cumulative frequency polygon: The cumulative frequency polygon or cumulative frequency curve is drawn on the basis of cumulative frequencies. The main difference between a frequency polygon and a cumulative frequency polygon is that the former is drawn by joining the midpoints of the intervals, whereas the latter is drawn by joining the end points of the intervals because cumulative frequencies interpret data in relation to the upper limit of an interval.

Dependability: Dependability in qualitative research is very similar to the concept of reliability in quantitative research. It is concerned with whether we would obtain the same results if we could observe the same thing twice: the greater the similarity in two results, the greater the dependability.

475

Dependent variable: When establishing causality through a study, the variable assumed to be the cause is called an independent variable and the variables in which it produces changes are called the dependent variables. A dependent variable is dependent upon the independent variable that is assumed to be responsible for changes in the dependent variable.

Descriptive studies: A study in which the main focus is on description, rather than examining relationships or associations, is classified as a descriptive study. A descriptive study attempts systematically to describe a situation, problem, phenomenon, service or programme, or provides information about, say, the living conditions of a community, or describes attitudes towards an issue.

Dichotomous variable: A variable which can have only two categories (e.g. male/female, yes/no, good/bad, head/tail, up/down and rich/poor).

Disproportionate stratified sampling: When selecting a stratified sample, if you select an equal number of elements from each stratum without giving any consideration to its size in the study population, the process is called disproportionate stratified sampling.

Dominant/less dominant studies: A mixed methods study where one methodology dominates the study is classified as dominant/less dominant study.

Double-barrelled question: A double-barrelled question is a question within a question.

Double-blind studies: A double-blind study is very similar to a blind study except that it also tries to eliminate researcher bias by not disclosing to the researcher the identities of experimental, comparative and placebo groups. In a double-blind study neither the researcher nor the study participants know which study participants are receiving real, placebo or other forms of interventions. This prevents the possibility of introducing bias by the researcher.

Double-control studies: Although the control group design helps quantify the impact that can be attributed to extraneous variables, it does not separate out other effects that may be due to the research instrument (such as the reactive effect) or respondents (such as the maturation or regression effects, or placebo effect). When you need to identify and separate out these effects, a double-control design is required. In a double-control study, you have two control groups instead of one. To quantify, say, the reactive effect of an instrument, you exclude one of the control groups from the 'before' observation.

Editing: Data editing involves scrutinising the completed research instruments to identify and minimise, as far as possible, errors in completeness, misclassification and gaps in the information obtained from respondents.

Elevation effect: Some observers when using a scale to record an observation may prefer to use certain section(s) of the scale in the same way that some teachers are strict markers and others are not. When observers have a tendency to use a particular part(s) of a scale in recording an interaction, this phenomenon is known as the elevation effect.

Equivalent status studies: A mixed methods study where both methodologies are equally applied is classified as an equivalent status study.

Error of central tendency: When using scales in assessments or observations, unless an observer is extremely confident of his/her ability to assess an interaction, s/he may tend to avoid the extreme positions on the scale, using mostly the central part. The error this tendency creates is called the error of central tendency.

Ethics: The moral values of professional conduct that are considered desirable for good professional practice.

Ethical practice: Professional practice undertaken in accordance with the principles of accepted codes of conduct for a given profession or group.

Evaluation: A process that is guided by research principles for reviewing an intervention or programme in order to make informed decisions about its desirability and/or identifying changes to enhance its efficiency and effectiveness.

Evaluation for planning: This addresses the issue of establishing the need for a programme or intervention.

Evidence-based practice: A service delivery system that is based upon research evidence as to its effectiveness; a service provider's clinical judgement as to its suitability and appropriateness for a client; and a client's preference as to its acceptance.

Experimental group: An experimental group is one that is exposed to the intervention being tested to study its effects.

Experimental studies: In studying causality, when a researcher or someone else introduces the intervention that is assumed to be the 'cause' of change and waits until it has produced – or has been given sufficient time to produce – the change. In experimental studies a researcher starts with the cause and waits to observe its effects.

Expert sampling: The selection of people with demonstrated or known expertise in the area of interest to become the basis of data collection. Your sample is a group of experts from whom you seek the required information. It is like purposive sampling where the sample comprises experts only.

Explanatory research: In an explanatory study the main emphasis is to clarify why and how there is a relationship between two aspects of a situation or phenomenon.

Exploratory research: This is when a study is undertaken with the objective either to explore an area where little is known or to investigate the possibilities of undertaking a particular research study. When a study is carried out to determine its feasibility it is also called a feasibility or pilot study.

Extraneous variables: In studying causality, the dependent variable is the consequence of the change brought about by the independent variable. In everyday life there are many other variables that can affect the relationship between independent and dependent variables. These variables are called extraneous variables.

Face validity: When you justify the inclusion of a question or item in a research instrument by linking it with the objectives of the study, thus providing a justification for its inclusion in the instrument, the process is called face validity.

Feasibility study: When the purpose of a study is to investigate the possibility of undertaking it on a larger scale and to streamlining methods and procedures for the main study, the study is called a feasibility study.

Feminist research: Like action research, feminist research is more a philosophy than design. Feminist concerns and theory act as the guiding framework for this research. The main characteristics of feminist research are a focus on the viewpoints of women, the aim of reducing the power imbalance between researcher and respondents, and attempts to change social inequality between men and women.

Fishbowl draw: This is one of the methods of selecting a random sample and is useful particularly when N is not very large. It entails writing each element number on a small slip of paper, folded and put into a bowl, shuffling thoroughly, and then taking one out till the required sample size is obtained.

Focus group: The focus group is a form of strategy in qualitative research in which attitudes, opinions or perceptions towards an issue, product, service or programme are explored through a free and open discussion between members of a group and the researcher. The focus group is a facilitated group discussion in which a researcher raises issues or asks questions that stimulate discussion among members of the group. Issues, questions and different perspectives on them and any significant points arising during these discussions provide data to draw conclusions and inferences. It is like collectively interviewing a group of respondents.

Frame of analysis: The proposed plan for analysing the data to operationalise your major concepts and the statistical procedures you intend to use.

Frequency distribution: The frequency distribution is a statistical procedure in quantitative research that can be applied to any variable that is measured on any one of the four measurement scales. It groups respondents into the subcategories in which a variable has been measured or coded.

Frequency polygon: The frequency polygon is very similar to a histogram. A frequency polygon is drawn by joining the midpoint of each rectangle at a height commensurate with the frequency of that interval.

Graphs: Graphs are a way of displaying analysed data that makes it easier to understand and effectively communicate.

Group interview: A group interview is both a method of data collection and a qualitative study design. The interaction is between the researcher and the group with the aim of collecting information from the group collectively rather than individually from members.

Guttman scale: The Guttman scale is one of the three attitudinal scales and is devised in such a way that the statements or items reflecting an attitude are arranged in perfect cumulative order. Arranging statements or items to have a cumulative relation between them is the most difficult aspect of constructing this scale.

Halo effect: When making an observation, some observers may be influenced to rate an individual on one aspect of the interaction by the way s/he was rated on another. This is similar to something that can happen in teaching when a teacher's assessment of the performance of a student in one subject may influence his/her rating of that student's performance in another. This type of effect is known as the halo effect.

Hawthorne effect: When individuals or groups become aware that they are being observed, they may change their behaviour. Depending upon the situation, this change could be positive or negative – it may increase or decrease, for example, their productivity – and may occur for a number of reasons. When a change in the behaviour of persons or groups is attributed to their being observed, it is known as the Hawthorne effect.

Histogram: A histogram is a graphic presentation of analysed data presented in the form of a series of rectangles drawn next to each other without any space between them, each representing the frequency of a category or subcategory.

Holistic research: is more a philosophy than a study design. The design is based upon the philosophy that as a multiplicity of factors interacts in our lives, we cannot understand a phenomenon from one or two perspectives only. To understand a situation or phenomenon we need to look at it in its totality or entirety; that is, holistically from every perspective. A research study done with this philosophical perspective in mind is called holistic research.

Hypothesis: A hypothesis is a hunch, assumption, suspicion, assertion or idea about a phenomenon, relationship or situation, the reality or truth of which you do not know, and you set up your study to find this truth. A researcher refers to these assumptions, assertions, statements or hunches as hypotheses and they become the basis of an enquiry. In most studies the hypothesis will be based either upon previous studies or on your own or someone else's observations.

Hypothesis of association: When as a researcher you have sufficient knowledge about a situation or phenomenon and are in a position to stipulate the extent of the relationship between two variables and formulate a hunch that reflects the magnitude of the relationship, such a hypothesis formulation is known as a hypothesis of association.

Hypothesis of difference: A hypothesis in which a researcher stipulates that there will be a difference but does not specify its magnitude.

Hypothesis of point-prevalence: There are times when a researcher has enough knowledge about a phenomenon that he/she is studying and is confident about speculating almost the exact prevalence of the situation or the outcome in quantitative units. This type of hypothesis is known as a hypothesis of point-prevalence.

Independent variable: When examining causality in a study, there are four sets of variables that can operate. One of them is a variable that is responsible for bringing about change. This variable which is the cause of the changes in a phenomenon is called an independent variable. In the study of causality, the independent variable is the cause variable which is responsible for bringing about change in a phenomenon.

In-depth interviewing: is an extremely useful method of data collection that provides complete freedom in terms of content and structure. As a researcher you are free to order these in whatever sequence you wish, keeping in mind the context. You also have complete freedom in terms of what questions you ask of your respondents, the wording you use and the way you

478

explain your questions to your respondents. You usually formulate questions and raise issues on the spur of the moment, depending upon what occurs to you in the context of the discussion.

Indicators: An image, perception or concept is sometimes incapable of direct measurement. In such situations a concept is 'measured' through other means which are logically 'reflective' of the concept. These logical reflectors are called indicators.

Informed consent: implies that respondents are made adequately and accurately aware of the type of information you want from them, why the information is being sought, what purpose it will be put to, how they are expected to participate in the study, and how it will directly or indirectly affect them. It is important that the consent should also be voluntary and without pressure of any kind. The consent given by respondents after being adequately and accurately made aware of or informed about all aspects of a study is called informed consent.

Interrupted time-series design: In this design you study a group of people before and after the introduction of an intervention. It is like the before-and-after design, except that you have multiple data collections at different time intervals to constitute an aggregated before-and-after picture. The design is based upon the assumption that one set of data is not sufficient to establish, with a reasonable degree of certainty and accuracy, the before-and-after situations.

Interval scale: The interval scale is one of the measurement scales in the social sciences where the scale is divided into a number of intervals or units. An interval scale has all the characteristics of an ordinal scale. In addition, it has a unit of measurement that enables individuals or responses to be placed at equally spaced intervals in relation to the spread of the scale. This scale has a starting and a terminating point and is divided into equally spaced units/intervals. The starting and terminating points and the number of units/intervals between them are arbitrary and vary from scale to scale as it does not have a fixed zero point.

Intervening variables: In certain situations the relationship between an independent and a dependent variable does not eventuate till the intervention of another variable – the intervening variable. The cause variable will have the assumed effect only in the presence of an intervening variable.

Intervention-development-evaluation process: This is a cyclical process of continuous assessment of needs, intervention and evaluation. You make an assessment of the needs of a group or community, develop intervention strategies to meet these needs, implement the interventions and then evaluate them for making informed decisions to incorporate changes to enhance their relevance, efficiency and effectiveness. Reassess the needs and follow the same process for intervention–development–evaluation.

Interview guide: A list of issues, topics or discussion points that serves as a reminder of what you want to cover in an in-depth interview. Note that these points are not questions.

Interview schedule: A list of questions, open-ended or closed, prepared for use by an interviewer in a person-to-person interaction (this may be face to face, by telephone or by other electronic media). Note that an interview schedule is a research tool/instrument for collecting data, whereas interviewing is a method of data collection.

Interviewing: One of the commonly used methods of data collection in the social sciences. Any person-to-person interaction, either face to face or otherwise, between two or more individuals with a specific purpose in mind is called an interview. It involves asking questions of respondents and recording their answers. Interviewing spans a wide spectrum in terms of its structure, from highly structured to extremely flexible.

Judgemental sampling: The primary consideration in this sampling design is your judgement as to who can provide the best information to achieve the objectives of your study. You as a researcher only go to those people who in your opinion are likely to have the required information and are willing to share it with you. This design is also called purposive sampling.

Leading question: A question which, by its contents, structure or wording, leads a respondent to answer in a certain direction.

479

Likert scale: The Likert scale, also known as the summated rating scale, is one of the attitudinal scales designed to measure attitudes. This scale is based upon the assumption that each statement/item on the scale has equal attitudinal 'value', 'importance' or 'weight' in terms of reflecting attitude towards the issue in question. Comparatively it is the easiest to construct.

Literature review: This is the process of searching the existing literature relating to your research problem to develop theoretical and conceptual frameworks for your study and to integrate your research findings with what the literature says about them. It places your study in perspective to what others have investigated about the issues. In addition, the process helps you to improve your methodology.

Longitudinal study: In longitudinal studies the study population is visited a number of times at regular intervals, usually over a long period, to collect the required information. These intervals are not fixed, so their length may vary from study to study. Intervals might be as short as a week or longer than a year. Irrespective of the size of the interval, the information gathered each time is identical.

Matching: is a technique that is used to form two groups of patients to set up an experiment–control study to test the effectiveness of a drug. From a pool of patients, two patients with identical predetermined attributes, characteristics or conditions are matched and then randomly placed in either the experimental or control group. The matching continues for the rest of the pool. The two groups thus formed are supposed to be comparable, thus ensuring uniform impact of different sets of variables on the patients.

Maturation effect: If there is a significant time lapse between the before and after data sets, the study population may change simply because it has grown older. This is particularly true when you are studying young children. The effect of this maturation, if it is significantly correlated with the dependent variable, is reflected in the after observation.

Maxmincon principle of variance: When studying causality between two variables there are three sets of variables that impact upon the dependent variable. Since your aim as a researcher is to determine the change that can be attributed to the independent variable, you need to design your study to ensure that the independent variable has the maximum opportunity to have its full impact on the dependent variable, while the effects that are attributed to extraneous and chance variables are minimised. Setting up a study to achieve the above is known as adhering to the maxmincon principle of variance.

Measurement scales: A system of classifying objects, responses, characteristics and attributes into different categories. These categorisations could be very subjective or objective depending upon the scale used. The four commonly used scales are nominal, ordinal, interval and ratio.

Mixed/multiple methods approach: In extremely simple terms, the mixed methods approach to social research is when you combine two or more methods to collect and analyse data pertaining to your research problem. When these methods are from both paradigms, that is, when a study uses both quantitative and qualitative methods, it is classified as mixed methods approach. However, when these are from one paradigm only, it is called multiple methods approach. The approach is based upon the rationale that for certain situations qualitative techniques are better and for others quantitative ones are better. Hence, to get the best outcome for a research study you need to combine both approaches or use more than one method.

Narratives: The narrative technique of gathering information has even less structure than the focus group. Narratives have almost no predetermined content except that the researcher seeks to hear the personal experience of a person with an incident or happening in his/her life. Essentially, the person tells his/her story about an incident or situation and you, as the researcher, listen passively, occasionally encouraging the respondent.

Nominal scale: The nominal scale is one of the ways of measuring a variable in the social sciences. It enables the classification of individuals, objects or responses based on a common/shared property or characteristic. These people, objects or responses are divided into a number of subgroups in such a way that each member of the subgroup has the common characteristic.

Non-experimental studies: There are times when, in studying causality, a researcher observes an outcome and wishes to investigate its causation. From the outcomes the researcher starts linking causes with them. Such studies are called non-experimental studies. In a non-experimental study you neither introduce nor control/manipulate the cause variable. You start with the effects and try to link them with the causes.

Non-participant observation: When you, as a researcher, do not get involved in the activities of the group but remain a passive observer, watching and listening to its activities and interactions and drawing conclusions from them, this is called non-participant observation.

Non-probability sampling designs: These do not follow the theory of probability in the selection of elements from the sampling population. Non-probability sampling designs are used when the number of elements in a population is either unknown or they cannot be individually identified. In such situations the selection of elements is dependent upon other considerations. Non-probability sampling designs are commonly used in both quantitative and qualitative research.

Null hypothesis: A hypothesis stipulating that there is no difference between two situations, groups, outcomes, or the prevalence of a condition or phenomenon; it is usually written as Ho.

Objective-oriented evaluation: This is when an evaluation is designed to ascertain whether or not a programme or a service is achieving its objectives or goals.

Observation: is one of the methods for collecting primary data. It is a purposeful, systematic and selective way of watching and listening to an interaction or phenomenon as it takes place. Though predominantly used in qualitative research, it is also used in quantitative research.

Observer's bias: is when, as an observer, you purposely do not accurately report what you observe because of your own vested interest. It is both illegal and unethical.

Open-ended questions: In an open-ended question the possible responses are not given. In the case of a questionnaire the respondent writes down the answers in his/her words, whereas in the case of an interview schedule the investigator records the answers either verbatim or in a summary describing a respondent's answer.

Operational definition: When you define concepts used by you either in your research problem or in the study population in a measurable form, they are called working or operational definitions. It is important to understand that the operational definitions that you develop are only for the purpose of your study.

Online survey: Online surveys have become reasonably common in collecting data and, in some situation, its analysis. There are three common options for data collection through online: e-mail, websites and mobile phones.

Oral history: More a method of data collection than a study design; however, in qualitative research, it has become an approach for studying a historical event or for gaining information about a culture, custom or story that has been passed on from generation to generation. It is a picture of something in someone's own words. Oral histories, like narratives, involve the use of both passive and active listening. However, they are more commonly used for learning about cultural, social or historical events whereas narratives are more about a person's own experiences.

Ordinal scale: An ordinal scale has all the properties of a nominal scale plus one of its own. Besides categorising individuals, objects, responses or a property into subgroups on the basis of a common characteristic, it ranks the subgroups in a certain order. They are arranged in either ascending or descending order according to the extent that a subcategory reflects the magnitude of variation in the variable.

Outcome evaluation: The focus of an outcome evaluation is to find out the effects, impacts, changes or outcomes that the programme has produced in the target population.

Outcome variable: see Dependent variable

481

Panel studies: These are prospective in nature and are designed to collect information from the same respondents over a period of time. The group of individuals selected becomes a panel that provides the required information. In a panel study the period of data collection can range from once only to repeated data collections over a long period.

Participant observation: This is when you, as a researcher, participate in the activities of the group being observed in the same manner as its members, with or without their knowing that they are being observed. Participant observation is principally used in qualitative research and is usually done by developing a close interaction with members of a group or 'living' in with the situation which is being studied.

Participatory research: Participatory research and collaborative enquiry are not study designs per se but signify a philosophical perspective that advocates an active involvement of research participants in the research process. Participatory research is based upon the principle of minimising the 'gap' between the researcher and the research participants. The most important feature is the involvement and participation of the community or research participants in the research process to make the research findings more relevant to their needs.

Pie chart: The pie chart is a way of representing data graphically. A full circle of 360 degrees can be used to represent 100 per cent or the total population. The circle is divided into sections in accordance with the magnitude of each subcategory comprising the total population. Hence each section is in proportion to the size of each subcategory of a frequency distribution.

Pilot study: see Feasibility study

Placebo effect: A patient's belief that s/he is receiving a treatment plays an important role in his/her recovery even though the treatment may be fake or ineffective. The change occurs because a patient believes that s/he is receiving the treatment. This psychological effect that helps a patient to recover is known as the placebo effect.

Placebo study: A study that attempts to determine the extent of a placebo effect is called a placebo study. A placebo study is based upon a comparative study design that involves two or more groups, depending on whether or not you want to have a control group to isolate the impact of extraneous variables or other treatment modalities to determine their relative effectiveness.

Plagiarism: Use of someone else's work, academic or non-academic, claiming it to be yours, is called plagiarism and is considered unethical in research.

Polytomous variable: A variable consisting of more than two categories, for example religion (Christian, Muslim, Hindu), political parties (Labour, Liberal, Conservative) and attitudes (strongly in favour, in favour, uncertain, against, strongly against).

Population mean: From what you find out from your sample (sample statistics) you make an estimate of the prevalence of these characteristics for the total study population. The estimates about the total study population made from sample statistics are called population parameters or the population mean.

Predictive validity: This form of validity is judged by the degree to which an instrument can correctly forecast an outcome: the higher the correctness in the forecasts, the higher the predictive validity of the instrument.

Pre-test: In quantitative research, pre-testing is a practice whereby you test something that you have developed before its actual use to ascertain the likely problems with it. Mostly, the pre-test is done on a research instrument or on a code book. The pre-test of a research instrument entails a critical examination of each question as to how clear it is and how it is understood by potential respondents with a view to removing possible problems with it. It ensures that a respondent's understanding of each question is in accordance with your intentions. The pre-test of an instrument is only done in structured studies. Pre-testing a code book entails actually coding a few questionnaires/interview schedules to identify any problems with the code book before coding the data.

Primary data: Information collected for the specific purpose of a study either by the researcher or by someone else.

Primary sources: Sources that provide primary data such as interviews, observations and questionnaires.

Probability sampling: When selecting a sample, if you adhere to the theory of probability, that is you select the sample in such a way that each element in the study population has an equal and independent chance of selection in the sample, the process is called probability sampling.

Process evaluation: The main emphasis of process evaluation is on evaluating the manner in which a service or programme is being delivered in order to identify ways of enhancing the efficiency of the delivery system.

Programme planning evaluation: Before starting a large-scale programme it is desirable to investigate the extent and nature of the problem for which the programme is being developed. When an evaluation is undertaken with the purpose of investigating the nature and extent of the problem itself, it is called programme planning evaluation.

Proportionate stratified sampling: In proportionate stratified sampling, the number of elements selected in the sample from each stratum is in relation to its proportion in the total population.

Prospective studies: refer to the likely prevalence of a phenomenon, situation, problem, attitude or outcome in the future. Such studies attempt to establish the outcome of an event or what is likely to happen. Experiments are usually classified as prospective studies because the researcher must wait for an intervention to register its effect on the study population.

Pure research: is concerned with the development, examination, verification and refinement of research methods, procedures, techniques and tools that form the body of research methodology.

Purposive sampling: see Judgemental sampling

Qualitative research: This is embedded in the philosophy of empiricism; follows an open, flexible and unstructured approach to enquiry; aims to explore diversity rather than to quantify; emphasises description and narration of feelings, perceptions and experiences rather than their measurement; and communicates findings in a descriptive and narrative rather than analytical manner, placing no or less emphasis on generalisations.

Quantitative research: This is rooted in the philosophy of rationalism; follows a rigid, structured and predetermined set of procedures to explore; aims to quantify the extent of variation in a phenomenon; emphasises the measurement of variables and objectivity of the process; believes in substantiation on the basis of a larger sample size; gives importance to validity and reliability of findings; and communicates findings in an analytical and aggregate manner, drawing conclusions and inferences that can be generalised.

Quasi-experimental studies: Studies which have the attributes of both experimental and non-experimental studies are called quasi- or semi-experiments.

Questionnaire: A written list of questions, the answers to which are recorded by respondents. Respondents read the questions, interpret what is expected and then write down the answers. The only difference between an interview schedule and a questionnaire is that in the former it is the interviewer who asks the questions (and, if necessary, explains them) and records the respondent's replies on an interview schedule, while in the latter replies are recorded by the respondents themselves.

Quota sampling: The main consideration in quota sampling is the researcher's ease of access to the sample population. In addition to convenience, the researcher is guided by some visible characteristic of interest, such as gender or race, of the study population. The sample is selected from a convenient location, and whenever a person with this visible relevant characteristic is seen, that person is asked to participate in the study. The process continues until the required number of respondents (quota) have been contacted.

Random design: In a random design, the study population groups as well as the experimental treatments are not

483

predetermined but randomly assigned to become control or experimental groups. Random assignment in experiments means that any individual or unit of the study population has an equal and independent chance of becoming a part of the experimental or control group or, in the case of multiple treatment modalities, any treatment has an equal and independent chance of being assigned to any of the population groups. It is important to note that the concept of randomisation can be applied to any of the experimental designs.

Random sampling: For a design to be called random or probability sampling, it is imperative that each element in the study population has an equal and independent chance of selection in the sample. Thus the probability of selection of each element in the study population is the same, and the choice of one element is not dependent upon the choice of another element in the sampling.

Random variable: When collecting information from respondents, there are times when the mood of a respondent or the wording of a question can affect the way a respondent replies. There is no systematic pattern in terms of this change. Such shifts in responses are said to be caused by random or chance variables.

Randomisation: In experimental and comparative studies, you often need to study two or more groups of people. In forming these groups it is important that they are comparable with respect to the dependent variable and other variables that affect it so that the effects of independent and extraneous variables are uniform across groups. Randomisation is a process that ensures that each and every person in a group is given an equal and independent chance of being in any of the groups, thereby making groups comparable.

Ratio scale: A ratio scale has all the properties of nominal, ordinal and interval scales plus a property of its own: the zero point of a ratio scale is fixed, which means it has a fixed starting point. Therefore, it is an absolute scale. As the difference between the intervals is always measured from a zero point, arithmetical operations can be performed on the scores.

Reactive effect: Sometimes the way a question is worded informs respondents of the existence or prevalence of something that the study is trying to find out about as an outcome of an intervention. This effect is known as reactive effect of the instrument.

Recall error: Error that can be introduced in a response because of a respondent's inability to recall its various aspects correctly.

Reflective journal log: This is a method of data collection in qualitative research that entails keeping a log of your thoughts as a researcher whenever you notice anything, talk to someone, participate in an activity or observe something that helps you understand or add to whatever you are trying to find out about. This log becomes the basis of your research findings.

Reflexive control design: In experimental studies, to overcome the problem of comparability in different groups, sometimes researchers study only one population and treat data collected during the non-intervention period as representing a control group, and information collected after the introduction of the intervention as if it pertained to an experimental group. It is the periods of non-intervention and intervention that constitute control and experimental groups.

Regression effect: Sometimes people who place themselves on the extreme positions of a measurement scale at the pre-test stage may, for a number of reasons, shift towards the mean at the post-test stage. They might feel that they have been too negative or too positive at the pre-test stage. Therefore, the mere expression of the attitude in response to a questionnaire or interview has caused them to think about and alter their attitude towards the mean at the time of the post-test. This type of effect is known as the regression effect.

Reliability: A research instrument that is able to provide similar results when used repeatedly under similar conditions is described as 'reliable'. Reliability indicates accuracy, stability and predictability of a research instrument: the higher the reliability, the higher the accuracy.

Replicated cross-sectional design: This study design is based upon the assumption that participants at different stages of a programme are similar in terms of their socioeconomic-demographic characteristics and the problem for which they are seeking intervention. Assessment of the effectiveness of an intervention is done by taking a sample of clients who are at different stages of the intervention. The difference in the dependent variable among clients at the intake and termination stage is considered to be the impact of the intervention.

Research: One of the ways of finding answers to your professional and practice questions. It is characterised by the use of tested procedures and methods and an unbiased and objective attitude in the process of exploration.

Research design: A research design is a procedural plan that is adopted by the researcher to answer questions validly, objectively, accurately and economically. A research design therefore addresses questions that determine the path you are proposing to take for your research journey. Through a research design you decide for yourself and communicate to others your decisions regarding what study design you propose to use, how you will collect information from your respondents, how you will select your respondents, how the information you will collect is to be analysed and how you will communicate your findings.

Research instrument: Anything that becomes a means of collecting information for your study is called a 'research instrument' or a 'research tool', for example interview schedules, questionnaires, notes on field observations, field diaries, information collected from secondary notes, interview guides.

Research journey: The process that you follow to find answers to your research questions.

Research objectives: Specific statements of goals that you set out to be achieved at the end of your research journey.

Research participants: Those respondents or subjects who participate in a research study.

Research problem: Any issue, problem or question that becomes the basis of your enquiry. It is what you want to find out about during your research endeavour.

Research proposal: A research proposal details your operational plan as to how you are going to find answers to your research questions. It outlines the various tasks you plan to undertake to fulfil your research objectives or obtain answers to your research questions.

Research questions: Questions that you would like to find answers to through your research, such as 'What does it mean to have a child with ADHD in a family?' or 'What is the impact of immigration on family roles?'. Research questions become the basis for research objectives. The main difference between research questions and research objectives is the way they are worded. Research questions take the form of questions whereas research objectives are statements of achievements expressed using action-oriented words.

Retrospective study: A retrospective study investigates a phenomenon, situation, problem or issue that has happened in the past. Such studies are usually conducted either on the basis of the data available for that period or on the basis of respondents' recall of the situation.

Retrospective-prospective study: A retrospective-prospective study focuses on past trends in a phenomenon and studies it into the future. A study where you measure the impact of an intervention without having a control group by 'constructing' a previous baseline from either respondents' recall or secondary sources, then introducing the intervention to study its effect, is considered a retrospective-prospective study. In fact, most before-and-after studies, if carried out without having a control – where the baseline is constructed from the same population before introducing the intervention – will be classified as retrospective-prospective studies.

485

Row percentages: are calculated from the total of all the subcategories of one variable that are displayed along a row in different columns.

Sample: A sample is a subgroup of the population which is the focus of your research enquiry and is selected in such a way that it represents the study population. A sample is composed of a few individuals from whom you collect the required information. It is done to save time, money and other resources.

Sample size: The number of individuals, usually denoted by the letter n, from whom you obtain the required information.

Sample statistics: Findings based on the information obtained from your respondents (sample) are called sample statistics.

Sampling: The process of selecting a few respondents (a sample) from a bigger group (the sampling population) to become the basis for estimating the prevalence of information of interest to you.

Sampling design: The way you select the required sampling units from a sampling population to obtain your sample is called the sampling design or sampling strategy. There are many sampling strategies in both quantitative and qualitative research.

Sampling element: Anything that becomes the basis of selecting your sample such as an individual, family, household, members of an organisation, residents of an area, is called a sampling unit or element.

Sampling error: The difference in the findings (sample statistics) that is due to the selection of elements in the sample is known as sampling error.

Sampling frame: When you are in a position to identify all elements of a study population, the list of all the elements is called a sampling frame.

Sampling population: The entire group, such as families living in an area, clients of an agency, residents of a community, members of a group, people belonging to an organisation about whom you want to find out about through your research endeavour, is called the sampling population or study population.

Sampling strategy: see Sampling design

Sampling unit: see Sampling element

Sampling with replacement: When you select a sample in such a way that each selected element in the sample is placed back into

the sampling population before selecting the next, this is called sampling with replacement. Theoretically, this is done to provide an equal chance of selection to each element so as to adhere to the theory of probability to ensure randomisation of the sample. If an element is selected again, it is discarded and the next one is selected. If the sampling population is fairly large, the probability of selecting the same element twice is fairly remote.

Sampling without replacement: When you select a sample in such a way that an element, once selected to become a part of your sample, is not placed back into the study population, this is called sampling without replacement.

Saturation point: The concept of saturation point refers to the stage in data collection where you, as a researcher, are discovering no or very little new information from your respondents. In qualitative research this is considered an indication of the adequacy of the sample size.

Scale: This is a method of measurement and/or classification of respondents on the basis of their responses to questions you ask of them in a study. A scale could be continuous or categorical. It helps you to classify a study population in subgroups or as a spread that is reflective on the scale.

Scattergram: When you want to show graphically how one variable changes in relation to a change in another, a scattergram is extremely effective. For a scattergram, both the variables must be measured either on an interval or ratio scale and the data on both the variables needs to be available as absolute values for each observation. Data for both variables is taken in pairs and displayed as points in relation to their values on both axes. The resulting graph is known as a scattergram.

Secondary data: Sometimes the information required is already available in other sources such as journals, previous reports, or censuses, and you extract that information for the specific purpose of your study. This type of data is called secondary data.

Secondary sources: Sources that provide secondary data are called secondary sources. Sources such as books, journals, previous research studies, records of an agency, client or patient information already collected and routine service delivery records all form secondary sources.

Semi-experimental studies: see Quasi-experimental studies.

Sensitive information: Any information that a respondent considers personal or private, and does not want to share, is considered as sensitive information. This could be about drug use, sexuality, income, criminal history, etc. Asking for sensitive information may upset or embarrass a respondent and should be done skilfully and having developed a good rapport.

Simple random sampling: This is the most commonly used method of selecting a random sample. It is a process of selecting the required sample size from the sampling population, providing each element with an equal and independent chance of selection by any method designed to select a random sample.

Snowball sampling: A process of selecting a sample using networks. To start with, a few individuals in a group or organisation are selected using purposive, random or network sampling to collect the required information from them. They are then asked to identify other people in the group or organisation who could be contacted to obtain the same information. The people selected by them become a part of the sample. The process continues till you reach the saturation point in terms of information being collected.

Stacked bar chart: A stacked bar chart is similar to a bar chart except that in the former each bar shows information about two or more variables stacked onto each other vertically. The sections of a bar show the proportion of the variables they represent in relation to one another. Such a chart can be drawn only for categorical data.

Stakeholders in research: Those people or groups who are likely to be affected by a research activity or its findings. In research there are three stakeholders: the research participants, the researcher and the funding body.

Stem-and-leaf display: The stem-and-leaf display is an effective, quick and simple way of displaying a frequency distribution. The stem and leaf for a frequency distribution running into two digits is plotted by displaying digits 0 to 9 on the left of the display, representing the tens of a frequency. The figures representing the units of a frequency are displayed on the right.

Stratified random sampling: One of the probability sampling designs in which the total study population is first classified into different subgroups based upon a characteristic that makes each subgroup more homogeneous in terms of the classificatory variable. The sample is then selected from each subgroup either by selecting an equal number of elements from each subgroup or selecting elements from each subgroup equal to its proportion in the total population.

Structured interviews: Interviews in which the questions that you ask of your respondents, their wording and sequence are predetermined. Everything that forms part of the interview is fixed and predetermined and any deviation from it is not permitted.

Stub: The stub is a part of the structure of a table. It is the subcategories of a variable, listed down the left-hand column of the table. Information about these subcategories is provided to the right of the stub.

Study design: This term is used to describe the type of design you are going to adopt to undertake your study; that is, if it is going to be experimental, correlational, descriptive, or before and after. Each study design has a specific format and attributes.

Study population: Every study in the social sciences has two aspects: study population and study area (subject area). The people you want to find out about are collectively known as the study population or simply population; the size of the population is usually denoted by the letter N. It could be a group of people living in an area, employees of an organisation, a community, a group of people with special issues, etc. The people from whom you gather information, known as the sample, are selected from the study population; the sample size is usually denoted by n.

Subject area: Any academic or practice field in which you are conducting your study is called the subject or study area. It could be health or other needs of a community, attitudes of people towards an issue, occupational mobility in a community, coping strategies, depression, domestic violence, etc.

Subjectivity: This is an integral part of your way of thinking that is 'conditioned' by your educational background, discipline, philosophy, experience and skills. Bias is a deliberate attempt to change or highlight something which in reality is not there but you do it because of your vested interest. Subjectivity is not deliberate, it is inherent in the way you understand or interpret something.

Summary of literature: A summary of literature is a description of the significant findings of each relevant piece of work that you have gone through as a part of your literature search. The summary basically entails listing, under each pertinent source, the major findings of relevance to your study. The sources searched can be listed in any order.

Summated rating scale: see Likert scale.

Systematic sampling: A way of selecting a sample where the sampling frame, depending upon the sample size, is first divided into a number of segments called intervals. Then, from the first interval, using simple random sampling, one element is selected. The selection of subsequent elements from other intervals is dependent upon the order of the element selected in the first interval. If in the first interval it is the fifth element, the fifth element of each subsequent interval will be chosen.

Table of random numbers: Most books on research methodology and statistics have tables that contain randomly generated numbers. These tables can be used to select a random sample.

Tables: A useful way of presenting analysed data in a small space that brings clarity to the text and serves as a quick point of reference. There are different types of tables for data pertaining to one, two or more variables.

Thematic writing: A style of writing which is written around main themes.

Theoretical framework: As you start reading the literature, you will soon discover that the problem you wish to investigate has

its roots in a number of theories that have been developed from different perspectives. The information obtained from different sources needs to be sorted under the main themes and theories, highlighting agreements and disagreements among the authors. This process of structuring a 'network' of these theories that directly or indirectly have a bearing on your research topic is called the theoretical framework.

Theory of causality: The theory of causality advocates that in studying cause and effect there are three sets of variables that are responsible for the change. These are: cause or independent variables, extraneous variables and change variables. It is the combination of all three that produces change in a phenomenon.

Thurstone scale: The Thurstone scale is one of the scales designed to measure attitudes in the social sciences. Attitude is measured by this scale by means of a set of statements, the 'attitudinal value' of which has been determined by a group of judges. A respondent's agreement with the statement assigns a score equivalent to the 'attitudinal value' of the statement. The total score of all statements is the attitudinal score for a respondent.

Transferability: The concept of transferability refers to the degree to which the results of qualitative research can be generalised or transferred to other contexts or settings.

Trend curve: A set of data measured on an interval or a ratio scale can be displayed using a line diagram or trend curve. A trend line can be drawn for data pertaining to both a specific time and a period. If it relates to a period, the midpoint of each interval at a height commensurate with each frequency is marked as a dot. These dots are then connected with straight lines to examine trends in a phenomenon. If the data pertains to an exact time, a point is plotted at a height commensurate with the frequency and a line is then drawn to examine the trend.

Trend studies: These studies involve selecting a number of data observation points in the past, together with a picture of the present or immediate past with respect to the phenomenon under study, and then making certain assumptions as to the likely future trends. In a way you are compiling a cross-sectional picture of the trends being observed at different points in time over the past, present and future. From these cross-sectional observations you draw conclusions about the pattern of change.

Triangulation: Triangulation involves the use of the same set of data from multiple sources to best achieve the objectives of your study. It is based upon the belief that use of the same set of data, collected through different approaches to draw conclusions, and its examination from different perspectives will provide a better understanding of a problem, situation, phenomenon or issue. There are different types of triangulations; data, investigator, theory and methodology.

Type I error: In testing a hypothesis, for many reasons you may sometimes commit a mistake and draw the wrong conclusion with respect to the validity of your hypothesis. If you reject a null hypothesis when it is true and you should not have rejected it, this is called a Type I error.

Type II error: In testing a hypothesis, for many reasons you may sometimes commit a mistake and draw the wrong conclusion in terms of the validity of your hypothesis. If you accept a null hypothesis when it is false and you should not have accepted it, this is called a Type II error.

Unethical: Any professional activity that is not in accordance with the accepted code of conduct for that profession is considered unethical.

Unstructured interviews: Interviews in which, you as an interviewer, have every flexibility in terms of questions that you ask of your respondents, explanation you provide, wording you use, and the sequence in which you ask them.

Validity: The concept of validity can be applied to every aspect of the research process. In its simplest form, validity refers to the appropriateness of each step in the research process. However, the concept of validity is more associated with measurement procedures. In terms of the measurement procedure, validity is the ability of an instrument to measure what it is designed to measure.

Variable: An image, perception or concept that is capable of measurement – hence capable of taking on different values – is called a variable. In other words, a concept that can be measured is called a variable. A variable is a property that takes on different values. It is a rational unit of measurement that can assume any one of a number of designated values.

Working definition: see Operational definition.

489

BIBLIOGRAPHY

Ackroyd, Stephen & John Hughes, 1992, *Data Collection in Context*, New York, Longman.

Alkin, Marvin C. & Lewis C. Solomon (eds), 1983, *The Costs of Evaluation*, Beverly Hills, CA, Sage.

Alwin, Duane F. (eds.), 1978, *Survey Design and Analysis: Current Issues*, Beverly Hills, CA, Sage.

Babbie, Earl, 1989, *Survey Research Methods* (2nd edn), Belmont, CA, Wadsworth.

Babbie, Earl, 2007, *The Practice of Social Research* (11th edn), Belmont, CA, Wadsworth.

Bailey, Kenneth D., 1978, *Methods of Social Research* (3rd edn), New York, Free Press.

Barton, Ruth, 1988, *Understanding Social Statistics: An Introduction to Descriptive Statistics*, Perth Editorial/ Publication Unit, Division of Arts, Education and Social Sciences, Curtin University of Technology.

Bernard, H. Russell, 1994, *Research Methods in Anthropology: Qualitative and Quantitative Approaches* (2nd edn), Thousand Oaks, CA, Sage.

Bernard, H. Russell, 2000, *Social Research Methods: Qualitative and Quantitative Approaches*, Thousand Oaks, CA, Sage.

Bilson, Andy (ed.), 2005, *Evidence-based Practice in Social Work*, London, Whiting & Birch.

Black, James A. & Dean J. Champion, 1976, *Methods and Issues in Social Research*, New York, Wiley.

Blaikie, Norman, 2007, *Approaches to Social Enquiry* (2nd edn), Cambridge, Polity Press.

Bogdan, Robert & Sari Knopp Biklen, 1992, *Qualitative Research for Education: An Introduction to Theory and Methods* (2nd edn), Boston, Allyn & Bacon.

Bradburn, M. Norman & Seymour Sudman, 1979, *Improving Interview Method and Questionnaire Design*, San Francisco, Jossey-Bass.

Brewer, J. & A. Hunter, 1989, *Multimethod Research: A Synthesis of Styles*, Newbury Park, CA, Sage.

Brewer, J. & A. Hunter, 2006, *Foundations of Multimethod Research: Synthesizing Styles* (2nd edn), Thousand Oaks, CA, Sage.

Brinberg, David & Joseph E. McGreth, 1985, *Validity and the Research Process*, Beverly Hills, CA, Sage.

Bryman, Alan, 1988, *Quantity and Quality in Social Research*, London, Routledge.

Bryman, Alan, 2004, *Social Research Methods* (2nd edn), Oxford, Oxford University Press.

Bryman, Alan, 2012, *Social Research Methods* (4th edn), Oxford, Oxford University Press.

Bulmer, Martin (ed.), 1977, *Sociological Research Methods: An Introduction*, London, Macmillan.

Burns, Robert B., 1997, *Introduction to Research Methods* (2nd edn), Melbourne, Longman Cheshire.

Butcher, Judith, 1981, *Copy-Editing: The Cambridge Handbook for Editors, Authors and Publishers* (2nd edn), Cambridge, Cambridge University Press.

Carr, Wilfred & Steven Kemmis, 1986, *Becoming Critical: Education, Knowledge and Action Research*, Lewes, Falmer Press.

Cherry, Nita, 2002, *Action Research: A Pathway to Action, Knowledge and Learning*, Melbourne, RMIT Publishing.

The Chicago Manual of Style (14th edn), 1993, Chicago and London, University of Chicago Press.

Cohen, Morris R. & Ernest Nagel, 1966, *An Introduction to Logic and Scientific Methods*, London, Routledge & Kegan Paul.

Coffey, A. & P. Aikinson, 1996, *Making Sense of Qualitative Data: Complementary Research Strategies*, Thousand Oaks, CA, Sage.

Collins Dictionary of the English Language, 1979, Sydney, Collins.

Commonwealth of Australia, 2002, *Style Manual* (6th edn), Milton, Qld, Wiley Australia.

Cozby, C. Paul, 1985, *Methods in Behavioral Research*, Palo Alto, CA, Mayfield.

Crano, William D. & Marilynne B. Brewer, 2002, *Principles and Methods of Social Research* (2nd edn), Mahwah, NJ, Lawrence Erlbaum.

Creswell, J.W., 1995, *Research Design: Qualitative and Quantitative Approaches*, Thousand Oaks, CA, Sage.

Creswell, J.W., 2003, *Research Design: Qualitative, Quantitative, and Mixed Methods Approaches* (2nd edn), Thousand Oaks, CA, Sage.

Creswell, J.W., 2007, *Qualitative Inquiry and Research Design: Choosing among Five Approaches* (2nd edn), Thousand Oaks, CA, Sage.

Creswell, J.W., 2009, *Research Design: Qualitative and Quantitative Approaches* (3rd edn), Thousand Oaks, CA, Sage.

Creswell, John W. & Vicki Clark, 2011, *Designing and Conducting Mixed Methods Research* (2nd edn), Los Angeles, Sage.

Crotty, Michael, 1998, *The Foundations of Social Research*, St Leonards, NSW, Allen & Unwin.

Cunningham, J. Barton, 1993, *Action Research and Organizational Development*, London, Praeger.

de Vaus, David, 2002, *Surveys in Social Research* (5th edn), St Leonards, NSW, Allen & Unwin.

Denzin, Norman K. & Yvonna S. Lincoln (eds), 1994, *Handbook of Qualitative Research*, Thousand Oaks, CA, Sage.

Denzin, Norman K. & Yvonna S. Lincoln (eds), 1998a, *Collecting and Interpreting Qualitative Materials*, Thousand Oaks, CA, Sage.

Denzin, Norman K. & Yvonna S. Lincoln (eds), 1998b, *Strategies of Qualitative Inquiry*, Thousand Oaks, CA, Sage.

Denzin, Norman K. & Yvonna S. Lincoln (eds), 2005, *The Sage Handbook of Qualitative Research* (3rd edn), Thousand Oaks, CA, Sage.

Denzin, Norman K. & Yvonna S. Lincoln, 2008, *The Landscape of Qualitative Research* (3rd edn), Los Angeles, Sage.

Denzin, Norman & Yvonna S. Lincoln, 2012, *Collecting and Interpreting Qualitative Materials* (4th edn), London, Sage.

Denzin, Norman & Yvonna S. Lincoln, 2012, *Strategies of Qualitative Inquiry* (4th edn), London, Sage.

Dixon, Beverly & Gary Bouma, 1984, *The Research Process*, Melbourne, Oxford University Press.

Duncan, Otis Dudley, 1984, *Notes on Social Measurement: Historical and Critical*, New York, Russell Sage Foundation.

Elliott, Jane, 2005, *Using Narrative in Social Research*, London, Sage.

Engel, R.J. & R.K. Schutt, 2009, *The Practice of Research in Social Work* (2nd edn), Thousand Oaks, CA, Sage.

Festinger, Leon & Daniel Katz (eds), 1966, *Research Methods in Behavioral Sciences*, New York, Holt, Rinehart and Winston.

Flick, U., 1998, *Introduction to Qualitative Research*, Thousand Oaks, CA, Sage

Flick, U., 2007, *Managing Quality in Qualitative Research*, London, Sage.

Foreman, E.K., 1991, *Survey Sampling Principles*, New York, Marcel Dekker.

Gilbert, Nigel (ed.), 2008, *Researching Social Life* (3rd edn), London, Sage.

Gray, Mel, Debbie Plath & Stephen Webb, 2009, *Evidence-based Social Work*, London, Routledge.

Greene, J.C., 2007, *Mixed Methods in Social Inquiry*, San Francisco, Jossey-Bass.

Greene, J.C., V.J. Caracelli & W.F. Graham, 1989, Towards a conceptual framework for mixed methods evaluation designs, *Education Evaluation and Policy Analysis*, 11(3), 255–274.

Grinnell, Richard Jr (ed.), 1981, *Social Work Research and Evaluation*, Itasca, IL, F.E. Peacock.

Grinnell, Richard Jr (ed.), 1988, *Social Work Research and Evaluation* (3rd edn), Itasca, IL, F.E. Peacock.

Grinnell, Richard Jr (eds), 1993, *Social Work Research and Evaluation* (4th edn), Itasca, IL, F.E. Peacock.

Guba, E.G. & Y.S. Lincoln, 1994, Competing paradigms in qualitative research. In N. Denzin & Y.S. Lincoln (eds), *Handbook of Qualitative Research* (pp. 105–117), Thousand Oaks, CA, Sage.

Hakim, Catherine, 1987, *Research Design: Strategies and Choices in the Design of Social Research*, London, Allen & Unwin.

Hall, Irene & David Hall, 2004, *Evaluation and Social Research: Introducing Small Scale Practice*, Basingstoke, Palgrave Macmillan.

Hawe, Penelope, Deirdre Degeling & Jane Hall, 1992, *Evaluating Health Promotion*, Sydney, Maclennan+Petty.

Hessler, Richard M., 1992, *Social Research Methods*, New York, West Publishing.

Johnson, R.B. & L. Christensen 2004, *Educational Research: Quantitative, Qualitative, and Mixed Methods* (2nd edn), Boston, Pearson.

Johnson, R.B., A.J. Onwuegbusie & L.A. Turner, 2007, Towards a definition of missed methods research, *Journal of Mixed Methods Research*, 1(2), 112–133.

Kaplan, David (ed.), 2004, *The Sage Handbook of Quantitative Methodology for the Social Sciences*, Thousand Oaks, CA, Sage.

Kazdin, Alan, 1982, *Single-case Research Designs*, New York, Oxford University Press.

Kerlinger, Fred N., 1973, *Foundations of Behavioral Research* (2nd edn), New York, Holt, Rinehart and Winston.

Kerlinger, Fred N., 1979, *Behavioral Research: A Conceptual Approach*, Sydney, Holt, Rinehart and Winston.

Kerlinger, Fred N., 1986, *Foundations of Behavioral Research* (3rd edn), New York, Holt, Rinehart and Winston.

Kirk, Jerome & Marc L. Miller, 1986, *Reliability and Validity in Qualitative Research*, Newbury Park, CA, Sage.

Krippendorff, Klaus, 2012, *Content Analysis*, Los Angeles, Sage.

Krueger, Richard & Mary Anne Casey, 2000, *Focus Groups: A Practical Guide for Applied Research* (4th edn), Thousand Oaks, CA, Sage.

Kvale, Steinar & Svend Brinkmann, 2009, *Interviews* (2nd edn), Thousand Oaks, CA, Sage.

Lancy, D.F., 1993, *Qualitative Research in Education: An Introduction to Major Traditions*, New York, Longman.

Leary, Mark R., 1995, *Introduction to Behavioral Research Methods* (2nd edn), Pacific Grove, CA, Brooks/Cole.

Lincoln, Y. S. & E.G. Guba, 1985, *Naturalistic Inquiry*, Beverly Hills, CA, Sage.

Longyear, Marie (ed.), 1983, *The McGraw-Hill Style Manual, A Concise Guide for Writers and Editors*, New York, McGraw-Hill.

Lundberg, George A., 1942, *Social Research: A Study in Methods of Gathering Data* (2nd edn), New York, Longmans, Green.

Marczyk, Geoffrey R., David DeMatteo & David Festinger, 2005, *Essentials of Research Design and Methodology*, Hoboken, NJ, Wiley.

Marshall, Catherine & Gretchen B. Rossman, 2006, *Designing Qualitative Research*, Thousand Oaks, CA, Sage.

Martin, David W., 1985, *Doing Psychological Experiments* (2nd edn), Monterey, CA, Brooks/Cole.

Matthews, Bob & Liz Ross, 2010, *Research Methods: A Practical Guide for the Social Sciences*, New York, Pearson.

Maxwell, Joseph A., 2013, *Qualitative Research Design: An Interactive Approach* (3rd edn), Los Angeles, Sage.

May, Tim, 1997, *Social Research: Issues, Methods and Process* (2nd edn), Buckingham, Open University Press.

Minium, Edward W., 1978, *Statistical Reasoning in Psychology and Education* (2nd edn), New York, Wiley.

Monette, Duane R., Thomas J. Sullivan & Cornell R. DeJong, 1986, *Applied Social Research: Tools for the Human Services*, Fort Worth, TX, Holt, Rinehart and Winston.

Moser, Claus A. & Graham Kalton, 1989, *Survey Methods in Social Investigation* (2nd edn), Aldershot, Gower.

Nachmias, David & Clara Nachmias, 1987, *Research Methods in Social Sciences*, New York, St. Martin's Press.

Newman, Isadore & Carolyn R. Benz, 1998, *Qualitative-Quantitative Research Methodology*, Carbondale, IL, Southern Illinois University Press.

Padgett, Deborah K., 2008, *Qualitative Methods in Social Work Research* (2nd edn), Thousand Oaks, CA, Sage.

Patton, Michael Quinn, 1990, *Qualitative Evaluation and Research Methods*, Newbury Park, CA, Sage.

Plano Clark, Vicki L. & John W. Creswell, 2009, *Understanding Research: A Consumer's Guide*, Melbourne, Pearson (Merrill).

Poincaré, H., 1952, *Science and Hypothesis*, New York, Dover.

Powers, Gerald T., Thomas M. Meenaghan & Beverley G. Twoomey, 1985, *Practice Focused Research: Integrating Human Practice and Research*, Englewood Cliffs, NJ, Prentice Hall.

Punch, K.F., 1998, *Introduction to Social Research: Quantitative and Qualitative Approaches*, Thousand Oaks, CA, Sage.

Ritchie, Donald A., 2003, *Doing Oral History: A Practical Guide*, Oxford, Oxford University Press.

Robson, Colin, 2002, *Real World Research* (2nd edn), Oxford, Blackwell.

Robson, Colin, 2011, *Real World Research*, Chichester, Wiley.

Rohlf, F. James & Robert R. Sokal, 1969, *Statistical Tables*, San Francisco, W.H. Freeman.

Rossi, Peter H. & Howard E. Freeman, 1993, *Evaluation: A Systematic Approach*, Newbury Park, CA, Sage.

Rossi, Peter H., Howard E. Freeman & Mark W. Lipsey, 1999, *Evaluation: A Systematic Approach* (6th edn), Thousand Oaks, CA, Sage.

Rutman, Leonard (ed.), 1977, *Evaluation Research Methods: A Basic Guide*, Beverly Hills, CA, Sage.

Rutman, Leonard, 1980, *Planning Useful Evaluations: Availability Assessment*, Beverly Hills, CA, Sage.

Rutman, Leonard, 1984, *Evaluation Research Methods: A Basic Guide* (2nd edn), Beverly Hills, CA, Sage.

Sandefur, Gary D., Howard E. Freeman & Peter H. Rossi, 1986, *Workbook for Evaluation: A Systematic Approach* (3rd edn), Beverly Hills, CA, Sage.

Sarantakos, S., 2005, *Social Research* (3rd edn), New York, Palgrave Macmillan.

Schinke, Steven P. & Lewayne Gilchrist, 1993, Ethics in research. In R. M. Grinnell (ed.), *Social Work, Research and Evaluation* (4th edn), Itasca, IL, F.E. Peacock.

Selltiz, Jahoda, Morton Deutsch & Stuart Cook, 1962, *Research Methods in Social Relations* (rev. edn), New York, Holt, Rinehart and Winston.

Siegel, Sidney, 1956, *Nonparametric Statistics for the Behavioral Sciences*, New York, McGraw-Hill.

Silverman, David, 2004, *Qualitative Research: Theory, Methods and Practice* (2nd edn), London, Sage.

Silverman, David, 2005, *Doing Qualitative Research* (2nd edn), London, Sage.

Simon, Julian L., 1969, *Basic Research Methods in Social Sciences: The Art of Empirical Investigation*, New York, Random House.

Smith, Herman W., 1991, *Strategies of Social Research* (3rd edn), Orlando, FL, Holt, Rinehart and Winston.

Somekh, Bridget & Cathy Lewin (eds), 2005, *Research Methods in the Social Sciences*, Los Angeles, Sage.

Stake, Robert E., 1995, *The Art of Case Study Research*, Thousand Oaks, CA, Sage.

Stevens, Stanley Smith, 1951, Mathematics, measurement, and psychophysics. In S.S. Stevens (ed.), *Handbook of Experimental Psychology*, New York, Wiley.

Strauss, A. & J. Corbin, 1998, *Basics of Qualitative Research: Techniques and Procedures for Developing Grounded Theory* (2nd edn), Thousand Oaks, CA, Sage.

Stufflebeam, Daniel L. & Anthony J. Shinkfield, 1985, *Systematic Evaluation: A Self-Instructional Guide to Theory and Practice*, Boston, Kluwer-Nijhoff.

Sue, Valerie M. & Lois A. Ritter, 2012, *Conducting Online Surveys*, Los Angeles, Sage.

Tashakkori, A. & C. Teddlie, 1998, *Mixed Methodology: Combining Qualitative and Quantitative Approaches*, London, Sage.

Tashakkori, Abbas & Charles Teddlie (eds), 2003, *Handbook of Mixed Methods in Social & Behavioral Research*, Thousand Oaks, CA, Sage.

Taylor, Steven J. & Robert Bogdan, 1998, *Introduction to Qualitative Research Methods: A Guidebook and Resource* (3rd edn), New York, Wiley.

Teddlie, C. B. & A. Tashakkori, 2009, *Foundations of Mixed Methods Research: Integrating Quantitative and Qualitative Approaches to Social and Behavioural Sciences*, Los Angeles, Sage.

Thyer, Bruce A., 1993, 'Single-systems research design', in R. M. Grinnell (eds), *Social Work Research and Evaluation* (4th edn), Itasca, IL, F.E. Peacock, pp. 94–117.

Trochim, William M.K. & James Donnelly, 2007, *The Research Methods Knowledge Base* (3rd edn), Mason, OH, Thomson Custom Publishing.

Walter, Maggie (ed.), 2006, *Social Research Methods: An Australian Perspective*, Melbourne, Oxford University Press.

Walter, Maggie, 2010, *Social Research Methods*, Melbourne, Oxford University Press.

Webster's Third New International Dictionary, 1976, G. & C. Company, Springfield, MA.

Willis, J.W., 2007, *Foundations of Qualitative Research: Interpretive and Critical Approaches*, Thousand Oaks, CA, Sage.

Wolcott, H.F., 1994, *Transforming Qualitative Data: Description, Analysis, and Interpretation*, Thousand Oaks, CA, Sage.

Yegidis, Bonnie & Robert Weinback, 1991, *Research Methods for Social Workers*, New York, Longman.

Yin, R. K., 2003, *Case Study Research: Design and Methods* (3rd edn), Thousand Oaks, CA, Sage.

Young, Pauline V., 1966, *Scientific Social Survey Research* (4th edn), Englewood Cliffs, NJ, Prentice Hall.

INDEX

100 percent bar chart 430
ABI/INFORM 64
accidental sampling 307
action research 200
active variables 114
after-only designs 182-4
Alexander 22
alternative hypothesis 134
ambiguous question 233
applications of research 8-9
applied research 13
approaches to research enquires 16-19
    differences in the methods 214-44
area chart 439
attitudes and qualitative research 261
attitudinal scales 252-62
    calculating attitudinal score 257-9
    difficulties in developing 254
    functions 253
    measurement in qualitative and quantitative research 252
    relation to measurement scales 261
    types of scales 254-60
attitudinal score 257-9
attitudinal value 254
attitudinal weight 254
attribute variables 114
authenticity 276

Bailey, K.D. 359
bar chart 429-30
before-and-after studies 174-6
Bernard 21
bias 9, 360
bibliography, styles 463

Biklen 200
bivariate tables 425
Black & Champion. 105, 131, 133
blind studies 195
Bogdan 200
books, reviewing 61-2
Brewer 21
Bulmer, M. 11
Burns, R.B. 11, 196, 197, 456

calculation of sample size 310-11
Carr 200
case studies 196
categorical variable 116
causal relationship 107
    dependent variable 107, 157, 160
    independent variable 107, 157, 160
    total 160
cause variable 107
Champion, D.J. 131, 133
chance variables 157
chapterisation, report outline 457-61
CINAHL 64
Clark 21, 28, 29
closed questions 229-32, 380
cluster sampling 303-6
code book 380-93
code of conduct 356
coding 393-4
coding qualitative data 402-12
Cohen and Nagel 105, 130
cohort studies 194-5
column percentage 428
community forums 199

computers in research 413-14
concept of sampling 291-2
concepts 105
    converting into variables 106-7
    measurement of concepts 107
    and variables 105-6
conceptual framework 67
concurrent validity 272
conditioning effect 177
confidentiality 360
confirmability 276
constant variable 116
construct validity 272
content analysis 379, 402
content validity 272
continuous variables 116
control group 157
control studies 181
convenience sampling 306
correlational research 13, 15
credibility 276
Creswell 21, 28, 29
Cronin 22
cross-sectional studies 171-2
cross-tabulations 399
cumulative frequency polygon 432
cumulative scale 261

data collection in qualitative studies 238-42
    focus-group interviews 239-40
    in-depth interviews 239
    narratives 240
    oral histories 240-1
    secondary sources 241
    unstructured interviews 238-41
    unstructured observations 241
data collection in quantitative studies
    differences in quantitative 214-15, 238
    structured interviews 221-2
    structured observation 217-20
    structured questionnaires 222-34
data collection, main approaches 214-15
    attitudinal scales 252-62

differences 214-15
    primary sources 215-37
    secondary sources 242-3
data collection, prerequisites 237
data display 422-42
data presentation
    graphs 428-41
    tables 423-8
    text 422-3
data processing 376-415
    coding 378-94, 393
    computers and data processing 413-14
    content analysis 403-12
    developing a code book 380-93
    editing 376-8
    frame of analysis 394-400
    mixed methods studies 413
    pre-testing the code book 393
    in qualitative studies 402-12
    in quantitative studies 376-402
    verifying the coded data 394
data saturation point 306, 312
Denzin and Lincoln 276
dependability 276
dependent variables 107
descriptive research 15
dichotomous variables 115, 116
difference between primary and secondary data 215
differences in quantitative and qualitative study designs 170-1
disproportionate stratified sampling 306
Donnelly and Trochim 277
double-barrelled questions 233
double-blind studies 195
double-control studies 186
Duncan, O.T. 117

editing, data 376-8
elevation effect 219
equal-appearing interval scale 261
ERIC 64
error of central tendency 219
ethics 356-7
ethics in research 356

concept 356-7
issues: participants 358-60
 researcher 360-1
 sponsoring organisation 362
secondary sources 362
stakeholders, in research 357-8
evidence-based practice 8
experimental group 181
experimental study designs
after-only 182-4
before-and-after 184
comparative 186-7
control-group 184-6
cross-over comparative 192
double-control 186
matched-control 187-9
placebo 189-91
prospective studies 179
random experiments 181
replicated cross-sectional 192-3
trend studies 193-4
expert sampling 306
explanatory research 13, 15
exploratory research 13, 15
external consistency procedures 275
extraneous variables 107, 108

face validity 272
feasibility study 15
feminist research 200-1
Festinger and Katz 42
fishbowl draw 298
focus group 239-40
formulation of research problem 80-95
frame of analysis 394-400
frequency distributions 399
frequency polygon 431

Gilbert 196
Gilchrist, L. 359
graphs, data presentation 428-41
100 percent bar chart 430
area chart 439

bar chart 429-30
cumulative frequency polygon 432
frequency polygon 431
histogram 429
line diagram 438-9
pie chart 438
scattergram 440
stacked bar chart 430
stem-and-leaf display 436
Grinnell, R. 11, 131, 192, 196
Guba and Lincoln 277
Guttman scale 260

halo effect 219
harm, caused by research 360
Hawthorne Effect 218
HEALTHROM 64
histogram 429
holistic research 198-9
Humanities Index 63
Hunter 21
Huxley, T.H. 130
hypothesis 130
alternative 134
of association 137
characteristics 133
definition 130-1
of difference 134
error in testing 137
formulation of (qualitative) 138
functions 131-2
null 134
of point-prevalence 135
testing of 132
types 133-7

in-depth interviews 220, 238
incentives, providing 359
independent variables 107
indicators 107
information rich sampling 307
informed consent 358
inquiry mode 11

497

internal consistency procedures 275-6
internet 63-4
interval scale 115, 116, 117
intervening variables 108, 114
interview guide 241
interview schedule 222
interviewing 220-2
    advantages 227-8
    constructing schedule 234-5
    definition 220
    disadvantages 228
    forms of questions 229-31
    formulating effective questions 232-4
    versus questionnaires 226
    schedule 222
    structured 222
    unstructured 220-1

Johnson 22
journals, reviewing 62-3
judgemental sampling 307

Katz, D. 42
Kerlinger, F.N. 105, 131, 154
Kemmis 200

leading questions 233
Likert scale 254-9
limitations, research 342
line diagram 438-9
literature review 58-72
    conceptual framework 67
    reviewing selected 65-6
    searching exiting literature 61-4
    theoretical framework 66-7
    how to review 61
    why 58
    writing, literature review 68-71
Lundberg, G.A. 11

matching 187-9
maturation effect 175

'maxmincon' principle 162
Maxwell 170
measurement of concepts 105-6
measurement scales 9, 116-20
    interval 117
    nominal or classificatory 117-19
    ordinal or ranking 117-19
    ratio 117
MEDLINE 64
methods of data collection
    approaches 215
    difference approaches 214-15
    primary sources 215-37
    qualitative studies 238-41
    quantitative studies 215-37
    using secondary sources 242-3
methods of drawing a random sample 298-301
methods of written communication 422
    graphs 428-41
    tables 423-8
    text 422-3
mixed sampling 309
mixed/multiple methods 21-33
    advantages 30-2
    considerations 32
    definition 21-7
    disadvantages 30-2
    introduction 21
    rationale 27
    when to use 27-9
    ways of mixing 29-30
multi-stage cluster sampling 306
multiple responses 390
multivariate tables 425

narratives (information gathering) 240
negative statements 257
neutral items 257
nominal scales 115, 116
non-discriminatory items 257
non-experimental studies 181
non-participant observation 218
non-probability sampling 296, 298, 306-9

non-random sampling 296, 298, 306–9
null hypothesis 134
numerical scale 256

observation 217–20
    non-participant 218
    participant 198, 217–18
    problems 218
    recording 219–20
    situations 218
    types 217–18
observer bias 218
online questionnaires 223
online survey 191–2, 223
open-ended questions 229–32, 380
operational definitions 92–4
oral histories 240–1
ordinal scales 116–17
outline (chapterisation) 457–61

panel of experts 308
panel studies 195
paradigms of research 33–4
participant observation 217–18
participatory research 202
percentages 426–8
    column 428
    row 427
    total 428
philosophy-based designs 199–202
    action research 200
    feminist research 200–1
    participatory and collaborative research 202
pie chart 438
pilot study 15
placebo effect 189–91
plagiarism 362
planning a research study 21
Poincaré 116
polygon 431–2
polytomous varables 115, 116
population mean 293
population parameters 293

positive statements 257
pre-test
    code book 393
    research instrument 237
prediction 291
predictive validity 272
primary data 215
primary sources 215–37
principles of sampling 293–5
probability sampling 302–6
problems vs limitations 342
processing data, qualitative
    studies 402–12
processing data, quantitative
    studies 376–402
professional practice 4–7
proportionate stratified sampling 303
prospective studies 179
pure research 13
purposive sampling 308

qualitative research 16, 195–9
qualitative–quantitative study designs
    differences 170–1
quantitative research 16, 171–95
quasi-experimental studies 181
questionnaires 222–34
    administering 223–6
    advantages 226
    collective 223
    covering letter 228–9
    disadvantages 226–7
    versus interviews 226
    mail 223
    online 223
questions, open-ended and closed 229–32
    advantages 231–2
    close ended 229–32
    developing questions 234–5
    disadvantages 231–2
    formulating effective questions 232–4
    open-ended 229–32
    order of 235, 237

personal 235
pre-testing 237
sensitive 235
quota sampling 306-7

random
error 161
numbers 298-301
sampling designs 302-6
variable 157
randomisation 181-2
ratio scale 115, 116, 117
raw data 376
reactive effect 175
reconstructing the main concepts 400
referencing 463
regression effect 176
reliability 273
concept 273
factors affecting 274
methods of determining 274-6
in qualitative studies 276-8
report writing 456
about a variable 461-2
bibliography 463
outline 457
referencing, systems 463
research
applications 8-9
characteristics 12
definitions 8-9
design 46-7
differences between approaches 16
meaning 8-9
operational steps 42-6
paradigms 33-4
phases 42
process 43
proposal 48-9
reasons for doing 4-7
types 13-19
a way of thinking 4
what does it mean 9-11

writing 48-9
research design 46-7, 154
definition 154
functions 155
and theory of causality 155-62
research, journey 42-6
research, problem formulation 46, 80
aspects 82
considerations in selecting 83-4
formulation of objectives 91
narrowing 83
operational definitions 92-4
in qualitative research 94-5
sources 81-3
steps in formulating 84-91
study population 92
research proposal 48-9, 324-44
contents 325-42
data analysis 337-40
ethical issues 336
hypotheses 332-3
measurement procedures 336
objectives 330-2
preamble 326-8
problem and limitations 342
research problem 329-30
sampling 336-7
setting 335
structure of the report 340-2
study design 333-5
work schedule 342
research report writing 49, 456-64
characteristics 458
draft outline 457-61
referencing 463
writing a bibliography 463
writing about variables 461-2
researcher, ethical issues 360-1
retrospective studies 177
retrospective-prospective studies 179
Ritchie 197
Ritter 192
row percentage 427

500

sampling 48, 292
    accidental 307
    cluster 303-6
    concept of 291-2
    convenience 307
    designs 296-8
    difference in qualitative/quantitative research 290
    disproportionate sampling 303
    element 292
    error 293
    expert 308
    frame 292
    judgemental 307
    methods of drawing a random sample 298-301
    mixed sampling 309
    non-probability 306-9
    non-random 306-9
    with or without replacement 302
    population 292
    principles of 293-5
    probability 302-6
    proportionate 303
    purposive 307
    in qualitative research 311-12
    quota 306-7
    random 302-6
    simple random 302
    size 310-11
    snowball 308-9
    statistics 293
    strategies 296-8
    stratified 303
    systematic 309
    terminology 292-3
    types of sampling designs 296-8
    unit 293
saturation point 309, 312
scattergram 440
schedule, work 342
Schinke, S.P. 358
search engines 63-4
secondary data 215
secondary sources 215, 242-3

self-selecting bias 227
Selltiz, J. 154
semi-experimental studies 181
sensitive information 235, 359
simple random sampling 302
Smith 117
snowball sampling 308-9
Social Sciences Citation Index 63
split-half technique 276
sponsoring organisation, ethical issues 362
stacked bar chart 430
stakeholders in research 357-8
statistics and research 400
stem-and-leaf display 436
Stevens, S.S. 117
stratified random sampling 303
structure of a table 423-4
    body 424
    column headings 423
    stub 423
    supplementary notes 424
    title 423
    types 424-6
structured enquiries 16
structured inquiries 16
structured interviews 221-2
stub 423
study designs 171
study designs in qualitative research
    case study design 196
    community discussion forums 199
    focus groups/group interviews 197-8
    holistic design 198-9
    oral history design 197
    participant observation 198
    reflective journal log 199
study designs in quantitative research 171
    after-only designs 182-4
    before-and-after 174-6, 184
    blind studies 195
    cohort studies 194-5
    comparative study designs 186-7
    control studies 184-6

501

cross-over comparative designs 192
cross-sectional 172–4
double blind studies 195
double-control designs 186
experimental 181
longitudinal 176–7
matched-control designs 187–9
non-experimental 181
online survey 191–2
panel studies 195
placebo design 189–91
prospective 179
random studies 181
replicated cross-sectional designs 192–3
retrospective 177–9
retrospective–prospective 179
semi-experimental or quasi-experimental 181
semi-experimental studies 181
trend studies 193–4
study designs, quantitative vs qualitative 170–1
study population 82, 92, 293
subject area 82, 91
subjectivity 9
Sue 191
summated rating scale 254–9
systematic sampling 309

tables, data presentation 423–8
Tashakkori & Teddlie 21, 22
text, communication 422–3
thematic writing 68–71
theoretical framework 66–7, 457
theory of causality 155–62
Thurstone scale 259–60
Thyer, B.A. 154
time-frame 343
total percentage 428
transferability 277
treatment group 181
trend curve 438–9
trend studies 193–4
triangulation 33
Trochim and Donnelly 277

type I error 137
type II error 137
types of percentage 426–8
types of sampling 296–8
    mixed 309
    non-probability 306–9
types of study design 171–99
    others 199–202
    qualitative 195–9
    quantitative 171–95
types of table 424–6
    bivariate or cross 425
    polyvariate or multivariate 425
    univariate or frequency 424

unethical 358
unit of measurement 115–16
univariate tables 424
unstructured inquiries 16
unstructured interviews 220–1

validity
    concept 270–1
    concurrent 272
    construct 272
    content 272
    credibility 277
    dependability 277
    face 272
    predictive 272
    in qualitative research 276–8
    in quantitative research 276–8
    transferability 277
    types 271–3
variables
    active 114
    attribute 114
    categorical 116
    chance 157
    change 114
    and concepts 105–6
    connecting 114
    continuous 116

converting concepts into variable 106-7
definition 104
dependent 114
dichotomous 116
extraneous 114
independent 114
intervening 114
measurement scales 116–20
outcome 114

polytomous 116
typology from different
    perspectives 107–16
writing about 461–2

work schedule 342
working definitions 92–4

Young, P.V. 105